THE CRUCIBLE OF WAR
VOLUME III
MONTGOMERY AND ALAMEIN

Barrie Pitt served in both the European and Middle East theatres in the war, and later edited the enormous partwork *History of the Second World War*. He was also Editor-in-Chief of *Ballantine's Illustrated History of World War 11*. He is the author of *Zeebrugge, St George's Day, 1918, Coronel and Falkland, 1918 - The Last Act, The Battle of the Atlantic, Churchill and the Generals* and a novel, *The Edge of Battle*.

Montgomery and Alamein is the third of the three volumes of *The Crucible of War*. Its companion volumes *Wavell's Command* and *Auchinleck's Command* are published by Cassell in uniform editions.

THE CRUCIBLE
OF WAR

VOLUME III
MONTGOMERY AND ALAMEIN

BARRIE PITT

CASSELL&CO

Cassell & Co
Wellington House, 125 Strand
London WC2R 0BB

The Crucible of War was first published in two volumes by Jonathan
Cape, 1980 and 1982
This three-volume edition published 2001

British Library Cataloguing-in-Publication Data
A catalogue record for this book is available from the British Library

ISBN 0-304-35952-1

Printed and bound in Great Britain by
Creative Print & Design (Wales), Ebbw Vale

To Frances

with love and gratitude

Contents

Illustrations

PLATES

1 The Cairo Conference, August 5th, 1942
2 Churchill with Generals Alexander and Montgomery
3 After Alam Halfa: Brigadier Roberts
4 Montgomery with his corps commanders
5 Lieutenant-General Leese with his divisional commanders
6 Montgomery watches the progress of the battle
7 Montgomery with Leese and Lumsden
8 Sherman tank
9 Tank commanders
10 General Montgomery
11 Capture of a German strongpoint
12 Infantry hold the ground taken
13 Australians approach a German strongpoint
14 Silhouettes at a minefield gap
15 Rommel and Hitler
16 General von Thoma surrenders

MAPS

FIGURES

The author and publishers would like to thank Mr John Batchelor for permission to use his line drawings, figures 1–4.

Author's Note

In addition to those fellow-students of warfare to whom I have been indebted all my professional life – librarians, archivists, historians and survivors – I must on this occasion acknowledge my debt to and also express my affection for the late Field Marshal Viscount Montgomery of Alamein, K.G., G.C.B., D.S.O., whose kindness to me, albeit peppered with occasional acerbity, remains amongst my fondest memories.

In the same way my memories of the kindness and sound advice given me by the late Major-General Douglas Wimberley will always remain a comfort in dark days, as will the hospitality of Mrs Wimberley.

To Field Marshal Lord Carver, General Sir John Hackett and Major-General G. P. D. 'Pip' Roberts I must repeat my thanks for help already expressed in a previous volume of this work, and again I must thank Generals Walther Nehring and Walter Warlimont, and Professor Lucio Ceva, for their help in understanding attitudes and problems faced by Generalfeldmarschall Rommel and his men of Panzerarmee Afrika.

Finally, I must again thank Jane Caunt for retyping the book, Deborah Shepherd for editing it so thoughtfully, and Frances Mary Moore for drawing the maps and compiling the index.

Prologue

To a neutral observer in July, 1942, it did not appear that the Allied cause was flourishing. In the Pacific, the Battle of Midway had been fought and, as its deeper consequences were not to be appreciated for some time, the losses of American aircraft and ships loomed largest in the public consciousness; in Russia the implacable eastern drive of Hitler's armies continued, Sevastopol had been captured and now the Panzer spearheads were pointing ominously towards the Volga at Stalingrad, with the hint too a drive southwards into the Caucasus.

But it was in North Africa that the Allies had suffered their worst setbacks. Despite the experience of the British and Commonwealth forces there, despite the armour and artillery that had been sent to them around the Cape, Rommel's Panzerarmee Afrika had recently driven them back across Cyrenaica from their fortified lines at Gazala and deep into Egypt itself, until they managed a scrambling halt in the narrow space between El Alamein on the coast and the Qattara Depression, a scant hundred miles from the Nile and the huge bases at Alexandria and Cairo.

Worst of all, especially from the point of view of morale, Rommel's troops had captured Tobruk in a fierce two-day battle – Tobruk, which during 1941 had withstood siege for nine months and won a place in fame alongside Lucknow and Mafeking in the past and Leningrad in the present. It had been an especially cruel stroke of Fate that Mr Churchill had been actually sitting in conference with Mr Roosevelt at the time the news was brought to him. 'Tobruk has surrendered', the telegram read, 'with twenty-five thousand men taken prisoner'.

It was, Churchill was later to write, one of the heaviest blows he received during the war, and the kindness and understanding he received from all sides in Washington in the days that followed did nothing to alleviate either the hurt or the Prime Minister's determination that strong measures must be taken to ensure that such a débâcle did not occur again. He would go out to the Middle East himself and take whatever drastic steps were necessary to this end.

What with the closing stages of the conference in Washington and matters to attend to in London, it was August 3rd before Churchill arrived in Cairo, escorted by the Chief of the Imperial General Staff, General Sir Alan Brooke. At six o'clock that evening the first of a series of working conferences took place, and to attend it the Commander-in-Chief, General Sir Claude Auchinleck, had come in from his headquarters in the desert. One matter upon which agreement was quickly reached was that the place for the Commander-in-Chief was in Cairo, not up in the desert, and that a new Eighth Army Commander must quickly be appointed to direct the actual fighting.

During the days that followed many suggestions were put forward, many plans discussed, but the overwhelming and most pressing problem was how soon could the Eighth Army recover from its traumatic experiences since Gazala, go over to the offensive and drive Rommel back out of Egypt? And in order to examine this question more closely, Churchill and the C.I.G.S. spent a day at the front, the first few hours in the wire-mesh cage which constituted Auchinleck's advanced H.Q., or the overheated and arid caravan in which Auchinleck and his Chief of Staff kept their maps and plans, the rest of the day at the R.A.F. advanced H.Q. at Burg el Arab on the coast, where an excellent lunch served on tables with white napery and gleaming silver, preceded by brandy in goblets, awaited Churchill.

Rightly or wrongly, the impression Churchill received was of an atmosphere of despondency in the army but of hope and victory among the R.A.F. Radical changes were, he decided, essential; and at speed.

As a result of long discussion with Sir Alan Brooke, and with both General Wavell and the South African Jan Smuts, the decision was taken that the Middle East Command must be split into two, and that a new Commander-in-Chief would be appointed to the Cairo Command from which the desert battles would be directed. General the Hon. Harold Alexander was the immediate choice of all concerned, and a message was sent to London requesting his early despatch to Cairo.

Churchill's first choice for command of the Eighth Army was a matter of some dispute. Lieutenant-General W. H. E. 'Strafer' Gott was one of the old desert hands who had been there from the beginning, had commanded the 7th Support Group, the 7th Armoured Division and recently the XIII Infantry Corps; he was greatly admired throughout the whole Middle East Command. Moreover, he was there on the spot, and despite Brooke's feelings that he might be too tired for the job, Churchill over-rode him and insisted upon his appointment.

But on the afternoon that Gott flew back from the front to take up his new command, the Bombay aircraft in which he was travelling was forced down by German fighters, Gott was killed and Churchill was informed that he must choose again. That night a cable was sent to Whitehall asking that General Montgomery be sent by special aircraft and at the earliest moment to take command of the Eighth Army.

As he was to play so vital a part in the remainder of the Middle East campaign and the eventual defeat of the Afrika Korps it will be as well to find out what kind of man, and soldier, he was.

Lieutenant-General Sir Bernard Law Montgomery was at the time of his appointment to command Eighth Army some three months short of his fifty-fifth birthday, and had spent most of his time on earth as a non-conformist.

This would seem at first sight somewhat unexpected, for he came of unblemished 'establishment' stock, his paternal grandfather being Sir Robert Montgomery, Commissioner of Lahore at the outbreak of the Indian Mutiny and as a result of the absence in Kashmir of the Chief Commissioner, Sir John Lawrence, virtually in command of the Punjab throughout those early, crucial days. His immediate disarming of the Native Infantry Regiments in the vicinity undoubtedly saved great bloodshed, for they were later proved to have been deeply involved in the planning of the rebellion; this example of swift thought and direct action would be echoed in some of his grandson's more ebullient achievements.

His mother's father was the celebrated Dean Farrar whose best known work was the novel *Eric, or Little by Little*, which in its Victorian heyday rivalled *Tom Brown's Schooldays* as a popular call to manliness, cold baths, the straight bat and a spirit of collaboration with the Almighty made easier by the unassailable tenet that He was an Englishman. One of Dean Farrar's curates was Henry Montgomery, Bernard's father, who later became Bishop of Tasmania (Bernard spent the years between his second and fourteenth birthdays there), ending his service to the Church as Secretary for the Propagation of the Gospel in Foreign Parts, Prelate of the Order of St Michael and St George (of which he wore the insignia of the Knight's Grand Cross), Prebendary of St Paul's Cathedral and a favoured preacher to the Royal Family.

From such a stock one would have expected orthodox attitudes, acceptance of one's place in the hierarchy and unquestioning obedience to authority, all contained in an ethical macedoine with muscular Christianity, strenuous physical activity and not a great deal of mental concentration.

But Montgomery's mother was a remarkable woman who had become engaged to her father's curate at the age of fourteen (Henry

was then thirty-two), married at sixteen and had borne her husband
five children by the time she was twenty-five, with four more still to
come. Photographs of her at the time show a remarkably good-
looking young woman with dark hair, high forehead and straight
features, but with a strong jaw and a mouth which would be a
recommendation for a commanding officer. During the family's stay
in Tasmania she had had to cope with entire strange surroundings,
bring up a growing family, and perform the many pastoral duties
expected of a bishop's wife, for long periods entirely on her own as
her husband's duties frequently took him away on protracted and
arduous journeys.

It all made for an undoubtedly hard life for her, and like many
another parent before and since she took it out on the children; in
particular, she seems to have taken it out on her fourth child,
Bernard, whom, in the opinion of one of his sisters, 'she did not love.'

Cause and effect in these circumstances is impossible to establish
(and anyway an unfair and irrelevant exercise), and whether or not
Bernard was a more than unusually unpleasant and bloody-minded
small boy, such a sorry station in the family pecking order was bound
to produce a reaction of disturbing violence. If he could not secure his
mother's love and attention by being dutiful and good, Bernard
would, and did, secure it by other means – and was as a result in a
continual state of bondage and disgrace.

'My early life was a series of fierce battles,' he was later to say,
'from which my mother invariably emerged the victor.'[1] And it does
not seem that he received any support from his elder brothers (his
older sister died at the age of nine in Tasmania), who both accepted
their mother's iron rule with more docility than he did, and tended to
exclude their naughty brother from their company with all the
ruthless beastliness of the very young and immature. His only friend
and companion in those early years was his young sister Una who
thus, though an extremely attractive child, drew upon herself her
mother's dislike and her brother's fiercely protective spirit.

Bernard adored his father, but the bishop was present only rarely
and with perhaps an inadequate knowledge or insight into the family
condition (and anyway a typically Victorian attitude to authority)
tended to support his wife against his unruly son. Despite therefore
the undoubtedly satisfactory social standing of being a member of the
bishop's family, despite also the carefree Tasmanian background in
which he grew up, Montgomery's statement that he had an
unhappy, indeed miserable, childhood, is unlikely to be much of an
exaggeration.

It was certainly to form ineradicable impressions upon his mind,
and thereafter to influence his attitudes to life and its problems. One
such impression would seem to have been that authority near at hand

was evil and to be resisted at all times, though authority at a distance (with occasional closer visitations) was not only acceptable but often to be welcomed. Another was that the unfortunate ones in life could only depend upon each other.

The Montgomery family returned to England in 1902 and Bernard and one of his brothers were immediately sent to St Paul's School, Hammersmith, where, on the first day, Bernard was asked if he wished to go into the 'Army Class'. This was, in fact, not so much a class exclusively for boys who had already made up their minds to follow a military career, as one for boys to whom practical as opposed to academic pursuits were more attractive; but it is doubtful if Bernard or his brother fully appreciated this and quite certain that their parents did not. It is also doubtful if Bernard had given the matter a great deal of thought beforehand, but quite certain that his immediate decision on the matter – without the slightest consultation with either of his parents or indeed anyone else – would provoke a scene of almost Apocalyptic fervour when he returned home that evening. And so it proved.

His mother had apparently intended that he should follow his father into the Church – as uncomfortable and thoroughly unsuitable a profession as she could choose for him, one suspects – and although the bishop, once he had expressed surprise and initial disagreement, made no attempt to change his son's mind, this was not a matter upon which she was disposed to agree without violent protest.

But there was a great deal of her own intransigence in her son, and her treatment of him had done much to give it a positively adamantine quality. 'I want to be a soldier,' he announced flatly, and no remonstrances, no threats, no arguments, no cold vituperation (she would not stoop to tears or cajolery) would weaken his determination. He remained in the Army Class and, after five years at St Paul's, entered the Royal Military College at Sandhurst in January 1907.

This at last removed him from his mother's immediate thraldom, and although much later in life he would claim that at this point he broke almost completely with her, it seems in fact that relations between them improved. Certainly his letters home for many years were mostly addressed to 'My Darling Mother', though whether she replied so affectionately is doubtful; even when fame crowned his efforts to attract her attention, it seems that he was never anything but the least favourite child.

Such a relationship between mother and son was unlikely to produce in the latter a relaxed, stable individuality, imbued with natural courtesy, an abundance of charm, or inexhaustible good nature.

*

Montgomery passed into Sandhurst 72nd in an intake of 170 and at first did well, so that after six weeks he was among the selections for promotion to the rank of lance-corporal – an honour which normally indicated bright prospects and further advancement.

It went, however, to his head, possibly because to obtain it he had had to overcome disadvantages other than those of personality. Judged by today's standards Sandhurst at that time was a focus of the most appalling snobbery, the majority of its intake being sons of serving army officers and often from old-established military families whose sons had provided senior army officers for decades. They came mostly from the public schools of Eton, Harrow, Wellington, Cheltenham, Clifton or Bedford, and thus formed close coteries which regarded those suffering the paralysing inconvenience of having been educated at other centres of learning as 'outsiders' if not actually 'bounders'; and they were generally in receipt of greater financial allowances than Bishop Montgomery could afford, for everyone entering the British Army would need a private income of at least £100 per annum, and in the case of those destined for the fashionable regiments of the Household Brigade of £400 or more.

Montgomery's allowance of £2 per month was derisory in comparison and he has recorded how jealous he was of most of his fellows at Sandhurst, for they possessed wristwatches; but his prowess at games, combined with the undoubted acuteness of brain when he cared to use it, was enough at first to override these quite significant disadvantages. At St Paul's he had been captain of both the School cricket XI and the rugby XV and would probably have captained the swimming team had not that position already been held by his brother – and during his first term at Sandhurst he was not only picked to play rugger for the College, but was a member of the team which then inflicted a notable defeat upon their traditional rivals from the Royal Military Academy at Woolwich.

He was thus at first accepted, albeit with some scepticism, into the upper hierarchy at Sandhurst. In a society in those days as robust and philistine as any in a robust and philistine age, his promotion and indeed notoriety then led to his becoming, in his second term, the leader of a gang of young thugs, who, had their ancestors been more plebeian and their circumstances more commonplace, would certainly have ended in front of the Bench of Magistrates and quite possibly in prison.

The culminating episode in a brief career of undiluted ruffianism reminiscent of Flashman, Westward Ho! or the gun-room in a ship of the line during the Napoleonic Wars, concerned the pinioning of an unpopular cadet by five of Montgomery's associates while Montgomery himself set fire to his shirt-tails. This resulted in severe burns and hospitalisation for the victim, and although the latter was to behave impeccably and refuse to divulge the names of his attackers, the authorities easily guessed their identities and Montgomery was reduced to the rank of 'Gentleman-cadet' and, one imagines, lost whatever credit he had won from the College élite.

It taught him a severe lesson. It also removed him from the company of the unambitious hell-raisers who were quite content to waste their time at Sandhurst, and as he had no money with which to pursue a social life outside the Academy, he was faced with the alternatives of either being idle on his own or occupying his time by working hard.

He worked – perhaps because of his Victorian upbringing and Irish-Scots ancestry (the family home set up by his great-great-grandfather was at Moville on the Inishowen peninsula north of Londonderry) among whom the 'work ethic' played so large a part; certainly because of his realisation that only by passing high enough in the final examinations could he hope to secure a commission in the Indian Army, the only force in which as a young subaltern he would be able to live on his pay.

But he had left it just too late. His final passing-out place was 36th (out of 150) and only those who passed out among the first thirty were accepted for the Indian Army; but at least his comparatively high placing allowed him choice of such English regiments as would accept an officer with the minimal private income of £100 per annum, which his father was prepared to find. He chose the Royal Warwickshire Regiment ('because I liked the cap-badge'), a sound county regiment with an excellent reputation but into whose officers' mess he hardly fitted.

He had no social, family or even local connections with the Warwickshires; he lacked any form of social or military polish, Sandhurst having failed completely to impart the slightest gloss to his abrasive personality; he was too slight in build, too unremarkable in feature (except for a pair of level grey eyes often so cool as to be frigid) to cut a dashing figure, and his performance on horseback was mediocre; and he had no conversation outside the military world (which had by this time already become his overmastering interest), failing completely to understand why 'shop' was not talked in the mess. Keenness is not a quality which has ever provoked much admiration in officers' messes, but the advantages of having one member who possessed it are obvious. Montgomery soon found himself Sports Officer, posted to the first battalion in India (which did not, however, put his pay up to parity with that of Indian Army officers) and appointed assistant adjutant with the rank of lieutenant.

He seemed to enjoy the minutiae of military life – the drills, the parades, the eternal weapons training and marches – and he certainly enjoyed the sport, excelling still at cricket, taking up hockey and proving a more than capable performer, even buying a cheap horse and winning a race on it, though falling off at both the beginning and the end. He was undoubtedly a hard-working, capable and probably happy young officer, and if his unshakeable conviction that he knew better than anyone else the best way of getting anything done upset many of his fellows, there were quite a number who were prepared to let him get on and do it. Three years passed very rapidly in Peshawar and Bombay, and in 1913 the whole battalion returned to England where Montgomery not only passed out top of the musketry course at Shorncliffe, but also, under the spur of a new acquaintance, a Captain Lefroy, nourished his capacity for hard work with a study of Clausewitz and long talks upon the almost forbidden (for junior officers) subjects of strategy and military theory.

He was soon to see whether they bore any relationship to practice, for in August 1914 the battalion were mobilised for war and within four weeks he was in action in France.

His experiences between 1914 and 1918 were to leave an ineradicable mark upon his entire personality – as happened, of course, to hundreds of thousands of other young men. But whereas so many of those who survived spent the rest of their lives imbued with a deep hatred of war and all its beastliness, Montgomery's repugnance was directed almost solely towards the waste of men and material which had occurred through incompetence at the top. So many men had died as a result of poor planning – or unnecessary deviation from a good plan – that for the rest of his life his first question upon being faced with any problem would be, 'What's the plan? Must have a good plan!'

His first experience of action was during the Battle of Le Cateau, and his own description is as revealing as any:

> Our battalion was deployed in two lines; my company and one other were forward, with the remaining two companies out of sight some hundred yards to the rear. The C.O. [Commanding Officer] galloped up to us forward companies and shouted to us to attack the enemy on the forward hill at once. This was the only order; there was no reconnaissance, no plan, no covering fire. We rushed up the hill, came under heavy fire, my Company Commander was wounded and there were many casualties. Nobody knew what to do, so we returned to the original position from which we had begun to attack. If this was real war it struck me as most curious and did not seem to make any sense against the background of what I had been reading.[2]

Montgomery took two men out to try to bring in the wounded company commander, but there were no stretchers and eventually the unfortunate officer had to be left to be taken prisoner and spend the rest of the war in a prison-camp.

Meanwhile, the rest of the battalion took part in the retreat to the Marne, followed by the subsequent formation of the trench-line up to the Channel coast and the first sanguinary battles around Ypres. It was here that Montgomery's military career, and indeed his life, were very nearly abruptly terminated.

During one of the many futile attempts to break through the opposing lines, Montgomery was ordered to take his platoon forward to occupy a group of buildings on the outskirts of Meteren. Drawing his sword (recently sharpened) he shouted, 'Follow me!' in the approved fashion and ran forward, very quickly to be confronted by a trench full of German soldiers, one of whom brought his rifle around and pointed it at the sword-waving subaltern. As the only exercise with the sword he had ever been taught was saluting-drill and having, as he later wrote, 'read much about the value of surprise in war', Montgomery uttered a loud yell, launched himself through the air and kicked the unfortunate man in a very tender spot 'in the lower part of his stomach'. He had taken his first prisoner.

But later during the day when he was reorganising his men for another advance and standing up to do it, he was hit in the chest by a German rifle bullet which passed completely through him. One of his men bent over to put on a wound dressing, was himself hit and fell across his officer's body, thus protecting it throughout the rest of the daylight hours and against several more rifle and machine-gun bullets. The soldier was killed and Montgomery was hit again in the knee, and when eventually stretcher-bearers found them both (some five hours after he had first been hit) he was judged so far gone that a grave was dug for him; but with a lack of co-operation which some would call typical, he refused to die, was eventually transported back to a hospital in England where he recovered to find that he had been promoted captain and awarded the Distinguished Service Order.

This was a most unusual award for any officer below the rank of major to win, and for a lieutenant to win it has become generally accepted as a 'near miss' for a Victoria Cross; no one during either war was ever to suggest that Montgomery possessed anything but a high degree of physical courage.

Upon recovery, his organising talents were recognised and he spent the remainder of the war 'on the staff' – as brigade major, as General Staff Officer Grade 2 first to a division and then to a corps, and in 1918 G.S.O.1 to another division. But he was a most unusual staff officer for those days, bringing to his duties a philosophy from earlier times.

Many survivors of the First World War have written about the hatred induced by the sight of the red tabs of a staff officer among fighting troops, generally caused by the staff's lack of understanding of front line conditions, exacerbated by an attitude of superiority and condescension especially among the temporary officers, springing from their conscious belief that they were the elite of the army. Many in the higher formations gave the impression – often a true one – that they regarded the brigades, divisions, corps and armies as in the line simply to carry out their own grand designs, irrespective of any ideas the troops or their officers may have had themselves, and certainly unquestioning of such instructions as they received, especially when they demanded that an attack must be 'pressed home regardless of loss'. In the opinion of many of the staff, the regimental officers and men were simply there to do as they were told – and certainly not to reason why.

Montgomery's view was that the staff were the servants of the troops, and that it was the staff's job to see that whatever objective was given to fighting troops, it was within their capability and that they were provided with everything necessary to achieve it. Today this is accepted doctrine, but during the First World War such an attitude in some circles was enough to mark its holder as a maverick of unsound and possibly revolutionary views to be rigorously excluded from the cosiness of the staff coterie. As this was not an exclusion which gave Montgomery a moment's regret or even discomfort, his unpopularity increased and the suspicion with which he was generally regarded by his fellow-officers on the staff deepened.

But fortunately there were some General Officers who could appreciate efficiency and use a capacity for concentration and hard work, however abrasive the personality of its owner. At the end of the war Montgomery became a staff officer with the British Army of Occupation, already dedicated to his profession to a degree which allowed him no distractions – social, idiosyncratic or even sexual. He had no time for cocktails and his only conversation was professional; any facet of his personality which did not contribute to increasing professionalism – laziness, love of physical comfort, enjoyment of food or drink – was already being ruthlessly eradicated; and as for women, at worst they could be as tyrannical as his mother and at best they were a waste of time. Very soon he would be announcing to younger officers with the finality of a diktat that 'You cannot be both a good officer and a good husband.'

His progress up through the military hierarchy between the wars was slow – it could hardly be otherwise in a contracting army after a war fought 'to end wars' – but it was steady, though punctuated by episodes vividly illustrating his unorthodoxy and sometimes gravely threatening his career.

He spent 1920 undergoing the Staff Course at Camberley (the students between them had won seven V.C.s and 170 D.S.O.s and all had a tendency to argue with their instructors, so Montgomery's rumbustiousness was not particularly noticeable at that time) and was afterwards sent to Southern Ireland as brigade major to 17th Infantry Brigade at Cork, engaged upon that depressing duty of 'giving aid to the civil power'. This was followed by another stint as brigade major, this time to 3rd Division where he had the good fortune to serve with a Brigadier Holland who was prepared to let him take over the running of the entire brigade; after which he was given a Grade 2 appointment with 49th West Riding Division. Here he organised a series of lectures for young officers at which he was the sole instructor, and continued the process of teaching junior officers his theories of warfare – and, one suspects, looking for promising youngsters to support him when, as he was sure it would, his hour came. One of the young officers during that spell was a Lieutenant Francis de Guingand.

He then returned as company commander to the Royal Warwick-shires (not a popular appointment with some as he had been away from his regiment for over ten years) but in 1926 was sent back to the Staff College for three years as an instructor, and it was at this point that his true bent was revealed, for it was as a teacher and trainer of troops that Montgomery would always shine. The time passed quickly – and in the end profitably for among his confrères there were Alan Brooke and the Hon. Harold Alexander (as a student), both of whom were to support him in difficult times ahead, and Oliver Leese, John Harding and Miles Dempsey who were to hold critical positions under his command.

Then in 1930 came the most important appointment in the life of any infantry officer – command in his own regiment. Montgomery became a lieutenant-colonel commanding 1st Battalion, Royal Warwickshire Regiment, and was almost immediately involved in his first major conflict with Authority. In addition to his duties as battalion commander, he was appointed secretary of a committee of distinguished senior officers whose task was to rewrite the *Infantry Training Manual* – an appointment which Montgomery interpreted as an instruction for him to do the rewriting while the committee rubber-stamped his work without argument.

'I was', he wrote, 'selected by the War Office to rewrite the Manual of infantry training' – which was not exactly what the War Office had in mind, but what he proceeded to do. 'In it', he later concluded with Olympian simplicity, 'I dealt with the whole art of war.' When the distinguished officers on the committee presumed to question some of his pronouncements he ignored them until their protests became too vociferous, then listed their amendments, suggested the disbandment of the committee and completion of the book by himself working alone, and when by some mysterious means as yet unchronicled all this came about, he arranged the publication of the book without including a single suggested amendment, later recording that the book was considered excellent 'especially by the author'.

He then took his battalion to Palestine (at the beginning of 1932) and later in the year to Alexandria, where it was expected to fulfil the usual standards of smartness and barrack-room drill required of garrison troops. This it notably failed to do. It was reported scruffy in appearance and offhand in manner, and to the shock and dismay of the authorities Montgomery went so far as to abandon official church parades on the grounds that if the men really wanted to go to church on Sundays there was nothing to stop them, but if they did not they might as well have a day's rest and relaxation. They got little enough otherwise for he worked them very hard, and as a result on exercises out in the desert the Royal Warwickshires revealed a standard of infantry training that no other formation had envisaged, let alone achieved. On one occasion, encouraged by a far-sighted superior, Montgomery was given command of a brigade (with de Guingand, now a major, as his chief staff officer) and with his own battalion in the van, executed a complicated manoeuvre at night which not only thoroughly defeated the other side but also silenced those pundits who had long claimed that movement of troops during darkness was an impossibility. As Montgomery himself had been by no means certain of this point but thereafter became thoroughly converted, that was undoubtedly a significant night's work.

After Alexandria he was posted back to India for a three-year appointment to the Staff College at Quetta, this time as Senior Instructor (he was there during the dreadful Quetta earthquake of May 1935) and then at last in the summer of 1937 came his first senior promotion, to brigadier commanding 9th Infantry Brigade at Portsmouth.

Again followed that same pattern of impeccable performance in training and on manoeuvres (9th Brigade became one of the 'star' brigades in the British Army, chosen for many experiments in new equipment and fresh ideas) punctuated by incidents of almost grotesque provocation. The most spectacular of these was brought about when Montgomery decided that the Brigade Funds for providing his soldiers and their families with extra comforts and amenities was in need of replenishment, and hit upon an unusual method of achieving this.

On Southsea Common near Clarence Pier were some football fields owned by the War Department and upon one Bank Holiday when they would not be in use Montgomery offered to rent them to a circus proprietor, despite the fact that he had not the slightest authority to least W.D. land. The man offered a £1,000 fee and was somewhat surprised to find himself then engaged in a tough bargaining session with this most unusual army officer, who eventually settled for £1,500. At this stage, the Portsmouth City Council heard of the matter and, not particularly wanting a circus on their sea-front during the Bank Holiday, forbade the deal – whereupon Montgomery approached the mayor, who he knew was promoting some charitable project of his own, and offered to donate £500 of the £1,500 to it if he could persuade the council to change their minds.

This was all satisfactorily concluded, the fair took place, the brigade's funds were replenished and quickly spent; but then the War Office learned the details of the episode and were shocked to the cores of their amalgamated orthodox souls. That a senior officer should have the commercial acumen even to conceive the scheme was bad enough – that he should then bargain with a circus proprietor as though he were a Levantine merchant (and win!) and follow this with something perilously close to bribery of a civil functionary, was not to be borne. Or at least, not *quite* to be borne; if Montgomery were to hand over the £1,000 to the War Office, then the matter might be overlooked – though probably never forgotten – to which their bête noire replied with impeccable logic that such a course was no longer possible as the money had already been spent. He would, however, be quite willing to send them the receipts.

On this occasion, Montgomery was saved from the wrath of outraged authority by Wavell, who was commanding the whole area and had greatly appreciated the presence of so hard and efficient a worker within his bailiwick – and was himself blessed with a sense of humour. Shortly afterwards, wafted onwards by sighs of relief from certain quarters in Whitehall, Major-General B. L. Montgomery sailed again for Palestine to take command of 8th Infantry Division garrisoning the northern half of that strife-torn country; the division in the south was commanded by Major-General Richard O'Connor. It was the time of the Arab Revolt against ever-increasing Jewish immigration into the country (as a result of Nazi persecution), and the role of British troops was to attempt to keep the peace. They were thoroughly hated by both sides.

It was not, however, long before Montgomery and O'Connor between them had the area under control, Montgomery's methods being, as usual, often unconventional. Jewish shopkeepers on one occasion disapproved of one of his ordinances and closed their shops for twenty-four hours, so Montgomery sent for their senior representative and informed him that the shops would now remain closed for the whole week; and that method of exhibiting displeasure waned sharply in popularity from then on. But with the end of the Arab Revolt in 1939, and danger so obviously looming on another front, Montgomery indulged in some determined, single-minded lobbying and as a result was given command of 3rd Division, part of Southern Command in England and earmarked to go to France upon the outbreak of war. By the end of September 1939, he and his division were in France, training hard and digging that line of defences which almost everybody knew would be abandoned the moment Hitler's troops made the slightest signs of an advance and the British Expeditionary Force moved forward into Belgium to meet them.

That period was distinguished by two personal performances of almost unexampled but unconscious iconoclasm, sandwiching between them a piece of military bravura which went some way towards extricating II Corps – and indeed the entire B.E.F. – from sudden disaster.

His first *faux pas* was brought about, typically, by his concern both for the well-being of his men and, more importantly, for their efficiency as soldiers. Not surprisingly in an area populated by thousands of soldiers aware of the fact that they might soon be fighting for their lives in a foreign country, the local brothels were well patronised and the incidence of venereal disease rose. The view at the top of the British Army hierarchy was that such a situation really should not arise and should be strenuously ignored if it did, but Montgomery put the cat among the pigeons by issuing an ordinance above his own signature which admitted the facts, did nothing to impute guilt to those immediately concerned, and ordered that those soldiers who felt themselves in need of what he called 'horizontal refreshment' should be fully instructed of what safeguards to take and provided by the army with the means of doing so.

Inevitably, a copy of this document fell into the hands of the Royal Army Chaplains' Department, who *en masse* reacted with the fatuous unreality to be expected of them at that time. Unfortunately, the Commander-in-Chief, Gort (who afterwards became the Governor-General of Gibraltar), belonged to the school of military thought which considered a smart turn-out, good drill and gentlemanly conduct the only real essentials, so the padres found a receptive ear, and Montgomery's corps commander (Sir Alan Brooke) felt compelled to take corrective action and administer a severe rebuke. This Montgomery accepted with surprising humility, the Church Militant was assured that the disreputable officer's career would be suitably affected, and venereal disease remained unnecessarily high throughout the British Expeditionary Force.

Later, when the German armies were pouring through the Low Countries, Alan Brooke had cause to thank the gods that he had stood firm against more drastic action being taken against his unruly subordinate.

At midnight on May 27th/28th, the Belgian Army capitulated and a gap suddenly opened between II Corps's left flank and a French division to the north, through which the Germans could easily penetrate and thus cut off the retreat of the B.E.F. to Dunkirk. In this dilemma, Brooke turned to Montgomery and ordered him to execute a move which in the words of one of Montgomery's biographers, Lord Chalfont,

> will be recognised at once by any soldier as one of the most difficult and dangerous manoeuvres in the whole science of war – a movement to a flank by night across the front of an enemy position. Montgomery's task was to disengage from his position at Roubaix, get his division into transport and move in the dark, without lights, over twenty-five miles of minor roads and then get his troops dug in by dawn in an unfamiliar new sector, to meet the overwhelming German attack which was now inevitable.
>
> It was an operation which could at any moment collapse into a comprehensive shambles – it needed only one false move to have the whole division wandering aimlessly about the Belgian and French countryside . . . It needed a high standard of training, impeccable staff work and a commander with nerves of steel.[3]

Fortunately, 3rd Division had them all and Brooke's diary entry the following night, referring to Montgomery, stated, 'Found he had, as usual, accomplished almost the impossible.' Trust and cooperation were beginning to work both ways.

But shock tactics in dealing with uncomprehending superiors were still part of the Montgomery technique. Gort as Commander-in-Chief had been instructed by the Government to appoint a corps commander to control the final, most dangerous stages of the Dunkirk evacuation, and had chosen for the job the commander of I Corps, Lieutenant-General Michael Barker – to be confronted very quickly by a cold-eyed Montgomery informing him that Barker was in no mental or physical state to undertake so responsible and intricate a task, and that it should be given instead to Major-General the Hon. Harold Alexander.

Whether persuaded by Montgomery's logic or stunned into acquiescence by his presumption, Gort agreed and Alexander took control – and an unexpectedly large number of Allied soldiers got away to fight again; but Gort was never heard to express any gratitude to Montgomery for his advice, or indeed any great admiration for him.

Back in England, Montgomery was at first engaged in preparing defences along the southern coast in which his division were to immolate themselves if and when the German invasion occurred, and he did this with his customary efficiency, though continuing his harassment of authority with his repeated pronouncements that Dunkirk had not been a glorious victory for British arms but a defeat and a disgrace. He was also pointing out at the same time that every

Englishman killed on the beaches or on the landing-grounds would be one fewer to help in mobile defence, which was the only kind likely to be of any effect against a blitzkrieg of the type which had brought about the collapse of France.

Eventually, some of that summer's panic and confusion died, Montgomery was given command of V Corps in Hampshire and Dorset, then in April 1941 of XII Corps in the vital area of Kent, and at the end of that year of the entire South-eastern Command. The realities of the military situation during these months of danger had been such that however many people and institutions Montgomery had alienated on his way up, his military competence was so patent and so necessary that his employment and promotion were more vital to the nation than the smoothing of bruised feelings or ruffled feathers.

Not that he ceased increasing animosity against him at all levels.

His immediate superior during the first few months after Dunkirk was Auchinleck, and after his insubordination during that period it says much for the Auk's generosity of spirit (and acceptance of the military reality after the fall of Tobruk) that he would ever have Montgomery in his theatre of command. During the short time Montgomery served in 1940 as one of Auchinleck's divisional commanders he treated the orders he received with scant attention, and whenever he wanted anything of note he rejected the normal channels of military communication and went over Auchinleck's head – on two occasions directly to the Adjutant-General. It was something of a relief to all when Auchinleck went back to India as Commander-in-Chief, and one factor of an increasingly embarrassing conflict – albeit the innocent one – was removed.

Montgomery at this period did not restrict his alienating policies entirely to those above him.

Many officers had been taking advantage of the fact that they were stationed now in England to have their wives and families living close by – some, by coincidence, were serving quite close to their homes anyway – but Montgomery brought this cosy situation to an abrupt close by decreeing that no wives or families of serving soldiers were to be allowed to live within thirty miles of the Channel coast, or within the operational area in which their husbands were serving.

This was misconstrued by many of the sufferers as a piece of overbearing misogamy on the part of an arrogant and deprived general, but Montgomery's argument that if the invader did come those officers would be, not unnaturally, over-concerned with the fate of their nearest and dearest and thus would not concentrate exclusively on their duties, is by no means groundless. And there was another justification for his edict.

The vast majority of the men serving under Montgomery's

command at that time had been used – whether in the regular army or not – to fairly regular hours. If they had not followed 'nine to five' professions they had had 'eight to six' jobs – and with their families in the neighbourhood they tended to spend the day looking forward to 'knocking-off time', followed by an evening with their wives and children.

This was not a schedule likely to increase the efficiency and dedication of an army which might soon be fighting for its life and that of the nation, for not only did it detract from individual concentration, it also militated against the formation of communal spirit and that co-ordination and understanding which it is one of the chief purpose of officers', sergeants' and corporals' messes to inculcate and develop. An officers' mess which is sparsely attended upon anything but a temporary basis is the sign of an uncoordinated formation – and co-ordination was what Montgomery was aiming at throughout his command.

Another thing he was aiming at was physical fitness, so he insisted not only that the fighting troops were kept hard at work whatever the weather, but that even headquarters administrative staff were to do a seven-mile run every week – and one pear-shaped colonel who complained that such an effort would kill him was coldly informed that his death now in training would be less damaging to the army than his death after action had been joined. 'If you are going to die – die now and let us find a replacement.'

This then was the military career of the man who in August 1942 was to fly out to Egypt to take command of Eighth Army. But the picture would not be complete without mention of the few years during which love and some semblance of a family life had brought a new and unexpected factor into Montgomery's life.

Despite his repeated affirmations to young officers, he had apparently succeeded for ten years in being both a good soldier and a good husband.

He met the woman who was to bring – briefly – happiness and a softer approach to life in 1926, though whether this was accidental or the result of a deliberate decision on his part that it was time he married has often been argued. She was Betty Carver, a widow with two young sons whose first husband had been killed at Gallipoli – and she was also sister to that other irascible military genius, Major-General Patrick Hobart, the founder and original trainer of the 7th Armoured Division, with whom Montgomery's relations were never to be much more than civil.

They were married in July 1927, and Betty introduced Montgomery into a world of which he had before had no experience at all – a world of books and music, of amusing and friendly conversation ranging over wide horizons, of men such as the humorous poet A. P.

Herbert and the painter Augustus John. It was a world which Montgomery could make no attempt to join, but in which he appeared quite happy to sit in a corner and watch – and especially watch the woman he so obviously adored being happy and content.

She on her part was more than willing to re-enter the military social world in which she had to a great extent grown up, to play her part as a rising officer's wife, treating his more outré performances with a degree of gentle mockery and understanding affection, and bringing about for him what was undoubtedly an unexpected and recurringly delightful revelation – that life with a woman could produce not only friendship and happiness, but also understanding, loyalty and, incredibly, approval. Very few people beforehand, and certainly no women, had ever admitted to Montgomery that occasionally he might be right about something.

She bore him a son in 1928, went abroad with him to Palestine, Alexandria and India, travelled on leave with him through the Holy Lands and afterwards to Japan, and in 1937 came home with him to England when he was posted to command the brigade at Portsmouth. Then, because she was feeling rather run down, she went to Burnham-on-Sea for a holiday while her husband was concerned with manoeuvres on Salisbury Plain, and one morning while sitting on the beach was bitten by an insect on the leg. A few days later she felt weak and was admitted to the local hospital; and by the time Montgomery had been sent for and arrived, it was obvious that something was badly wrong.

The infection spread and in those days before antibiotics, multiplied with frightening rapidity until gangrene set in and the leg had to be amputated; and in her run-down state she was in no condition to withstand the shock. On October 19th, 1937, with her husband's voice reading from the 23rd Psalm the last sounds she would hear on earth, she died – and Montgomery's ten brief years of marital happiness were at an end.

The shock to Montgomery was traumatic. It marked the end of a period in which some of his attention had been directed away from military matters, and the beginning of another in which it was totally redirected into its old, habitual narrow arc. He drowned his tragedy in work, he numbed his sorrow with mental fatigue and, as mind and body recovered, his concentration on his profession brought its due reward of increasing technical expertise and understanding.

But he never forgot his experience, and almost certainly never lost a feeling that something important had been ripped brutally away from the pattern of his life. Even the success which later came to him seems not to have compensated for this, and he was on one occasion to say (forgetting perhaps his earlier comments on Life with Mother) – 'I have never lost. Except when my wife died.'

Other things he said were:

I went through the whole war on the Western Front, except during the period I was in England after being wounded; I never once saw the British Commander-in-Chief, neither French nor Haig, and only twice did I see an Army Commander. The higher staffs were out of touch with the regimental officers and with the troops. The former lived in comfort, which became greater as the distance of their headquarters behind the lines increased.[4]

By the time the 1914–18 war was over it had become very clear to me that the profession of arms was a life study.[5]

There are only two answers to most military problems. One of them is wrong.[6]

An army is a most sensitive instrument and can easily become damaged; its basic ingredient is men and, to handle an army well, it is essential to understand human nature.[7]

It is important to remember that all men are different . . . If a commander thinks that all men are the same and he treats the great mass of human material accordingly, he will fail.[8]

Every man who is worth his salt should have ambition.[9]

Study the individual soldier. Create the atmosphere of success. Morale means everything.[10]

You must learn to pick a good team of subordinates, and once you have got them stick to them and trust them. All men are different and all general are different; so are brigades and divisions.[11]

You must have the will to win; it is much more important to fight well when things are going badly than when things are going well.[12]

If you worry you merely go mad.[13]

The discipline demanded of the soldier must become loyalty in the officer.[14]

There are no bad soldiers; only bad officers. [He was aware that this was not a Montgomery original.]

Of equal significance, of course, were some of the things said about him:

He is clever, energetic, ambitious and a very gifted instructor. But to do himself justice he must cultivate tact, tolerance and discretion . . . very refreshing to meet. He revels in independence and responsibility.[15]

An officer of great military ability who delights in responsibility. He is very quick. He writes very clear memoranda . . . definitely above the average and should attain high rank in the army. He can only fail to do so if a certain high-handedness, which occasionally overtakes him, becomes too pronounced . . . He is really popular with his men whom he regards and treats as if they were his children.[16]

Brigadier Montgomery is one of the cleverest brains we have in the higher ranks, an excellent trainer of troops and an enthusiast in all he does. His work this year in the gas trials was of a very high order. He has some of the defects of the enthusiast, in an occasional impatience and intolerance when things cannot be done as quickly as he would like, or when he meets brains less quick and clear than his own.[17]

He could describe a complex situation with amazing lucidity and sum up a long exercise without the use of a single note. He had a remarkable flair for picking out the essence of a problem, and for indicating its solution with startling clarity. It was almost impossible to misunderstand his meaning, however unpalatable it may be. In an argument he was formidable and ruthless.[18]

Quick as a ferret; and about as likeable.

Nobody in those days ever said of him that he was a 'nice chap'.

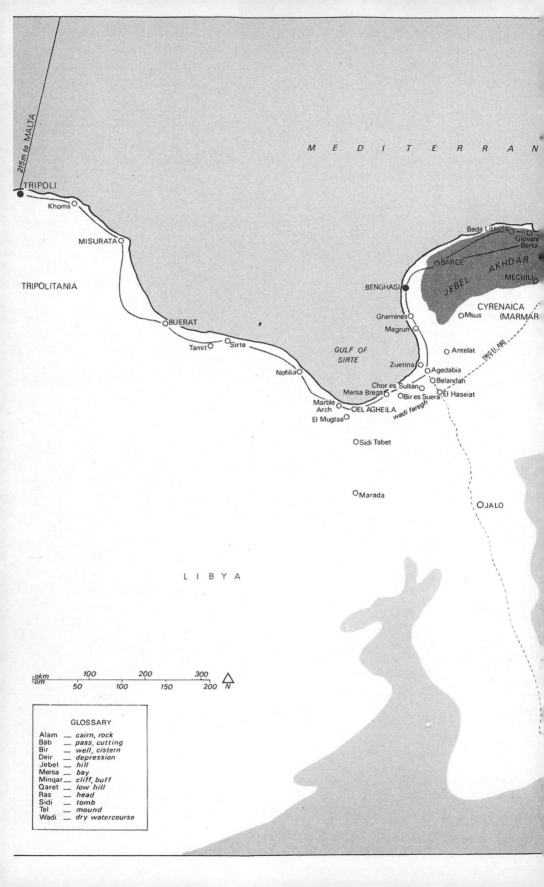

MEDITERRAN

215m to MALTA

TRIPOLI

Khoms

MISURATA

TRIPOLITANIA

BUERAT

Tamit Sirte

GULF OF
SIRTE

Nofilia

Mersa Brega

Chor es Sultan

Bir es Suera

Marble
Arch EL AGHEILA

El Mugtaa

wadi faregh

Sidi Tabet

Marada

JALO

LIBYA

Beda Littoria
Giovann
Berta

BARCE JEBEL AKHDAR

MECHILI

BENGHASI

CYRENAICA
(MARMAR

Ghemines Msus

Magrun

Antelat

Zuetina

Agedabia

Belandah

El Haseiat

TRIG EL ABD

okm   100   200   300
1om
       50   100   150   200   N

GLOSSARY
Alam — cairn, rock
Bab — pass, cutting
Bir — well, cistern
Deir — depression
Jebel — hill
Mersa — bay
Minqar — cliff, buff
Qaret — low hill
Ras — head
Sidi — tomb
Tel — mound
Wadi — dry watercourse

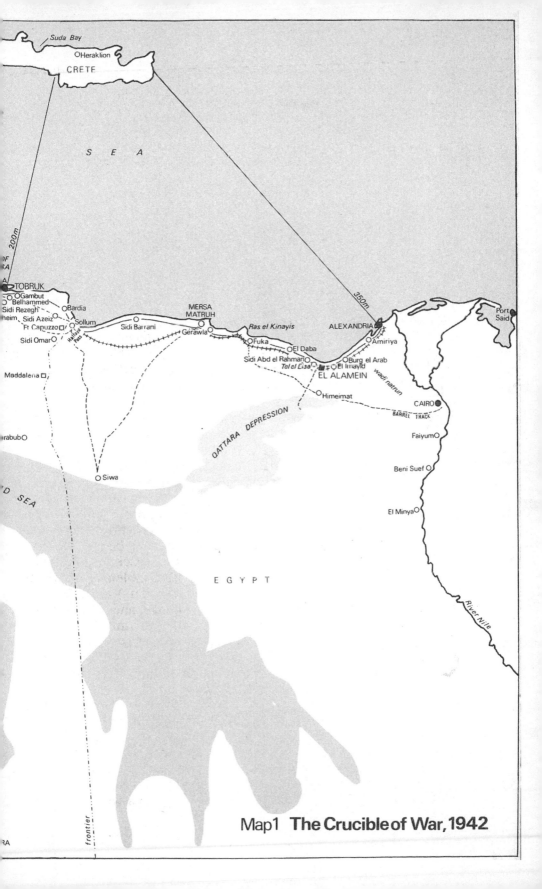

Map 1 **The Crucible of War, 1942**

Map 28 Breakout and Pursuit, November 4th-6th

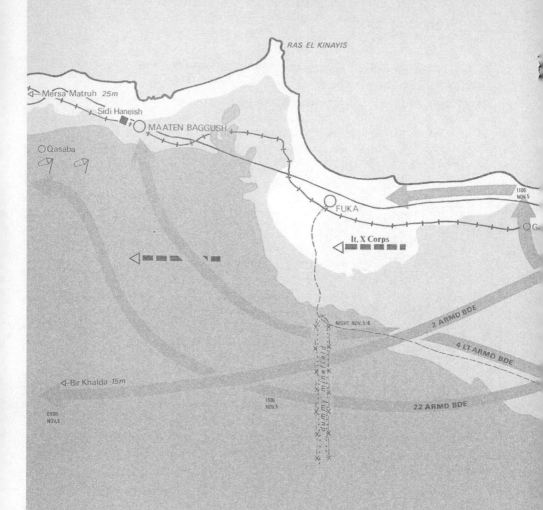

RAS EL KINAYIS

Mersa Matruh *25m*

Sidi Haneish

MAATEN BAGGUSH

Qasaba

1100
NOV.5

FUKA

Ga

lt. X Corps

2 ARMD BDE

NIGHT NOV.5/6

4 LT ARMD BDE

Bir Khalda *15m*

1800
NOV.5

22 ARMD BDE

0900
NOV.6

| 0km | | 8 | | 16 | | 24 | N |
| 0m | 5 | | 10 | | 15 | |

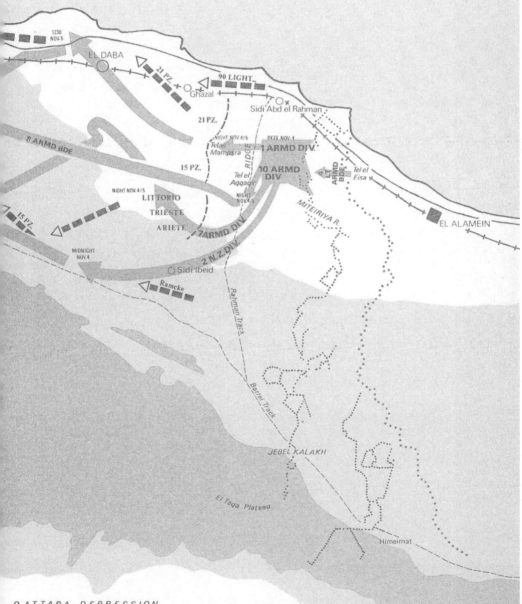

DITERRANEAN   SEA

QATTARA DEPRESSION

1 · 'A cool and refreshing breeze'

With both armies relatively quiescent after the July battles, the fighting at Alamein was largely lifted in early August into the third dimension, where the Royal Air Force, augmented by sixteen South African Air Force squadrons and eight from the Royal Australian Air Force, dominated the skies.

During the retreat from Gazala they had at first been unable to offer the armies much protection as their fighter squadrons had been busily skipping backwards out of danger from desert airstrip to desert airstrip, while the bombers could give little help in the face of the inextricable entanglement of the Army units with each other and the similarity of their appearance to that of the Axis formations. But with the stabilising of the line south of Alamein, the rapid development of bases for fighters and light bombers around Amiriya and for mediums and heavies back in the Levant, the Desert Air Force began to play an increasingly crucial role in the conflict.

During the latter part of the retreat they had already caused Rommel considerable trouble by bombing concentrations of Panzer-armee vehicles, and had won the everlasting gratitude of the Eighth Army by keeping dive-bombers away from the long columns of slow-moving trucks and lorries; 'Thank God you didn't let the Huns Stuka us,' Freyberg had said to Tedder when he got back from hospital, ' . . . we were an appalling target.' Now as Eighth Army reorganised and Rommel awaited supplies and planned his next stroke, the Wellingtons, Albacores and Bostons were out all night and often all day, bombing the harbour installations at Sollum, Matruh, Derna and Tobruk, searching for tankers bringing Rommel his vital fuel, or coasters creeping up with his ammunition, and strafing and bombing the Axis convoys making their increasingly perilous way along the narrow ribbon of the coastal road.

Above the battlefield itself, Hurricanes, Kittyhawks, Spitfires and Tomahawks ranged continuously, machine-gunning every movement they saw, chasing away the occasional Stuka or Me 109, and carrying out the essential reconnaissance which the armoured cars, blocked at one end of the line by the sea, at the other end by the Qattara Depression and along its length by the ever thickening belts of mine-fields, were finding increasingly difficult to carry out.

Plain statistics can in this instance give a clear indication of the growing Allied air strength and activity. During the twenty-two days following the opening of the Gazala battle on May 26th, the Desert Air Force had flown 5,732 sorties; between July 1st and 27th over 15,400 sorties were flown, all in direct support of Eighth Army or of attempts by the Royal Navy to help the Army. Inter-Service co-operation had become the vital factor under the pressure of im-mediate danger, and four times during July, cruisers and destroyers based on Haifa or Port Said had bombarded the port at Matruh with the aid of flares dropped by Albacores, sinking two merchant ships, wrecking port installations and thus further aggravating Rommel's already precarious supply situation.

Obviously all this had been carried out at some cost – the Allies lost 113 aircraft in the area during July, in most cases complete with pilots and crews for they had been operating either over the sea or over parts of the desert in hostile hands; but Air Marshal Tedder's greatest need at this time was for machines, not men. As a result of the Empire Air Training scheme he often found himself with crews for several squadrons standing by awaiting aircraft (to their great disgust) while many promised Hurricanes and Tomahawks had been diverted to India in the face of the Japanese onslaught, and now more aircraft were being held back in America to equip the rapidly growing U.S.A.A.F.

Even the announcement that Major-General L. H. Brereton was coming out to the Middle East in order to establish complete American formations to take part in the coming battles was not unalloyed good news, for such formations would not be ready for action for some time to come whereas their aircraft were needed now.

So what machines there were in the area had to fly all the time – often with alternating crews. Engines and airframes were subjected to enormous strain as the machines flew out on seven or eight sorties every day, the pilots and crews making half that number – which was almost as great a strain on the men as on the machines in the conditions in which they had to live and fly. Intense heat, continual dust and grit, sweat and sand caking every exposed part of the body, flies everywhere; and in the air, sandstorms blocking out the targets, choking the gun-barrels, turning the cockpits into in-dividual furnaces.

But at least the Desert Air Force was spared one horror to be continually endured by the troops on the ground – the sight of the dead lying among the minefields, obscene and swollen in the blazing sun until they burst, to drench the neighbourhood with the reek of putrefying flesh.

During the early days of August, Eighth Army had drawn wearily back from immediate contact with the enemy, thankful that for the moment it seemed unlikely that they would be called upon for much more active duty than patrolling and occasional raids, bitter at the waste of life and effort of the last few weeks, and sceptical of promises of better times to come. Hopes raised by the news that Auchinleck had replaced Ritchie had fallen again in the face of the evident failure of the attacks mounted in July, and the fact that the advance of the Afrika Korps had at least been ended was a negative benefit which did little to improve morale or to lift any but the most volatile spirits.

Dour dissatisfaction was the mood of the mass of the army, cynical in its attitude to authority, doubtful of the ability of any formation other than the individual soldier's own to perform well in either attack or defence, over-ready to blame other units or arms for every failure. This mood of pessimism had reached such a stage that despite the disappointments of July, the information that Auchinleck was himself to be replaced was greeted with even more bitterness by some; few had ever heard of the new general from Britain who in Eighth Army opinion would be unlikely to possess desert experience, would have to be carried by Eighth Army until his 'knees were brown' and until then could be expected to make the same mistakes that all the other commanders had made in the past – at the cost of Eighth Army sweat and blood.

Even the news of Churchill's presence caused only the slightest alleviation of discontent, for comparatively few of the fighting troops saw him and most of his time had been spent talking to senior officers. So the men observed the comings and goings of the staff cars bearing newcomers forward and taking old hands away with cynical detachment, and one of the first observations made by their new Commander-in-Chief, General the Hon. Sir Harold Alexander, was that although the men looked tough and fit, they showed little sign of cheerfulness, many of them turning their backs on his car as it went by, and very few making the slightest attempt to salute it.

Realising, however, that it was more important for him to inspire a proper respect in the future than to attempt to enforce its outward signs in the present, he concentrated for the moment upon the terse but extremely comprehensive directive he had just been given, written in the Prime Minister's own handwriting upon Embassy notepaper, for his future conduct of the Middle Eastern conflict:

1. Your prime and main duty will be to take or destroy at the earliest opportunity the German–Italian Army commanded by Field-Marshal Rommel together with all its supplies and establishments in Egypt and Libya.
2. You will discharge or cause to be discharged such other duties as pertain to your Command without prejudice to the task described in paragraph 1 which must be considered paramount in His Majesty's interests.[1]

Well, at least it was not clouded by ambiguity.

The changeover in command was to take place officially on August 15th, and there would inevitably be a certain measure of upheaval and disjuncture which not even the studiously polite and civilised behaviour of all but one of the participants could disguise.

On August 8th, with the final changes as a result of Gott's death agreed with the War Cabinet, Mr Churchill had written to Auchinleck:

Cairo
8th August 1942

Dear General Auchinleck,
1   On June 23 you raised in your telegram to the C.I.G.S. the question of your being relieved in this Command, and you mentioned the name of General Alexander as a possible successor. At that time of crisis to the Army His Majesty's Government did not wish to avail themselves of your high-minded offer. At the same time you had taken over effective command of the battle, as I had long desired and suggested to you in my telegram of May 20. You stemmed the adverse tide and at the present time the front is stabilized.
2   The War Cabinet have now decided, for the reasons which you yourself had used, that the moment has come for a change. It is proposed to detach Iraq and Persia from the present Middle Eastern theatre. Alexander will be appointed to command the Middle East, Montgomery to command the Eighth Army, and I offer you the command of Iraq and Persia including the Tenth Army, with headquarters at Basra or Baghdad. It is true that this sphere is today smaller than the Middle East, but it may in a few months become the scene of decisive operations and reinforcements to the Tenth Army are already on the way. In this theatre, of which you have special experience, you will preserve your associations with India. I hope therefore that you will comply with my wish and directions with the same disinterested public spirit that you have shown on all occasions. Alexander will arrive almost immediately, and I hope that early next week, subject of course to the movements of the enemy, it may be possible to effect the transfer of responsibility on the Western battlefront with the utmost smoothness and efficiency.
3   I shall be very glad to see you at any convenient time if you should so desire.

Believe me,
Yours sincerely,
Winston S. Churchill[2]

This epistle was conveyed to Auchinleck that same morning by one of Churchill's staff, feeling 'as if I were just going to murder an unsuspecting friend,' and after Auchinleck had read it with typical impassivity, he asked a few questions and indicated that he doubted whether he could accept command of the new theatre, for a number of reasons.

These reasons he detailed during a 'bleak and impeccable' interview with Churchill the following day, Sunday, August 9th. Although he accepted the grounds given for a change in command, Auchinleck felt that the reduction of his responsibilities to such a small proportion of those he had lately been shouldering would look to the public too much like the appointment of an unsuccessful general to an operational sinecure – a policy of which he would thoroughly disapprove had it happened to anyone else and which he could therefore not accept himself. He also voiced strongly the opinion that such a division of the Middle East Command would prove impracticable, as the new zone would rely for its supplies and reinforcement upon passage through either the new Middle East theatre or through India and a crisis in either of those areas would affect delivery, however crucial the situation in Iraq or Persia might be.

In the circumstances he asked to be allowed to retire into oblivion (in the event he was to become Commander-in-Chief in India within a year) though at Mr Churchill's urgent bidding he agreed to give the matter a few more days' thought; but he warned the Prime Minister that he would be unlikely to change his mind between then and Churchill's return from Moscow in ten days' time. In the meantime, he would return to the desert to hand over his command.

That day Alexander arrived and the interview between the interchanging Commanders-in-Chief was as polite and friendly as the inevitable embarrassment would allow; but on August 12th Montgomery arrived and the atmosphere became much less cordial. As neither Alexander nor Montgomery was due to take up his respective command for another three days, Montgomery's superior at that moment was Auchinleck and to him he must first report.

It was a prickly, thoroughly uncomfortable interview in which Montgomery made little attempt to ease the situation either by trying to gloss over the past and pretend that his recent insubordination to Auchinleck had been mere misunderstanding, or even doing much to disguise his attitude of thinly veiled contempt for all military command as it had been exercised to date in the Middle East. It is doubtful whether he took in much information from the War Map he was shown or from the situation outline as given by Auchinleck, and he got out of the room as quickly as he decently could. But within a matter of hours, it became evident that he was again paying scant attention to any instructions Auchinleck had given him, and also that an entirely new set of conditions would henceforth apply in the Desert War.

John Harding was then Deputy Chief of General Staff at the Cairo H.Q. and has given an illuminating account of the immediate effect of Montgomery's arrival in the establishment, and of his own first meeting with his two new superior officers on that portentous afternoon.

> The first I knew of the changes in command was one afternoon (August 12th) when my orderly came in and said,
> 'The Commander-in-Chief wants to see you.'
> So I said, 'Who is the Commander-in-Chief?'
> I went along to the C-in-C's room, and there, sitting at the desk, was Monty: and sitting on the desk, drumming his heels against it, was Alex. I didn't know what their respective appointments were. Nobody had told me. Monty introduced me to Alex:
> 'You know General Alexander?'
> It was the first time I had ever met him, but I knew all about him of course. Monty said,
> 'Well John, you've been out here a long time. Tell me everything.' And then he put me through a catechism for about an hour, with Alex not taking any real part in the discussion, and I was quizzed on all the formation commanders down to brigades. At the end he said,
> 'From all this muckage, can you organise for me two desert-trained armoured divisions and a mobile infantry division?'
> I asked, 'And hold the front too, presumably?'
> 'Yes, of course.'
> 'Yes, I think I can.'[3]

According to Montgomery, the formation of this *corps de chasse* as an equal opponent to the Afrika Korps and a means of exploitation of the breakthrough at Alamein he was already planning, was a result of deep thought on his part during his journey out from England, and the agreement by Harding that its formation was a practicability became the basis upon which many plans for the future were to rest. But having given a significant glimpse of how he saw the relationship between himself and his eventual Commander-in-Chief, Montgomery then travelled up into the desert the following day to visit Eighth Army advanced headquarters. On his way he picked up his old acquaintance Freddie de Guingand who had been acting since the beginning of July as Auchinleck's B.G.S. at the front, and questioned him closely on recent events there and again on the performance of various commanders and their formations.

As de Guingand and Montgomery had worked together success-fully before, it was not surprising that there was great similarity in their points of view, and as the former expressed the doubts he had already begun to feel for the methods and intentions of the present command, he found his sentiments echoed with redoubled fervour by the newcomer. De Guingand's account of what followed sparkles with an enthusiasm noticeably absent from his narrative of previous events:

> He [Montgomery] then went through his proposals for the future. It was extraordinary how he had spotted most of the weaknesses even before his arrival. And he gave out his ideas to a gathering of all the Headquarters Staff officers that very evening as the sun was setting below the Ruweisat Ridge . . .
>
> That address by Montgomery will remain one of my most vivid recollections . . . We all felt that a cool and refreshing breeze had come to relieve the oppressive and stagnant atmosphere.
>
> He was going to create a new atmosphere . . . The bad old days were over, and nothing but good was in store for us. A new era had dawned.

Above all,

> Any further retreat or withdrawal was quite out of the question. Forget about it. 'If we cannot stay here alive, then let us stay here dead!'[4]

This was unquestionably what everyone present wanted to hear – as did the rest of Eighth Army, and Montgomery was determined that they should indeed all hear it during the next few days. But in the meantime there was an opportunity for another blatant swipe at that particular manifestation of authority of which his mother had been the primal fount, and of which Auchinleck was now the most immediate representative.

Dismissing Ramsden (who had been appointed temporary Eighth Army commander until the time of Montgomery's official assumption of command) back to his corps, Montgomery had as early as two o'clock that afternoon sent a signal back to Cairo H.Q. ordering the immediate destruction of all plans within Eighth Army for withdrawal, and then announced that he was not waiting for the elapse of two more days before taking up his command, but was doing so immediately. He then left for an inspection of XIII Corps and a talk with their temporary commander Freyberg (in whom he found a sympathetic ear, especially when he laid it down as an ineluctable principle that from now on divisions would fight as divisions and that the day of the Jock Column or even battlegroup was over), trusting that any violent reaction to this latest piece of discourtesy would be expended by the time of his return.

There seems, in fact, to have been no immediate or obvious riposte by Auchinleck, however bitter that moment may have been for him, so Montgomery could later write of that night, 'It was with an insubordinate smile that I fell asleep: I was issuing orders to an Army which someone else reckoned he commanded!'[5]

There was undoubtedly an element of gratuitous arrogance, perhaps even of brutality, in the method adopted by Montgomery in taking command of the Eighth Army when he did, but those who criticise him for not waiting that extra forty-eight hours should remember the part time can play in warfare. Had Auchinleck taken over first from Cunningham and then from Ritchie two days earlier than in fact he did, who can say what benefits might have accrued or losses been avoided? Even more important is a lesson to be drawn from the whole catalogue of war, that a general driven always by a desire to get things done quickly is more likely to be granted victory than one whose habit of mind allows him to accept the passage of time with easy acquiescence.

Montgomery, as has been suggested, was not the model of the 'nice chap' so popular at all levels of the British regular army – charming to his equals, authoritative to his subordinates and especially to 'the men', preferably big, handsome and splendidly filling his immaculate uniform; vested, except to his staff, with a degree of Olympian remoteness.

Montgomery was none of those things; indeed, had he possessed any of these attributes he would possibly have attempted to discard them because he sensed that, at that moment, those very qualities which the British were supposed traditionally to admire were stained in the eyes of Eighth Army with defeat – and in some cases with disgrace. His very physical insignificance would be an asset now, and he would make the men of the desert accept him quickly by his own identification with them – by adopting their own style of informal dress, by being seen by them all, by talking to them in the language they understood, above all by saying the things they wanted to hear even though some of them might not stand up to strict examination.

In this last category came, then and later, many statements or inferences with regard to the past in which, according to him, everything had always been done wrongly whereas from now on-wards everything would be right. All the past, according to Montgomery, had been a dismal catalogue of weakness, muddle, bad training, bad planning and low morale, with leadership mediocre at best and abysmal in general; and if such a simplification was unfair to Auchinleck and to many of the other officers who were soon to find themselves sent back to England under the cloud of Montgomery's stinging disfavour, these could presumably hardly have arrived at their various stations in life without having recognised that life itself is not a condition in which justice or fairness plays an appreciable part.

It had been, after all, not very fair that so many brave young men had lost their lives, their limbs or their freedom as the result of mistakes made, time and time again, by some of the men now gloomily complaining of Montgomery's lack of good breeding as they made their way back to a civilian comfort and security denied, sometimes for ever, to the victims of their own professional incompetence.

The first to feel the impact of the new man's personality were of course the corps and divisional commanders and the staff, and to these Montgomery made his intentions crystal clear in a very short time. As he had told Freyberg, the expressions 'Jock Column' and 'battlegroup' were to disappear from the lexicon of the Eighth Army as henceforward they would fight as they had been organised and trained – in divisions and corps. Another expression to go must be the term 'box', which so far as their new commander was aware was a contraption with a lid on it to hold the occupants down; this would be replaced by the term 'defended area' – and as 'consolidation' had in the past been a term often interpreted as an excuse for sitting down and doing nothing, the new expression would be 'reorganising', with its emphasis on gathering strength for future action.

If some well-used terms were to be replaced by others, certain practices one above all – were to disappear completely. A total embargo was placed upon what the new Army Commander called 'bellyaching' and in case any present were not aware of his own interpretation of that expression he spelled it out for them. 'Bellyaching' meant arguing about orders and would cease forthwith; in future, orders issued from Army Headquarters – almost invariably through Freddie de Guingand who was quickly confirmed as Montgomery's Chief of Staff – would be obeyed without question, and would certainly not be regarded, as seemed to have happened in the past, as little more than a basis for discussion. And when Major-General Callum Renton, who since the first desert victory in 1940 had worked his way up from command of the 2nd Rifle Brigade to command of 7th Armoured Division, made the mistake of believing that the new man did not mean what he said and argued about the employment of armour during the forthcoming battle, he found himself the recipient of a tongue-lashing from his new corps commander which left him white-faced and shaken, and when the battle was over was relieved of his cherished command.

For preparations for the forthcoming battle – and everyone was quite certain that Rommel must either strike soon or abandon any hope of reaching Cairo – were obviously Montgomery's first preoccupation. There was general agreement that Rommel would try to break through during the moonlit period at the end of August, probably in an attempted repeat of his success at Gazala with a right hook through the bottom half of the opposing line, followed by a drive up to the coast in order to cut off the infantry of XXX Corps around and in the Alamein defences, and then the final triumphant advance to Alexandria and Cairo.

These potential dangers had already been foreseen by Auchinleck and Dorman-Smith, and their plans to deal with them had entailed the consolidation of the defences from Tel el Eisa past the El Alamein box down to Ruweisat Ridge (held from north to south respectively by 9th Australian, 1st South African and 5th Indian Divisions) with an extension by 5th and 6th New Zealand Brigades of XIII Corps further southwards down to Bare Ridge on Alam Nayil. Behind the XXX Corps positions were held the Valentines of 23rd Armoured Brigade, while further south on a ridge named Alam Halfa leading back north-eastwards from behind the New Zealanders was ensconced the 21st Indian Infantry Brigade, taking the place under Freyberg's command of 4th New Zealand Brigade, recuperating in the Delta from their recent heavy losses and undergoing training as the first Commonwealth armoured brigade.

Also under XIII Corps command were the two armoured brigades and one motor brigade of 7th Armoured Division, 22nd Armoured Brigade in the wide gap between the New Zealanders and Alam

Map 3   Auchinleck's dispositions for Alam Halfa

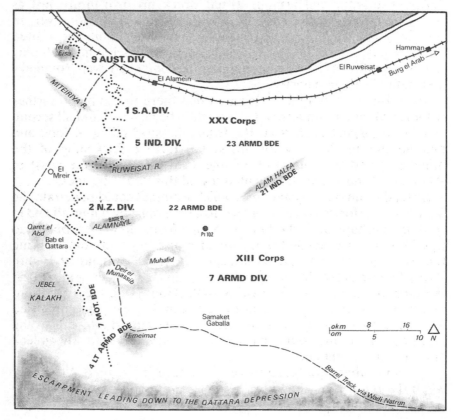

Halfa, 7th Motor Brigade patrolling from the southern edge of the New Zealand positions down to Himeimat, and the armoured cars and light tanks of 4th Light Armoured Brigade operating west of the minefields and around Himeimat itself.

In accordance with Auchinleck's plan to keep Eighth Army mobile and capable of manoeuvre, transport was held available close to every defensive position, with the general philosophy that Rommel's forces should be contained and channelled during a fluid battle, revolving around the fulcrum of the Alam Halfa position. Whether 7th Armoured Division would close up into the gaps to the east of the New Zealanders or instead stay out to the south and threaten the outer flank of Rommel's advance was a matter which had apparently not been thrashed out before Montgomery arrived and was, as has been mentioned, the subject of some initial disagreement.

Montgomery did not think much of these plans for a mobile battle. On past form Rommel's men were likely to be better at it than his own, and he was well aware that yet another disaster which could be blamed upon armoured incompetence or upon lack of co-operation between infantry and armour would wreck his own future just as surely as it had wrecked Ritchie's and Auchinleck's. Moreover, in this particular battle he did not want his men to be mobile; he wanted them to stay where they were and fight, thus bringing into full play that one quality of British troops which had compelled even Rommel's admiration – their tenacity.

Montgomery had already declared that there would be no further withdrawal, and to underline this assertion he now ordered all second echelon transport back from the front, the stockpiling of food and ammunition in the forward areas, the further thickening of the minefields and the formation of one solid front from the coast to Alam Nayil, no longer fragmented 'by all this "box" business'.

Instead of an open system into which Rommel could penetrate, he would form a fortress against which Rommel must hurl himself and in so doing perhaps dash the famous Afrika Korps to pieces; but to do this Montgomery needed more infantry and more armour. During the evening after he had so brusquely taken command of Eighth Army he instructed de Guingand to ring up Cairo H.Q. and request the immediate despatch forward of 44th (Home Counties) Division, and when the staff replied that the division was still unacclimatised and could not move up until the end of the month, Montgomery rang Harding who in due course passed on the request first to Auchinleck and then to Alexander.

'If that's what Monty wants, let him have it,' replied Alexander when the request reached him, setting a precedent he was to follow for many months.

The bulk of the division arrived on Alam Halfa ridge two days later, its third brigade coming up the following day; and quite soon afterwards, Major-General Gatehouse was instructed to bring up the H.Q. of his 10th Armoured Division, together with the seventy-two Grants and twelve Crusaders of 8th Armoured Brigade to take positions along and to the south of the ridge.

Now the fortress could take shape – a solid defence stretching down from Tel el Eisa on the coast as far as Alam Nayil (with thick minefields going further on down to Himeimat) and an equally solid flank stretching back from Alam Nayil along the Alam Halfa Ridge. And to give added toughness to the defence and added striking power to the artillery, the orders to the troops were quite unequivocal – in itself a factor to boost morale considerably. All Corps positions were to be fought to the last man and the last bullet, as were the New Zealand and 44th Divisional positions of XIII Corps, while the Valentines, Grants and Crusaders of 22nd Armoured, 23rd Armoured and 8th Armoured Brigades were to be regarded for the most part as mobile artillery fighting alongside the infantry from hull-down positions. They were only to move forward in charge or counter-

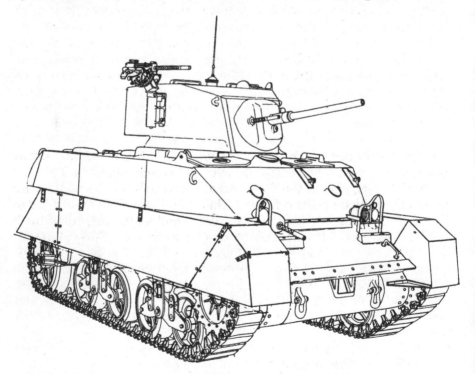

Figure 1   Light tank M3 (Stuart): weight 12·3 tons; armour 25mm.–40mm.; engine 250 h.p.; maximum speed 35 m.p.h.; armament one 37mm., three ·30 in. machine-guns; crew 4

attack if specifically ordered to do so by their new corps commander, Lieutenant-General Brian Horrocks, a protégé of Montgomery's who had been especially flown out at the Army Commander's request to take over Gott's old command.

As for the 7th Armoured Division, despite recent pronouncements 22nd Armoured Brigade was to be detached for the battle and placed under Gatehouse in 10th Armoured Division, while the Stuarts, Crusaders and armoured cars of 7th Motor Brigade and 4th Light Armoured Brigade would endeavour to stop Rommel on the mine-fields south of the New Zealanders, and if this proved impossible then to harass the southern flanks of any breakthrough to the greatest possible extent. To give an impression of greater strength down in that area and thus perhaps to impose an extra degree of hesitation upon the Afrika Korps, two dummy tank battalions were moved down to the east of Himeimat, dummy infantry positions were dug around Samaket Gaballa and some stretches of dummy minefield laid; and with memories of Allenby's device before the third battle of Gaza in 1918, a false map of the terrain showing a hard level surface below the Alam Halfa Ridge where there was in fact a patch of soft sand was planted in an old scout car which then 'accidentally' blew up on a mine just east of Himeimat and was abandoned by its crew.

By August 25th all formations were moving into position, and somewhat to the surprise of a number of the troops, they all knew what was expected of them. Much more had happened to Eighth Army than just the reinforcement and redisposition of its constituent corps, for Montgomery had begun reshaping it to his own specifications.

He had also begun – rather unexpectedly in view of his strong puritanical strain – by easing the lives of his immediate staff.

'What's this, a meat safe?' he had asked as soon as he saw the wire mesh cage which had so offended Churchill. 'You don't expect me to live in a meat safe, do you? Take it down and let the poor flies out!'[6]

And very soon his headquarters had moved to Burg el Arab, close – to Air Marshal Tedder's great relief – to the R.A.F. head-quarters, and alongside the sea in which all could wash away the sweat and grime of desert living. A large mess tent arrived, white tablecloths and shining cutlery appeared, a good cook was found and competent servants to help lift everyone's morale and capacity for work.

'Let us be at least as comfortable as we can,' Montgomery said, and saw to it that this precept was obeyed not only at his own head-quarters. Every soldier in his command was soon to learn, often to his surprise, that the new general considered him worth looking after and likely to fight better after a good night's sleep.

Montgomery never pretended that he did not thoroughly enjoy the methods by which he both made himself known to his troops and excited their enthusiasm; and the fact of his enjoyment should not obscure the necessity for the process. For too long the men of Eighth Army had been expected to endure the hardship of desert life, the heat, the thirst and the boredom, then to walk forward into appalling danger, towards death, wounds or captivity, all at the behest of remote Olympian figures whose names they hardly knew, who were rarely seen except as shadowy figures on the back seats of large cars rolling past swathed in dust, who never spoke to them except in reproof for some military solecism such as appearing before them with their shirts unbuttoned, and whose ignorance of military reality they felt had been so often demonstrated by themselves, and paid for in their own blood.

Now the most senior officer in their army, the man who most closely controlled their own personal destinies, was suddenly coming out to see as many of them as possible – not only to talk but apparently also to listen to them; to tell them not only that they each had an important part to play in his plans, but what that part was; to tell them what they had long believed was true – that they were as good soldiers as their opponents in the Afrika Korps – and what they now hoped to be true – that in the next battle he was going to prove himself to be as good a general as Rommel.

'We are going to hit Rommel for six out of Egypt!' he said, in his high, slightly lisping voice – stressing, however, that this was to be the long-term aim and that the immediate prospect was for a purely defensive, stone-walling battle – and when he walked along the ranks inspecting them, he looked deliberately and coolly into every man's eyes so that all felt, in that sudden, surprising moment, the creation of a personal bond. It might not be a bond which everyone welcomed, but whoever found himself looking back into those clear, grey-blue eyes felt irrevocably that military authority could never again lie elsewhere. Here, undoubtedly, was the man in command; whether he was competent to fulfil his promises would remain to be seen but of one thing all felt immediately certain. If he failed, he would fall with them himself. There would be no buck-passing with Montgomery.

The fact that he was prepared not only to be known but also instantly recognised was unusual enough among British regular officers who, once they had been promoted beyond regimental service, seemed generally to prefer a cult of anonymity except among themselves; but the methods he used to advertise his presence caused amusement throughout the bulk of the army at first, and shocked disgust followed by glum acceptance in some of the more exalted circles. From the beginning in the desert he adopted the woollen pullover, the corduroy or khaki drill trousers, the desert boots of the old Eighth Army hands, not bothering to display his badges of rank and relying at first instead upon warning and expectation to establish his identity. By the time the staff car or truck bringing Montgomery to visit a new formation drew up in its cloud of dust, everyone in the area knew who was arriving.

And then, of course, there was the matter of his headgear. His first unorthodoxy in this respect was to accept an Australian slouch hat while visiting their 9th Division, and to claim that in view of his childhood in Tasmania he was entitled to wear the Australian sunburst badge in addition to his own General Officer's insignia; but as the hat was so large and as he had so many units to visit, it soon became covered with the badges of almost every formation under his command and the result was slightly ridiculous. Eventually he changed it for the headgear which was soon to become indissolubly linked with his name – a black beret with the badges of the Royal Tank Corps and the General Staff – in itself a perhaps subconsciously significant combination, holding out as it did the promise of co-ordination between infantry and armour under a command knowledgeable of both.

Inevitably, as more and more men saw him and heard what he had to say, the stories began to circulate, the myths accumulate; and as Montgomery was in fact satisfying what de Guingand has described as a 'craving throughout the army for guidance and inspiration', they were all, whatever element of ridicule or mockery they may seem to contain, favourable. Rommel was reputed to be anxiously scouring the Afrika Korps for someone with knowledge of the rules of cricket in order to explain which six he was to be hit for, and after one of Montgomery's addresses at which he had mentioned – as he frequently did – 'the Lord, Mighty in Battle,' one young officer blandly inquired whether He could be presumed to be actually under command, or merely in support.

But Montgomery's sincerity, his clarity of vision (and few were then to question its width) and the total lack of ambiguity with which he expressed himself won enormous loyalty and enthusiasm.

'He told us everything:' one hard-bitten Regimental Sergeant Major told Vladimir Peniakoff, 'what his plan was for the battle, what he wanted the regiments to do, what he wanted *me* to do. And we will do it, sir. What a man!'[7]

It was not long, either, before he was being talked about on the opposite side of the front, among the German and Italian commanders planning for the next attack. But not much was known about him then, and certainly no one suspected that within eight months one of them would deliver himself of one very striking judgment: 'The war in the desert ceased to be a game when Montgomery took over.'[8]

For Rommel, the war in the desert had ceased to be a game well before July and by mid-August it had become something of a nightmare.

For one thing, he was himself very ill. He had now spent nineteen months on active service in Africa, which for a man of over fifty was a remarkable feat, even taking into consideration the care lavished upon him by his devoted staff. The elation of victory and advance had sustained him until July (as it had done a large proportion of his army) but with the development of the stalemate his spirits drooped and he began to be subject to fainting fits which he tried to hide from his staff, and especially from his medical adviser.

But with no improvement during August in the military situation (in fact, an exacerbation of problems of all kinds) there came no relaxation of tension for him and his physical deterioration became so evident that Professor Hörster insisted upon a complete examination. This revealed circulation and blood pressure problems, chronic stomach and intestinal catarrh and, of all incapacitating complaints in such circumstances, nasal diphtheria. The blocking of the nose and sinuses and consequent irritation of the throat which this infection causes in a cool and temperate climate is sufficiently debilitating to put most people to bed for several days; in the heat, dust, grime and general lack of sanitation of the war-time desert in August the resulting discomfort must have been excruciating – and the effort of will required to keep going at all, let alone to retain command of an army in the field, extraordinary.

Moreover, ill health was rife throughout his entire army, for however adaptable German Army training and doctrine were for the actual fighting of battles, it had not often been called upon to deal with tropical or sub-tropical conditions and the medical problems they bring. Panzerarmee Afrika lacked the historical experience of fighting in such intemperate climes as those of the North-West Frontier of India, for instance, which sustained the British Army, and German standards of hygiene were insufficiently rigorous while the diet was in general lacking in both variety and balance. Jaundice was widespread, desert sores universal (as they were in all armies, for no one found a complete cure for them), trachoma and amoebic dysentery commonplace; and with the halt after the sweep forward from Gazala and the gradual fading before their eyes of the enticing vision of delights ahead for them in Cairo and Alexandria, the Afrika Korps were beginning to show on their faces and in their bearing the strain of the last months.

And for the old hands of 90th Light, and 15th and 21st Panzer Divisions, the relative calm on the battlefield brought little or no alleviation of their discomforts for the supply situation seemed to become, if anything, worse as day followed day. At first they had welcomed the arrival at last of more German comrades to share the rigours of the desert war – units of 164th Division were now in the line with them, as were the Ramcke Parachute Brigade – and they were even prepared to welcome the Italian Folgore Parachute Division who had a good reputation and appeared to bear themselves well; but then it transpired that all these formations had come out to North Africa by air, so they possessed almost no lorries or other forms of transport of their own. Their rations, fuel, ammunition and everything else they would need to live and fight in the desert would therefore have to come forward on the existing supply mechanisms, already grossly overburdened by the tasks of supplying just the original Afrika Korps.

Now it became evident that there had been a serious incipient disadvantage in those large hauls of British supplies which had seemed so heaven-sent a few weeks before – in the sequestered batteries of 25-pounders so quickly put to efficient use by German artillerymen, in the capture of the massed parks of British lorries; for when the dumps emptied there were no factories behind German lines to manufacture British ammunition, or spare parts for the British trucks and lorries – and these by the end of July made up 85 per cent of Afrika Korps transport.

Most crucial of all, with the battle line now static there were no more reservoirs of British petrol to be gathered into their hands, and every drop to reach their fuel tanks must first cross the Mediterranean, then survive the unloading operation, often under heavy R.A.F. attack, then make the long and arduous journey forward from Tobruk, Benghasi or even Tripoli – journeys which themselves used up as much of the precious fluid as actually arrived.

As always happens in conditions of strain unrelieved by action or immediate danger, relations between the two Axis partners now worsened rapidly. To German eyes the weight of supplies arriving in North Africa for Italian formations appeared grossly out of proportion, not only in relation to military worth, but even out of proportion to plain numbers. Rommel was to claim to the German representative in Rome, von Rintelen, that Panzerarmee Afrika contained 82,000 Germans and but 42,000 Italians – yet during August only 8,200 tons of supplies arrived for the German element while 25,700 tons came in for the Italians; and in view of the dominance of the skies above Panzerarmee by the R.A.F., Rommel found it an additional annoyance that 8,500 tons had arrived safely for the Luftwaffe.

There were thus several matters of disagreement to upset even further the Generalfeldmarschall's uncertain blood pressure, perhaps the most serious being the arrival in Libya of two-thirds of the Italian Pistoia Division with over two hundred of their vehicles but with orders that they were not to cross the frontier into Egypt – while his own 164th division, already in the line, had to bring their supplies forward with a total of sixty vehicles, many of them already showing signs of the battering they were taking as they rolled and shuddered under excessive loads over disintegrating desert roads and tracks.

Cavallero on his occasional visits to the front would make promises to have such matters put right. 'But it just as frequently happened that on his next visit he would say with a laugh that he had made many a promise in his time and not all of them could be kept.'[9]

But it was not all the fault of the Italians, two of whom had specifically warned Rommel after the fall of Tobruk that to attempt the advance to the Delta while Malta remained to threaten his communications was to court disaster; and Malta during July and August was again justifying its description as the 'windlass of the Allied tourniquet' on Rommel's supply lines. R.A.F. reconnaissance aircraft based on the island kept the Allied Command fully informed about the movements of supply convoys, and these were attacked by submarines and by surface craft during their voyages and by R.A.F. Wellingtons and R.N.A.S. Albacores as soon as they arrived at their destinations.

In this activity both the R.A.F. and the Navy were now being aided to a significant extent by another service; the Ultra Intelligence was at last 'coming on stream' in an astonishingly effective manner.

A study of Military Intelligence in the First World War and the opening months of the Second can draw cynical reflections from even the most eager student of such recondite affairs. In the majority of cases its products always seemed to be either inaccurate or too late to be of use: and on the rare occasions when they were both correct and delivered in time, then they were ignored by the generals commanding the battles either because they did not believe them, or because the armies were already committed to a plan of battle and for one reason or another the generals were unwilling to modify it.

There were, of course, other reasons why the full benefit of the remarkable breakthrough achieved by the Bletchley organisation could not be reaped during the early months of the war. The knowledge in April 1941 that twelve panzer divisions were about to sweep down through the Balkans, and the routes they were to take, was in the hands of Maitland Wilson's headquarters in Greece by the end of March – but with the forces and equipment available to the Allies at that time, there was nothing they could do but skip out of the way when the panzers came through. You cannot stop military force with just the knowledge of its strength and intention.

Moreover, it was vitally important that nothing should reveal to the German authorities that their Enigma codes were being broken, for in German belief in their inviolability lay one of Britain's best hopes for eventual victory; and the shielding of this Enigma-breaking capability imposed delay and sometimes total embargo on the use of the information it gathered until organisations could be devised and set up to ensure that the dissemination of that information did not reveal the secret of its origin.

By the end of 1941 such an organisation was in being in the Middle East, and had, in fact, foreseen the arrival of the German merchant-ship *Ankara* at Benghasi in mid-December, with her cargo of twenty-two panzers. Unfortunately, consultations between the head of the relevant Intelligence section, Brigadier John Shearer, and his naval advisers convinced him that the *Ankara* would never be able to reach the Benghasi quays through the wrecks and debris with which the waters of the harbour were now choked, in order to unload her cargo.

He reckoned without the luck, the determination and the sheer expertise of the master of the *Ankara*; he was also ignorant of the fact that, to quote the words of Mr Ronald Lewin who first revealed the story in his book *Ultra Goes to War*, 'A current working into the blocked channel at Benghazi had gouged out enough space for *Ankara* to reach the quayside and get her tanks ashore. It was a feat characteristic of so indomitable a ship.'

The whole episode was itself characteristic of something else – the misfortune which dogs inexperience, especially of a new weapon or technique; but such episodes tend in themselves to provoke intense activity towards their correction, and so it proved in this case. One of the officers in the Intelligence section at Middle East Headquarters concerned with the analysis of the Afrika Korps logistics, and who was also one of the few in receipt of Ultra intelligence, was Major Enoch Powell, who after the *Ankara* affair brought to bear on the problem that cold, incisive and totally logical brain which has since brought him political notoriety together with considerable un-popularity among those not so intellectually endowed.

At his suggestion and with his participation, a small and secret inter-service committee was set up which met early every morning and analysed all the previous twenty-four hours' information, mostly from Ultra but also from other sources, regarding the Panzerarmee's supplies crossing the Mediterranean either by sea or by air. Time and systematisation inexorably built up a picture of Rommel's logistic service from which not only could the size of the supply convoys and the dates and ports of departure be provided, but also the names, specifications and past record of achievement of individual ships – and from this information the cargoes they were most likely to be carrying were deduced.

This knowledge was comparable to that provided by radar to R.A.F. Fighter Command during the Battle of Britain, for it meant that instead of flotillas of submarine or surface craft patrolling the wide seas in the hope of finding a convoy and perhaps sinking some of the more valuable cargoes, a single submarine or a flight of aircraft could now be directed to an exact destination, certain that they would find there a convoy amongst which would be the specified ships they were to attack and sink. As a result, the still exiguous forces at the disposal of Admiral Sir Henry Harwood and Air Marshal Sir Arthur Tedder were able to obtain results far out of proportion to their size, so that of thirty ships, fourteen barges and six supply submarines to leave Italy for North Africa during August, seven of the largest ships were lost taking with them to the bottom 1,660 tons of ammunition, 2,120 tons of general supplies, 43 guns, 367 assorted vehicles and, most crucial of all, 2,700 tons of petrol and oil – and although 12,800 tons of fuel did arrive, this was hardly enough to sustain the Panzerarmee in its positions, let alone to build up reserves for a battle.

The most crippling disadvantage under which Rommel now laboured was the abrupt switch after the fall of Tobruk of Hitler's attention from the North African to the Russian front. The massive drive through Southern Russia was gathering strength – Maikop fell on August 9th, Piatigorsk on the 10th, Mosdok was under threat by the 15th, and already just beyond the tips of the arrows marking the direction of advance for von Paulus's Sixth Army there beckoned the irresistible lure of Stalingrad – and the Afrika Korps was now a minor formation fighting an unimportant campaign against a secondary enemy. Rommel might still attract favourable comment whenever the Führer could spare a thought for him, but his requirements did not at that moment warrant even the momentary distraction of the High Command's attention from the Russian Front, and when Professor Hörster reported to O.K.W. that Rommel was 'not in a fit condition to command the forthcoming offensive' and his message was accompanied by the suggestion that Guderian should be sent out to command Panzerarmee Afrika on an acting basis until Rommel was fit again, the curt response 'Guderian unacceptable' arrived that night and no other replacement was suggested.

The message was quite clear; Rommel must make do with what he had in the area, bearing in mind all the time of course that under no circumstances would Hitler countenance a retreat – even as far as the Egyptian frontier.

But Rommel could see quite clearly that the longer he stayed where he was, the greater would be the strength built up against him (he already knew that a 100,000-ton convoy bringing every sort of supply for Eighth Army would arrive in the Suez Canal at or before the beginning of September) until a point would be reached after which it would be totally impossible for him to advance and his army would be able only to wait where it was until the British decided that their strength was so overwhelming that they could just move forward and crush it.

He must, therefore, advance – and soon, or the British minefields now growing thicker every day between Qaret el Abd and Himeimat would become as impassable as the defences the British had already formed from the coast down past Ruweisat Ridge.

The plan for battle he therefore evolved during the second half of August would rely for its success upon secrecy and, above all, on speed of execution. During one of the moonlit nights at the end of August, the two Afrika Korps panzer divisions, with Ariete and Littorio on the left flank and the combined German and Italian reconnaissance battalions on the right, would smash through the southern half of the British line, throw back the armoured cars and tanks of the 7th Armoured Division, and drive flat out for the area just south-west of El Hamman, arriving there before dawn. On the left of the Italian armoured division, 90th Light would move forward through the Munassib and Muhafid Depressions towards the gap between the rear of the New Zealanders and the new British division on the Alam Halfa Ridge. In the northern section of the line, the attention of the Australians, South Africans and Indians would be held to their front by pressure from the Italian divisions, plus local attacks by the 164th on the coast and the Ramcke Parachute Brigade in the centre.

By dawn the Afrika Korps divisions must be in position facing north for the breakthrough to the coast near Ruweisat Station and once this was reached von Bismarck's 21st Panzer were to turn east and race for Alexandria while 15th Panzer, back under command of von Vaerst and accompanied by 90th Light as soon as it had scattered the forces holding the Alam Halfa Ridge, were to drive south-east for Wadi Natrun and Cairo. Behind them the Italians would afford protection against any attempts the British might make to fall on the rear of the panzer divisions, and once these had turned east they would be able to wreak their usual havoc among the British supply depots, thus drawing off the British motorised forces who could then be defeated piece by piece as had so often happened before:

> We placed particular reliance in this plan on the slow reaction of the British command and troops, for experience had shown us that it always took them some time to reach decisions and put them into effect. We hoped, therefore, to be in a position to present the operation to the British as an accomplished fact.
>
> Things were then to move fast. The decisive battle was on no account to become static. With large British forces pinned down by repeated minor attacks by the German–Italian infantry left in the Alamein line, the decisive battle was to be fought out behind the British front in a form in which the greater aptitude of our troops for mobile warfare and the high

tactical skill of our commanders could compensate for our lack of material strength. Separated from their supply depots, the British would be left with the option of either fighting it out to the end in their line or breaking out and falling back to the east, thus relinquishing their hold on Egypt.

Summing up, the success of the operation depended – the supply question apart – on the following factors:

(a) The effectiveness with which our move into the assembly area was concealed.
(b) The speed with which the breakthrough of the British line and the thrust into their rear could be achieved – in other words on the accuracy of the reconnaissance.[10]

But of course the supply question was not one which could ever be 'apart' or anything but vitally important. Given that the German gunners were so accurate that very little ammunition would be wasted, given that with an overwhelming victory in sight they would be willing to go hungry for a few days – even so, with all the willingness in the world they could not move without petrol. The plan relied totally upon the timely delivery of at least four days' supply before the attack was launched, and a continuous supply coming up every day at least equalling the amount burnt the day before – and nothing which had happened since Panzerarmee's arrival at El Alamein evoked the slightest confidence that such a supply would be maintained.

Yet Rommel could not wait, for time was so evidently not on his side. Even had the Italians blandly announced that they could not provide what were obviously his minimum requirements, he could not remain where he was without courting disaster – a disaster which began to loom even more ominously when on August 21st the R.A.F. began 'round the clock' bombing, which shook the nerves of even the toughest Afrika Korps units, depriving them of sleep, gradually wearing down their numbers and reducing even further the amount of transport available to feed them.

He *must* attack – and on August 27th both Kesselring and Cavallero visited him and were forced to agree. Kesselring thereupon promised to fly out to him a minimum of 500 tons of fuel a day while Cavallero assured him that 6,000 tons would immediately be despatched from Italy; and on August 30th Rommel received 1,500 tons taken from the Luftwaffe by Kesselring which together with the amount already with the panzer divisions was considered enough for a week's battle. As for the main bulk, he received another message from Cavallero: 'You can begin the battle now, Herr Feldmarschall. The petrol is already under way.'[11]

The die was cast; that night the moon, five days past full, would rise just before midnight and by that time the panzer divisions must be waiting at the edge of the British minefields between Alam Nayil and Himeimat, ready to sweep forward through them as soon as the engineers pronounced it safe to do so. They had already moved forward to their assembly areas during the four previous nights – a quarter at a time, the places from which each quarter had moved being then occupied by supply vehicles to confuse the R.A.F. while the panzers themselves were hastily camouflaged in their new positions in the broken ground around Jebel Kalakh. On August 29th the wheeled vehicles had gone up in one bound.

Assembled and ready to move forward were 200 panzers including 26 of the new Mark IV Specials with the long 75mm. gun, and 243 Italian mediums – for what they were worth. If they could only break through the minefields quickly, then skirt the Alam Halfa Ridge and reach the coast, they should prove enough to create the required panic amid the British ranks and enable Afrika Korps to crash through to the Delta and the rich loot of the supply depots there. So long as the petrol arrived regularly and on time.

As darkness fell on the evening of August 30th the leading panzers moved off towards the western edge of the minefields, engineers in front with infantry to guard them and lead the way through the lanes as soon as these were clear. All seemed to go well for the first half hour, but above the rumble of the panzer engines could be heard the high whine of aircraft, and although the more optimistic proclaimed them to be Me 109s the older hands recognised them for what they were – Hurricanes on reconnaissance. They wondered how long it would be before the bombers arrived.

Not long. Even as the first troops reached the British minefields, Wellingtons droned in above the massed panzers still in the assembly areas, parachute flares lit up the scene like daylight and the bombs came down; and from then on the night was a calvary of exploding H.E., of burning lorries and panzers – and of even more ominous events at the front. The minefields were much more extensive and sewn much more thickly than had been expected or previously experienced, and it was taking more time than had been allowed to get through them. The artillery was making things worse by shelling the passages through which British armoured cars had been observed passing, and this brought immediate reaction from anti-tank guns and artillery of the British motor brigade opposite; as parachute flares floated down behind the attacking infantry and engineers, these were silhouetted and subjected to a remorseless hail of rifle and machine-gun bullets. There had certainly been no surprise . . . and by daylight it was only too evident that speed was lacking too, and the programme well behind schedule.

There was other bad news for Rommel when he arrived at the

advanced H.Q. at Jebel Kalakh at 0800 on the morning of August 31st; General von Bismarck, the gallant and enterprising commander of 21st Panzer Division, had been killed when his motor-cycle combination blew up on a mine, and General Nehring, commander of the Afrika Korps, had been badly wounded in an air attack. Already, the basic provisions for success seemed to be lacking and the portents ominous; but knowing – like every successful general – that matters are never as bad or as good as they first appear, Rommel decided to wait and see what progress Afrika Korps made that morning. Temporary command had been taken over by the Chief of Staff, Oberst Bayerlein, and Rommel and he had worked closely enough together already for each to know and trust the other's judgment; when Rommel went forward to find Bayerlein he was greeted with the first good news of the day – that Afrika Korps were at last through the minebelt and could now deploy.

However, adjustments must be made. With the British now thoroughly alerted, there was little or no chance of the panzer

Map 4   The Battle of Alam Halfa, August 31st

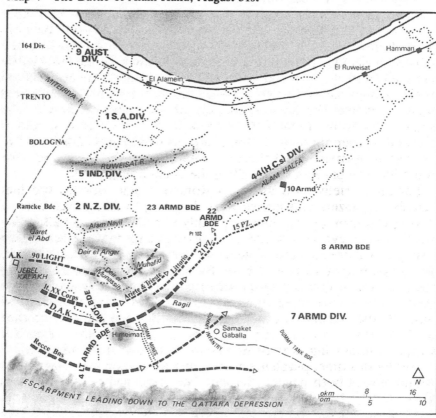

spearheads reaching that first objective south-west of El Hamman unassailed – probably from both north and south by 10th Armoured and 7th Armoured Divisions respectively – so the turn north must take place earlier. The best axis for the advance of the Afrika Korps would now be the line of telegraph poles which led up from Himeimat towards the centre of the Alam Halfa Ridge, while Littorio and Ariete could swing up on their left towards Point 102 in the gap between the New Zealanders' rear and whoever was on Alam Halfa, while 90th Light in their turn guarded the Italians' left flank.

There would undoubtedly be a tough battle for the ridge, but so long as the Grants of 10th Armoured Division were properly lured forward on to the 88mm. anti-tank screen and there destroyed in the usual manner, then the experience and expertise of 21st and 15th Panzer should be enough to deal with the holders of the ridge, who had just been identified by Intelligence as a new and unfledged division straight out from England. In the meantime, the reconnaissance battalions were successfully pushing back armoured cars south and east of Himeimat and would soon be free to cover the right flank of 15th Panzer. Things were not so bad, after all.

News from the north was quite satisfactory, too. Ramcke's parachutists had attacked the infantry opposite and destroyed one company before retiring, 164th Infantry Division had attacked the Australians and kept their attention firmly away from the main battle area and although the Italians opposite the South Africans and the Indian troops had scored no notable successes, they had at least held their positions. The greatest menace on that front, as here in the south, was from the R.A.F. who were still omnipresent, and if allowed to keep up their continual attacks would undoubtedly prove an embarrassment when the time came – as it shortly would – for refuelling the panzers and refilling the ammunition racks.

Fortune, briefly, was again on Rommel's side. Just as the fuel gauges in panzers and lorries were dropping to dangerous levels a dust storm blew up, thickening quickly into the choking yellow fog which made everyone's life miserable except those quick-witted enough to appreciate the protection it gave from the enemy aircraft, now impotently returning to base. By 1300, the panzer divisions were ready to move forward again with Littorio close alongside, though Ariete and Trieste were lagging behind – delayed, so they said, by more British minefields which had apparently been laid even thicker in the northern sector of the defences. It was thus 1500 before XX Corps were moving, well behind on the left flank of the advance.

But by this time, puzzlement and some frustration was nagging the commands of both panzer divisions. Soft sand had bedevilled them since shortly after their first move and already the petrol gauges were again dropping alarmingly; and where was the British armour? Two hours' sweat and slog through the sandstorm had brought the leading panzers (Mark IIIs with some of the Mark IV Specials) to the point where the line of telegraph posts veered east and some of them followed it, leading along almost parallel to the ridge, their commanders cursing the fog, their eyes sore from the grit and the perpetual strain of watching for the enemy.

Then at last from their rear came the sounds of battle; away to the north-west, from the foothills around Point 102 had suddenly appeared some Grants and some Crusaders, evidently about to attack the van of the panzer advance. The Mark IIIs swung left and moved out, the anti-tank screens formed up with their usual precision and waited for their prey to be lured forward. It all promised a repeat of the classical baited trap which had succeeded so often before – though it did seem that the panzers were having to move rather far forward and the Grants were strangely hesitant.

But the range closed, the Grants opened fire, the panzers halted and fired back and quite soon twelve of the Grants were burning furiously although anti-tank fire from out of the setting sun had knocked out some of the panzers too. But as the sun went down further, the wind dropped, visibility improved and the panzer crews could see that the destruction of the Grants had left a sizeable gap in the British defences. Gingerly, they moved towards it, waiting for the next wave of British tanks to appear, cursing the sun which, as it dropped, effectively blinded them; to such an extent that they were but three hundred yards from the waiting Rifle Brigade anti-tank screen before they saw it, and they thus caught the full blast of highly accurate and concentrated firing, augmented immediately by heavier artillery fire from behind the near foothills which screamed overhead and fell among the following waves and the waiting 88mms.

Instinctively, the panzers charged forward at the anti-tank screens and overran the forward platoons, but then at last saw what they had been waiting for; over the rise in front of them came the leading waves of a squadron of Grants, with more waves following, all exhibiting the usual panache of British armour, the speed, the waving pennons, the clouds of dust, the élan of the hunting field. Waiting only to fire off one hasty salvo, the panzers turned and sped for the protection of the 88mms, confident that behind them the field would soon be littered with the burning hulks of yet more British tanks. As the light was fading fast, this would be the last action of the day.

As far as ground action was concerned this was so – but it did not end quite as the panzer crews expected. As they reached their anti-tank screens, the only noise of battle they heard above the roar of their own engines was the crash of 25-pounder shells landing amongst them, and when they turned they saw that the British armour had only pursued them as far as the edge of the gap into which they had penetrated, and were now waiting there in defensive positions out of effective range of the 88mms. And very soon afterwards came news that an attempt by the leading panzers of 15th to attack the British infantry on the middle of the Alam Halfa Ridge had had the same unsatisfactory result, running first into minefields and then into such a concentration of artillery fire that they too had been forced back into the soft sand below the ridge, where they expended even more of their precious petrol retiring into the leaguer area.

By this time darkness had fallen, and precedent demanded that a decent silence should now fall upon the battlefield, the British withdrawing into remote leaguers, the Afrika Korps refilling their fuel tanks and replenishing their ammunition racks.

But somebody was making new rules. There was to be no respite for the Afrika Korps now, for all night long the British artillery on the ridge poured shells into the area just below while the R.A.F. carried out a long session of pattern bombing on the eastern flank, which caught the hapless reconnaissance battalions in the open desert, banished all hope of sleep for the entire Panzerarmee, wrecked several of their vehicles and killed and wounded a large number of their most experienced men.

And there was no petrol coming up. The lanes through the minefields were choked, attacked by marauding armoured cars and occasionally menaced by artillery fire, and moreover it would seem that the supply echelons were lacking in the enthusiasm necessary to get the supplies forward. This lack of initiative was noticeable elsewhere too, for many observers that day felt that Afrika Korps were not attacking with their usual fire, and Rommel was later to make a significant comment upon the new factor which had entered the desert war against him:

> Anyone who has to fight, even with the most modern weapons, against an enemy in complete command of the air, fights like a savage against modern European troops, under the same handicaps and with the same chance of success.[12]

So when the morning of September 1st came, only 15th Panzer had sufficient petrol to mount an attack – against the western end of Alam Halfa Ridge – and this was to prove as inconclusive and as puzzling as had been the attacks of the day before. The division moved off shortly after first light, probing between the scene of the previous day's fighting and the most western infantry positions on the ridge, to find themselves caught in yet another devastating artillery bombardment and then attacked from the east by a force of mixed Grants and Crusaders which again refrained from chasing the panzers as they fell back to the protection of the 88mms; the British tanks thus escaped their planned annihilation although the panzers themselves did manage to knock out seven of the Grants at a cost of a couple of their own Mark IIIs. By early afternoon, 15th Panzer were back to the positions from which they had started, but with rather less petrol and ammunition with which to face the immediate future.

And behind them, Rommel and his staff were becoming increasingly worried – and indeed, severely persecuted. The R.A.F. had hardly paused in their attacks all day, concentrating especially on the area around Ragil where one bomb had killed seven of the staff of 15th Panzer Division, whose commander von Vaerst had now as senior officer taken over command of the Afrika Korps from Oberst Bayerlein. All that night it was the same as the night before – a continuous thunder of artillery from the ridge and the crash of shells amid the dispersed lorries and panzers, the whole scene lit by parachute flares and the garish light of burning vehicles as Wellingtons and Albacores flew overhead in such perfect formations that the more cynical among the Afrika Korps men christened the attacks 'Party Rally raids', their high explosive bombs bursting with shattering effect on the hard desert floor, cutting down anything standing two feet above it with whining scythe-blades of steel. Besides the actual physical destruction, the effect on the officers and men of the Afrika Korps was becoming grave as lack of sleep, the strain of waiting for the next bomb, the consciousness of how helpless they were under skies so completely dominated by the enemy, all began to take their toll. By the following morning (September 2nd) Rommel was coming to the conclusion that he must abandon the operation.

The last three days had been for him a deeply disturbing experience. Excitement and the anticipation of battle had brought about a brief improvement in his health for a day or so before the advance began, but now the gnawing symptoms of stomach trouble were back, the nausea and the blocked nasal passages all adding to the problems with which he must wrestle. As he went forward to seek out von Vaerst for the morning conference, the signs of incipient defeat and demoralisation were all around him. Not only were the panzers unable to move forward because of empty fuel tanks, but the men were unwilling to come out of their slit-trenches because of the continual air attack – a condition vividly illustrated to Rommel when he was himself forced to dive into one, whereupon a huge shell splinter ripped through the blade of a shovel lying on the lip of the trench and a piece of red hot metal fell in beside him.

There was another ominous factor about the air attacks on this day, too. Amid the perfect formations of aircraft wearing the R.A.F. roundels were now appearing Mitchells and Liberators with the white star of the U.S.A.A.F. – a token of the force which would be thrown against Germany once the full industrial strength and manpower of America was mobilised.

But the most immediate problem for Rommel was still the shortage of petrol; and one piece of news brought to him that afternoon was that a supply convoy of nearly three hundred lorries had been caught just east of Himeimat by some marauding light tanks of 7th Armoured Division, which scattered them and destroyed fifty-seven of their number. This meant that there now remained in the advanced areas only one petrol issue for the depleted panzer and soft-skinned vehicles left to him – enough for a move of about one hundred kilometres over good going, perhaps half that distance over the kind of surface with which they were now surrounded. Would they, in fact, have enough fuel even to retreat to safety . . . wherever that might now lie?

That evening he went back to Jebel Kalakh and there found Kesselring awaiting him – sympathetic to his problems and willing to throw every aircraft at his disposal into the task of protecting the army on the ground, but nevertheless the bearer of bad news. The R.A.F. had been active over other places than the battlefield, and two of the tankers bringing petrol across from Italy had already been sunk; as for the five hundred tons per day promised by Kesselring himself, although this was being despatched from the various dumps in which it had been stored, it was 'consuming itself' on the way forward in the tanks of the vehicles bringing it up over the appalling roads and tracks.

The searching analysis of the supply situation which this provoked then unearthed more unpleasant facts. Of the 5,000 tons of petrol which Cavallero had promised would be in Rommel's hands by the following day, 2,600 tons had already been sunk, 1,500 tons was still in Italy (despite Cavallero's message on the eve of the attack) and the prospect of the remaining 1,000 tons arriving in time to be of use was limited indeed.

That night Rommel sent off a report to O.K.W. telling them of his decision to call off the operation, to withdraw his divisions gradually along their own tracks to the starting line, there to await either the necessary reinforcement and supplies to begin again . . . or whatever fate the Gods of Battle and the new British general had in store for them. As the report went off the R.A.F. arrived punctually over the battle area, the hapless troops around Ragil being especially subjected to relentless bombing, brilliantly illuminated by flares which they could not extinguish and which seemed never to die. A new terror was let loose upon them that night when down from the noisy darkness above came hurtling two 4,000-pound bombs which shook the floor of the desert and flung into the air huge lumps of stone to add to the death and destruction from bomb splinters.

The night of September 2nd/3rd was the bitterest to date in the history of the Afrika Korps and in the military career of their general.

From the new British general's point of view, of course, matters looked very different.

By noon of the first day of the battle, Montgomery had concluded that all the forecasts made by his intelligence staff had been correct, that the main Afrika Korps drive was in the south and that the attacks in the north were merely holding operations which could easily be beaten off. He thereupon ordered 23rd Armoured Brigade to move their Valentines down behind the New Zealanders to plug any gap which might exist there, and told Ramsden to start thinning out the forward troops of XXX Corps in order to form a reserve in case opportunity arose for unexpected exploitation.

He then checked that his staff were efficiently collecting all necessary information, and began himself a series of regular visits to his chief subordinates. Horrocks had been dissatisfied with the defence put up both by the 7th Motor Brigade and the 4th Light Armoured Brigade in the south, telling Renton that the 7th Armoured Division appeared more concerned to save their own skins than to fight the enemy – a comment which outraged all who heard of it and which in view of the comparative fragility of the vehicles then with both brigades was certainly unfair; but it ensured that from that moment on, every unit in the division hit as hard as it could whenever the opportunity presented itself.

But this attitude in itself had to be watched, for Montgomery's total embargo on piecemeal armoured forays remained and indeed he was at pains to emphasise it wherever he went. When by the morning of September 3rd the R.A.F. reported that all the enemy vehicles in the area were now pointing westwards and that over a thousand of them were driving in that direction just north of Ragil, the instructions issued to Horrocks were that XIII Corps could close up behind them but that offensive moves should be limited to patrol activity aimed at harrying enemy soft-skinned transport and supply columns.

Not only did Montgomery want as much of his armour as possible preserved for his future plans but, whether he had read it or not, he was in agreement with that part of Dorman-Smith's appreciation of July 27th which read, 'None of the formations in Eighth Army is now sufficiently well trained for offensive operations. The Army badly needs either a reinforcement of well-trained formations or a quiet period in which to train.'[13]

No such well-trained formations had arrived, and as for the 'quiet period in which to train' – both Dorman-Smith and Auchinleck had declared that no offensive could possibly be launched before mid-September even under ideal conditions, and this was another point with which Montgomery would have agreed. There would thus be no launching of armoured brigades into battle, however enticing the prospect might look, for there was too great a chance that the enticement might be deliberate, the prospect deceiving.

However, if the armour was judged lacking in the training and efficiency to carry out an assault, the same was not true of all of the infantry – and as it happened, some of the most experienced were exactly poised to deliver a perhaps lethal blow at what might still be Rommel's weakest point. If the New Zealanders could drive south as far as Himeimat, they might so choke the escape route of the Panzerarmee that an appreciable part of it might not get back. Freyberg was therefore instructed to mount such an attack during the night of September 3rd/4th, though as his men had already borne so much of the campaign in the desert, he was given 132nd Brigade of 44th Division to accompany his own 5th Brigade, still commanded by the redoubtable Howard Kippenberger.

Operation Beresford was a failure for a number of reasons, the chief being that however ill Rommel might be, he was not so distracted as to attempt to withdraw his main forces through a narrow gap without first ensuring that the sides of the gap were adequately stiffened. Defences had been prepared along the northern edge of both the Muhafid and Munassib Depressions and also of Deir el Angar further out to the west, and during September 2nd these defences had been occupied by elements of both the Ramcke Brigade and the Folgore Division, both in their first desert battle and both eager to prove their superiority as parachutists over ordinary infantry.

It was into these defences that the men of the 4th and 5th Battalions of the Royal West Kents (132nd Brigade) ran headlong, after a badly delayed start, a thoroughly confused advance garishly illuminated most of the way by a burning truck, and a complete breakdown of communications. Although the brigade commander, Brigadier C. B. Robertson, had taken the trouble to ask Kippenberger's advice upon some details of the attack, he then took little notice of it, advanced too quickly himself, was badly wounded and had to be evacuated, leaving his already disintegrating brigade without a commander.

On the eastern flank of the attack, the New Zealanders did rather better, though their two leading battalions lost touch and diverged leaving between them a gap into which trundled some supporting Valentines whose crews, under the impression that the infantry were still in front, drove unexpectedly into the German defences and lost twelve of their number before they could extricate themselves. Meanwhile, the Maoris on the left flank had charged rather over-enthusiastically out towards Muhafid and the morning found them in the open desert, while on their right the other New Zealand battalion was also unpleasantly exposed.

In all, *Operation Beresford* had that night advanced rather less than two miles into empty desert and Allied forces were now occupying exposed positions in front of defences manned by determined and enterprising troops – at a cost already of 700 casualties from 132nd Brigade and 124 from 5th New Zealand. Moreover, 6th New Zealand Brigade had mounted a diversionary attack on 132nd Brigade's right, and lost another 159 men including their commander, the ebullient and irrepressible George Clifton, who was taken prisoner. (He escaped a day or so later, was recaptured and sent to Italy where he then escaped four times, being recaptured close to the Swiss border on the last; after which he was sent to Germany where he broke out another four times, was badly wounded on his eighth attempt but finally made it on his ninth.)

By the evening of September 4th, it was thus evident that the attempt to close the gap had failed, and Montgomery ordered the exposed formations to withdraw out of danger during the night. The only offensive measures from then on were to be by the armoured cars and light tanks in the south which should continue their harrying activities; under no circumstances should the heavier armour be engaged.

Hindered only by continual shelling and the gradually subsiding attentions of the R.A.F., the remains of Panzerarmee were thus allowed to withdraw during the next day until they reached the edge of the British minefields, where their rearguards halted, 15th Panzer going back to Jebel Kalakh, 21st Panzer remaining further forward with some of its units occupying the edge of Munassib and others the only visibly worthwhile gains the battle had made for Rommel – the twin peaks of Himeimat from which good observation of the southern part of what became known as the Alamein Line was available. However, as Montgomery had already decided to mislead Rommel into a belief that when he at last attacked, he would do so in the south, this vantage point was later to provide nothing but bogus information, but quite a lot of that.

On the evening of September 5th Montgomery issued an Order of the Day which announced:

> The Battle of Alamein [sic] has now lasted for six days, and the enemy has slowly but surely been driven from 8 Army area. Tonight, 5th September, his rearguards are being driven west, through the minefield area north of Himeimat. All formations and units, both armoured and unarmoured, have contributed towards this striking victory, and have been magnificently supported by the R.A.F. I congratulate all ranks of 8 Army on the devotion to duty and good fighting qualities which have resulted in such a heavy defeat of the enemy and which will have far-reaching results.[14]

Like quite a number of war-time announcements by both sides, this one attained its purpose but does not stand up well to close examination. The main bulk of the infantry of XXX Corps had hardly seen action at all, and although the armour of XIII Corps had played some part in the battle, it had not been in the mobile role for which armour is intended. The gunners had done well, the R.A.F. magnificently; but it was petrol shortage which had contributed as much as any other factor to the defeat of the Afrika Korps, so perhaps Montgomery should have included the Royal Navy (and, privately, the Ultra Organisation) in his congratulations.

British losses in killed, wounded and missing amounted to 1,750, German losses to 1,859 and Italian to 1,051 – so from the point of view of the 'butcher's bill' it would seem that the British had done better. But the Germans had left the wrecks of only 38 panzers behind and the Italians had lost only eleven of their tanks, while despite Montgomery's caution, 67 British tanks had been so badly damaged that even with the ease of recovery after the battle they had to be written off. The difference in aircraft losses – 41 German and Italian against 68 British – was a reflection of far greater activity by the R.A.F. than by their opponents.

But these comparisons could not be made by the men on the battlefield, and they were busy making others. They were remembering the proclamation made to them before the *Crusader* operation and the Gazala Battles, and what validity those promises had afterwards proved to contain; and they reflected now that even if Rommel had not yet been 'hit for six', he had at least been adequately stonewalled, which was all that Montgomery had said would happen this time. The little man with the funny hats had been as good as his word on this occasion, and would thus certainly deserve a second chance; if he delivered as well next time, Eighth Army would begin to believe that he knew his job, and might then be prepared to follow him with some of the enthusiasm and confidence which they had given to some of his precedessors – and lost in a welter of incompetence and mismanagement.

There were now certainly grounds for hope – hope that in future their lives would not be sacrificed uselessly, hope that the machinery of the army would not break down as soon as it was exposed to the realities of battle, hope that they would be told the truth about their equipment and leadership before they had to trust their lives to either, and that in the future any exhortations to battle would not be so empty and meaningless as in the past.

Above all, there was hope that Rommel and his Afrika Korps were not, after all, invincible, and that in time Eighth Army could and would beat them.

In the circumstances, they were even prepared to believe their new commander when he said they needed more – and radically different – training.

2 · Daffodil, Hyacinth, Snowdrop and Tulip

There were some units in Montgomery's new command – or at any rate operating in the Eighth Army theatre – which were already committed to action and thus beyond reach of new training methods, which for some at least was to prove unfortunate and for many fatal.

During the early summer, Lieutenant-Colonel John Haselden (who had acted as guide for the famous Keyes Raid on Rommel's headquarters at Beda Littoria just before *Crusader*) had spent a great deal of time behind Axis lines disguised as an Arab, collecting and sending back much valuable information. He had come back to Cairo at the end of July and early in August had suggested, to a newly constituted command for raiding forces in Alexandria, that he return to Tobruk with a few picked saboteurs and there blow up the bulk fuel storage tanks which were so heavily concreted as to be virtually immune from air attack, his party then escaping south into the desert to a rendezvous with the Long Range Desert Group.

In the circumstances of August 1942, any suggestions for the destruction of more of Rommel's petrol supplies were welcomed with enthusiasm – but on this occasion with perhaps a little too much. Before many days had elapsed, a slightly bemused John Haselden found himself commanding a much larger force than he had ever contemplated, taking part in a combined operation of ever-increasing complexity.

The final plan for *Operation Daffodil*, as this attack on Tobruk was called, envisaged the penetration of the Tobruk defences along the El Adem–Tobruk road by a party of commandos with sappers and signallers attached, travelling in three lorries with Afrika Korps markings, the men disguised as prisoners-of-war, with members of the highly secret Special Interrogation Group (S.I.G.) dressed in German uniforms acting the part of lorry drivers and guards. The men from S.I.G. were mostly Jews who had escaped from Germany and were thus fluent German speakers, and their fate if taken prisoner was certain death, quick if they were fortunate.

Having entered Tobruk, this force (Force B) would seize the easternmost inlet at Mersa Sciausc under cover of the heaviest air raid the port had experienced up to that time, capture the coastal guns in the neighbourhood, and hold the inlet while a company of Argyll and Sutherland Highlanders with machine-gunners from the Royal Northumberland Fusiliers (Force C) came ashore from a flotilla of sixteen motor torpedo boats and three Fairmile motor launches which would have made the journey from Alexandria. The joint forces would then fight their way westwards, capturing the coastal and defence guns along the southern shore of the harbour, while in the meantime Force A, consisting of a battalion of Royal Marines with attached gunners and sappers, would be landed at Mersa Mreira to the north of Tobruk itself. This force would fight its way into the town, join hands with Forces B and C, and then capture the guns on the northern side of the harbour. With all the harbour protection guns then affectively silenced, the destroyers upon which the marines had travelled, H.M.S. *Sikh* and H.M.S. *Zulu*, would then enter the harbour and land specialist demolition parties to destroy the fuel tanks, harbour installations, any enemy shipping present and a tank repair shop. The destroyers would then evacuate the wounded and part of the attacking force, while the rest moved out into the area around the port, wrecking all Axis installations they could find, releasing British and South African prisoners-of-war believed still to be there, and sequestering all enemy transport, in which they would escape out into the desert.

Both the journey in and the escape out would be led by L.R.D.G. patrols who would be in complete control of timing and movement to and from the area, and these, while the main actions were being fought, would themselves wreck the radio direction-finding station along the El Adem road, destroy aircraft on the adjacent landing grounds, help release some of the prisoners, hold the main exits for the escaping forces and then lead them back to Kuffra when they had emerged.

According to the latest intelligence reports (gathered, according to one account, from a South African soldier who had been taken prisoner in Tobruk, put to work in a German officers' mess and had subsequently escaped), Tobruk was weakly held by only two battalions of Italian second-line troops, with a possible stiffening of not more than a thousand German technicians. Given complete surprise and the luck which normally attends youth and daring, it was by no means impossible that the operation would attain many of its objectives, and thus create enormous confusion behind the Axis lines in addition to destroying yet more of Rommel's precious petrol and his equally essential unloading facilities.

And this was not the sole operation to be mounted that same night, as a pattern of simultaneous raids had been planned. David Stirling was to take a large party of his S.A.S. mounted in forty heavily armed jeeps into Benghasi, which they were to take and hold for as long as necessary in order to sink all ships in the port, block the inner harbour and destroy oil storage and pumping plants; and the L.R.D.G. patrols which led them were at the same time to attack the airfield at Benina. This was *Operation Snowdrop*; *Operation Hyacinth* was a wholly L.R.D.G. affair at Barce where two patrols would attack the landing-ground and destroy all aircraft there, causing as much chaos and confusion among the Italian garrison as possible.

All parties would then endeavour to escape south to Kuffra (a distance of some 500 miles from Barce and Benghasi, be it said) and as they must all therefore pass close to the Jalo oasis, it would obviously be best if the oasis were in friendly hands. *Operation Tulip*, would therefore take place on the night after the main raids in the north, whereby Force Z – a detachment of the Sudan Defence Force, guided of course by another L.R.D.G. patrol – attacked the fort at Jalo and held it until all raiding forces had withdrawn through the gap and were well on their way to the south. The Sudan Defence Force would also send one motorised battalion from Baharia towards Siwa as a demonstration which might distract Axis attention – and especially Axis aircraft – away from the more vulnerable areas to the west.

John Haselden's original idea had therefore ballooned from a single operation carried out by a maximum of ten men, into four operations engaging a total strength of nearly seven hundred in the raids themselves, and at least as many in administration. Moreover, a considerable naval force would be engaged, as in addition to the two destroyers and the M.T.B.s and M.L.s mentioned it was obviously necessary to put heavier ships to sea to afford protection against both air and sea attack, especially during the withdrawal. The cruiser H.M.S. *Coventry* and eight Hunt class destroyers would accompany the forces attacking Tobruk, and another cruiser with five more destroyers would bombard Daba during the night of the raids in order to provide some form of diversion,. This deployment of naval strength was by no means popular with Admiral Harwood and his staff, for they were all well aware that the Royal Navy would shortly have an important part to play in a large-scale battle, and that losses which they could ill afford must inevitably occur during this previous – and comparatively unimportant – series of operations.

Other commanders were also worried. For instance, the successes which had attended S.A.S. operations to date had mostly been won by small groups of men, rarely of more than ten and usually of four or five; now David Stirling was required to take nearly two hundred men into action, quite a high proportion of whom were inexperienced in

DAFFODIL, HYACINTH, SNOWDROP AND TULIP

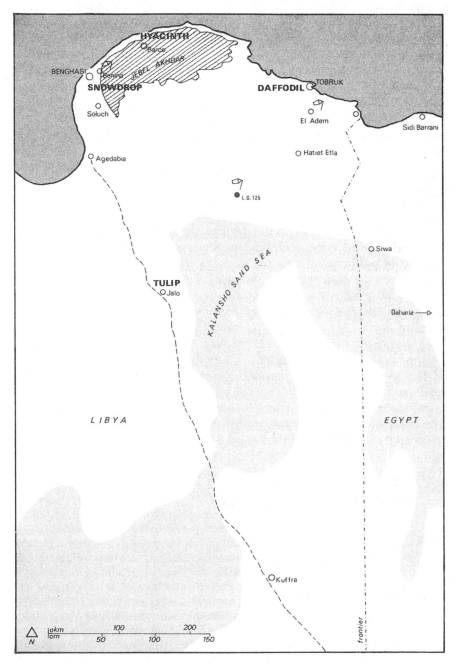

Map 5   The raids of September 13th

raiding, and some hastily – and thus perhaps inadequately – trained. Both the inexperience and the size of the force would rob it of the vital element of flexibility, for the first necessitated close control of every individual unit and vehicle, which with the second meant that the only approach to the target could be along a road, and through the inevitable roadblocks. Shock, speed and bluff had often sufficed in the past to burst through these, but many of Stirling's most experienced men viewed the accumulation of vehicles and equipment, recruits and armament with misgiving, wondering how so large a concourse could possibly escape enemy observation at some point in their fifteen-hundred-mile journey from base.

As for the naval officers in charge of the always tricky operation of putting the troops ashore, some of these were near to desperation. Neither *Sikh* nor *Zulu* had been spared from normal duties in order to concentrate on rehearsal for the landing operations, and not long before D-day itself it was realised that the two destroyers could not carry sufficient boats to put the marines ashore in one wave and that the landing-craft – so rudimentary in design and makeshift in construction that they had already been christened 'shoe-boxes' – would have to make two trips, putting half the force ashore each time. In the single rehearsal on Cyprus, the operation of putting just one wave ashore had taken far too long . . . with no enemy interference.

But perhaps the most serious aspect of the run-up period was the evident lack of security. The Argyll and Sutherland Highlanders, for instance, had practised landing from their M.T.B.s and M.L.s under the interested gaze of members of the Royal Egyptian Yacht Club in Alexandria, and Vladimir Peniakoff, who had been invited to join John Haselden's party but had hastily attached himself to the L.R.D.G. patrols going to Barce instead, later wrote a withering account of the pre-operational lack of control:

> The night of September 13th, 1942, might well have been a nightmare to the enemy if, out of the blue, his lines of communication had been attacked by mysterious forces in five different places spread over 250 miles. German and Italian headquarters would have been flooded with conflicting messages, reporting a party of parachutists on Benina landing-ground and an armoured division in Barce, and a certain amount of confusion might have resulted. As it was, unfortunately for us, our bright young men were far too excited to hold their tongues: when they were turned out of the Middle East H.Q. in the evening they gathered in the bars and night clubs of Cairo to discuss again their childish plans: their friends joined in with suggestions picked from boyish books that they had pored over in earnest only a few years before, Drake and Sir Walter Raleigh, Morgan and the Buccaneers were outbidden, new stratagems poured out in a stream of inventiveness, while circles of admiring Levantines formed round the excited youths, and the barmen's ears visibly stretched while they mixed their drinks in feigned aloofness.

Later at night lovely dark Syrian heads on crumpled pillows listened carefully to their blond bed-fellows: military plans mingled with the raw pleadings of inexperienced passion. Early next morning the telephones in Gezirah and Qasr el Dubara buzzed with shrill Levantine voices exchanging notes in French, Italian and Greek, mixed with English military expressions and names of units. The Cairenes loved to impress their friends with a knowledge of our future operations, and wasted no time in spreading around any scrap of information they had managed to collect: amongst them, indistinguishable, just another bridge-playing Levantine, was the Italian agent, sitting pretty with an easy job indeed. No romantic disguises for him, no purloining of secret documents, no treacherous accomplices to be kept in order – no risks at all, in fact, no expenses and no trouble: he just stayed at home and answered the telephone. A host of enthusiastic voluntary helpers, unwitting and unbidden, provided him with solid material for daily reports, which, enciphered, went on the air from a discreet wireless set in a villa off the Pyramids Road.[1]

There is, undoubtedly, a degree of imaginative fictionalisation about that picture, for many of the colourful details are unprovable; but in its essence it would seem to be accurate, bearing out the sentence in a letter written later by one of the more senior officers concerned: 'Security in these operations was quite appalling.'[2]

Nevertheless, the first stage of the main operations went quite smoothly. The commandos under John Haselden completed the trip down to Kuffra with ample time to spare and then, guided by two L.R.D.G. patrols under Captain David Lloyd Owen, travelled north along the western edge of the Kalansho Sand Sea, slipped past Jalo during the night of September 8th, and reached Hatiet Etla some ninety miles south of Tobruk by September 10th. There they rested, cleaning and checking their weapons, and Haselden briefed them all again on their individual tasks.

On the morning of Sunday, September 13th, they moved off to a wadi some thirty-five miles south of Tobruk, rested there briefly and were then guided by the L.R.D.G. to within sight of the by-pass, where they packed into three lorries, the men detailed as drivers and guards changed into German uniforms, all arms were hidden but kept ready for instant use, and the nerve-racking opening moves began. They were somewhat delayed by the difficulties of descending the escarpment, but once down drove smoothly along the road amid scattered and only slightly curious Axis traffic and, to their immense relief, were then waved casually through the roadblock at the entrance in the perimeter wire by Italian guards too bored even to bother to look at the papers one of the S.I.G. men had ready.

Inside, matters did not proceed quite so smoothly, as they quickly met a fast-moving convoy coming towards them and their middle lorry was struck a glancing blow by a German staff car carrying, according to another S.I.G. man, a high-ranking officer. None of the lorries stopped – indeed they accelerated away – while behind them the Axis convoy slowed to a halt, various angry voices shouted after them but eventually the convoy started off again, doubtless with someone writing down the lorry numbers for disciplinary action to be taken at some future date. For another uncomfortable period the commandos were accompanied by three motor-cycle combinations bearing German military police who seemed unnecessarily inquisitive, and for a time it seemed that Very lights erupted on every occasion they passed an important Axis installation, giving the impression that their course was being charted; but no attempt was made to stop them, and the most memorable moment in their journey into Tobruk came when Haselden nodded casually towards an impressive rock-face looming out of the near darkness (for it was by now nearly 2100) and said, 'That's the bomb-proof oil-storage depot we must destroy later tonight.'[3]

At least one officer swore bitterly to himself as they drove past for it seemed quite obvious that had the occupants of that one lorry baled

Map 6   The raid on Tobruk

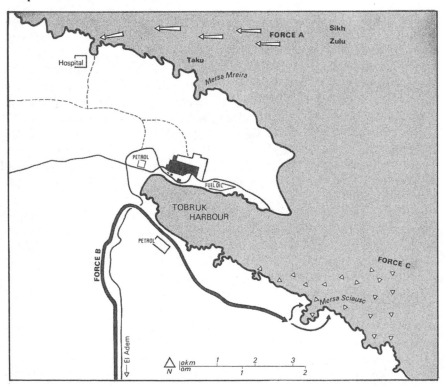

out there and then, the oil which was, after all, the prime target of the raid could have been destroyed within such a short time that little or no resistance would have been encountered. Haselden's original plan would seem to have been eminently feasible – and without such a large commitment of manpower and equipment.

They skirted Tobruk town, turned east and only a few minutes after the scheduled time were debussing at the head of the inlet which was their objective, sorting their weapons, those who had travelled in German uniforms quickly (and with some relief) changing into their own. Aircraft were droning in above them, one party moved off in the dark to the reported positions of two heavy coastal guns on the east shore of Sciausc Bay, and as the bombers arrived over Tobruk town and harbour the air raid alarms were given and the port area sprang to life. Everything was going according to plan.

It continued to do so for a little while longer.

The main commando party moved up through the wadi and had little difficulty in taking over the crucially important headland over-looking Sciausc Bay, the Italian gunners and support infantry making the fatal but very natural mistake of believing that they would be safer if they remained in their billets and did not venture out into the increasingly noisy night beyond. Many of them were thus killed by grenades thrown through barrack windows or dropped down ventilators into the underground shelter, and those who ran for it were hunted down amid the rocks and crannies of the steep-sided wadi and the majority killed – although a few prisoners were taken. From one of them, an N.C.O., was elicited the statement that the garrison had recently been increased to at least a brigade and that there were over two thousand extra German troops inside the perimeter waiting to go forward into the line at El Alamein; but little notice was taken of what a frightened prisoner was saying.

Within an hour the first success signal was fired indicating that the headland was secure, and once Haselden received a similar signal from the party looking for the coastal guns, he could raise Base H.Q., who would then order in the light craft with the Argylls to join him, and the destroyers now presumably off the Mreira inlet to send in their marines. But the second party was having a thoroughly frustrating time.

They had run into an unexpected minefield very shortly after setting out, and Haselden's success signal went up before they were even clear of it. But they pressed on, cursing the slowness of the sappers in front, gradually working down towards the beach until at last they reached it and could move more quickly in the shadows of the overhanging cliffs. They found a Spandau nest and a radio station, both of which they stormed and destroyed in sharp, vicious actions, and then at last one of a recce party sent out in advance reported back that they had found the heavy guns' positions – disused and unmanned. Their success signal went up just in time for Haselden to send off the code-word which would bring in the M.T.B.s and the destroyers.

But from then on everything went wrong.

The officer whose job it was to position and flash the light guiding in the M.T.B.s had also, incredibly, been sent off on a forward reconnaissance and had left his Aldis lamp behind; so in order to save time he tried signalling with his torch, which was not only far less powerful but white instead of red. It was hardly surprising that the men offshore were puzzled.

They were not only puzzled, but also out of communication with one another as a direct consequence of lack of training. The two columns had kept good formation throughout the daylight hours, but with darkness had been faced not only with the turn in towards Tobruk, but also with the need to increase speed from eighteen to thirty knots. One column snatched away into the darkness and lost all cohesion, and although the other column built up speed gradually and thus kept more or less together, when they reached the coastline from which should be shining the essential guiding light, they found complete blackness complicated by an almost total ignorance of their exact positions. It had proved impossible to hold a precise course at such high speeds in the choppy sea, for radar in those days was not available for such small craft and even their signal sets were so rudimentary as to be almost useless, especially when close under the cliffs.

By 0230 on Monday, September 14th, therefore, Force C had been reduced from an organised force to nineteen individual but blind units, probing like a small swarm of bees searching for an entry along the length of a darkened coastline, while ashore waited Haselden and his commandos, unable to move without the reinforcement the small boats were carrying. In the event, two M.T.B.s bearing machine-gunners from the Royal Northumberland Fusiliers eventually found the inlet at about 0400, discharged their cargoes of men and weapons with some difficulty but to the enormous relief of those awaiting them, then turned to leave, whereupon one stuck on the mud and had eventually to be abandoned. But this was all the reinforcement the commandos were to receive, and they were already nearly three hours late in opening their clearing operations along the southern shore of the harbour.

If anything, matters were even worse with Force A. Captain St J. A. Micklethwaite aboard H.M.S. *Sikh* had received the 'Proceed' signal on time, and also one from the submarine *Taku* off Mersa Mreira to the effect that weather conditions were acceptable for landing operations. Punctually at 0300 his two destroyers arrived two miles offshore and the complicated business of putting the 'shoe-boxes' over the side and filling them with the first wave of marines began.

It was an agonising task. Whatever the youthful captain of *Taku* thought, the seas were unruly enough to cause the destroyers to rock, the lifting wires to sway, the 'shoe-boxes' to bump on the decks and crash against the sides – and to buck and heave diabolically when in the water. A shackle broke, a man's hand was caught and crushed – and the marines were still penned out of the way below decks.

But eventually, all the landing-craft were alongside, the first party of marines, slung about with weapons of every sort, climbed perilously down into them, the towing craft carefully shepherded the bucking 'shoe-boxes' into position and the tow ashore could begin. *Sikh* and *Zulu* turned and steamed away into the darkness so as to be less easily detected should enemy suspicions be aroused, intending to turn back to meet the returning landing-craft as soon as the relevant signal was received from the marines' commanding officer in one of the power-boats.

Unfortunately, the signal Captain Micklethwaite received was to the effect that that particular power-boat (the only one carrying a signal set) had broken down, that it and its accompanying train of lurching landing-craft were drifting helplessly away to the west, while the other tows – minus their commanding officer – disappeared into the darkness towards their as yet unidentified landing place.

The landing place was to remain unidentified. Although the captain of the *Taku* had considered conditions good enough for the main landing operations, he then found that they were too rough for the launching from his craft of two folboats bearing specialists, whose job it had been to inspect the beaches for possible obstructions, find the entrance to the inlet and then signal in the landing-craft and the marines. Like the M.T.B.s and M.L.s further to the east, those landing-craft not wallowing helplessly out at sea were now slowly moving inshore, blind and uncertain of their position. Eventually, they drifted into beaches some two miles west of their intended landing place and quickly ran into trouble.

By this time both *Sikh* and *Zulu* had come back to meet the supposedly returning landing-craft, edging much nearer inshore than had been agreed in order to cut down the interval between the landings of the first and second waves; and at 0500 they suddenly saw lights flashing from the coast and heard the unmistakable sounds of battle. The seventy-odd marines who had managed to land were being attacked, while two hundred of their comrades waited at sea, totally unable to get ashore to help them.

Five minutes later, as the crew of *Sikh* were hauling aboard the cold and frustrated marines of two landing-craft and the broken-down power-boat, a searchlight beam shot out from the shore, wavered, touched *Sikh*, moved on, returned and held her. Within minutes coastal defence guns had opened up and among the first salvoes was a shell which smashed through the destroyer's thin side and exploded in the engine-room, wrecking the steering and the lubrication system to the main shaft. *Sikh* could now do nothing but circle slowly, and thus drew upon herself the attentions of every German and Italian gun along that stretch of coast that could be brought to bear. Coastal guns threw 5-inch shells into her, 88mm. anti-aircraft guns lowered their barrels and poured in their shot; by 0545 she was helpless – but *Zulu* was coming in to try to tow her out of danger.

Four times *Zulu* made the delicate manoeuvre to pass a line to *Sikh* – by now both ships were under concentrated enemy fire – and on the fourth was successful. The line brought across a rope, the rope the end of a hawser quickly made fast, and *Zulu* turned away with *Sikh* slowly veering after her. But by now it was daylight and the coastal guns were making very good practice; and just as *Sikh* was pulling clear into line behind her sister-ship, a shell exploded on *Zulu*'s quarterdeck and by the time the smoke and flame had cleared the end of the broken hawser had slipped overboard and *Sikh* was on her own again.

For another hour *Zulu* tried to protect *Sikh* with smoke in the hope that her engineers might get her moving again, but *Zulu* was taking punishment herself all the time and at 0708 Captain Micklethwaite decided that *Sikh* was lost. He ordered *Zulu* to rejoin *Coventry* at sea, gave the order to abandon *Sikh* at about 0800 and half an hour later, surrounded by the survivors of her crew and of the marines she had carried, the destroyer finally sank. She was about three miles offshore by then, and for several hours the survivors clung to pieces of wreckage, the badly wounded dying, all becoming weaker and weaker until, with the sounds of battle ashore subsiding, an Italian landing-barge came out to collect them.

By dawn it was quite clear to everyone in the area that *Operation Daffodil* had failed. For over two hours the M.T.B.s which had not found the entrance of Sciausc Bay had cruised up and down vainly searching for the guiding lights, but after 0530 were blinded by searchlights whose beams had been directed seawards once the diversionary nature of the R.A.F. activities had been realised at the Garrison Command. The M.T.B.s' speed had usually been enough to take them out of trouble even when caught by the searchlights, but their manoeuvring brought them no nearer their objective and their cargoes of Argylls and Northumberland Fusiliers became ever more vociferous in their demands to be put ashore to help their comrades, even if not in the agreed place.

But the M.T.B. commanders were unanimous in their refusal. Either the soldiers would be put ashore at the right place, or not at all; and when daylight began quickly to spread across the scene it was all too evident that little would be gained by throwing yet more men into a lost battle. Moreover, another and even more dangerous threat to the M.T.B.s became apparent; from the direction of El Adem airfield came the whine of engines as Stukas and Me 109s rose in an angry swarm and came hurtling across the bay at them. The Fairmile motor launches drew the first attack because of their size, but the volume of fire which rose from their decks as every automatic weapon aboard and most of the rifles opened up, deterred their attackers for a while, though near-misses rocked them like corks and flooded their decks. One M.T.B. was hit squarely and blew up with a roar which echoed around the bay.

Then, as they circled and their young commanders wondered what next they could do, H.M.S. *Zulu* came slowly towards them. It was evident that she had been hit hard and often and had developed a distinct list, but there was nothing they could do to help her and even less to help her sister ship. Orders were shouted to them from *Zulu*'s bridge and reluctantly the young M.T.B. commanders turned to obey. They were to return on their own to Alexandria – or at least as far along the coast in that direction as the petrol remaining in their tanks would take them – leaving Haselden and his men to their fate.

By dawn the commandos were penned into the bridgehead they had taken so triumphantly four hours before, by an Italian battalion which was swiftly being strengthened by German troops rushed across from the port area. Moreover, as *Sikh* sank and *Zulu* drew away, the guns which had been hammering them could turn their attention to the headland; a hastily constructed sangar, the Italian blockhouse which had served at first as headquarters for Haselden and aid post for the wounded, and the stranded M.T.B. down in the inlet served as nuclei around which the commandos gathered and which became the centres of resistance.

At first Haselden, ever the optimist, declared that although it was quite evident that the Argylls were not to arrive, it was the plain duty of the commandos to continue the fight in order to take pressure off the marines of Force A; but shortly after 0700 came a signal saying that Force A had failed to land, so he gave the orders for every captured gun, emplacement and hut to be destroyed and then for each man to try to make his own way south to the desert and escape.

But of course the second part was much easier said than done. An attempt was made to load the wounded on the last remaining truck, man the sides with heavily armed men and crash out through the ever-tightening ring – but the attempt was seen in preparation, an ambush was prepared for it and Haselden himself, who had spotted the trap, was killed trying to warn the truck of the danger and at the same time to disperse it. Down in the inlet, frantic efforts were made to shift the M.T.B. off its embracing mudbank, but first efforts were defeated by technical ignorance ('I just don't know which bloody buttons to push!' one officer was heard complaining) and when eventually someone did get the engines to start, the commandos were no more successful than the Navy had been in moving the craft. Two of them manned the twin Oerlikons throughout and kept the wadi ridges on each side clear of all but snipers – but these inevitably caused some casualties and in time the ammunition drums were empty.

There was then a short but curious silence (except for the curses of the men still trying to shift the hard-stuck hull), broken after a short while by the sounds of engines from seaward. Then, smoothly but powerfully, an E-Boat slid into the inlet, its decks crowded with German infantry, its deck guns covering the M.T.B. and the forlorn but grim group around it. As it was so obviously the end for them, the commandos laid down their arms and the German soldiers and marines poured ashore to take them prisoner. The wounded were gently and carefully carried aboard, the British weapons collected and piled on one side, the fit commandos congratulated and assembled aboard the E-Boat by Germans, obviously impressed by their performance and, they said, not unamused by the panic and chaos so small a band had sewn among their Italian allies. The commandos by the M.T.B. were among the luckier ones.

On the headland above, the groups fighting in the sangar and the Italian blockhouse were facing the same inevitable surrender and for the same reasons – growing casualties and rapidly decreasing stocks of ammunition; they were also subject to much heavier attack than those down in the inlet – from artillery, from mortars and from heavy machine-guns in addition to the ever-growing infantry strength being brought against them. Eventually, when the guns in the blockhouse fell silent and those in the sangar had an average of but three rounds left apiece, the giant sergeant-major who had been the soul of the defence since Haselden had been killed, rolled over, wriggled out of his by no means white shirt and, holding it above his head, rose slowly to his feet. He had already revealed on several occasions that he led a charmed life, but this latest exhibition astonished everyone who saw it, for despite the cease-fire in the defended area, rifle and machine-gun bullets continued to pour in from every side and they were quite evidently all aimed at him. Yet all that happened was that the off-white shirt between his hands was riddled, and eventually split apart.

But then there was heard above the sounds of firing an ever-increasing volume of German orders and rebukes, a tall Oberleutnant was seen to rise from behind some rocks and run across to them followed by a group of men wearing Afrika Korps insignia, and these, much to the commandos' relief but also to their astonishment, formed a ring around them to protect them from a horde of furious and vociferous Italians, obviously intent upon avenging the deaths of many of their comrades. A few Italians got through but were apparently too incensed to use their heads or their weapons and tried to club the commandos to the ground (one took a swing at the sergeant-major and although he left him with a bloody mouth was himself neatly felled by a colossal clip around the ear) but the Afrika Korps quickly threw them out and then began to steer the commandos away, rather like police escorting a football team off the field after one of today's more tumultuous soccer matches.

Even given the volatility of the Latins, it all seemed unusually ferocious, but as became evident afterwards, they felt they had cause.

Even the marines in the 'shoe-boxes' which remained in tow had had an appalling time. The hastily constructed landing-craft proved so unseaworthy that most of the men were violently sea-sick before they had gone far, and although their power-boats kept going, many of the tow-ropes snapped and had there not been double ties, some 'shoe-boxes' would undoubtedly have gone individually adrift. Even so, the task of finding and retying broken ends of rope between heavy-laden and unmanageable craft, yawing at every twist of a choppy sea in almost complete darkness, had called for enormous reserves of both strength and courage; by the time the power-boats were inshore and casting off, the marines were cold, wet and exhausted.

They were also under fire, but such was the turmoil of the breaking waves that none of the 'shoe-boxes' was hit. Too many of them, however, themselves hit rocks, splintered, rapidly filled and sank, or capsized and threw their living cargoes into the sea, where many of them were crushed between 'shoe-box' and rock, and many others dragged under by their heavy equipment and drowned. By the time Major Hedley, the most senior officer to land, could collect all the survivors together, he had fewer than sixty men including half a dozen officers left and so much time had been lost that darkness had gone, any element of surprise in their attack had long dispersed – as had any chance of reinforcement. Out to sea, *Sikh* was ablaze fore and aft, *Zulu* being repeatedly hit. As there was obviously no hope of succour or rescue from that direction, and equally little chance of attaining any of Force A's objectives, the unanimous decision of all officers present was that they should split up into three groups, fight their way out towards the perimeter and escape into the desert, in the hope that the L.R.D.G. would pick them up.

But first they had to climb up one or more of the wadis which seamed the cliffs, reach the high ground and somehow make their way through the enemy positions which obviously dotted the ridge. Each party found, as soon as it started, that even the wadis held small enemy groups, each of which had to be stormed and eliminated, so by the time the groups reached the ridge their numbers had already been severely reduced.

But then they saw in front of them a small level plain, clustered with palm trees under which were pitched neat lines of tents. As they reached the edge of the area, men broke from the tents and ran away towards a building on the far side and, assuming this to be either a headquarters or an armoury, the marines opened fire and gave chase. As they reached the clumps of trees and tents, they heard movement and shouting from inside, so they riddled them with tommy-gun and pistol fire as they rushed by, and threw grenades into the open flaps.

It was not until they reached the square in front of the building and saw the Red Cross on the door that they realised what they had done – shot up lines of hospital tents filled with sick and wounded. Had they gone much further they would have hit a compound with tents containing sick and wounded British and South African prisoners-of-war.

Clear of the hospital area, the marines now found themselves within sight of the road leading from the west into Tobruk, along which lorry-loads of both Italians and Germans were hurrying towards the main defences. It was quite obvious that they would not be able to cross it in daylight, but behind them, in the wadis they had just climbed, were several caves and dug-outs which had housed the Australians during their epic siege of the previous year; there they went into hiding, and from the mouth of one of the caves, Major Hedley watched the *Sikh* sink, and *Zulu* limp away out to sea.

But the Royal Navy had still not paid the full price for their part in this ill-fated operation.

H.M.S. *Coventry* and her eight Hunt class destroyers had duly trailed their coats along the African coast in order to confuse Axis radar, and by 0630 had returned almost to Alexandria when Captain Dendy aboard *Coventry* received a message reporting the fate of *Sikh*, and ordering him to return as quickly as possible to render what assistance he could to the battered *Zulu*. At least two of his destroyers were short of fuel so he ordered them into harbour, and with the others reversed course towards a given rendezvous.

It was quickly obvious that the night's activities had thoroughly aroused all Axis aircraft in the eastern half of the Mediterranean, and

long before the time for sighting *Zulu*, *Coventry*'s somewhat rudimentary radar screen was indicating unidentified groups of aircraft
approaching. A hurriedly summoned Beaufighter arrived from
Alexandria in response to requests for aid but at best the only help it
could give would be observation and advice; which shortly before
1124 it provided.

But hardly had its message been received and *Coventry*'s stern guns
swung on to a new bearing, than fifteen Ju 87s broke cloud just
behind her and by 1126 *Coventry* was a broken ship. One bomb
practically blew off her bows forward of No. 1 gun, two bombs
exploded on the forecastle deck just below the bridge demolishing
everything under the compass platform and starting a fire below, and
a fourth bomb smashed through the upper deck and exploded in a
boiler room, destroying the radar equipment at the same time.

After this it was evident that even if *Coventry* could be kept afloat,
the operation of towing her back to Alexandria would so hamper the
accompanying destroyers that one or more would inevitably be very
badly damaged, so the decision was taken that the cruiser must be
abandoned and sunk; but an almost unbelievable combination of
circumstances complicated this operation out of all reason.

Her scuttling charges had been unprimed as a result of experience
on previous convoy work, when it had been discovered that near-
misses from enemy aircraft or guns could make them explode, thus
completing the enemy's work for them; and the fires below caused by
the bombing made it impossible for anyone to approach and re-
activate them. Moreover, when Captain Dendy instructed one of the
accompanying destroyers to torpedo his stricken ship, he learned to
his bitter astonishment that of the flotilla appointed for this operation, only the two destroyers which he had ordered into harbour to
refuel carried torpedoes, the others being regarded and armed as
anti-aircraft and anti-submarine vessels.

The only destroyer in the vicinity carrying torpedoes was *Zulu*;
Coventry would therefore have to await her arrival before receiving
her death blow, while the other destroyers around picked up survivors and fought off more attacks by Ju 87s and 88s.

And *Zulu* was herself now in great danger. Stukas had found her
just before 0900 and by the time she reached the rendezvous point
and the stricken *Coventry* she had survived three concentrated
attacks, the last by four Ju 88s and five Ju 87s – and even as she
reached the circle of protective Hunt class destroyers and slowed to
aim her torpedoes at the wallowing but still floating *Coventry*,
another swarm of German aircraft dropped out of the clouds.

The next ten minutes produced one of the most concentrated
sea-actions of the Second World War, when, in a circle less than three
miles in diameter and in the air above it, seven destroyers fought off

sixteen aircraft while one of their number sank the crippled cruiser in their midst; and when, at 1505, *Coventry* at last slid under the waves, the battle continued as *Zulu* and her escort set off on the voyage back towards their own air cover based on Alexandria.

Two of the Hunts, loaded with wounded from *Coventry*, raced off at full speed, and the other four remained to help the by now badly hit older ship, whose ordeal was by no means over. At 1600, six Ju 88s and twelve Ju 87s arrived overhead and it was quite obvious that *Zulu* alone was their target. One of their bombs burst in the engine room, and it seemed at last as though the end had come, but Commander White was determined to save his ship if possible (Alexandria was but a hundred miles away now) and the destroyer *Hursley* tried to take her in tow. There were moments similar to those off Tobruk as the ships manoeuvred and the tows parted but at last *Hursley* and *Zulu* were linked and the slow, careful journey could begin, with the remaining three destroyers circling to keep off the now slackening air attack.

They were defeated by time and nature. By dusk *Zulu* was so deep in the water that *Hursley* could barely make ten knots and her captain was genuinely worried that if *Zulu* went suddenly, his own command might be dragged down before the tow broke; and Commander White saw his point. H.M.S. *Croome* was ordered alongside to take the last of *Zulu*'s survivors, and orders were given for the tow to be broken – and hardly had the last order been carried out when *Zulu* suddenly rolled to starboard, her commander and skeleton crew were thrown into the water and the destroyer vanished from sight in a maelstrom of bubbling and spewing turmoil from which, fortunately, all survivors were rescued. The rest of the journey was comparatively uneventful, and all four Hunt class destroyers were back in harbour by the following morning – but three more M.T.B.s and two of the motor launches had been caught and sunk on their trip back along the African coast, and every single craft was hit and damaged in some way. Admiral Harwood and his staff had been right to regard *Operation Daffodil* with scepticism.

So far as the land forces were concerned, the marines hiding in the old Australian dug-outs were rounded up by German infantry during the evening of September 12th, and most of the surviving commandos were under guard by nightfall, though a few were caught trying to make their way out into the desert during the next two days. Five men – including one of the S.I.G. men – eventually walked back eastward sufficiently far to reach the British lines, the last one being picked up, a wasted skeleton, long-haired, bearded but quite composed, on November 18th.

As for the only other formation concerned with *Operation Daffodil*

– the L.R.D.G. patrol under David Lloyd Owen – they had met and shot up an Italian patrol within an hour of despatching the commandos, had run into a number of hastily erected roadblocks on their way towards the perimeter and managed to dodge around them and, somewhat to the astonishment of all concerned, caught a lorry full of German soldiers under an Oberleutnant who had decided, not unreasonably, that Tobruk was becoming too noisy for a section en route to the main battlefront to enjoy a good night's sleep, and were therefore seeking one in the empty and comparatively peaceful desert to the south.

By this time it had become evident that the operation was not going according to plan, no contact with Haselden was possible despite the most expert attempts by the signallers, and David Lloyd Owen knew that his first duty was to keep his patrol intact and available for what promised to be complicated and perhaps desperate rescue operations. He abandoned the attempt to penetrate deep into the Tobruk area, leaving the radio stations and the aircraft unattacked, the prisoners unrescued.

In this he was well advised as his services were going to be urgently needed elsewhere in the near future.

Operation Snowdrop, the S.A.S. raid on Benghasi, had proved just as great a disaster as the raid on Tobruk, the only difference being the instant and spectacular way in which disaster struck.

An advance party under Paddy Mayne had gone up into the Jebel, contacted one of the resident agents there who was already troubled by movements of German and Italian units which seemed to suggest that the Benghasi raid was expected, and who now despatched one of his Arabs into the port to obtain specific information. The Arab returned thirty-six hours later with a report that Benghasi teemed with newly arrived Axis troops, that the whole population was talking about the impending raid, that civilians were being evacuated from danger spots and minefields, roadblocks and ambushes were being set up around the town perimeter – especially at the planned entrance-point for the attackers. The date for the attack – September 14th – was freely talked about, and even some fairly accurate figures discussed for the hour.

When David Stirling arrived with the main body and learned of all this, he signalled Base Headquarters in Alexandria and suggested that, although the raid itself should not be cancelled, at least the time and planned approach should be varied, but he quickly received a curt signal telling him to ignore 'bazaar gossip' and adhere closely to his schedule. The Arab had probably made up all the details of his report, the signal implied, possibly because of relations or property in Benghasi which might be harmed during the raid; perhaps he had not even gone into Benghasi, but had instead lurked in the foothills outside concocting his story.

Just after dusk on September 13th, the main party began the intricate descent of the escarpment above the Soluch–Benghasi road and found it so much more difficult for such a large convoy than had been expected that by the time they had reached the bottom they were well behind schedule and the R.A.F. raid, intended to attract enemy attention up into the air during the close approach, was over and the Wellingtons and Mitchells already on their way back to base. But on the road, speed was picked up and the head of the column made good time until suddenly it ran into a roadblock.

There was no light on the bar across the road and there appeared to be no sentry – circumstances themselves unusual enough to arouse suspicion – but what caused the gravest doubts were the signs of recent digging on each side of the road which seemed to indicate new minefields. Stirling called forward his chief sapper officer, Captain Cumper, who examined the disturbed surfaces, and then turned his attention to the roadblock. Here there was apparently no trouble for with an audible click a catch snapped back, the bar hinged upwards to leave a clear road, Captain Cumper stepped back and with a gracious wave of his hand invited the leading jeeps to go through.

'Let battle commence!' he announced in imitation of a well-known comedian of those days, and hardly were the words out of his mouth when it did, with quite astonishing ferocity.

Breda machine-guns opened up on the head of the column from

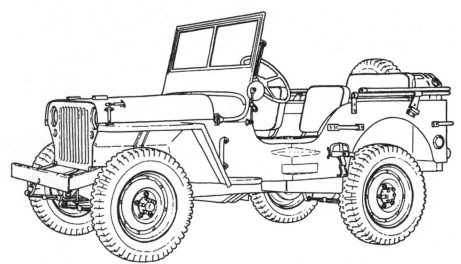

Figure 2   Willys jeep: overall length 131 ins; width 62 ins; weight unloaded 2,750 lbs; payload 800 lbs across country, 1,200 lbs on roads; speed 55 m.p.h.; fuel consumption (loaded) 17·5 m.p.g.

just beyond the roadblock, submachine-gun and rifle fire poured into the flanks while mortar-bombs exploded along its length. The leading jeeps raced forward through the block (there was nowhere else for them to go and to remain stationary would have been suicidal), one was hit by an incendiary bullet in the petrol tank, the resultant flames throwing a fiery, garish light over the whole diabolical scene, and every gun in the column – and each jeep was fitted with twin Vickers – opened up to add its rattle to the din. Many of the jeeps deployed off the road, their comparative lightness saving them from destruction on the new minefields, and as they came up abreast of the head of the column, the sheer weight of fire they were able to bring to bear began to turn the conflict in their favour.

But the overall situation was quite clear; the Arab had been right, their attack had been expected, they had been effectively ambushed and despite their momentary superiority on the field, they would be in severe trouble once reinforcements arrived – and these must assuredly be racing in from other points all along the perimeter. With the element of surprise gone there was no hope for the attainment of any of the raid's objectives and, reluctantly, David Stirling gave the order to withdraw.

It was, inevitably, a case of every man – or at least, vehicle – for himself in a race to reach the comparative safety of the escarpment wadis before daylight; and most of them just managed. But as they hastily camouflaged their vehicles and found what cover they could among the rocks and boulders of the wadi-sides, they could see in the growing light swarms of aircraft rising like angry wasps from the airfields around Benghasi (including Benina which in the light of the night's events had remained unattacked by the L.R.D.G. patrols). For over an hour the S.A.S. men remained unobserved and safe, but then a random burst from one of the searching aircraft hit the truck containing reserves of explosive and ammunition, and the resulting pyrotechnics attracted every Axis pilot in the area; for the rest of the day the wadis were combed, more men were wounded and killed and more trucks destroyed. Surprisingly, no ground force was sent out against them, so by nightfall the survivors could reassemble, assess the damage and begin a further stage of the withdrawal.

It was a nightmare journey back across the Jebel, worst of all for the wounded who were thrown about as the vehicles bucked along unmade tracks or no tracks at all, everyone endeavouring to reach by dawn the base wadi where the doctor waited, and there would be food and drink, more ammunition and good cover. One man had been shot through the lung, one had a badly shattered arm, and the resident agent who had insisted upon taking part in the attack had found himself too close to an exploding hand grenade and now carried several parts of it in his legs and body. There were a number of other minor wounds for the doctor to take care of when eventually they all arrived, and the vehicles were again dispersed and camouflaged, the men settling down for another uncomfortable day under what cover they would find.

Their presence was betrayed to the searching aircraft by what would appear to have been gross negligence or stupidity. Somebody during the morning drove in a jeep and a cloud of dust from one wadi to another, and the bored pilot of one of the CR-42s saw it; from then on the area was continually covered by at least twenty aircraft, combing wadis, shooting up every clump of bushes under which the S.A.S. might be sheltering, bombing the wadi sides to release boulders upon anyone underneath, raking every declivity or shadow which might hold a camouflaged vehicle. By the time the sun went down, 'with sickening deliberation' as Fitzroy Maclean was later to write,[4] there was barely enough transport left to carry the fit men as far as Jalo, let alone any of the badly wounded.

In the end, the resident agent and the corporal with the shattered arm were taken, the other wounded left with a medical orderly and one of the Italian prisoners, who went into Benghasi the following day and brought out an ambulance to take them to hospital. Nothing is known of their fate, for none of them, not even the medical orderly who was unhurt, lived to report upon events after the main body left the area.

Three days later on the evening of September 18th, the leading S.A.S. vehicles were less than thirty miles from Jalo, but as one of the trucks destroyed during the first day had been the signal truck, no one knew if the fort there was in the hands of the Sudan Defence Force or not. Fitzroy Maclean took a jeep to find out – and quickly found himself in the middle of a battle; like the men on *Operations Daffodil* and *Snowdrop*, the S.D.F. on *Operation Tulip* had been expected and were still, after four days, fighting in the area of the oasis for possession of the fort.

But at least contact with the Sudan Defence Force made possible the refilling of the empty S.A.S. petrol tanks and ammunition racks, the men at last had something more than a teaspoonful of bully beef for their day's ration, and their water-bottles could be filled. Moreover, the Sudan Defence Force signal sets were working and from H.Q. they then received news of a column of German armoured cars combing the desert behind them, together with orders that the whole joint force was to retire southwards towards Kuffra as quickly as possible. Although exhausting, the withdrawal was comparatively uneventful for the enemy armoured column was never seen, and by the evening of September 23rd, the survivors of *Operation Snowdrop* were arriving in Kuffra, many of them wondering whether their journey had been worth while.

The only operation of September 13th which could claim any worthwhile degree of success was *Operation Hyacinth*, the L.R.D.G. raid on Barce.

Three patrols under Major J. R. Easonsmith had left Faiyum on September 2nd and made their way across the Sand Sea to emerge into the open desert south of the Jebel Akhdar on September 10th – a route chosen on the grounds that no one in his senses would try to take twenty-two vehicles across such appalling country in September; the ruse seemed to have worked for no hostile aircraft or units at all were seen. By September 12th, the three patrols – one of New Zealanders, one of Rhodesians and a Guards patrol – were into the southern foothills and by the following morning two of them were but fifteen miles away from Barce, the Rhodesians having joined the S.A.S. in *Operation Snowdrop*. Arabs sent into the town by Peniakoff reported the presence of some Italian tanks, probably M13s, but no apparent expectation of immediate attack, so soon after dusk the patrols moved off.

They cut telephone lines en route, shot up an isolated police post, ran into two M13s just outside Barce and killed the crews, and at the entrance to the town separated into three groups each with a distinct task. The New Zealanders under Captain N. P. Wilder made for the airfield along the Maddalena road which they entered with no trouble, threw grenades into the nearest buildings and set fire with incendiary bullets to a large petrol bowser. In the glare of the towering flames which this produced, the nine trucks and single jeep of the patrol then circled the airfield, methodically shooting up the thirty-two aircraft parked around the edges, while from the last truck one of the sappers planted short-fused bombs on any aircraft not alight by the time he reached it.

Meanwhile, the Guards patrol under Sergeant Dennis (the officer commanding the patrol had been injured in an accident while crossing the Sand Sea) were attacking buildings and barracks at the other end of the town with grenades and machine-gun fire in order to deter the inhabitants from interfering with the New Zealanders, while around the main square of the small town, Easonsmith and Peniakoff were operating in a similar manner between buildings which were either administration blocks or officers' quarters. Neither the Guards nor Easonsmith encountered much opposition, and towards the end of his depredations, Easonsmith and his companion found an empty and unguarded transport park where they wrecked a dozen trucks and cars.

By this time, Wilder's objectives had all been achieved and his patrol were running short of ammunition, so he led them off the airfield and up the long main road towards the railway station – to find that the Italians had at last organised some resistance and two

M13s blocked the way, their shells fortunately aimed too high and screaming away into the darkness.

There was no possibility of retreat, so Wilder in the leading Chevrolet stamped on the accelerator and charged forward, pushing one M13 off the road, crashing into the second and wrecking it – and wrecking his own vehicle at the same time. He and his crew immediately leaped aboard the jeep racing up behind but as they roared off towards the station cross-roads, the driver was blinded by tracer pumped out of their twin machine-guns at an enemy post ahead, hit the curb and overturned the jeep. When it was righted, Captain Wilder was found underneath, unconscious and soaked in petrol, so the next truck behind collected him and the patrol then escaped out of town, except for the last truck with the sapper and his bombs, which had been cut off and was not seen again.

By now all parties were making their way back towards the base wadi where the doctor and spare vehicles and equipment had been left, and before dawn everyone had arrived although Peniakoff and Easonsmith had at one point run into a minor ambush and the former lost the little finger of his left hand. Wilder had recovered consciousness as the petrol in which he was soaked evaporated, and nobody for the moment was badly hurt so they dispersed the vehicles in rolling, scrubby ground, camouflaged the trucks and settled down for a hot but uneventful day's rest.

This they were not to enjoy. A group of Tripolitanian horsemen was seen riding towards the area and Easonsmith went off with a pair of jeeps to scare them away – and on return, decided that as their position might now be reported to the Italians, the group should move. During this operation they were seen and fired upon by two old Italian CR-42s which then hastily alerted the Italian command, and for the rest of the day the L.R.D.G. men were harassed by all the aircraft in the area not similarly engaged over the S.A.S. positions. By nightfall their doctor had six casualties to look after including Peniakoff and Captain Wilder who had been hit in both legs, and one of the men whose stomach had been torn open by a bullet which passed right through his body.

Twenty-seven fit survivors with one undamaged Chevrolet truck, one jeep in sound order and another with a punctured petrol tank and a torn tyre were now all the remaining effectives of Easonsmith's command, with enough petrol and water for about two hundred miles.

Fortunately, this was the kind of situation for which the L.R.D.G. had long made provision, and forty miles away was hidden a truck with water, petrol and rations, while nearly one hundred and fifty miles further south was a disused airfield, L.G. 125, which had been assigned as rallying point for stragglers from the operations and from which, with luck, the wounded might be flown out. The problem (apart from getting there) was communication, for one of the day's casualties had been the wireless truck.

Easonsmith now divided his group into a walking party of twenty-three plus himself, with the damaged jeep accompanying them to carry their gear, and a second party consisting of the six wounded men, the doctor, a navigator and a fitter, to travel as quickly as possible in the truck and the sound jeep first to the reserve truck in order to collect their portion of the rations, then to L.G. 125 and then, if necessary, down through the Jalo gap to Kuffra. In the doctor's opinion, Parker, the man with the stomach wound, would not live to reach that last destination by surface vehicle.

It was a warm, dark, moonless night and the going was so bad that for the first hour both parties kept together. Peniakoff, who had also been hit by splinters in the knee which in consequence was now stiffening up, was with the driving party and left a vivid description of that night's journey:

> Davis, our navigator, tried to keep a straight course and the driver did his best to follow his instructions, but the night was so dark that he could only just see far enough ahead to avoid crashing into trees and boulders. Of the general lie of the land he could see nothing: he drove ahead in a straight line as long as he wasn't stopped by an impassable obstacle. We found ourselves, at one time, driving along the steep side of a hill at such an angle that we could hardly cling to our seats and we expected the truck to topple over, but it righted itself; then some time later, we stopped dead with our front wheels nearly over a cliff, a vertical drop of forty feet or so to a wadi below. We drove round, followed the curving cliff edge for a long time, found a way down, slid and skidded to the wadi bottom and started climbing up the opposite bank. Night was wearing out, there was no time to send a man on foot to reconnoitre ahead: if dawn found us anywhere near our starting point, the planes would soon be on us and our adventures at an end. The climb out of the wadi proved difficult: it was steep and full of screes which had to be rushed, and protruding rocks which should be taken with care. The heavy truck rocked and swayed, the uphill wheels on rock, the downhill ones on shingle in which they spun, digging a hole which slowly brought the truck to a dangerous angle: suddenly the wheels gripped (having reached rock, I suppose) and sent us lurching forward, over boulders and through high bushes with a loud crash. We pulled up on a level keel, and while the fitter got down to inspect the damage, Lawson injected a dose of morphia to Parker, to whom the jolting was agony.[5]

There was no vital damage to the truck and as the ground was not now so broken they made better speed for about twelve miles, halted just after three o'clock for a rest (which by now both navigator and driver needed as badly as the wounded), carried on during the morning and eventually found the reserve truck in the Wadi Jerrari in mid-afternoon. Having helped themselves to food, water and petrol and left a note for the walking party, they continued in the direction of L.G. 125 until darkness fell, then halted and slept for ten hours.

Parker was still alive in the morning but in great pain for the morphia seemed to be losing its power to ease his sufferings. He could not be given anything to eat or – far worse – to drink, and he was conscious always of the limitations which under such circumstances a badly wounded man places on the movements and chances of escape of his comrades; almost the only words he spoke during the journey were in apology for the trouble he was causing them.

By the morning of September 17th, the navigator reckoned they were but thirty-miles from L.G. 125 – marked by the tail of a wrecked Hurricane standing upright – and they found it before noon, carefully reconnoitred to ensure that the area was not in enemy hands and then occupied the disused hangars and dug-outs, searched and found reserves of petrol which they did not need, and water, bully beef and biscuits which they did. But they still lacked means to communicate with base, and Lawson the doctor decided that they should stay at the landing-ground either until someone arrived who could order in aircraft, or until Parker died . . . which would surely be in but a few days.

Fortunately, aid was at hand.

Throughout September 16th, Easonsmith's walking party had trudged on towards the Wadi Jerrari, and on the morning of the 17th they heard the noise of vehicles over the crest of a hill. Judging them to be of another L.R.D.G. patrol, they fired Very lights, but these were not seen so it looked as though the walk was going to be a long one after all. An hour later, however, they reached the top of a rise to see the Rhodesian patrol which had accompanied them up from Faiyum to the Jebel and then joined the S.A.S. approach to Benghasi breakfasting in the hollow below.

Not only did this mean the end of their own immediate tribulations, but also that a situation report could be sent to H.Q. who took swift action to rescue the wounded at L.G. 125. David Lloyd Owen was still at Hatiet Etla and was ordered to the landing-ground where he arrived the evening of the same day as the wounded, and as a result of much radio traffic and some excellent organisation, a Bombay of 216 Squadron put down on the airstrip the following day at 1300. That night the wounded slept in Kuffra and the following day were flown back to Heliopolis, in due course arriving at the New Zealand General Hospital at Helwan. It is pleasant to be able to record that all survived their wounds.

By September 25th, the remaining L.R.D.G. men from *Operation Hyacinth* – including two Guardsmen who had been cut off in Barce and had walked out to L.G. 125 on their own – were back at Kuffra.

The operation had caused the destruction of a dozen Axis vehicles, thirty-two Axis aircraft and had probably killed the same number of Axis soldiers, at a cost of six Allied wounded, ten prisoners of war and fourteen assorted vehicles. Five decorations were shared among the participants – two D.S.O.s, one M.C. and three M.M.s.

Attempts to justify the raids of September 13th, 1942, read a little thin.

The raid on Tobruk alone had caused the loss of a cruiser, two destroyers, four motor torpedo boats, two Fairmiles and, according to the *Official History*, 280 naval officers and men, 300 Royal Marines and 160 soldiers; and the other raids caused losses among the S.A.S. and even more valuable L.R.D.G. men, not to speak of the vehicles and equipment destroyed.

According to Fitzroy Maclean, the signal received by the Sudan Defence Force ordering them to withdraw to Kuffra also claimed that the raids had achieved their main object, causing the diversion from the front or retention behind it of large numbers of enemy troops and aircraft – which was undoubtedly true at the time. But there is no point in causing an opponent to weaken his defences if advantage is not taken of that weakness. Not until the end of the month was any attack mounted on any part of the Alamein Line (by 131st Brigade at Munassib) – a hiatus which gave ample time for any of Rommel's strength which might have been withdrawn or withheld to cope with the raiding forces, to be returned to their original positions.

The stated main object of the raids before they took place had been destruction, not diversion – destruction of Rommel's petrol, of his harbour facilities, of aircraft, transport and key installations – and the proclamation of a different main object in the light of what actually happened smacks of sophistry. Only at Barce had any concrete results been achieved, and if the local profit and loss account there appeared quite reasonable, embodying that account into the overall balance sheet reveals an Allied disaster. The loss of *Coventry* alone outweighed the destruction of the Macchis and Capronis at Barce, and nothing had been achieved to offset the loss of the two destroyers, the commandos, the Royal Marines and the seamen or indeed anyone or anything else.

One lesson which might have been drawn was that in raiding operations, economy of force is essential; and another is that any planned pattern of separate attacks can easily be discerned by an intelligent foe, who can read a map as well as anyone else. Once the objectives of the various raids had been marked around the edge of the Cyrenaican bulge on the map at Panzerarmee H.Q., the escape routes of any raiders not evacuated by sea quite obviously funnelled down towards Jalo and the gap. The L.R.D.G. had pleaded for the

Sudan Defence Force to attack the fort there on the same night as the rest of the raids, but been overruled by the planners who had not yet learned to give their opponents credit for as much intelligence as they had themselves.

Overconfidence and lack of security in military affairs are marks of the amateur; and in Cairo a thorough professional was watching developments with a critical eye. Perhaps Montgomery should have vetoed the raids immediately he arrived in Egypt, but he had many other things to do, his personal experience and knowledge of such formations as L.R.D.G. and S.A.S. was minimal and their reputation so high that he allowed them to proceed despite his conviction that nothing should happen in his area of command which had not been controlled from the outset by himself.

The failures of the operations of September 13th confirmed him in this belief. He was to use raiding forces himself on many later occasions and in time he came to value both L.R.D.G. and S.A.S. very highly, but the brigadier in charge of the Raiding Forces H.Q. at Alexandria in September 1942 received no further promotion during his military career (though he remained in the Middle East until the end of the campaign) and when David Stirling went to see Montgomery to ask for a free hand in recruiting throughout Eighth Army, he received a very cold and firm refusal.

Montgomery had other plans for the best, the bravest, the most imaginative – in short, the most professional – of the men under his command, than allowing them to concentrate in small private armies of whose value he had still to be persuaded.

3 · *Prelude to Battle*

There is no doubt – even discounting General Montgomery's conviction that troops suffering the grievous disability of not having been trained under his personal direction would be unlikely to withstand the rigours of battle – that Eighth Army in August 1942 lacked certain military qualities essential for victory against so skilful a foe as the Afrika Korps, in any area of the desert and especially in the Alamein positions.

Enough examples of the lack of co-ordination between infantry and armour had already occurred for it to be obvious that that facet of battle-winning technique needed polishing, and indeed the whole principle which still to a great extent permeated the Royal Armoured Corps thinking – that their task was to eliminate the enemy panzers and leave the infantry to fight their pedestrian battles on their own – was in need of rectification. Moreover, with the arrival of the three hundred Shermans from America, many of the tank crews – especially those newly arrived from England – had now to learn how best to take advantage of a tank whose armament, power and reliability were well above any they had previously experienced.

There were also both general and particular aspects of infantry training in need of improvement, not least because among the divisions which had been out in the desert for some time there existed a belief that 'the best training is fighting' and as they had seen so much of it, they must already be well trained – a dictum which might have been truer had more of Eighth Army's fighting in recent weeks been successful. As it was, it seemed likely that some of the habits which had contributed to failure in the past might have become ingrained, instead of being eradicated; and in any case, many of the N.C.O.s and company officers now with Eighth Army had only recently been promoted as a result of casualties at Gazala and since, and thus lacked certain proficiencies – for it takes more than just a period of time as a good rifleman to make a satisfactory corporal or as a subaltern to make a good captain.

As for the new infantry divisions arriving in the desert, not only did they need to accustom themselves to the heat and the dust, but also to develop 'desert sense' – a lack of which was demonstrated with blinding clarity one night when Major-General Douglas Wimberley, commanding the newly arrived 51st Highland Division, left his caravan in a dust storm and took two hours to find his way to the mess tent four hundred yards distant. Moreover, like the men of the 44th Division at Alam Halfa, the Highlanders had for the most part never seen action, for their division had been almost totally destroyed in France in 1940, and since been reconstituted.

But there was an even more fundamental reason for retraining the desert army, as a totally new approach to battle was necessary at Alamein. For the first time in the desert fighting, there was no open flank for the attacking force to hook around – no Bir Enba Gap as for 7th Armoured and 4th Indian in 1940, no wide space as for XXX Corps during *Crusader* or Rommel's forces during the Gazala battles. By September 1942 the defences of both armies stretched all the way from the sea just north of Tel el Eisa down to the Qattara Depression south of Himeimat, and every day which passed saw those defences thickened. The mine-marshes between the opposing sides grew ever more extensive (the Germans referred to them picturesquely as 'devil's gardens') and if the shortages of barbed wire did not allow entanglements of the complexity of the Western Front of 1918, the overall situation would nevertheless demand an attack of 1918 style.

The keynote of this – and indeed of all attacks upon the First World War trench system once it had been firmly established – had been massive artillery bombardment followed by direct infantry assault, and the cornerstones of the philosophy which directed them had been the cold, grim facts of attrition. Only in April 1915 when the Germans had used gas at Langemark and in November 1917 when the British attacked the line at Cambrai with massed tanks had surprise alleviated the necessity for an attacking force to be at least three times the strength of a defending force, and to lose lives in a corresponding proportion; and no one was suggesting the use of gas at Alamein. As the use of armour on the field of battle had become commonplace and no other completely new weapon was available, Eighth Army had now to retrain for the type of battle which their fathers had fought, and of which most professional soldiers and every amateur soldier had prayed there would be no repeat. Strafer Gott had refused to allow his men to partake in the assault on the northern flank of the Cauldron at Gazala exactly because it would have borne too strong a resemblance to First World War tactics, and it is interesting to speculate upon how he would have faced up to the realities of the situation at Alamein had he lived.

But however Gott might have reacted, Montgomery was quite

prepared to draw the inevitable conclusions from his analysis of the problem, and with those conclusions the equally inevitable fact that in order to break through the Alamein positions and defeat the Afrika Korps, many brave men – probably the best in Eighth Army – were going to lose their lives. Some warning of this was given in one of his memos:

> This battle will involve hard and prolonged fighting. Our troops must not think that, because we have a good tank and very powerful artillery support, the enemy will all surrender. The enemy will NOT surrender, and there will be bitter fighting.
> The Infantry must be prepared to fight and kill, and to continue doing so over a prolonged period . . . [1]

But if his training directives to the rank and file stressed the toughness of the battle ahead, his directives to senior officers were to ensure that within the overall context of defeating the Afrika Korps, the minimum of lives were to be lost *unnecessarily* – and to those two ends, victory and the most economical expenditure of lives, all training was to be directed. Not every training programme in the annals of the British Army had been based upon such clearly defined principles.

In one important aspect the forthcoming battle would differ fundamentally from those of the closing stages of the First World War. Along the trench lines of the Ypres Salient and the Somme battlefields, barbed wire entanglements had been the chief impediments to attack, and in the great Allied assaults the first task for the lumbering tanks had been to crush paths through them for the infantry to follow. Now the main obstacles were the minefields and the roles must be reversed; infantry and engineers must now make gaps for the armour to pass through and so an essential new element of training for the desert army must be that of mine-lifting on a large scale. During the O'Connor offensive small units from the Royal Engineers had been employed on this task for the assaults on Bardia and Tobruk, but now with mine-marshes several hundred yards wide to be gapped – under fire and at night – it was evident that deep thought and considerable practice would be necessary before the obstacle they represented could be overcome.

Infantry patrols and aerial observation had given quite an accurate picture of the extent and basic pattern of the Axis minefields, but there were obviously some factors about them only known before the attack to the German engineers who had sewn them. These engineers, under command of a Colonel Hecker, had by the end of September sewn nearly half a million 'devil's eggs', as they called them (a large number of them British, collected from Gazala and Tobruk), in a regular pattern from north to south with variations resulting from the lie of the land. The front edge of the German defences was both wired and mined to a width of between 500 and 1,000 yards, and within this band were dug battle outposts to hold a company of machine-gunners and riflemen, often accompanied by watch-dogs, for every 1,500 yards.

Behind this first belt was an empty space between 1,000 and 2,000 yards wide and behind that another mined strip some 2,000 yards wide, within which were posted the remaining two companies of each defending infantry battalion, with their heavy machine-guns, mortars, anti-tank guns and other supporting weapons.

The open space between the two mine-belts was cut into irregular shapes by lateral belts crossing between the outer and inner fields in the form of narrow triangles, with their apices to the front and passages up in the median lines for counter-attacking infantry and reinforcement for the battle outposts. The main purpose of these lateral belts was to channel any force breaking through the outer belt into the enclosed quadrangles where they would run on to smaller, haphazard minefields, and also find themselves under heavy bombardment from guns previously ranged into the area.

Over 95 per cent of the mines were anti-tank mines which would not necessarily destroy a tank but would certainly cripple it, probably by blowing off a track; and would certainly wreck a wheeled vehicle and kill the majority of its occupants. Many of the mines were interconnected so that a string of them would explode if a tank or lorry went over one, many were booby-trapped to explode at any but the most expert attempts to defuse them, and some large British aircraft bombs and heavy-calibre shells which had fallen into German hands at Tobruk had been buried in the open spaces and ingeniously connected to trip-wires with 'push-pull' igniters to explode them at either an increase or a release of tension on the wire.

Fortunately for the attacking infantry, only some 3 per cent of the mines available at that time were anti-personnel mines – though even this known proportion was enough to make the task of walking across a mine-belt one of particular sensitivity. These S-mines, as they were called, consisted of metal cylinders from which protruded small wire horns, almost invisible in the dust even in daylight. When the horns were trodden on, a charge blew the cylinder into the air to about waist-height where it exploded in a spreading circle of shrapnel and ball-bearings. Frequently several of these, too, were interconnected.

Such then was the pattern of the defences through which the infantry of the attacking divisions would have to walk (not run, for the impact so generated could set off an anti-tank mine) with tingling feet and weapons not heavier than a light machine-gun, while behind them the engineers must clear wide passages before even the infantry support weapons – heavy mortars, heavy machine-guns or anti-tank guns – could come up to join them.

As for the passage of armour through the minefields, the plan of attack would call for three wide corridors to be opened up for them during the first night, and as along most of the front the mine-marsh net covered an area over three miles deep, it was soon obvious that a very large number of highly trained engineers would be required, every one working to a carefully conceived plan.

The first problem for each team would be to find each separate mine – and although nearly five hundred of the newly invented electronic mine-detectors (called, after the nationality of their inventors, Polish detectors) would arrive in time for the battle, these had been hastily manufactured and many of them were to prove defective. In any case their method of usage – the operator standing upright, wearing earphones to detect the change in tone and sweeping the ground ahead from side to side with the instrument on the end of a pole – seemed likely to lead to an unacceptably high casualty rate.

The alternative method and the one which was mostly to be used, called for the careful prodding of each square foot of ground, generally with a bayonet, the scraping away of the sand when the bayonet point struck metal, the gentle exploration around the base of the mine for booby-traps or trip-wires, and then either the explosion of the mine from a distance or the careful removal of its igniter. Anti-personnel mines could be neutralised by inserting a nail into the hole in which had sat the safety-pin, removed when the mine had been planted.

It would all be a matter of very cool nerves and very steady hands, neither being ruffled or disturbed by the violence of battle raging on all sides. As protective infantry would have aroused the enemy at least in the battle outposts, the violence was likely to be extreme.

By mid-August the Eighth Army School of Mine-clearance had been set up near Burg el Arab under a Regular Royal Engineer, Major Peter Moore, who had already distinguished himself during the first battles on Ruweisat Ridge, was one of the few men who had shot his way out of trouble with a revolver and one of the even fewer who had actually wrestled with an armed antagonist in the dark. Together with a New Zealand engineer, Major A. R. Currie, Moore worked out the requisite composition of teams for mine-clearance and a drill for them to follow – and even in an armchair nearly forty years later without the slightest possibility of personal involvement, reading the drill instructions can evoke feelings of cold discomfort; how it looked and sounded to the men under training and faced with the realisation that theory would become practice in but a few days requires little imagination.

The team would be led into action (after the infantry) by an officer and four men, marching on a compass-bearing and unrolling a white tape which would eventually mark the median line of the gap. Upon reaching the area in which it had been deduced (from foot patrols and aerial photographs) that the forward edge of the minefield lay, a stake would be driven into the ground and a blue light mounted to shine to the rear. The whole leading party would then spread out in line abreast and advance in a stooping position rather like the popular impression of a gorilla on the move, with fingers brushing the ground, backs of hands to the front feeling for trip-wires, eyes anxiously scanning every inch of ground for the treacherous S-mine horns. Direction would still be controlled by the man with the compass who would also unravel the tape.

Behind them would come first a jeep or, more often, a small utility truck, with a heavily sand-bagged floor and steering wheel extended to avoid impaling the driver when the almost inevitable explosion took place. The main purpose of this vehicle was to discover if the forward edge of the minefield really was where it had been suspected, or nearer – and the evidence of the latter would be the truck's destruction.

Behind the vehicle came three teams of nine men, each team to clear a width of eight feet making a twenty-four-foot wide gap in all.

The first three men of each team were the trail-blazers – unrolling more tapes as guides, and the ones on the outside of each twenty-four-foot width planting stakes eventually to hold guiding lights for the heavy vehicles and tanks coming through afterwards. (In all, 88,775 lamps were to be used!) These three teams of three men, working abreast, also dealt if they had time with the trip-wires, booby-traps or S-mines found and marked by the first team to go through if these had not already been defused.

The second trio in each of the three teams were the detectors – sweeping the ground with the electronic brooms if these were available, painstakingly prodding every foot of the ground across and forward if they were not; and upon every mine they found, they planted a white metal cone for the teams behind them.

These teams defused the mines – first scraping away the sand, then beginning the heart-stopping process of feeling for booby-traps under or close by, finding and tracing the connecting wires to other mines, praying that no heavy-footed moron was jumping up and down on another in the string. When eventually the mine was proved isolated, a length of wire was looped around it and with the area cleared of friends, it was pulled out – and if it did not explode during this operation, the job of removing the igniter was undertaken.

Disarmed, the mines could then be piled at the side of the passage to await further clearance and the team moved forward. And as the twenty-four-foot wide passage behind the last trios lengthened, lights could be lit on the cross-bars of the stakes marking the outside edges, green on the inside, orange on the outside, and support weapons for the infantry in front – still trying to force their way forward with nothing heavier than their rifles and light machine-guns – could come through to join them.

During training it was found that 200 yards could be cleared in an hour using the electronic detectors, 100 yards prodding with bayonets. As the main inner and outer mine-belts were known to be respectively 500 and 1,000 yards deep *at least*, and the extent of the minefields inside the quadrangles was not known at all, it can be seen that a very large number of teams would be needed, and that every member of every team would need, in action, a remarkable degree of concentration. As one trainee was heard to remark reflectively at the end of one of Peter Moore's opening lectures, it was quite likely that under certain circumstances, the whole business could become 'bloody hazardous'.

One other method had been devised for clearing the lanes, and the principle behind it was successfully used eighteen months later during the invasion of France – that of Flail Tanks. 'Scorpions', as they were called in the desert, consisted of elderly Matildas with drums fitted forward which would revolve, and in doing so flail the ground with whirling chains; several were manufactured at Abbassia and tested near Wadi Natrun, but the tanks were indeed old, the extra engines fitted to revolve the drums still experimental, and the columns of dust which arose from the operations blinded the operators and choked the filters and tank engines after a very short period. A few Scorpions were to be used by XIII Corps in the south, and had one unexpected gain. According to one badly shaken prisoner, the sight of the slowly advancing pillars of dust from which emerged such dreadful clanking noises and random, violent explosions, was far more frightening than even the preceding barrage, despite the fact that most of the Scorpions ground to a smoking halt long before they reached the Axis lines.

So far as infantry training was concerned, all divisions carried out detailed and rigorous rehearsals, typified by those of two brigades of the New Zealand Division – the 5th and 6th, to which was attached the 9th British Armoured Brigade as the conversion of 4th New Zealand Brigade to armour was progressing too slowly for it to be ready for the forthcoming battle.

General Freyberg had by this time been given some detail of the part his division was intended to play in the forthcoming battle together with particulars of the location, so he was able to have laid out in the desert lines of token weapon pits, and wire and dummy mine-belts in fairly accurate reproduction of the area over which his men would be fighting – taking at the same time, of course, stringent precautions against security leakages.

For a few days the separate units carried out ordinary weapon-training and night marches, then on September 24th the entire division moved ten miles in formation to an assembly area where battle headquarters were set up and communications laid out as for action. At 2030 the division moved off along lines of guide lights – 5th Brigade on the right and 6th on the left with the armour of 9th Brigade waiting for the signal to move – but soft sand delayed many of the lorries, and morning mist and fog blinded some units which thus failed to arrive at their correct destinations; at the afternoon conference Freyberg had several trenchant criticisms to deliver.

But that night the two infantry brigades moved forward in bright moonlight to a lying-up area, dug themselves in and dispersed all transport by dawn, to spend the whole of that day (26th) lying concealed. At 2200, the riflemen rose from their pits and preceded by a token live barrage set off through the dummy minefields, followed closely by engineer teams clearing real but unfused mines. Bofors guns fired tracer along the boundary between the two brigades, 25-pounder tracer marked the outer edges of the divisional area, pre-posted instructional teams and umpires fired live ammunition over the heads of the advancing infantry and detonated carefully sited explosive charges to give extra realism to the exercise; and as the infantry battalions leap-frogged through each other's positions, and the support weapons came up, the Shermans of 9th Brigade moved into the prepared corridors to pass through the infantry and offer them dawn protection.

As dawn broke, the anti-tank gun screens opened up with live ammunition on dummy panzers ahead massed as though for a counter-attack.

It constituted a very realistic exercise and many lessons were learned from it. Traffic jams had occurred as soon as vehicles in any number had reached even the widest bottle-neck, armour had jammed almost solid at the entrance to the corridors and the chaos when one tank had broken down would obviously prove fatal in battle; it had also been realised that British tank crews and signallers used different jargon and expressions from the New Zealanders and the resultant misunderstanding shook everybody, a situation not improved by yet more evidence of cavalry disdain for foot-sloggers.

Perhaps the greatest lesson learned from the exercise, however, was the degree of truth behind Montgomery's maxim that everyone in battle must know what is going on. To some extent because of security, but more because of a human desire to give the impression that they were members of an elite who knew more than the commonalty, junior officers and N.C.O.s had not passed on sufficient information about the purpose of the exercise in general, and the parts each unit had to play in particular, to the men expected to carry it out. As a result, many of them had become bored with marching and counter marching, with lying in fly-infested trenches throughout a long, hot day, with abjuring cigarettes at night and driving vehicles either with wind-shields removed or smeared with wet sand which had frequently to be renewed to avoid reflection of the bright moonlight – and often the inevitable periods of chaos had been extended by practical jokers alleviating monotony. As a result, Freyberg decreed that the armoured brigade and certain other units would remain in the area for further indoctrination, and his instructions for all future operations were very clear indeed upon the necessity for better communication at all levels.

But another weakness noted by one pair of eagle eyes was that too many of the men had shown signs of distress during the approach marches and had been forced to fall out of the exercise through sheer exhaustion. Soon commanding officers throughout Eighth Army were reading a memo from the Army Commander, containing the passages:

> This battle for which we are preparing will be a real rough house and will involve a very great deal of hard fighting . . . There must be no weak links in our mental fitness.
>
> But mental fitness will not stand up to the stress and strain of battle unless troops are also physically fit.
>
> This battle may go on for many days, and the final issue may well depend on which side can best last out and stand up to the buffeting, and ups and downs, and the continuous strain, of hard battle fighting.
>
> There will be no tip and run tactics in this battle; it will be a killing match; the German is a good soldier and the only way to beat him is to kill him in battle.
>
> I am not convinced that our soldiery are really tough and hard. They are sunburnt and brown, and look very well; but they seldom move anywhere on foot and they have led a static life for many weeks.
>
> During the next month, therefore, it is necessary to make our officers and men really fit; ordinary fitness is not enough, they must be made tough and hard.[2]

This point received even further emphasis at the end of the month when the new commander of XIII Corps, Lieutenant-General Brian Horrocks, decided to capture an area of ground near Deir el Munassib for extra artillery deployment during the coming battle, and used the unblooded 131st Brigade of 44th Division to obtain it.

On the morning of September 30th the brigade advanced under heavy morning mist and equally heavy artillery cover (which did more to neutralise the advantages of the mist than it was worth) with tanks of 4th Armoured Brigade in support. Two battalions of the Queen's (1st/6th and 1st/7th) met no worthwhile opposition in the north but the unfortunate 1st/5th ran into positions still held by the Italian Folgore and the Ramcke parachutists and were brutally handled, losing in killed, wounded and captured nearly three hundred officers and men before evening.

Attempts to relieve the survivors and renew the assault by the armoured brigade broke down in confusion caused by inexperience and misunderstanding, and on the morning of October 1st Horrocks called off the operation, sending 132nd Brigade in to take over the occupied ground in the north. Here the newcomers found that even though the two Queen's battalions there had had little fighting there were a number of cases of exhaustion and heat-stroke, that although no one had been wounded several men had lost direction and were not seen again, and the ambulances were full for the trip back.

This and other episodes demonstrated only too clearly the evident unfitness for battle of some brigades, and Montgomery's expressed intention that all divisions were to be kept intact and fight together as they had been trained had perforce to be modified – a move made even more complicated by the proclaimed readiness for battle of a Greek infantry brigade and two French infantry brigade groups.

The result during the training period was a bewildering interchange of formations between divisions which continued through the opening days of the battle, and produced such improbabilities as two of 44th Division's brigades joining armoured divisions as support infantry, and at one time 50th (Northumbrian) Division consisted of Percy's brigade of Durham Light Infantry, plus the Greek Brigade and one brigade group of Fighting French.

If this was rather unsettling for the troops themselves it posed acute problems to the command, especially as two of the corps commanders were new to the theatre. Horrocks had joined Eighth Army to take Strafer Gott's place at the head of XIII Corps before Alam Halfa, and on September 10th Lieutenant-General Oliver Leese came out from England (again, at Montgomery's request) to take over XXX Corps from General Ramsden who, it will be remembered, had figured in Churchill's signal to the War Office of August 6th for replacement. A big, solid but quick-witted ex-Guardsman, Leese provided a complete contrast to the mercurial Horrocks, but had at least the advantage that as his corps would consist largely of Dominion troops – Australian, New Zealanders and South Africans, plus the 51st Highland Division – no one was to suggest the transposition of any of their brigades in view of native sensitivities.

Command of X Armoured Corps – the *corps de chasse* which

Montgomery had instructed Harding to form as a riposte to the Afrika Korps – was, however, to present some problems. The senior armoured commander in the theatre was Lieutenant-General Herbert Lumsden, recently promoted, a cavalryman who had at no time been closely involved with Montgomery's previous career and who had voiced strong objection to his superior's decision to wear the black beret of the Armoured Corps.

It is hardly surprising that Montgomery wanted him replaced, but on this occasion Alexander stood firm against his subordinate as he felt that too clean a sweep was being made of the old desert commanders – a stand in which Alexander was supported by his own Chief of Staff, Major-General Richard McCreery, another ex-cavalryman and indeed one from Lumsden's regiment, 12th Lancers. It was not to prove the happiest of Alexander's decisions, possibly because Montgomery resented it and was not prepared to try very hard to make it work.

It is also possible that Lumsden was not prepared to try very hard either, and as a result, Montgomery on October 6th had to make changes in his plans for fighting the battle.

He had announced his original plan for *Operation Lightfoot*, as he chose to call it – with, in view of the extent of the minefields, perhaps rather macabre flippancy – to the corps and divisional commanders and some of their staff on September 15th, and the essence of the tactics to be used was that infantry and engineers would cut passages through the enemy defences in both northern and southern sectors through which the armour should pass *unopposed* (the main bulk, X Corps under Lumsden, in the north), then break clear of all Axis positions and when well behind them, wheel and place themselves across the enemy lines of communication on 'ground of their own choice'. Here they would form a defensive block and fight off Rommel's panzer divisions, who must attack or face swift starvation. In view of the large numerical superiority of the British armour over the panzer strength, it was felt that they could afford if necessary to trade tank for tank – and still have enough left at the end to be able to round up the isolated Axis infantry and thus eliminate at least the German presence on Egyptian soil. There would then be little trouble from the Italians in Tripolitania, especially in view of the imminent Anglo-American invasion at the other end of the Mediterranean.

But during the days which followed it became increasingly evident that among the Commonwealth commanders at least, there was deep scepticism as to whether the armour possessed the ability to carry out their part in the plan or perhaps even the will to try very hard. Freyberg made it his business to have long discussions with both Morshead and Pienaar (whose voice of protest had been curiously muted since Montgomery's arrival) which he followed with other talks with both Lumsden and Gatehouse, whose 10th Armoured Division was the one scheduled to pass through the New Zealand sector of the line. These convinced him that, as in the recent past, the armour was more likely to act with caution than with determination.

As a result, the three Commonwealth commanders requested an interview with Oliver Leese and voiced their disquiet – greatly to Leese's astonishment as, with no previous experience of the desert war, he could not believe that the armour would not obey the Army Commander's orders to the letter. However, a few days later Leese's own B.G.S. attended a X Corps conference and could hardly believe his eyes and ears at the general atmosphere of casual disregard for Montgomery's edicts, amounting almost to insubordination, which ruled there.

He reported this impression to Leese who in due course talked to Montgomery about it, and within a few hours the armoured commanders had been told quite clearly that Montgomery's orders allowed them no latitude whatsoever, and must be obeyed to the letter. The Commonwealth commanders were then told that they need have no further qualms as the armour would do as it was told, and Freyberg's blunt comment, 'They won't!' even at this reassurance, was enough greatly to diminish his popularity at the top of Eighth Army.

It was also enough, however, to prompt Montgomery to examine much more closely the type and state of training now being carried out in the X Corps area, and as a result, to quote the *Official History*, 'He feared that he might be asking too much of his "somewhat untrained troops",' and abruptly reversed the principles behind the original plan.

Instead of breaking clear through all the Axis positions, bursting into open country and thus leaving a gap between British armour and British infantry, X Corps would now deploy as soon as they had passed through the corridors, form a screen to cut the Axis armour off from *their* infantry – and behind this screen the infantry battle would be fought. In other words, instead of first eliminating the panzer divisions so that the Axis infantry would wither, he would now eliminate first the Axis infantry so that, with no front holding, the Axis armour could be isolated; and when, inevitably, the panzers tried to break through the shield to aid their own infantry, X Corps would at least be close enough to XXX Corps for mutual support, and both would be kept tightly under Montgomery's personal control.

Distrust between infantry and armour was not, however, a one-way affair, and Lumsden made no secret of his belief that the passages through the minefields would not be completed during one night, and that dawn would catch his armour penned in narrow, blocked lanes, probably under concentrated anti-tank fire; and he received

Montgomery's instructions upon this point with blank incredulity. Should XXX Corps infantry and engineers fail to clear the passages entirely during that first night, the Army Commander ordered that X Corps would complete the job themselves with their own attached infantry and engineers, and fight their way forward to their designated positions on their own – a proposition so far opposed to Lumsden's thinking and the cavalry traditions requiring mobility, space in which to manoeuvre and a certain freedom to improvise, that even in the face of the Army Commander's specific instructions he still told his brigade and regimental commanders that they were not to try to rush anti-tank guns, and to make sure that the exits from the passages were not under anti-tank fire when they attempted to pass through them. What they were to do instead seems not to have been specified.

There was undoubtedly much to be said for Lumsden's point of view, especially in view of the difficulties which were attending X Corps's training. Originally intended to consist of three armoured divisions – 1st, 8th and 10th – one armoured division – the 8th – had been disbanded as no support infantry could be found for it, and as a result the 10th Armoured Division faced the problem of absorbing two extra brigades – one armoured from the disbanded 8th Division, and 133rd Brigade from 44th Division, which had itself hurriedly to adapt not only to a lorried infantry role but also to attachment to armour – a prospect undreamed of before departure from England only two months earlier.

Moreover, it was common practice throughout the Armoured Corps that new and reconditioned tanks should be concentrated by types in squadrons – a reasonable arrangement in most circumstances, but one which that summer entailed constant transfers of tanks and crews from squadron to squadron – and often transfers back a week later when newer or better reconditioned tanks arrived from the depots. Needless to say, every commander was trying to get the new Shermans, and often these were promised but Grants or even Crusaders turned up in their place; and some Shermans were actually delivered to their squadrons the day the battle began, lacking many important pieces of equipment.

Lumsden thus undoubtedly faced greater problems than Leese with his intact Commonwealth divisions and eager Highlanders, or Horrocks down in the south with only feint operations to organise; but it does not appear that Lumsden grappled with those problems with either the solid faith of the former or the enthusiasm of the latter – indeed the differences in attitude between Lumsden and Montgomery, amounting in the end to mutual antipathy, probably deepened the cavalryman's air of scornful disbelief to contrast with his superior's incisive certainty. This was not the frame of mind in which to weld the main thrust of Eighth Army's attack into a solid, homogeneous force.

That this was evident to others became clear when Leese informed de Guingand that the Commonwealth commanders were still dubious about the armour's intentions, but when de Guingand reported this to Montgomery he was told that there would be no more changes of plan. Bellyaching had to stop; orders would be obeyed, not discussed.

Not that General Montgomery felt that he himself must so slavishly obey directions from above.

It will be remembered that one of the main reasons for Auchinleck's removal from command of the Middle East theatre was his unshakeable conviction that Eighth Army would not be ready to attack the Afrika Korps positions before mid-September, and his refusal to allow the Prime Minister to persuade him otherwise. It was an opinion with which Auchinleck's successor not only agreed, but extended.

As soon as the Battle of Alam Halfa had been won and Montgomery's prestige at home as a result considerably increased, he announced that he needed a full moon for his attack at Alamein, that the army would not be ready in time for the September moon but would instead attack on the night of October 23rd. The response from Whitehall was immediate and expected – that the attack must be made in September in order to synchronise with various Russian attacks and preface *Operation Torch* by sufficient time for real advantages to accrue – but Montgomery, loyally backed by Alexander, declared that it would be suicide to attack so soon, that he would guarantee victory in October and that if Churchill insisted on the previous date then he must get somebody else to command the Army.

It was, as Montgomery was later to agree, pure blackmail . . . but it worked, and Churchill, after some ritual growling, accepted the situation despite the fact that once more Malta was under heavy attack by the Luftwaffe and unless supplies reached the island it would be starved into submission by November. His acceptance was perhaps made easier by a message from Roosevelt to the effect that the American military commanders were experiencing unexpected difficulties and that they now felt that the North African invasion could not take place, after all, until early November.

There was therefore to be a gap of seven weeks between the end of the Battle of Alam Halfa and the beginning of the Battle of Alamein. The time might not have been spent with total efficiency, but no one could say that much of it was wasted.

Very few battles in history have been won unless they included in their preparations and plans an element of surprise – but from neither the strategic nor geographical factors in Egypt in 1942 would it be possible to extract any high degree of this valuable quality. Nothing could hide the enormous build-up of men and material now arriving in the Suez ports, and it was obvious to all that an attack on the Panzerarmee was intended; there was nowhere for this to happen except at Alamein, and no practical alternative to a frontal assault.

Only in timing and local tactics could deception be practised and a degree of surprise thus perhaps achieved, and Montgomery's preparations from the beginning were meant to extract as large an element here as possible.

He had already determined that the main stroke would take place somewhere along the northern half of the line, so from the beginning everything was done to give the impression that it would occur in the south. The twin peaks of Himeimat had been left in German hands after Alam Halfa, and from their heights a great deal of activity could be seen, while in the early days of September at least, Axis observation aircraft found it far easier and safer to penetrate here than nearer the coast.

Dummy administration camps were erected in XIII Corps's area to the south of Ruweisat Ridge, existing dumps were expanded by empty cases and tentage while totally empty ones were erected in between, and a dummy fresh-water pipeline was laid complete with three dummy pumphouses, leading from Bir Sadi in the north and obviously aiming for Gaballa in the south. Each night a trench was dug about five miles long and a dummy pipe made from old petrol cans laid alongside it. During the following night a similar trench was dug and the one dug the night before was filled in (by troops who knew what was happening, otherwise there could have been trouble) and the length of tin piping shifted south; and after a comparatively short time it became evident to the morning Luftwaffe observation plane that the project would not reach its destination until early in November.

But the main deceptive operation was mounted in the north, and such was its scope and size that it even achieved an operational code name – *Bertram* – of its own. Here an early decision had been taken by one of Montgomery's staff officers, Lieutenant-Colonel C. L. Richardson, and followed throughout with admirable consistency – that every evidence of concentration of force would be openly displayed as quickly as possible so that, when no assault immediately developed, the enemy would grow used to its existence and notice no change when fact replaced fiction.

Numerous slit-trenches were dug in advanced positions and then left unused; thousands of dummy vehicles, guns, tanks and dumps were erected during the first weeks of October – enough to give the concentration needed for an attack – but as day followed day they either remained static or were moved around enough by the deception staff to add verisimilitude to their existence, while back around Wadi Natrun the real tanks, guns and lorries arrived, were tested and the crews given at least some training in their use. When eventually these moved into the operational area they did so under cover of darkness, took the place of the dummies and these or others were erected in the training areas to give the impression that no change in concentration had taken place.

This routine was followed when the New Zealand Division had finished their exercise and moved to battle positions, men and vehicles disappearing into the previous concentration while in the dummy camp they left behind, small detachments moved about, lit fires, drove vehicles around and kept up a flow of routine signals. Maintaining a consistent signals density was an essential part of the plan, and this was achieved when the divisions moved forward by imposing wireless silence upon them in their new positions but keeping a nucleus signal section behind sending out bogus messages; when eventually X Corps moved up, the entire signals organisation of the disbanded 8th Armoured Division, which had been retained for just this purpose, continued the wireless traffic.

There was even a special section formed under a hurriedly commissioned world famous illusionist, Jasper Maskelyne, to conceive and execute the more *outré* effects. A dummy railhead was set up with a dummy oil-discharging point nearby, and around these locations were piled inflammatory materials in which were buried remotely controlled igniters; when the Luftwaffe bombed the areas the igniters fired the heaps, and following waves of bombers dumped their loads on what appeared to be worthwhile targets. Alongside a dummy oil-jetty, they erected a convertible tanker which one day presented the picture of a one-funnelled ship to aerial observers, and the next day two funnels and a mast on a lengthened hull or some other variation. The main water pipeline from Alexandria was replaced by one with a larger bore, but all the work was done at night and the old one left apparently undisturbed, and the new water-point thus supplied concealed in El Imayid Station and not used until the opening of the battle.

All the time this activity in the rear areas was taking place – the armour training, the specialists carrying out their own esoteric duties, the supply services building up the dumps – the bulk of Eighth Army infantry had of course, despite brigade training exercises, still to hold the line. They were at times very thinly spread, for not only were the entire New Zealand Division absent but in turn each of the Australian brigades also went back for training exercises, as did brigades from the South African Division. Some relief was provided by substituting individual brigades from the 51st Highland Division for those with-drawn from the front, and indeed the practice not only gave the Jocks some invaluable experience, it also formed a bond between them and the Australians in whose area they did most of their replacement duties which was to prove very valuable in the near future.

But there were times for the men in the foremost positions – patrolling and exploring the minefields in front, fighting off the occasional foray by Afrika Korps or Ariete armoured cars, digging their slit-trenches deeper or building up their sangar walls – when it seemed that they were alone in a hot, dusty, fly-ridden and dangerous world, very much at the sharp end of the war.

During the day along most of the line, they lay in their trenches trying to sleep unless they were on guard, cursing the flies, the dust and the heat, wriggling into whatever shade they could contrive, wondering if they could afford to smoke another cigarette; and when the time came for their own spell of duty, they watched the enemy positions through dancing heat-waves or listened anxiously for ominous sounds beyond the blur of the daily sandstorm. Despite the dangers it could easily bring, everyone longed for nightfall.

Once darkness had fallen, everything began to happen. Picks and shovels rose and fell as everyone – especially in the areas closest to the enemy – tried to deepen his own shelter, with compressors in the rocky areas if he was lucky, sometimes with explosive. Behind the immediate front positions, gun-pits, medical posts, headquarters and supply positions had to be dug out, while in front the barbed wire was strung on pickets driven into rock or sand, with mines somehow concealed among it all. Sweat was being used to save blood.

Above them all, R.A.F. or U.S.A.A.F. bombers either roared close and dropped their bombs ahead on Axis gun-flash or pre-recorded target, or zoomed away high in the sky towards Benghasi, or Tobruk, or Benina or any other of the nodal points behind Rommel's lines; and occasionally the Luftwaffe would come over, and if Junkers or Heinkel was low and slow enough, everyone would pause in their tasks, listening for the faint whisper of a falling bomb before diving into shelter. And all the time the work was punctuated by the staccato rattle of machine-gun and rifle fire as patrols met and fought brief actions amid the minefields, creeping silently about their duties of search and reconnaissance until their own target areas coincided with those of the enemy. Every morning there were new corpses out in no-man's-land, lying unburied, quickly to swell up and blacken in the daytime heat.

Reinforcements came up during the night, units returned from training in the rear areas, men came in from leave or hospital, passing as they did so the ones going back – the lucky ones with just minor injuries, desert sores, 'Gyppo tummy' or even better still a temporary posting; the not so lucky in swaying ambulances en route for base hospitals. Trucks brought up rations and, most welcome of all, water; staff cars brought up an occasional visitor of greater or lesser importance, despatch riders would bump their way through tangles of trenches to find battalion and sometimes company headquarters. The traffic during the night was continuous – but slow and cautious, picking its way through the maze of gun-pits, haphazard dumps and random training areas still infested with unexploded bombs or mines, each vehicle trailing its plume of dust to add to the gloom.

With dawn came a cessation of all this activity. Patrols would by now be back in their own lines, the privates into their slit-trenches, officers or N.C.O.s reporting to the headquarter positions and if they were lucky enjoying an early cup of rather chemical-tasting tea. And as the sun came up behind them, the whole Eighth Army stood to against the possibility of a dawn attack, infantry waiting tensely, gunners already into action as the light grew, for with the sun behind them the first hour of a fine morning gave them the best visibility of the day; and from then on, the artillery would boom and bang away all day at known enemy positions or along tracks known to carry supplies for the Panzerarmee, for by mid-September the big Allied convoys had arrived at Tewfik and there was no shortage of ammunition.

But the infantry were back in their 'slitties' again, cursing the flies.

Yet despite the hardship and monotony of the life, Eighth Army morale was good again, and rising. The sense of purpose and grip which had started with Alam Halfa strengthened every day, many more men were seeing much more of their divisional and corps commanders than ever before in the desert war, and a large number had even seen and been talked to by Montgomery himself. Moreover, there were visible and concrete signs that their new Army Commander really did have their welfare at heart, an instance of this being that despite the fact that he was a non-smoker himself the cigarette ration arrived regularly, and if a platoon, company or battalion did particularly well an extra issue might arrive for them with a message of appreciation.

Even more importantly, the water ration (of at least one water-bottle per day per man) arrived with reassuring regularity, and although it usually tasted of chlorine and was never cold enough, it was always drinkable; and to palates long used to chemical adulterants, sometimes positively 'sweet'. And then there were those eagerly awaited short spells of leave back in the peace and comfort, not to say luxury, of Cairo or Alexandria.

Every division made their own arrangements, but those of the New Zealanders were typical. A 'Four day' leave consisted in fact of six days away from the unit, the first and last days being devoted to travel back and forth, the days between spent as each man chose. There had been little chance of spending accumulated pay for weeks and sometimes months past, so if the men wished they could stay at their own expense in clubs or in selected hotels; or they could stay for nothing at rest camps designed and organised expressly to free them from the usual constraints of army discipline. Meals were available at almost any hour, beer was on sale with little regard for licensing hours, canteens and cinemas were there in the camp, transport into Cairo provided at hourly intervals and for those who wanted them, conducted tours to places of interest.

There were baths, tennis courts, swimming pools, laundries and even friendly quartermasters who would replace torn or sweat- and sand-caked clothing without demur. There were cabarets in the cities in the evening, the vast Pole Nord bar in Cairo and many smaller establishments like it; Groppi's for cakes and ice cream, for officers the cool though musty lounge at Shepheard's with gin slings and servants in white gallabiyas. And for those who wished to take advantage of them and who could avoid the vigilance of the military police, there were also, of course, the forbidden delights of the Burka or Sister Street in Alex; otherwise there was little chance of feminine company, for what there was had long been appropriated by the Base Staff.

One interesting development for the front line infantry was that, having been made up by reinforcements to full strength, some formations by the end of September were finding themselves over-strength. The news of Alam Halfa and the possibility that the new Army Commander might know his job had combined to persuade some absentees that perhaps the time had come for a return to their units, and most commanding officers were content to exact retribu-tion in the form of extra duties without referral to a higher authority which might have felt it encumbent to take more drastic or even penal action. The numbers were not yet great, but the rate of return was increasing.

On October 6th Montgomery issued to the corps and divisional commanders and their immediate staff the bones of the overall final plan. There were five main points:

1 The main attack by XXX Corps in the north would take place on a frontage of four divisions. Two corridors were to be cleared through the minefields, and through these lanes X Corps would pass.
2 XIII Corps in the south were to stage two attacks, one directed past the Himeimat Peaks and on to the Taqa Plateau, the other into the area of Jebel Kalakh, both with the object simply of disguising the main thrust of the assault and thus holding in the south enemy forces

which might otherwise be transferred to the main attack front.
3 On both fronts the enemy forward positions were to be destroyed though heavy casualties in the south, especially among the tanks of 7th Armoured Division, were to be avoided.
4 Once X Corps were through XXX Corps positions and the main enemy defences, they were to deploy so as to prevent interference with XXX Corps operations against the Axis infantry. Offensive action against the enemy armour would only be undertaken when the infantry battles had been won.
5 The battle would commence at night during the full moon period.

As the recipients could read calendars as well as Montgomery himself there was little doubt in any of their minds as to the date of the attack, so few of them were surprised when Montgomery called for an assembly of all XXX and XIII Corps officers down to the rank of lieutenant-colonel on October 19th, with one for X Corps officers the following day. They proved memorable occasions.

Speaking clearly and incisively but with his curiously flat, almost metallic voice, the Army Commander first explained the reorganisations which had taken place throughout Eighth Army since the end of August, then outlined his plans in some detail – the break-in, the 'crumbling' process behind the X Corps shield, the break-out. He then went on to specify the almost overwhelming superiority in guns and tanks which Eighth Army held over Rommel's forces, but warned strongly against any belief that the battle would be a walk-over. It would be very tough, he stressed repeatedly, and every man in the army must be prepared to kill the enemy and go on killing until the battle was won – even chaplains, he announced to some amusement, 'one on weekdays and two on Sundays!'

Spectacular results must not be expected too soon, for in the final analysis a battle such as this promised to be would only be won by prolonged and consistent effort, directed from firm bases, maintained with offensive eagerness by men of high morale. The whole affair would last, he told them, for twelve days – and one point of interest is that in the notes from which he delivered these addresses he had originally written '10 days' and that at some time very shortly before beginning to speak, he had crossed out '10' and pencilled '(12)' in the margin.

It would therefore seem that despite his instructions to both XXX and X Corps that they were to force their way through the minefields during the first night, and that X Corps must form the shield by dawn on the first morning, he did not really expect them to do so; Panzerarmee could hardly last eleven days after so decisive a separation of their infantry from their armour.

The officers were then dismissed with instructions that every one of their men was to be told of the overall plan and the part he was to play in it, but not for obvious reasons until October 21st after which all leave would be stopped and Eighth Army virtually sealed off from the outside world. By then, the final moves up to their start lines for the attacking troops would be well under way.

The main tasks for the commanding generals were completed by October 20th (if they were not, as one of them later commented, it was by then too late to do anything about them) but from that time until the opening of the battle the lives of the staff officers were of immense concentration, constant activity and for some of them, nightmarish worry. Theirs was the responsibility of ensuring that by the morning of October 23rd, over 2,000 guns, 1,000 tanks and some 220,000 men were all in their assigned positions, and that all the ammunition, petrol, helmets, ambulances, shell-dressings, shovels, haversacks, full water-bottles, guiding beacons, searchlights, tins of bully beef, matches and mortar-bombs, Very pistols and bagpipes, mine-detectors and paybooks and everything else that the soldiers would need to fight a battle lasting twelve days would be instantly available to them when and where required. And at least 60 per cent of all these men and all this material had to be moved during four successive nights, in such a manner that no trace of its passing would remain on the desert floor to be observed by hostile eyes during the hours of harsh desert light in between.

On October 18th the 450 assorted tanks and 2,000-odd lorries of X Corps moved openly down into positions well south of Alam Halfa behind XIII Corps headquarters, carrying with them canvas replicas of every vehicle on strength. These were carefully erected, and during the next four nights the corps moved north again to its final assembly area around El Imayid, slipping into the dummy positions which had been there since the beginning of the month, carefully obliterating all tracks left by this prodigious move – which had perforce been meticulously dovetailed into another taking place across its axis by the two infantry brigades of the New Zealand Division, with their Divisional Cavalry and the 9th Armoured Brigade which was attached to them and had come up from Wadi Natrun. Both moves had also to be correlated with the moves of isolated brigades of the other XXX Corps infantry divisions, rejoining the line after training exercises in the rear areas.

Parallel tracks led to the last staging areas before the move into the front lines – Diamond, Boomerang, Two-bar and Square leading off the coast road into the northern section of the line and the positions held by the 9th Australian Division, running from the coast to about two miles south of Tel el Eisa. Sun, Moon and Star tracks fed the positions of 51st Highland Division to the south of the Australians, a short spur off Star plus the Bottle and Boat tracks fed the New Zealanders on the left of the Highlanders, while the single Hat track fed the South African Division holding the left flank of the XXX Corps attack front. It was along these tracks, each identified at night by their symbols cut into the sides of lamps shining to the rear, that first the infantry element of Montgomery's striking force must make their separate and dusty ways to their attack positions; and it was through the eight-mile front which these comprised that the two lanes must be cut for the passage of the armoured divisions – 1st and 10th – of X Corps. To the south of the South African Division stood the 4th Indian Division holding the left flank of XXX Corps, stretching down for nearly another twelve miles across Ruweisat Ridge to the junction with XIII Corps.

Thousands of men laboured day and night in the rear areas, tens of thousands marched and countermarched, climbing in and out of vehicles, coughing in the thick, swirling dust-clouds, sweating under the weight of pack and shovel and rifle or machine-gun – a few not understanding or even caring what it was all about, but most knowing full well that they were taking part in as significant a piece of administrational expertise as the modern world had seen up to that time, the move of the Eighth Army into position for the Second Battle of Alamein.

Its successful execution in broad daylight would rank as a feat of organisation to compare with any; its completion at night is a matter for perpetual wonder, especially when its successful concealment is taken into consideration. Every track made by a vehicle was brushed away before daylight, the military police who had spent the preceding hours directing the blacked-out convoys in ever-increasingly complicated moves through ever-thickening dust-clouds hastily snatching up the pickets holding the guiding lamps, while alongside them engineers replaced the fence lines, the dummy huts and dummy minefields which they had removed a few hours before, to disguise once again the very existence of the tracks to the front.

And there was vital work to be done – and disguised – much further forward. Start and guide-lines were laid out on every divisional front during the four nights before the attack – nearly nine miles for every division – accurately surveyed, meticulously plotted, and laid down first in near-invisible telephone wire, to be covered during the last hours by white tape. One battalion commander spent over eighty hours by himself out in no-man's-land on this chore alone, on occasion narrowly avoiding death at the hands of friendly patrols; but the work was done, and at least during the opening hours of the battle the leading troops would know where they were and where they were going.

If Lieutenant-General Horrocks in the south felt any disappoint-

Map 7   The Alamein Line, October 23rd, 1942

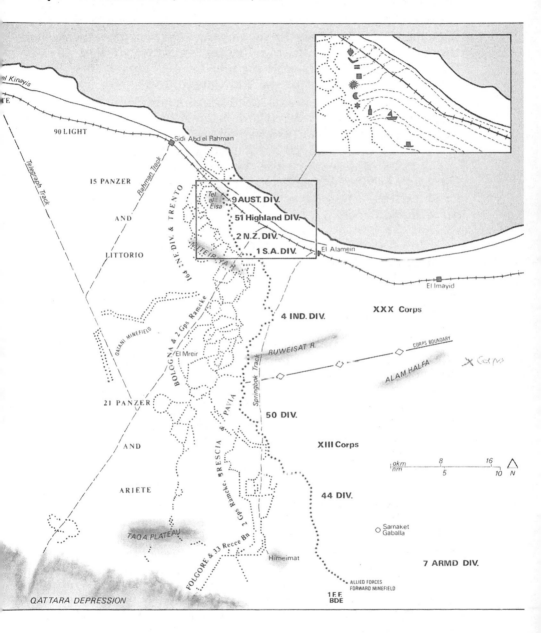

ment about the comparatively minor part his own command was allotted in the forthcoming battle, it did not in any way affect his energy or activity. Here in the XIII Corps area was played out the reverse side of the deception plan. Here, day and night, Axis aircraft might perceive a constant swarm of activity, Rommel's intercept service could listen to the stream of signals between the various brigade and divisional headquarters, many of them fictional but some from the 50th Division on the right next to the corps boundary, down through 44th Division positions in the centre to those of the 1st Fighting French Brigade near the edge of the Qattara Depression; behind these the units of the old adversary, the 7th Armoured Division, gravely manoeuvred, chattering unceasingly as they did so. Huge and badly camouflaged dumps grew daily, massed parks of vehicles accumulated and occasionally moved a little nearer to the front, the pipeline from the north edged ever closer to Gaballa.

The cloak of deception over the whole enterprise never slipped, *Operation Bertram* was meticulously carried out. Ironically, it may in some part have been unnecessary, for the Desert Air Force now commanded the skies.

Since the end of August they had possessed the capability of 'round-the-clock' bombing for limited periods, but both logistics and common sense had held them back and to some extent dispersed their effort until the last, vital period – at least so far as the activities of the fighters and day-bombers were concerned. Too much attention was not to be drawn to the battlefield itself, though prime targets further afield were continually attacked. Every night there were twenty or thirty Wellingtons over Tobruk, and on most nights Sollum, Bardia and Mersa Matruh received a visitation – as did Suda Bay whenever reconnaissance revealed worthwhile concentrations of Axis shipping. Benghasi was the chosen target for the Liberator squadrons of the Middle East detachment of the U.S.A.A.F. as theirs were almost the only aircraft capable of the return journey; altogether they dropped over a hundred tons of bombs on the port.

On October 9th there was an exception to the partial ban on daylight attacks when reports came in of the flooding of some Axis airfields. Baltimores of 55th and 223rd Squadrons and South African fighter-bombers of 2nd and 4th Squadrons, all escorted by British and American fighters, attacked the airfields at El Daba, and that night Wellingtons attacked the field at Fuka – but except for that occasion the Desert Air Force held itself in check until the morning of October 19th, its prime activity over the battlefield merely to chase away Axis reconnaissance from the northern section.

Then, during the last four days before zero hour, Air Vice-Marshal Coningham set out to achieve two main aims – to clear the air above the entire battleground of Axis aircraft, and to destroy the potential of both the Luftwaffe and the Regia Aeronautica to interfere with Eighth Army activities or even to contribute very much to those of the Panzerarmee. During the day the Hurricanes and Spitfires ranged the desert strip between El Alamein and Himeimat, while further west Baltimores and Kittyhawks struck again and again at El Daba and Fuka and at night Wellingtons and Bostons continued the attack. To the north Albacores and Seafires of the Fleet Air Arm swept the coastal waters, and the Liberators pounded the areas further west along the Egyptian frontier and beyond – and all the time they kept the eyes of the Axis forces watching upwards, every day more fearfully. An average of over five hundred and fifty sorties were flown every twenty-four hours by the aircraft of the Royal Air Force, the South African Air Force, the Royal Australian Air Force and the United States Army Air Force, and there were few members of the Eighth Army who were not aware of their activities and profoundly grateful for them. The resentment that the soldier had felt for the airman since the desperate days of Dunkirk vanished and never returned; at last it was evident to all that both arms were fighting the same war and the days of the Luftwaffe's domination of the battlefield were gone.

By dawn on Friday, October 23rd, the Eighth Army was in position. All along the front soldiers lay in their slit-trenches, sweating, roasting in the concentration of heat from which they might not escape for any reason at all, plagued the whole day by the flies. Behind them, the artillery banged away occasionally, neither increasing nor decreasing the weight of fire that had been thrown at the Axis positions every day for the past few weeks; occasionally a machine-gun would chatter, a motor-bike would roar off into the distance, trucks would trail dust-clouds back towards the headquarter areas. Above them, the air squadrons cruised and sometimes roared low overhead; and the air shimmered and the sun blazed.

And then, at last, it began to sink. The heat drained from the sky, the air lightened, sometimes shifting slightly to give the first of the cool evening breezes. Suddenly the flies were gone, movement could be sensed all around, a hum of low voices. The stars were out. It was dark.

Out of the ground climbed the Eighth Army, stretching its limbs, coughing, swearing, still keeping voice low. Rifles clunked on the ground, webbing creaked, metal lids on cooking-pots clanked as hot food came up, mugs slurped into the tea dixies; out in front the forward patrols moved cautiously back, passing as they did so the hurrying figures laying out the white tape. And everyone glanced at their watches every few minutes.

Back at his tactical headquarters by the coast into which he had moved that morning, the Army Commander talked briefly with his corps commanders, and satisfied himself among other things that his message to the troops ending with the confident assertion that 'The Lord Mighty in Battle will give us the victory' had reached every one of them. He had a cup of tea with de Guingand at about half past four, then settled down with a book to read until retiring to bed, which he did earlier than usual in the hope of getting solidly to sleep before the barrage began. It seems that he was now quite confident of the readiness for battle of the army under his command.

It is at least likely that he may have wondered briefly about the state of the enemy.

The condition of the Panzerarmee by this time was serious – so serious indeed that a proportion of even the Afrika Korps itself was becoming despondent. With the obvious rebuff to Axis hopes at Alam Halfa, dreams of rest and recuperation amid the fleshpots of the Delta had faded abruptly, and the resultant fall in spirits was accompanied by an inevitable recrudescence of the physical ills which had plagued the army during July. An extra depressant to Afrika Korps morale had been the news that the health of their heroic commander had suffered as much if not more than their own, and on September 23rd he had left for extended leave and treatment at his home near Wiener-Neustadt. It says much for the regard in which he was held that no one doubted that he would return.

His replacement, General der Kavallerie Georg Stumme, had arrived on September 19th and proved to be a large, good-humoured man, lately commander of a panzer division on the eastern front, who announced that after the rigours of a Russian winter he positively relished the climatic conditions in the desert. This hardly recommended him to the men newly under his command, unlikely to view any replacement for Rommel with much favour, and now disgruntled and inclined towards contempt for one so totally unversed in the grim realities of desert warfare. And although Stumme was to find little room for criticism in the disposition of the forces under his command or with the proposals for fighting the battle which so obviously loomed, his position was not made easier by Rommel's announcement just before he left, that he would abandon his cure and return to take command the moment the battle began.

As for Rommel's condition, it was in many ways both physically and mentally worse than that of his army. He was, of course, much older than the majority of the men under his command and had been in the theatre longer than most – but now a totally new factor was added to the psychological burdens he already bore. He was not used to circumstances forcing him to admit that he might have been wrong, but after Alam Halfa he could not disguise from himself the fact that the position of the army under his command would have been far more secure were it back on the Egyptian frontier, with its supplies arriving regularly and unmolested by enemy forces operating from Malta; and many voices would be raised in chorus should he so much as hint at his acceptance of this fact, pointing out that he had only himself to blame for the fact that they were not.

His main battlefield concern was the total dominance of the air above it and above the vital supply lines feeding it, by the enemy. Not only did this curtail his own possibilities for reconnaissance and at the same time reveal every movement of his own troops to hostile eyes, but it wore down the nerves and hopes of his men even further. Perhaps most important of all, by limiting large-scale movement of every kind to the hours of darkness, it wasted a great deal of that essential element in warfare – time.

It was thus with a heavy heart that he set out for home on September 23rd, calling first at Derna where he depressed his spirits even further by undertaking what he knew in his heart to be a pointless exercise. From the Italian headquarters there he obtained promises that 3,000 workmen would be immediately provided to repair the road surfaces, which had by then become so pitted and worn that daily wastage on his already exiguous transport had become unacceptable; that 7,000 tons of rails and sleepers would be brought to the area to aid that condition even further, and that in view of the recent events at Tobruk and in the Jebel, the Italians would immediately assemble and despatch a sufficiently large and aggressive force down to Kuffra to capture the oasis, and thus eliminate it as a base for British commando raids. (He was not surprised to learn, upon his eventual return to Africa, that none of the promises had been kept.)

At Rome, his experiences were in similar vein. Il Duce welcomed him warmly, expressed some surprise at his tale of supply shortages and lack of logistical support and promised to rectify the matter, then sent him on his way with assurances of his continued and complete confidence, expressed in the bland but hardly encouraging exhortation, 'You have done the impossible before, Herr Feldmarschall. We are all sure you will do it again!'[3]

And when eventually he arrived at the Führer's 'Wolf's Lair' in East Prussia, he found a similar atmosphere, the whole place aglow with unfounded optimism. Praise and congratulation were poured upon him, he was surrounded by beaming and sycophantic headquarter personnel (his old enemy Halder had been dismissed the day after Rommel left North Africa for introducing an unwelcome note of cold realism into this febrile climate) but his attempts to get across some understanding of the parlous condition of Panzerarmee Afrika were total failures. Goering, in particular, brushed aside all tales of difficulties present or future, assured Rommel that despite the evidence of his own eyes, the Luftwaffe and not the R.A.F. dominated the skies everywhere, and as for the possibility of significant aid for the Allies from America: 'Quite impossible! Nothing but latrine rumours! All the Americans can make are razor blades and Frigidaires!'⁴

The only note of genuine help or understanding seemed to come – as usual – from the Führer himself, who did spare time to listen without interruption to Rommel's by now somewhat tired and cautious list of grievances, promising to send to the Mediterranean a large number of Siebel ferries – a type of craft which had proved fairly immune to air and torpedo attacks. Moreover, 'In the near future I'll be sending you in Africa a heavy-mortar brigade, five hundred barrels, as well as forty of the newest Tiger tanks, to be followed by several assault gun units!'⁵ And even Rommel's by now engrained scepticism was not proof against promises from so high an authority.

As a result, the next few days spent as guest of the Goebbels family in Berlin passed happily, both his spirits and health improving under the stimulus of good food and continual, indeed lavish, admiration amounting to flattery. On the last day of the month, after a brief ceremony in the Reich Chancellery at which the recently returned Führer presented him with the baton of his new and exalted rank, he was quite able to present to the world the picture of a supremely capable and confident Army Commander.

The occasion was a mass rally at the Berlin Sportpalast Stadium at which Rommel was the guest of honour, Hitler making to the assembled Party and Wehrmacht notables a speech in praise of the new Generalfeldmarschall – all duly recorded and then broadcast throughout the Axis-dominated and much of the neutral world by the whirring press cameras and the German radio networks.

At Goebbels's request, the whole rodomontade was repeated three days later in the Ministry of Propaganda, when, his hand still holding the knob of the door through which he had just made a somewhat theatrical entrance, Rommel delivered himself of the following defiant – and in view of the realities of the situation, surely unwise – announcement: 'Today, we stand just fifty miles from Alexandria and Cairo, and we have the door to all Egypt in our hands . . . We have not gone all that way to be thrown back again . . . what we have, we hold.'⁶

A few hours later, he left at last for home, for rest and recuperation, and for Dearest Lu.

For the remainder of Panzerarmee there was, of course, not the faintest hope of leave at home, only at best the relaxation of widely spaced two-day visits to rest camps on the coast where, although their food was prepared by trained army cooks and not just by the appointed member of the platoon, it was basically the same as that available in the line; not for the Afrika Korps the delights of hotel cuisine or even a well-stocked city bar, and they were fortunate if their visit to the rest camp coincided with a delivery of beer. Even the water was becoming more and more unpalatable, for the bulk came from old wells and cisterns along the coast, many of which had been damaged during the various stages of the 'Benghasi Handicap' and again during early October when heavy rainstorms washed sand and dirt into the caverns and further polluted the already murky liquid. But at least there was swimming in the sea, and clothes could be washed in it; though there was very rarely any new linen or drill to replace the now worn and sand-clogged uniforms.

If life was Spartan in the rest camps, it was grim indeed at the front. Hygiene had still not improved even among the German contingent – and with the desperate water shortage, lice infestation was common throughout the whole Panzerarmee – while the ordinary Italian soldier was by now so tired of the war that only such obviously life-preserving measures as the digging of shelters or the thickening of minefields in front were willingly undertaken. Washing, disposal of waste or even of dead bodies was a chore to be avoided, flies and stench being accepted as preferable to physical exertion; in this the Italians at least contributed to the additional discomfort of their enemies wherever the opposing lines were close together.

Not surprisingly in these circumstances the sick rate rose every week, but as all forms of transport were limited both because of petrol shortage and vehicle deterioration the severity of sickness which would justify release to a base hospital rose all the time, and jaundice, dysentery and scabies were rife throughout the divisions in the line. Food for all was dull and unvaried – tinned meat, hard biscuits, a small bread ration of uncertain quality, little margarine, fewer vegetables of any sort and none fresh – and for the Germans it was on occasion so short that battalion commanders had to go cap-in-hand to neighbouring Italian units. The almost offensive magnanimity adopted by the latter on these occasions did nothing to improve relations between the allies, already strained by the events of the last few months.

These relations could not be alleviated by keeping the two nationalities apart either, for Rommel had decreed that the Italian units should be 'corseted' by German units down sometimes to company level. This meant, for instance, that the German 164th Infantry Division and the Italian Trento Division both occupied the whole length of the line from the coast down to the end of the Miteiriya Ridge (and facing Montgomery's XXX Corps's main attack front), their fighting troops thoroughly intermingled, their various headquarters situated close together so that German control, euphemistically designated 'help and advice', would be constantly available, certainly down to battalion level and sometimes lower. To the south of this conglomerate, the Bologna Division with two groups (Heydte and Schweiger) of the stout Ramcke Brigade of German paratroops faced the 4th Indian Division positions down to Ruweisat Ridge – almost exactly opposite the junction of XXX and XIII Corps – while immediately south of this lay two more groups of German paratroops (Burckhardt and Hubner) with the Italian Brescia and Pavia Infantry Divisions holding the line opposite the 50th and 44th Divisions. The Folgore Division held the southern end of the line down to the Qattara Depression, but even these were supported by Rommel's 33rd Reconnaissance Battalion.

The 15th Panzer and the Littorio lay behind the northern sector and the 21st Panzer and the Ariete behind the southern, their respective command units also situated so close as to be practically united; and along the coast back from Sidi Abd el Rahman almost to Ras el Kinayis lay the 90th Light and the Trieste Divisions in reserve. In theory, no one was going to move anywhere without complete agreement between two equal partners; in practice, no one was under any illusions as to who would be in control.

Rommel's original philosophy behind this deployment of his forces was based upon the realisation that British preponderance of men and weapons had now reached such a stage that in any form of mobile battle it would outweigh the superior skills of even the Afrika Korps. The battle therefore must be fought as a static slogging match . . . but this would give an even greater advantage to the enemy, as it would bring out the finest qualities of the British infantry, and especially of the Australians and New Zealanders for whom Rommel had the highest admiration.

As there was no way in which he could defeat the Eighth Army by brawn, they must be beaten by brain. He must out-think the new Army Commander.

In this task, Rommel considered that he possessed certain advantages. While writing what had become the German Army's standard manual of infantry tactics, he had spent much time in deep study of British methods of attack in the First World War, and he now felt that the situation at Alamein would see a repetition of their use. With this in mind he had designed his forward defences to absorb the shock of the artillery barrage and the initial impetus of the infantry assault, keeping his main defensive positions back out of artillery range.

His whole front, he considered, would be subject at the outset of the battle to powerful attacks at many points, which would continue until General Montgomery made up his mind as to which attack looked most promising and began to reinforce it. During the pause for the redeployment which this would necessitate – unduly prolonged by German standards by the almost traditional slowness of thought at British command level – Rommel would have time to move his panzer divisions behind the most threatened areas, and indeed, once he was certain of his antagonist's choice, concentrate his main strength there first to block the danger and then to counter it. He must, however, be correct in his interpretation of Montgomery's decision for with supply conditions as they stood, once he had moved one pair of armoured divisions north or south, there would not be enough petrol to move them back again.

This original plan had, however, been modified in the light of the crippling shortages of petrol and transport. There was just not enough of either adequately to feed the forces in the southern half of the line – and the suspicion grew that this was where the main blow would fall. Every indication seemed to confirm that the British would attempt a massive attack south of Ruweisat Ridge, and by the beginning of October it was evident to all at Panzerarmee Head-quarters that they could not make the defences there impregnable without an enormous increase in logistic support – and in the possi-bility of such support no one any longer believed. The probability of the southern half of the line breaking must therefore be faced, and plans laid to cope with the development.

Although everything must still be done to absorb and slow the impetus of this southern assault, if and when it broke through the infantry defences the panzer divisions behind must be preserved, swinging back to the south and west, while what remained of the southern defences themselves must hinge back along the Ruweisat Ridge–El Mreir line, to find shelter behind the 'Qatani minefield' which would now be thickened and run east–west from the Ramcke Brigade positions in the line back as far as the Rahman Track. In this position, they would block any attempt by the attacking forces to drive northwards, channelling them instead westward into the desert where they would then be attacked from both sides by the combined German and Italian armour, with the reserve divisions deployed down from the coast as necessity dictated.

As for the northern half of the line from Ruweisat up to the coast, this of course would be made as impregnable as German military expertise could make it with the materials available. As there was, in fact, rather more material than Rommel ever admitted in his despatches and reports to Berlin (for obvious reasons), this should prove effective in blocking any British attack north of Ruweisat Ridge, even if Panzerarmee's fears were unfounded and the main attack fell there instead of in the south.

This then was the prospect and these the probabilities facing General Stumme and his immediate subordinates as October passed – and few of them faced the future with much optimism, especially as with only one exception they were all new to the desert. The Afrika

Korps itself was now commanded by Generalleutnant Ritter von Thoma after Nehring's wounding during Alam Halfa; Generalleutnant von Randow commanded 21st Panzer in von Bismarck's place and Generalleutnant Graf von Sponek the 90th Light in Kleeman's. Of the divisional commanders only von Vaerst and Lungershausen of 164th Division were still in Africa (and the latter was hardly an old hand) while of the chief staff officers, Gause and von Mellenthin had both gone back to Europe, the first as a result of wounds and the second with acute amoebic dysentery, Westphal was ill with jaundice and even the indestructible Bayerlein viewed the immediate future with deep foreboding.

One of the psychological reasons for the mood of depression at the top could have been that there were no plans at all for any form of offensive action. Not even a vague date for the possible resumption of the drive to the Nile was discussed – perhaps because no one could conceive of such a prospect under any but Rommel's command, perhaps because of ever-growing conviction of the Panzerarmee's weaknesses. Not enough fuel, not enough transport, shortage of ammunition for a prolonged battle, disheartened allies, even the German element of the Panzerarmee no longer the elite fighting force of earlier days, for the old hands were showing signs of strain and the newcomers were of neither the physique nor standard of training of the original Korps.

Yet the Germans were still the nucleus of the force which must somehow hold back the growing power of the Eighth Army. As such they could not be risked night after night before the main battle in deep patrols probing the enemy defences, and as the Italians were not willing to undertake anything but sporadic and small-scale reconnaissance, and as command of the air had passed so irrevocably to the enemy, this meant that the intelligence section had very little sound material to work on – and with the departure of the brilliant von Mellenthin no intuition or long desert experience to guide them. In this respect the High Command had received yet another blow; Colonel Bonner Fellers had been recalled to Washington and no longer broadcast his nightly messages from which the Rome codebreakers had been able to extract the details of British plans and deployment.

General Stumme and his staff were not therefore in receipt of a continuous stream of accurate information, but he was not himself yet affected by the general air of pessimism and indeed for the moment all felt fairly secure. The minefields were already thick and work was progressing on them all the time – to such an extent that of one aspect of the attack when it came they could be absolutely certain; it must take place in moonlight. As every piece of evidence which came into intelligence hands indicated that neither an increase in logistical support behind the enemy lines nor a forward movement of troops into attack positions was taking place during the week or so before the October full moon, then at least they had until the end of November to finalise their defensive plans, to hope that Berlin and Rome would at last appreciate their position and do something constructive about it.

They might, for instance, send out some more of the new Mark IV panzers, for although there were a few with both the 15th and 21st Divisions, most of the 220 panzers they held between them were the old Mark IIIs with the 50mm. gun. Ariete and Littorio added between them 340 Italian tanks, but some of these were too light to be counted as much more than armoured cars, and singularly ineffective ones at that. As usual, the most valuable contribution the Italians were making lay with their artillery, over half of the 500-odd field guns in the Panzerarmee being theirs and nearly 300 of the anti-tank guns. This together with the 550 German anti-tank guns – including 86 of the 88mms (although nearly half of these were at the moment assigned to anti-aircraft duties) – should prove effective in blocking if not destroying the British armour, especially if the tanks' cautious tactics at Alam Halfa were just a passing phase and they could be tempted back into their old, amateur, hunting-field follies.

Not, of course, that the Panzerarmee artillery would match that of the Eighth Army in any way. There were no false hopes on that score, for since their arrival at Alamein back in July they had all had ample experience of the British predilection for gun-fire, of their present possession of overwhelming superiority and of their skill in using it.

So, as the October weeks passed and the nights became colder, both the command staffs and the 50,000-odd German and 62,000 Italian soldiers at Alamein, however dolefully they might view their ultimate prospects, were not particularly anxious about the immediate future. The staffs continued to plan and to hope, the troops passed their days lying in the forward trenches watching the minefields in front or, if they were in the armoured divisions, working on their vehicles or practising battle drills – bearing in mind all the time the shortage of fuel and ammunition. October 23rd was exactly the same as every other day, and like the men a few thousand yards away to the east those at the front watched the sun go down and felt the first breaths of the evening breeze with relief.

Then they too, climbed out of their trenches, stretched luxuriously, grumbled among themselves, waited for and then consumed their evening meals and went about their allotted night-time tasks. Picks and shovels rose and fell, relief parties moved up to the forward positions and those who had watched all day moved back, rubbing their eyes and looking forward to a few hours' sleep. Along the front, a few patrols moved out along the known paths through their own minefields.

Occasionally those who possessed watches glanced at them to see how much of their stag had passed, how much remained. Just after the hands registered eight o'clock there were sounds of gun-fire at the northern end of the line, those up there cursed the Australians who were obviously about to launch one of their large-scale raids, those to the south blessed their good fortune and hoped it would last the night. Like the day, it promised to be an ordinary one.

Forty minutes later, the eastern horizon suddenly turned pink and for a few brief seconds an astonished silence gripped the world.

4 · El Alamein: The Onslaught

The opening barrage at Alamein remained or will remain in the memories of those who heard it to the end of their lives. It was not so much the sheer volume of sound – though this was surely great enough – as the impact it made, sweeping over the ranks of waiting men like a solid, moving force, shaking the very foundations of the desert floor.

Eight hundred and eighty-two field and medium guns opened up along the length of the front, raining steel and high explosive on the known enemy artillery positions and their ammunition dumps, and within minutes of the opening of the barrage Wellington bombers were overhead to drop an additional 125 tons of explosive upon them. Every now and then the vast clamour would be marginally increased by a deep roar as bomb or shell found its target, and red flame shot like a violent tropical flower into the sky – to the grunted satisfaction of the XXX Corps artillery commander standing next to de Guingand on a slight rise close to Tactical Headquarters.

Some six miles to the west of them as they stood there, the infantry of XXX Corps were already marching forward through the made gaps in the British minefields – line upon line of steel-helmeted figures, bayoneted rifles held at the high port, Bren-guns at the carry, boots crunching the desert gravel, grenades, shovels, picks or entrenching tools slung from their webbing. Behind the leading companies the engineers were already moving up to begin their intricate tasks as soon as the forward edge of the enemy minefields was reached, while behind them the heavy Valentine infantry support tanks of the 23rd Armoured Brigade waited impatiently for assurance of clear lanes.

Fifteen minutes after the opening rounds had been fired, the guns paused, their crews readjusting the ranges, and then – precisely on the hour (2200 British time; nine o'clock Axis time) – the guns roared out again and this time the barrage fell close in on the line of known enemy forward defence posts. On towards the curtain of exploding shell the leading infantry marched now into hostile ground, cutting their way through enemy wire, tramping with tingling feet over enemy minefields, listening for the crack of enemy bullet, the crash of enemy shell or mortar-bomb.

Every three minutes the line of the barrage lifted forward one hundred yards and the infantry closed up, sometimes to see just in front of them an enemy post to be charged and silenced, sometimes to see the remains of one wrecked by the barrage, sometimes to hear away on their flank the harsh clatter of a Spandau awaiting its fate at the hands of comrades abreast of them, or of the mopping-up parties following close behind. They prayed that their support tanks would be up soon.

The further the infantry advanced, the thicker became the fog of battle, for in addition to the smoke of the explosions every shell which landed flung up clouds of dust, and the whole area of the main advance was quickly shrouded in dense obscuration. Along each brigade boundary coloured tracer from specially sited Bofors guns kept separate the main bodies and at the rear searchlight-beams lanced the sky to intersect above specified orientation points, but within brigade, battalion and especially company areas, direction had to be maintained by lonely navigating officers (generally subalterns) marching unhesitatingly forward with eyes glued to compasses, counting steps and constantly adjusting for stumbles on uneven ground, for occasional lapses of concentration caused by whiplash crack or nearby crash. These men were indeed the very pin-point of the sharp end of battle, and far too many of them were to lose their lives during that first, dramatic night.

The other navigational aid for blinded infantry was, of course, the barrage itself, dropped immaculately on to carefully calculated grid lines lifting regularly and inexorably towards the final objectives as the night wore on. If the infantry could keep close behind it – and live – they should be on those objectives by 0245, giving them three more hours of darkness in which to dig themselves in, for their mortars, heavy machine-guns and anti-tank guns to come up, for the engineers to clear the corridors and for the armour to pass through and form that vital protective screen behind which the infantry would 'crumble' the Axis infantry.

But before that they would have a pause for adjustment and reorganisation. Just over half-way to the final objective was an area variously called the Red Line or the First Objective, to be reached by the barrage and the forward infantry by just before midnight. Here there was an hour's wait while bypassed enemy strongpoints were destroyed, while wounded were tended and evacuated, while platoons and companies sorted themselves out and refilled their ammunition pouches, while second wave battalions came up and prepared to take over the lead; and in many ways most important, while commanding officers tried to find out exactly what had happened and conveyed that vital information to the anxiously waiting divisional commanders at their posts at the rear.

To the Australian General Morshead in the north, to General Wimberley of the Highland Division next to him, to General Freyberg to his left and to the South African commander General Pienaar, these were indeed the most testing moments. How were their men doing? What sort of opposition were they encountering? Had the British artillery done their work? And at first reports seemed

Map 8   *Operation Lightfoot*, northern sector, October 23rd–24th

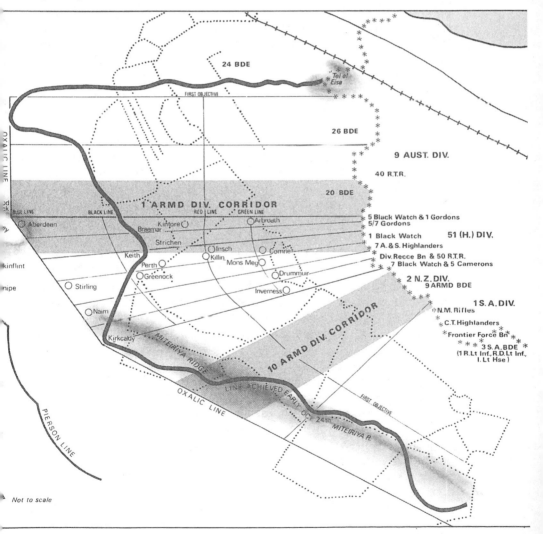

too good to be true for there was little sign or sound of enemy artillery, and the first casualties to come limping back spoke more of accident, of occasional mortar-bomb or random machine-gun fire, as the cause of their wounds. By midnight, it seemed, the Red Line had been reached all along its length, the support companies were moving up to take over the next stage of the advance, the mopping-up companies were clearing the by-passed opposition and the engineers were already at work deep into the minefields.

The Australians, in particular, were making excellent progress. Their 24th Brigade had, in fact, undertaken the raid which had begun at 2100 and might be called the prelude to the battle. In the coastal sector north of the railway line they had attacked known enemy positions, captured five German infantrymen, added to the diversion by use of smoke-screens, by cut-out models of crouching figures silhouetted by searchlight beams, and by continual machine-gun and mortar fire. In addition, Hudson aircraft added to the confusion by dropping self-destroying dummy parachutists and flares further back along the coast, and naval small-craft had run close in under destroyer fire to simulate attempted landings.

To the south of the 24th Brigade positions, two battalions of the 26th Brigade drove expertly and aggressively forward, wiping out all opposition as they went and arriving not only on their first objective exactly on time, but then sending their follow-up battalion (2nd/28th) in a storming rush onwards to the final objective, the northern corner of the 'Oxalic Line' as it was called. During the night the Australians advanced over 7,000 yards from their original start line – but with only the first 3,000 through no-man's-land, that last 4,000 yards thus left an open flank on their right. Along this line, facing north, were now hastily dug a line of anti-tank and heavy machine-gun posts each deeply wired in for all-round defence and manned by a special 'Composite Force', who now waited for what dawn would bring, conscious of the fact that they held the northern hinge of the great 'break-in'.

Immediately to the south of the 26th Brigade sector was the wider section of the Australian front, the responsibility of the 20th Brigade. Here too, the two leading battalions had fought their way to the Red Line in time though the battalion on the left had been caught by mortar and machine-gun fire on the way, and lost some eighty men in the fierce battle which followed. But by the appointed time, the follow-up battalion, 2nd/13th, were in position and waiting to go forward on the last stretch, awaiting only their own support, the forty-two Valentines of the 40th R.T.R.

Here was the first set-back. The Valentines were still blocked in a deep minefield some 1,500 yards to the rear, and with the 26th Brigade attack ready on the north, the whole divisional artillery

opened exactly on time and, *faute de mieux*, the 2nd/13th followed –
but a few minutes late and without their support. Not surprisingly,
this part of the Australian advance proved the most costly for that
few minutes' lag lost much of the protective effect of the barrage, and
there was now an opening flank on their left where the Highlanders
were also falling behind in their time schedule. Machine-gun fire
harassed the 2nd/13th from enemy strongpoints ahead and on the
flank, and as their numbers dropped, the pace inevitably slowed,
despite both expert teamwork and individual gallantry.

With the young subalterns so exposed it was not long before
several platoons were commanded by sergeants, and one of these,
blinded by smoke and dust, adopted the age-old tactic of marching to
the sound of the guns; on the way he found and obliterated one
enemy strongpoint, then set out alone to make contact with the rest
of his company and in doing so captured nine German prisoners on
his own.

But by this time Australian experience had come into force, and
the 2nd/13th battalion commander decided that with dawn approaching he must use the remaining dark period to dig in and prepare for
counter-attack, wherever he might be – so, some 1,000 yards short of
Oxalic, he regrouped his men. To his relief, some of the Valentines
arrived in time, 'looming up like battleships' out of the murk, and
took position among his defences.

Thus by dawn the northern corner of the 'break-in' was achieved,
the upper half of the Australian sector of Oxalic held, the line then
bending back about 1,000 yards to the 2nd/13th positions, in front of
which one strong German post had been attacked and almost
destroyed, the ground 'carpeted with German dead' but then left as
enemy fire poured into it. The first night of Alamein for the
Australians was at least an 80 per cent success.

General Wimberley's Highlanders had been faced with a much more
difficult task than the Australians on their right, and in the event they
came up against tougher opposition. Whereas the flanks of the
Australian attack had been parallel and they fought along the length
of a rectangle, the Highland Division was to move forward from a
start line less than a mile and a half long into an expanding funnel five
miles long towards a final objective line just over three miles long.
Moreover, although many of the Jocks had been briefly attached to
Australians for raids and 'line experience', it was, for all except the
few survivors from the First World War, their first taste of battle.

It was extremely fortunate for them that Douglas Wimberley was
not only a professional soldier of long experience, but one whose
basic military philosophy insisted that in battle the morale of the
infantry soldier was the factor of highest importance. He had

therefore used his not inconsiderable powers of persuasion at all levels to ensure that over 90 per cent of his division were genuine born and bred Scotsmen (thus overriding the tendency of Army Administration to regard all soldiers as 'bodies' and thus interchangeable) and also that too zealous security regulations should not deprive his division of their identity. His men wore the kilt whenever conditions allowed, and every one of them went into action that night with a St Andrew's Cross of white scrim tied across the back of his pack as both a means of identification and a proclamation of nationality. And to underline the point even further, alongside each platoon officer marched his piper, so that throughout that night in the centre section of the main attack the wild skirls of the most eerie, exhilarating and frightening music the battlefield knows would pierce the din of shell and mine exploding and the hoarse racket of gun-fire.

To aid control of the advance Wimberley had inserted extra intermediate objective lines – Green Line some two miles from the start and nearly a mile short of the Red Line, and Black Line half-way between the Red and the final objective Blue Line. He had also given all known enemy strongpoints Scottish names, chosen moreover from the localities from which their designated attackers came. The Gordons and the Black Watch on the right, for instance, would find Arbroath, Montrose and Forfar barring their way to the Green Line, Dufftown and Braemar on the second stretch and Aberdeen their final objective, while the Argyll and Sutherland Highlanders would storm Paisley and Renfrew, Greenock and Stirling.

To demonstrate his complete confidence that his men would take their objectives, General Wimberley had moved his own Battle H.Q. as far forward as possible and in the silence preceding the barrage he had stood in one of the gaps watching his Jocks file past in the moonlight:

> Platoon by platoon they filed past, heavily laden with pick and shovel, sandbags and grenades – the officer at the head, his piper by his side. There was nothing more I could do now to prepare them for the battle, it was only possible to pray for their success, and that the Highland Division would live up to its name and the names of those very famous regiments of which it was composed.[1]

On the outside flanks of the Highland Division sector were two battalions, one to leap-frog through the other at the Red Line – 1st Gordons passing through the 5th Black Watch on the right next to the Australians, 7th Black Watch passing through the 5th Camerons on the left next to the New Zealanders. Between them were four lanes along each of which one battalion would fight the whole way – 5th/7th Gordons on the right, then the 1st Black Watch, then the 7th

Argyll and Sutherland Highlanders while the lane next but one to the New Zealanders was to be taken by the divisional reconnaissance battalion supported by Valentines of the 50th Royal Tank Regiment.

As they moved forward, one of the officers whose job it had been to check the guiding tapes for the last time, turned to watch the barrage and the first advance:

> Through the din we made out other sounds – the whine of shells over-head, the clatter of machine-guns . . . and eventually the pipes. Then we saw a sight that will live for ever in our memories – line upon line of steel-helmeted figures with rifles at the high port, bayonets catching the moon-light, and over all the wailing of the pipes . . . As they passed they gave us the thumbs-up sign, and we watched them plod on towards the enemy lines, which by this time were shrouded in smoke. Our final sight of them was just as they entered the smoke, with the enemy's defensive fire falling among them.[2]

There was not a great deal of enemy fire at the beginning for it seemed that the weight of the British barrage had numbed the faculties of those unfortunates upon whom it had fallen, when it had not killed them. The first enemy posts the Highlanders encountered yielded but a few prisoners, all half-stunned and acquiescent to control – one Italian officer wearing pyjamas. But inevitably, the further the advance penetrated, the more resistance grew and it must be said that the pipe music attracted fire. Piper Duncan McIntyre of the 5th Black Watch was quickly hit twice but hardly faltered in his step, but a third shot brought him to the ground and when later his nineteen-year-old body was found, his fingers were still on the chanter.

But soon the code-words began coming back to Wimberley's head-quarters – Inverness was the first, telling Wimberley that the Camerons, his own regiment, had taken their first objective and were nearly on the Red Line. From then on the names came in regularly – Drummuir and Mons Meg on the left, Killin, Comrie and Insch in the centre, Arbroath on the right; but as the names came in so did the first casualty figures and these mounted inexorably.

Now began the first of many arguments with which the whole period of the battle was plagued, as to which positions had been reached. Not only had shell-fire shrouded the entire area with dust and smoke while enemy mortar and machine-gun fire had taken its toll of navigating officers, but a line drawn on a map can mean very little to men moving across a flat surface almost totally devoid of identifying features. When the 5th Black Watch on the right paused at what they considered to be the Red Line, the Colonel of the 1st Gordons who were to take over the advance from them swore they were still 400 yards short – and that the barrage falling just in front of them was an Italian defence and not British support.

In this it seems possible that the Gordons colonel was right, for when eventually he led his men towards it – after a pause for nine minutes in the hope that it would lift, they disappeared into the curtain of fire and it was morning before news of their exploits came back. Two companies of the Gordons had by-passed a strong enemy post at Kintore and gone on to attack Braemar, and although they captured all but a small corner they had by this time been reduced to three officers and sixty men. Another company supported by Valentines attacked Kintore, but even when dawn broke the position there was still uncertain – though General Wimberley believed that some of his men had reached Aberdeen, despite the fact that the tanks which had gone forward had found themselves blocked by minefields.

The 'Fog of War' was certainly thick on the morning of October 24th on the right flank of the Highland Division – as indeed the Australians had discovered; and to the immediate south of the 1st Gordons, their 5th/7th Battalion had also suffered severely from machine-gun posts in the Keith and Strichen areas short of the Black Line. One company had been cut to pieces while trying to outflank a minefield, and another pinned down by accurate machine-gun and mortar fire so that by dawn the whole of the right flank of the Highland Division was still short of the Black Line and with a serious casualty rate.

On the left flank, however, although casualties had still been high, better fortune had attended the efforts and sacrifices of the attacking battalions. The 1st Black Watch had swept on past the Red Line, cleared all the opposition through the Black Line and were on the way towards the Blue Line when it was realised that their strength had been so reduced that a withdrawal to the Black Line positions would be wise. Only one officer was left of the company which had cleared Perth, and in the confusion of the fighting it had lost touch with the rest of the battalion.

To their left, Lorne Campbell's Argyll and Sutherland Highlanders had run into fierce opposition once they passed the Red Line, one company had lost contact, two in the lead had been reduced to a quarter of their strength and the squadron of Valentines which had been attached to help them storm their final objective, Stirling, had been blocked by an unexpected minefield. Like the Australians to the north, the Argylls dug in short of their main objective, but dawn found them in positions strong enough to hold. Fortunately, both their flanks were secure.

On the left flank of the Highland Division front, 7th Black Watch had passed through the 5th Camerons on the Red Line and at first it seemed that bad luck was haunting them. Within an hour six navigating officers had been killed or wounded, and by the time the

Black Line was reached the two leading companies had been reduced almost to platoon strength. But this lane of the attack had one advantage over the others – their final objective, Kirkaldy, lay on the north-western end of the Miteiriya Ridge and as such was identifiable – and with the fire coming from it, visible. Captain Cathcart led his company and the survivors of one of the other leading companies forward in a probing, cautious advance which developed into a wild charge at the end and the mad confusion of hand-to-hand fighting; and by 0400 the final objective on the left flank of the division had been captured – the only final objective to be won by the Jocks during that first, traumatic night. But only fifty men were left of Cathcart's company, one officer had been killed and all the rest wounded, and there was for a time some doubt as to whether they were out there all on their own. Where were the New Zealanders?

The nearest New Zealanders were, in fact, some way out in front of them and to the left, for their long experience of desert fighting and their undoubted ardour had swept them along close behind the barrage – and in some cases through it.

Like General Wimberley's men, General Freyberg's had advanced into an opening funnel, from a start line barely a mile long to a final objective three miles long – beyond the crest of the Miteiriya Ridge. Unlike the Jocks to the north, however, the New Zealanders' two infantry brigades were supported by the 9th Armoured Brigade actually under Freyberg's command – and their commander, Brigadier John Currie, had no intention of allowing the trust which had been built up during training between his tank crews and the New Zealand infantry to be dissipated.

But the first advances had, of course, to be made by the infantry battalions – 23rd on the right and 24th on the left, both as far as the Red Line with the 28th Maori Battalion mopping up behind them – then 21st and 22nd Battalions following through after 23rd, and 26th and 25th battalions on the left after 24th. Close behind them would come the mine-clearing parties, then the infantry support vehicles bringing up heavy mortars and anti-tank guns, then the Crusaders and finally the Grants and Shermans of the Armoured Brigade.

It was as well that their time fighting together in North Africa had bred in the New Zealanders a spirit of trust and confidence between themselves which in no way hampered their individual independence. On the right flank the commander of the 23rd Battalion, Lieutenant-Colonel Reginald Romans, found himself and the majority of his command on the Red Line so exactly on time and having experienced so little strong opposition that he decided upon Nelsonian tactics despite the fact that he was out of contact with both his left hand company and brigade headquarters (the rear-link signals jeep had run on to a minefield). Announcing that casualties among the pace-counters had confused the extent of the advance and anyway that 'We can't stop here; we haven't fought yet!' he ordered and led a further advance of the three remaining companies through his own barrage, past several well-manned enemy posts, and only admitted that they might all be too far forward when they found themselves on the slope of Miteiriya Ridge.

The fact that he had now to lead the survivors back through his own barrage again and possibly through the ranks of the 21st and 22nd Battalions who might not immediately recognise them as friends in view of the direction in which they were moving, disturbed him not at all; and they were, in fact, safely back on the Red Line by 0300, in contact again with their missing company and with 24th Battalion on their left, but not with the Camerons on their right.

This situation daunted nobody, especially as the Maori companies had already cleared the area behind of all overrun opposition. The Maori company commanders had been slightly puzzled to find no sign of Romans's men on the Red Line but would seem to have accepted the possibility of unorthodox behaviour on the part of 23rd Battalion, and had continued mopping up along their whole front, their left hand company helping the flanking platoons of 24th Battalion clear up some enemy points across in the South African sector, where progress had not been so rapid.

Despite the rather puzzling reports reaching Freyberg's head-quarters at first from the Red Line, the general saw no reason to delay the advance of the second wave, so the four follow-up battalions lined up in the dust and smother shrouding the Red Line positions, with their intelligence and provost sections in front to carry out the tasks of navigation and pace-counting. To the planned second, the infantry rose to their feet and moved forward into the dark haze, and so close did they stay to their barrage that they overran several enemy posts with the defenders still crouching in their trenches; and on the right the men of 21st Battalion also came across the debris of some enemy posts wiped out by Romans's men or mopped up by the Maoris, still hunting across the ground in front.

But as the funnel widened, the battalions separated, within them the gaps between the companies grew and even platoons risked losing touch with their neighbours. Still undaunted, however, they pressed forward and by 0200 the 25th Battalion on the extreme left were on the crest of Miteiriya Ridge, to find in front of them on the forward exposed slope a thick and extensive minefield. Here they dug in, discovered the presence of 26th Battalion some 600 yards to their right and swiftly and efficiently organised the filling of the gap with two companies of the Maori Battalion, happy to be up at the front with their compatriots.

The 21st and 22nd Battalions had been even more successful and by 0230 the New Zealand battalions were all either on the Miteiriya crest or further on down towards the bottom of the forward slope, digging in furiously, their heavy weapons slowly coming through. On the right flank, there had been briefly some concern as the subalterns of the 21st Battalion and the 7th Black Watch who had commanded the outer platoons of their respective divisions, who knew each other and agreed passwords with which to communicate during the crucial times, had both been killed – and so had been the first runner sent out by the New Zealanders to make contact. But he had been seen by one of the Black Watch privates who, although already wounded, went out under fire, found the message, brought it in to Captain Cathcart and then went out again to find and reassure their neighbours of Scottish presence on their flank. From the north-west tip of Miteiriya Ridge, therefore, across the whole of the New Zealand three-mile front, the crest and most of the forward slope were in XXX Corps's hands well before dawn broke. By 0300, the main concern of Brigadier Gentry, commanding the left hand, 6th Brigade, was lack of contact with the South Africans on his left flank.

The South Africans had been delayed by a combination of bad luck and poor communications. On their right flank the Natal Mounted Rifles were given the task of taking the Red Line, and this they achieved with few casualties and deceptive ease, for there had been few enemy posts directly in the path of their advance and no immediately apparent dangers on the flanks. But the dangers nevertheless existed and when the Cape Town Highlanders began moving up to take over the second stage of the advance to the ridge, they immediately ran into concentrated fire which killed the two leading company commanders and pinned down the forward platoons until a reserve company could be brought up. There then followed frantic attempts to reorganise the available men for the advance from the Red Line, and to postpone the artillery cover until they were ready. Such checks to an agreed time-table seem inevitably to expand into lengthy pauses, it was 0200 before an effective creeping barrage began again and nearly 0400 before the men from Cape Town had effectively cleared their original start line.

From then on, they had a fairly clear run – due in some cases to New Zealand raids from the right flank on enemy posts in the path of the South African advance – and they were on the crest of the ridge by dawn and at least in contact with the New Zealanders some 600 yards away on their right.

But on their left, the Frontier Force Battalion had had perhaps the worst time of any of the Commonwealth Divisions; not only had they run on to an uncharted minefield only 1,200 yards from their start line, but a position identified as a 'dump' by their photographic interpreters proved instead to be a well-fortified strongpoint manned by stalwart and unshaken German troops of the 164th Division.

The leading Frontier Force platoons were quickly cut to pieces, and attempts by the survivors of A' and 'B' Companies to outflank the post foundered on booby-traps and mines, while machine-gun fire extracted its inevitable price. One platoon appeared at first to be succeeding in working its way along the northern flank, only to find that it was then cut off, subject to merciless mortar and rifle attack and reduced eventually to one corporal and seven men.

In the end, with only some fifty men of the Frontier Force Battalion still effective they were reinforced with a company of the Natal Mounted Rifles, and supported by brigade mortars and heavy machine-guns they stormed the post. In fifteen minutes of desperate close-quarter fighting they overcame a stubborn and courageous resistance, but the battalion suffered 189 casualties that night, capturing only 36 exhausted but defiant German prisoners in exchange. The action undoubtedly constituted the most bitter fighting they had experienced in two years of desert warfare, and even with reinforcements from the Natal Mounted Rifles, they were still a mile short of their objective when they were forced to dig in before dawn.

The left hand half of the South African advance was undertaken by the 3rd South African Brigade, consisting of the 1st Rand Light Infantry, the Royal Durban Light Infantry and the Imperial Light Horse. The task for the R.L.I. was to take the Red Line, and as on the South African right flank, this proved more difficult than expected owing to an unidentified strong post manned by yet more Germans of the 164th Division. In the end, Bangalore torpedoes were used to blow apart the wire defences, and a murderous engagement then followed with three attacking platoons charging in with bayonet and bomb while on the flanks other platoons waited and picked off the few Germans who attempted to escape.

The battalion was well under strength when it eventually reached the Red Line, and the two follow-up battalions had also been delayed by anti-personnel mines and the survivors of by-passed enemy posts; but the delay in the barrage for the second advance gave them time to assemble on their new start line. Here, on the right the Royal Durban Light Infantry quickly became aware of the problems facing the Frontier Force Battalion and were obliged to form a defensive flank, and it was still held in place when the delayed barrage came down again at 0200, and the advance towards the eastern edge of Miteiriya Ridge could be recommenced.

Like the New Zealanders, the South Africans tried to keep as close behind the barrage as possible, and the Imperial Light Horse on the left were especially successful in this, not meeting serious opposition until within 600 yards of their final objective. Here they were delayed by another lone enemy post surrounded by an anti-personnel mine-field, but they were through and on to their objective past the eastern end of Miteiriya Ridge by 0430, with the R.D.L.I. firmly in position on their right – though with nearly a mile of the ridge in 2nd Brigade's sector still in enemy hands and the survivors of the Frontier Force Battalion blocked well short of it.

Thus the marching infantry of XXX Corps had reached their final objectives – the Oxalic Line – at both the northern and southern ends, were dug in about a mile short of it in the southern half of the Australian sector and three-quarters of the Highland Division sector, had captured three-quarters of the crest of the Miteiriya Ridge, and in the New Zealand right hand sector were down at the bottom of the forward slope.

Moreover, in the New Zealand sector the 9th Armoured Brigade had realised some though not all of its ambitions, and at least the New Zealand infantry had not lost their faith in them. Nevertheless,

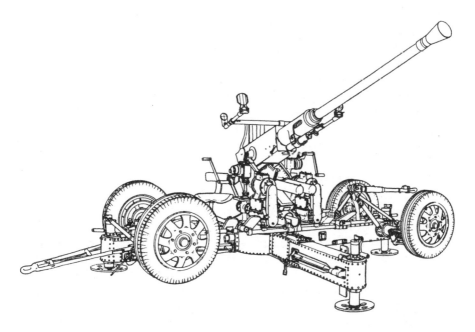

Figure 3   40mm. A-A gun (Bofors): overall length 21 ft; weight 2·4 tons; vertical range 12,000 ft; weight of projectile 2 lbs; rate of fire (practical) 60/90 per min.; crew 6

the armour had had a frustrating time, for it was 0300 before word came that gaps had been opened in the first minefield and even these were partially blocked by blown-up Scorpions which, despite all the efforts of their crews and the basic soundness of the idea behind them, had proved too old and decrepit for the tasks which faced them. Many were stuck deep in the minefields, sometimes with the mines they had flailed out of the ground lying on their carapaces, unexploded and threatening.

The 9th Brigade Crusaders had gone forward close behind the infantry (as had the 50th R.T.R. Valentines with the Australians and the Highlanders), but the problems of getting the heavy Grants and Shermans forward in worthwhile numbers were to prove more difficult. On the right behind the 21st and 22nd New Zealand Battalions the heavy squadrons of the Royal Wiltshire Yeomanry pressed forward through the murk following its lighter guiding vehicles, but when these dodged around the dead Scorpions, many of the Grants or Shermans following blew up on uncleared mines and added to the blockages. But they stayed where they were and the gunners engaged enemy posts harassing the mine-lifting parties, and as the gaps widened, more tanks could edge past.

On the left, Shermans of the Warwickshire Yeomanry with their Grant squadrons close behind slowly but surely picked their way through the maze (the small isolated minefields proved more of a problem than the large, foreseeable ones) and by 0400 they began at last to climb the eastern slope of the Miteiriya Ridge. Once on the crest they found the 25th New Zealand Battalion slightly to their left – and the thick minefield which had held up the infantry extending across their own front. Six Shermans of the leading squadron blew up within minutes of attemping to go through, and however hard the engineers laboured (and Major Moore himself was in the area urging them on) it was soon evident that there would be no way through before dawn. Regretfully, the Warwickshires pulled back to hull-down positions behind the 26th Battalion.

But on their right the Wiltshires had had more luck.

By 0400 both the 21st and 22nd New Zealand Battalions were well dug in at the bottom of the forward slope of Miteiriya Ridge, the 21st had received their heavy mortars and anti-tank guns, the 22nd some mortars but only two anti-tank guns, and it was while endeavouring to clear a wider route for more support weapons to come up that their commander, Lieutenant-Colonel Campbell, learned of the approach of the armour behind him. He immediately brought more of his men back to clear and mark a wider route and to the relief of everyone, just after 0600 the leading squadron of the Royal Wiltshire Yeomanry breasted the crest and drove on down towards the New Zealand front line. Nine of them blew up on the left flank where they caught the edge of the thick minefield, but fifteen swept on down the slope, past the New Zealanders and ahead towards the known positions of more enemy posts.

But dawn was breaking and one factor becoming ominously clear. Infantry and artillery might be able to live on the forward slope of the ridge or the broken ground at the bottom, if they had arrived in darkness with sufficient time to dig in; but tanks in daylight must either find 'hull-down' positions from which to act as semi-static artillery – or keep moving.

Soon after the Wiltshires began engaging the enemy posts, they came under fire from leading units of the 15th Panzer Division which were moving up into the battle area – at a time, moreover, when fuel tanks were running low. Prudently, they retired up the face of the ridge and by full daylight the tanks of 9th Armoured Brigade were refuelled, ready to repeal any counter-attack the enemy might mount – but behind the crest and behind the infantry. It would seem that the idea of tanks forming a screen in open country behind which infantry could fight infantry battles – or even just find protection – might be in need of revision.

Nevertheless, to the Royal Wiltshire Yeomanry went the honour of being the first – and only – armoured regiment to break out beyond the infantry's final objective on the first day of the Battle of Alamein.

If the infantrymen of XXX Corps had reason to feel some satisfaction with their performance, the same could not be said of the tank crews of X Corps, who had spent a thoroughly frustrating and unhappy night.

The tasks for the two divisions of X Corps (1st and 10th) in detail were as follows: they were to leave their assembly areas after dark and move forward until their respective leading units reached the Springbok Track at half past midnight, whereupon they would pause to refuel and then begin their main move forward at 0200. The 1st Division – 2nd Armoured Brigade followed by the 7th Motor Brigade – were to make their way along the Sun, Moon and Star tracks and on through their designated main gap straddling the Australian southern and the Highland Division northern flanks, while the 10th Armoured Division – 8th Armoured Brigade, 24th Armoured Brigade and 133rd Lorried Infantry Brigade – would use Bottle, Boat and Hat tracks to reach their own main gap through the New Zealand sector, up to and over the Miteiriya Ridge.

The plan called for the leading tanks of 2nd Armoured Brigade to burst out in the north through the Australian and Scottish positions along the Oxalic Line before dawn, and establish themselves in position about a mile further west. In the south, first the 8th

Armoured Brigade and then the 24th would cross the Miteiriya Ridge, pass through the New Zealand-held portion of the Oxalic Line, swing west and join the 2nd Armoured Brigade to form the 'Pierson Line', 8th Armoured Brigade in the centre and 24th Armoured Brigade anchoring the southern end of the line about three miles south-west of Miteiriya.

In the north the riflemen of the 7th Motor Brigade would form a flank guard with their anti-tank guns and heavy weapons on the right, while the infantry of the 133rd Brigade did the same in the south, the massed armour of the entire corps between them, well concentrated to guard XXX Corps and to annihilate the panzer divisions if they attacked.

In the next stage, the whole corps would move forward into an area known as Skinflint which would lie across the Rahman Track, while the corps's armoured cars ranged forward to the north-west to locate 15th Panzer Division, and to the south in order to give due warning of any northward move of the 21st Panzer Division.

It was undoubtedly a very ambitious programme, especially as it had now been accepted that the responsibility for clearing the wide gaps through which the armoured divisions would move would rest with their own engineers, the mine-clearance by XXX Corps engineers being expressly for the benefit of the infantry and only coincidentally of value to the X Corps armour.

Obviously the tasks of the engineers and leading armour of the 1st Armoured Division were going to be complicated by the fact that both the left flank of the Australians and the right flank of the Highland Division were dug in some way short of the Oxalic Line – but in the event this did not greatly affect the issue, for minefields, misfortune, confusion and the almost indescribable dust-clouds which enshrouded the armour as soon as it moved forward *en masse*, combined to delay them to such an extent that by dawn they had hardly reached the Red Line.

Again, as with the New Zealanders' armoured brigade, it was the scattered, unidentified minefields which caused the most trouble, three Shermans on the extreme right blowing up on them early in the move forward, thus displacing those behind off the marked gaps, causing them either to blow up themselves or often to crush down the flimsy pickets holding the essential signal lamps. Tempers and tank-engines both became overheated, dust-clouds blanketed the heads of the columns and billowed back over those trying desperately to see what was happening ahead . . . and time crept inexorably by.

And whereas the infantry had at least some idea as to how many paces they had marched forward, the armour gauged its progress by a combination of time elapsed, fuel consumed, landmarks recognised and some degree of faith and hope; and under the conditions reigning behind XXX Corps's front after midnight on October 24th, in none of those factors could much reliance be placed. When therefore the leading tanks came under fire from Kintore and Strichen – both of which were presumed to have been reduced by the Jocks – the assumption immediately made was that the fire must be coming from enemy posts much further west – from beyond the infantry final objectives, which they themselves must now be close behind. Soon, therefore, the armour reasoned, once the sappers had cleared whatever mines there were immediately in front, their Grants and Shermans would be able to break out towards the Pierson Line. But until then they must stay where they were.

Armoured opinion in the northern sector when dawn broke was therefore convinced that their spearheads were some 3,000 yards further forward than they actually were, and in the arguments which soon began to rage it would seem that as old desert-worthy veterans they were not going to yield their opinions to those of a lot of newly arrived foot-sloggers from outer space . . . or north of the border, or wherever it was they came from.

It was a difference of opinion which was to cause difficulties and high words for some time to come.

In the south, down in the New Zealand sector, 10th Armoured Division faced problems of a different order. Here they had a comparatively clear run as a result of the successes of the New Zealand infantry, at least as far as the crest of the Miteiriya Ridge for the whole width of the proposed armoured front. Their problems, however, sprang from an *embarras de richesse* – two armoured brigades and a lorried infantry brigade trying to get forward through a comparatively narrow passage in order to reach their positions on the Pierson Line all at more or less the same time.

But in addition to the clear run given them by the New Zealanders, the clearance of the minefield gaps had also been attended by remarkable success. The planned routine worked well, not too many of the Polish detectors broke down, and the teams probing with bayonets worked efficiently and coolly despite the darkness and the danger – and on the left flank under the personal supervision of their chief trainer Peter Moore himself. There were only two occasions when infantry had to be summoned to attack unsubdued enemy posts, and only one serious check to plans when two lorries bearing Military Police with the essential pickets were blown up. Incredibly, the tasks of the entire section were then carried out by the one lone survivor, staggering forward beneath a crushing load of pickets, running backwards and forwards all night and showing a total unconcern for the bullets which hissed by his ears with increasing frequency as the night wore on. Before dawn that particular route was lit all the way through.

Mine-clearance along all the lanes was steady across the width of 10th Armoured Division's front until the crest of the ridge was reached – and on the right where the New Zealand battalions had gone forward, the sappers followed on down the slope. But the same minefield which held up the left hand infantry battalions obviously presented an even greater problem to the sappers who now, if they wished to use their detectors, had to stand upright and ignore the hail of bullets and later of shells which whistled and screamed close by them. But the job had to be done, and a gap cleared for the tanks of the leading armoured brigade (the 8th under Brigadier Custance) to break out into the open and drive for their place in the Pierson Line; so the divisional C.R.E., Lieutenant-Colonel McMeekan, despite having already been blown up and as a result almost completely deafened, collected five more of his sappers and, in the hope of finding a possible German gap through the mines, led the group slowly down the forward slope of Miteiriya Ridge – thus forming, at that moment and in that place, the tiny lead force of the Eighth Army.

They had progressed some 150 yards when they were seen by an enemy machine-gun post which promptly pinned them to the ground until McMeekan decided that time was passing too quickly, where-upon he crawled back through the field to the shelter of the crest. Here he found that his own signals set had been broken by the same blast which had deafened him, and his efforts to contact the leading armour and call them forward were frustrated by bad luck and a degree of bureaucratic incomprehension among those he first came across which it is surprising to find so far forward.

As a result vital minutes were lost and when the leading tanks of the Nottinghamshire Yeomanry, guided now by Peter Moore, came up over the crest of the ridge, they were silhouetted against the greying eastern sky. In five minutes of furious action six of their Crusaders were knocked out, the Grants behind them attempted to deploy and ran on to the minefield and within a short time the survivors were all forced back to hull-down positions behind the ridge, leaving sixteen of their number smoking wrecks on the forward slope. To their right they found their divisional comrades of the Staffordshire Yeomanry similarly sheltered, and these in their turn had the Grants and Shermans of the New Zealand 9th Armoured Brigade on their right.

On the left of the Nottinghamshire Yeomanry the line was eventually extended by the late arrival of the 3rd Royal Tanks – who had been badly held up by unexpectedly thick minefields and did not climb the eastern slope until well after daybreak – but then the whole of 8th Armoured Brigade at least were close up behind the New Zealand infantry.

But behind them, the light was growing to reveal a scene of such confusion as to stun the mind.

Down the reverse slope of Miteiriya Ridge and the flat ground at the bottom were congregated the ammunition and fuel trucks, the water-carriers, the artillery and ambulances, staff cars and pick-ups and all the heterogeneous manpower which made up the 'tail' of an armoured brigade, while behind them the whole of 24th Armoured Brigade under Brigadier Kenchington – 140 tanks of the 41st, 45th and 47th Royal Tank Regiments, plus the vehicles and personnel of *their* tail – were stretched back through the old no-man's-land as far as the original British minefields.

As for divisional headquarters and the three battalions of the 133rd Lorried Infantry Brigade intended to form by morning the protective screen at the southern end of the Pierson Line, these were all still back in the area of the Springbok Track, about three miles south of El Alamein Station. They had hardly moved all night and now accepted their orders to disperse as the light grew, with frustration but phlegmatic resignation.

The same orders given to the men of 24th Armoured Brigade, however, were greeted with a certain degree of incredulity. Not only was there very little room to 'disperse' in, but what there was was pocked with slit-trenches, sewn with as yet unplotted minefields, still shrouded with dust and only too often stained with the blood of wounded men still awaiting evacuation. Moreover, their own dispersal had to be superimposed upon the dispersal of the tail of the New Zealand Division and – more crucially – across the lines of communication and supply along which the New Zealand administration services were frantically trying to get food, water, ammunition and reinforcements to the heroic companies holding the forward and most exposed positions reached by the main assault of the entire army. They were not going to be thwarted in their tasks by the domestic convenience of units from another division – which was not even a member of the same corps – especially when those same units were the ones who should have been forward protecting the very men whose lines of supply they were now blocking!

The scene has been most aptly described by an observer as looking 'like a badly organised car park at an immense race meeting held in a dust bowl'.[3] But few race meetings have been attended by so many men in so impatient a frame of mind.

One of the most impatient, not surprisingly, was Bernard Freyberg – already himself on Miteiriya Ridge – who not only wanted to see the gallantry and success of his men thoroughly exploited, but also to see them protected by rather more than their own Armoured

Brigade, doughty though its performance had been. Soon after 0700 he got word to Leese back at XXX Corps H.Q. that in his opinion the moment had come for a supreme effort to be made by 10th Armoured Division to break out and reach their intended position on the Pierson Line – and three-quarters of an hour later he was inquiring acidly why so little seemed to be happening.

The answer he received was to the effect that everything possible was being done but the armour was held up by the congestion on the eastern flank of Miteiriya Ridge, complicated by the fact that the only completely mine-free lane had been commandeered by the New Zealand supply services; but two hours later there was still no sign of movement, and perhaps with the hope of shaming the 10th Armoured Division forward, Freyberg's Chief of Staff informed Leese's that Currie had been ordered to take his brigade up over the crest again and down through the forward infantry positions. As they would be grossly outnumbered, would Lumsden please order at least 8th Armoured Brigade after them in support?

The answer when it came was that Lumsden considered that the operation was 'not on', that 10th Armoured Division must remain where it was for the moment reorganising itself and clearing wider paths forward, and that any attempt to cross the ridge except at night or perhaps under cover of a sandstorm would be suicidal.

In this opinion the commander of X Corps was undoubtedly correct, for heavy and accurate anti-tank fire met every sign of movement forward by Currie's tanks, and by midday attempts by the Wiltshire Yeomanry to repeat their exploits of a few hours before had reduced their strength to one Sherman and three Grants.

It was time for a reassessment of the situation.

First reports to reach the Army Commander were, not surprisingly, somewhat confused, but by 0845 a fairly clear picture had emerged and half an hour later he had issued orders to the corps commanders. Along XXX Corps's front, the greatest priority was to be given to clearing the 'northern lane' to get 1st Armoured Division through and on to its position on the Pierson Line; on their right, the Australians would strengthen their present positions and be prepared to begin 'crumbling' operations against the enemy infantry that night. In the south, Freyberg's New Zealanders would begin exploiting their success beyond Miteiriya ridge by driving down across the South African front, the reserve brigade from Wimberley's Highland Division coming up to take their place along and in front of the ridge. Wimberley's first job, however, would be to clear the remaining enemy posts in front of his other two brigades, advance up to the Oxalic Line and let the armour in the north through.

So far as Gatehouse's 10th Armoured Division were concerned,

Montgomery would issue orders for their further employment when he had investigated their situation more closely, with which object he left de Guingand in charge of his own H.Q. and went forward through the dust and confusion to find Freyberg's.

By this time both Leese and Freyberg had visited Miteiriya Ridge and satisfied themselves that it was at least safe from counter-attack, although they were still in the dark as to what the armour of X Corps intended. This to a great extent was due to the fact that they had been unable to contact either Lumsden or Gatehouse, but the former now arrived from the northern sector and Montgomery, after listening to what all three had to say, issued his orders.

There would be no change in the plan or the main objectives, despite twenty-four hours' delay. The formations in the northern sector already had their orders, and now he laid it down specifically that Gatehouse's armour must break out as soon as possible through the New Zealand positions and reach the Pierson Line, and in order to assist them Leese must quickly organise the support of every piece of his artillery which could be brought to bear. Montgomery then returned to his headquarters, but immediately rang up Lumsden's Chief of Staff and stressed that the armour must get out through both fronts quickly, and in the southern one in time for the New Zealanders to get on with their southern exploitation. He was quite prepared to accept casualties to ensure that success was achieved.

But it was not to be as easy as that. After the conference, Leese returned to the ridge and at last found Gatehouse, grimly surveying the burnt-out remains of the 9th Brigade tanks and some of his own, watching the immediate response by the waiting German anti-tank guns to the slightest sign of movement above the crest-line. To Leese's explanation of the Army Commander's intentions, Gatehouse replied that his tanks had been trained for a static role, not for charging forward over uncleared minefields at well-entrenched enemy positions – a response which Leese was quickly reporting to Montgomery by telephone from New Zealand headquarters.

He also reported wide expectation of attacks and the steps being taken – especially by Gatehouse – to repel them, together with Freyberg's continued belief that with the support of one of Gate-house's brigades, the New Zealand Divisional Cavalry and the remains of John Currie's 9th Brigade could break out – perhaps under smoke? – if only somebody would give the word. Freyberg apparently also believed that the barrage of fire which descended on Miteiriya Ridge at the slightest signs of movement was the result of an enemy decision to shoot off all their remaining ammunition before retiring; nobody could ever accuse the New Zealand commander of pessimism.

By this time de Guingand had been able to analyse the first intelligence reports to come in. Neither 21st Panzer Division nor 90th Light seemed to have moved from their positions in the south or in reserve, the latest count gave a total of nearly 1,000 prisoners taken of whom over 300 were German, and it seemed that the whole of one Italian regiment and the larger part of one German regiment had been completely destroyed.

First estimates of the cost gave an overall figure for killed, wounded and missing from XXX Corps of approximately 2,500 – 350 each from the Australians and the South Africans, 600 from the New Zealanders and nearly 1,000 from the Highlanders – which on the face of it did not seem unduly high. However, the vast majority of the killed and badly wounded had obviously come from the rifle companies, for whom among the Commonwealth divisions and especially the New Zealand Division there were very few available reinforcements. And XXX Corps's infantry had still to close up to several critical lengths of the Oxalic Line before the armour could break out – after which the infantry 'crumbling' battle would have to be fought.

It was fortunate that infantry casualties down in XIII Corps's area had been comparatively small.

The basic ambiguity about the tasks given to XIII Corps – to bring such pressure on their portion of the front as to hold 21st Panzer in position, yet not to hazard the Grants, Stuarts and Crusaders of 7th Armoured Division (they had no Shermans) – called for a nicety of judgment difficult to exercise amid the chaos of battle. The situation was also complicated by two other factors, one being the direction that despite the necessity to conserve the armour, every opportunity must be taken to exploit to the fullest extent any weaknesses found in the opposing defences. The wish both to have cake and eat it is apparently as common among Army commanders as it is among more ordinary humans.

The second complicating factor was brought about by the pre-battle phase of the planning, for if opportunities are freely given to the enemy to observe one's own manoeuvres and assembly of force, it becomes exceedingly difficult to obtain at the same time an accurate picture of the defences against which that force must operate. The result had been that the supposition that Panzerarmee's main defence line in the south was still that from which they had advanced at Alam Halfa had not been challenged, and the fact that it instead now lay along the line of the most westerly of the old British minefields, codenamed February, had gone unnoticed. Horrocks's corps thus faced a much tougher task than was realised, especially as Rommel had deliberately stationed there the toughest of the Italian infantry, the Folgore parachutists, together with a strong leavening from the German Ramcke Parachute Brigade.

The basic plan of attack for XIII Corps was for the main strength of 7th Armoured Division – 22nd Armoured Brigade – preceded by a minefield task force and supported by a creeping barrage provided by the combined artillery of 7th Armoured Division and 44th Division, to break through both the January and February minefields south of the Munassib depression and there form a bridgehead into which would follow the armoured cars, Stuarts and Grants of the 4th Light Armoured Brigade and the infantry of 44th Division. Meanwhile, 1st Fighting French Brigade as part of 7th Armoured Division would hook around to the south of the Himeimat peaks and capture the ground to the west and, it was hoped, the peaks themselves. Then, with the bridgehead firmly held, both brigades of 7th Armoured plus the French would drive westwards as far as Jebel Kalakh and the Taqa Plateau, while to the north of the attack area 50th and 44th Divisions acted together to straighten out the line.

All units were faced with a long approach march – in the case of

Map 9   Southern sector, October 23rd–24th

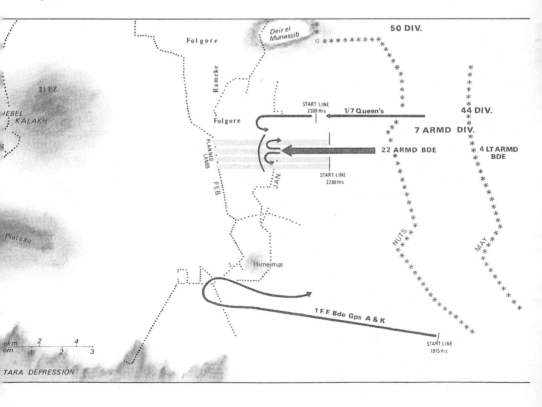

the armour one of over ten miles, for after Alam Halfa two extra protective minefields, Nuts and May, had been laid by Royal Engineers east of January. Four and a half miles separated those two from each other, and another six miles of no-man's-land had to be crossed befo e the minefield task force arrived at the front edge of January, to begin cutting the four gaps for the tanks to pass through. January was known to be nearly 500 yards wide, two miles separated it from February, which was itself now reputed to be nearly 1,000 yards wide.

It looked like being a long journey, and with this in mind Brigadier Roberts sent off the lead units of 22nd Armoured Brigade at 1845. In brilliant moonlight they made such good time through their own Nuts and May minefields that Roberts called a halt at 2000 to avoid congestion on the start line itself, but the carrier platoons, the reconnaissance regiment from the 44th Division, the sappers and the two companies of protective infantry which made up the minefield task force went on ahead, their six Scorpion flail tanks clanking along with them. Behind them soon stretched the trail of lamps on pickets, alight to guide the following armour, while on their right flank the infantrymen of the lead battalion of 131st Brigade (44th Division) – the 1st/7th Queen's – marched stolidly forward, awaiting the on-slaught, trusting in the guns and the armour for protection:

> The barrage began. It was a shattering fantastic sound, drowning the subdued whispering of boots in the sand and the occasional clink of a rifle or bayonet as the infantry moved up. The din of nearly 1,000 field guns firing along the front was like gigantic drum-beats merging into one great blast of noise. As we went forward we could hear the sighing whistle of the shells overhead and the flicker of their bursts on the dark horizon and beyond . . . Bofors guns on fixed lines were lobbing tracer shells in a lazy curve towards the enemy lines ahead of us, to help the Queen's Brigade maintain the correct axis of advance.[4]

But the enemy reaction here was to be quicker than further up north, and shells crashed down among the unfortunate battalion even as they waited on the start line, giving the erroneous but demoralising impression that their own artillery were firing short. Three officers of the 1st/7th Queen's including the second-in-command were killed instantly, but the C.O. rallied the companies and led them forward and across the January minefield into the gap beyond. Here, how-ever, they ran into positions manned by Folgore and Ramcke units and lost many men and all the company commanders. The com-manding officer was taken prisoner shortly afterwards and then shot while trying to escape, but the survivors early in the morning were collected together by the adjutant to form small bridgeheads guard-ing the exits of the gaps now cleared through January.

The fate of the 1st/7th Queen's exemplified the bad luck which had dogged 44th Division since its formation, and would do so until its eventual disbandment.

On the left of the Queen's advance through January, the minefield task force had met with varying fortunes. Soft sand had made the work heavy and the job slow, and at one time and another all the Scorpions broke down through overheating and time was lost while the engines cooled and the crews carried out repairs. Number 1 lane in the north gave the greatest trouble, its location dominated by an enemy post almost immediately opposite. As a result it was not through despite the utmost gallantry until nearly 0430, but number 2 on its left was through nearly three hours before as was the most southerly lane number 4, while number 3 lane was through by 0215 although the sand along its whole length was so soft as to render it unusable by wheeled vehicles. Unfortunately – and ironically – dead Scorpions partially blocked every one of the three lanes which had been opened early, causing delay when the time came for the Grants and Crusaders to edge gingerly around them.

The price paid by the minefield task force had been high, and when their commander, Lieutenant-Colonel Lyon Corbet-Winder, assembled the survivors in the gap between January and February, he quickly concluded that he had only enough men to attempt two gaps through February. Fortunately Brigadier 'Pip' Roberts, bringing 22nd Armoured through as quickly as possible, was not unduly disturbed at the prospect of such limited passage for his tanks through what he still thought to be an unmanned minefield, concentrating as he was for the moment on getting his squadrons together after their passage through January.

They were by no means unscathed. Their ten-minute delay had served to bring them to the start line exactly on time – but their guides had not waited and when the time came for the bulk of the armour to begin passing along the marked gaps, some of the lights had already gone out. Moreover, the alert enemy artillery caught the supply lines and set alight many of the soft-skinned vehicles, all of which caused delay, resultant loss of the protective effect of the barrage, casualties in men and machines among the minefields, and when they eventually cleared January, some of the congestion which was proving so dangerous in XXX Corps's area.

By 0400 most of the 5th Royal Tank Regiment were through January on the right, and with Corbet-Winder's force ahead they cautiously moved westward towards the near edge of February. Soft sand and breakdowns again held up the right hand squadrons, while those on the left reached February but immediately came under heavy fire which not only held them back, but also made it almost impossible for the task force to clear the gaps for them – and by now it was nearly 0500 and the eastern sky was lightening. A bridgehead between January and February was obviously all that was to be achieved during this first night, and with the object of stabilising it, all units drew back from February and began the tasks of consolidation – well aware of the fact that unless the Fighting French had been successful in all their tasks, the bulk of 7th Armoured Division would face the daylight hours penned in a comparatively small area under the direct observation of enemy forces on the Himeimat peaks.

Brigadier-General Koenig had divided his force into two groups – Group A under Colonel Amilakvari consisting of two battalions of the Foreign Legion, and Group K under his own command consisting of a squadron of Moroccan Spahis with Crusader tanks, and a company of anti-tank guns. Soft going and several deep wadis slowed up the entire force but the Foreign Legionnaires reached their forming-up areas to the south-west of Himeimat well on time. At 0230, supported by what little artillery they had been able to bring up with them and under a smoke-screen put down by the R.A.F., the 1st Battalion on the right advanced against strong opposition but forced their way forward until their left flank became exposed. Amilakvari then ordered 2nd Battalion to move up to protect them, but as they did so they were themselves attacked in flank by the German Kiel group in eight captured Stuarts, who had managed to evade (or were not seen by) the Crusaders of Koenig's Group K, also held back by the bad going.

As Amilakvari's force thus lacked even the protection and support of the anti-tank guns in Koenig's command and as darkness was fading, the orders were given for a withdrawal of about three miles to the south-east – but an admirable but unfortunate reluctance to retreat on the part of the Legion caused delay, and when eventually they came back it was in broad daylight and across open desert. All their vehicles were lost together with over a hundred of their men and, most unfortunate of all, the commander was killed; and the loss of the gallant Amilakvari who since Bir Hacheim had seemed to epitomise the very spirit of the Foreign Legion, so deeply affected the regiment's morale that no further French contribution to the fighting was to take place for several days.

Himeimat peaks therefore remained in German hands, and during October 24th no element of 7th Armoured Division could make the slightest move in daylight without immediate observation and response.

To John Harding, at last free of staff duties and with his first divisional command, the situation was so criticial as to call forth every facet of his considerable military talent. General Horrocks visited him shortly after daybreak to discuss whether his 7th Armoured could even now break through the February minefields without incurring the prohibited degree of losses, and they agreed that it probably could, but not until after nightfall – and for the proposed attack the remaining two battalions of the Queen's Brigade from 44th Division would be placed directly under Harding's command.

Harding's day was therefore one of almost feverish activity. Not only had he to ensure that as little damage as possible was suffered by his exposed formations, but they must also be marshalled as far forward as possible without betraying too obviously their plans for further operation – not that they had many alternatives. He held a short conference with his brigade commanders during the morning, crouched in the lee of a tank amid the heat and dust of continual shelling, some of which exploded uncomfortably close, and worked out the details of the night's attack. Warning orders were issued by midday to bring the 1st/5th and the 1st/6th Queen's down from the north, and for them quickly to establish close liaison with the remains of Corbet-Winder's force. Artillery cover for the operation had to be carefully planned, and all the time, despite attempts by the R.A.F. to bomb known or observed enemy gun positions, shells burst among the tanks and supply vehicles of the formations in the bridgehead, while at one time panzers were seen massing as though for a counter-attack in the north – which, however, remained nothing but a threat.

The Queen's battalions had a long march down to their start line, and there would seem to have been some administrative delays on the part of the Queen's Brigade staff – so that it was not until 2230 that the infantry advanced behind their artillery barrage. At first all seemed to go smoothly and they thrust through the width of the February minefield and nearly half a mile beyond it, but then, when they tried to consolidate they found that the ground was rock-like, slit-trenches difficult to dig and sangars almost impossible to build; rifle and machine-gun fire opened on them from the flanks, mortar-bombs exploded amongst them, and their losses rose sharply as they anxiously awaited the arrival of the armour – or at least of some protective artillery.

But some of the enemy guns which had been shelling the gap between January and February during the day concentrated their fire into the area through which the minefield parties were trying to clear gaps, and the northern sector especially erupted continually under shell-burst or mortar-bomb. This gap was nevertheless cleared by 0230, although the pickets bearing the lamps were too far apart and the gaps between them not filled with wire which was the usual practice in such cases. The result was that when the tanks of the 4th County of London Yeomanry began following through, some of them lost their way and wandered off the cleared path, blowing up in the minefield. Others were knocked out by the efficient anti-tank guns opposite the end of the gap, and in all the C.L.Y. lost twenty-six of their tanks together with their colonel and second-in-command. In the confusion the idea spread that the gap had not in fact been properly cleared, and as the exit from the gap cleared in the southern area was covered by an 88mm. firing along the edge of the minefield, catching tanks of the 1st R.T.R. in flank as they came through, a bleak picture began to emerge from the reports as the night wore on.

Harding, who had already narrowly escaped death when a shell landed just in front of his jeep, killing his A.D.C. who would normally have been driving it instead of Harding himself, now intervened personally. Highly conscious of the need to conserve his armour, he stopped their further attempts to pass through February, and in the light of the reports he had received ordered the colonel commanding the sappers personally to ensure the clearance of the gaps. After registering a formal protest, the colonel called for volunteers, took them to the entrance to the northern gap where they were immediately subjected to such heavy fire that he dispersed them. He then commandeered two tanks in which he and one of the engineer squadron-commanders set off, and together they drove through the gap.

The leading tank was hit five times but not penetrated, both tanks reached the far side of February, then turned around and drove back – one of them losing a track and being abandoned when almost home – after which the colonel reported to Harding and told him in no uncertain terms that the gap *was* clear, that the tanks which had been blown up had left it, and that the majority of casualties had been – and undoubtedly would be – caused by the accurate anti-tank fire which dominated the gap exits.

In the circumstances, Harding thus had no choice but to halt the attempts to pass the armour through February, hold the bulk of 22nd Armoured Brigade where it was between January and February, allow the remains of the battered 4th County of London Yeomanry to retire through January and join the still practically immobile 4th Light Armoured Brigade – and leave the unfortunate Queen's battalion alone in their highly exposed bridgehead some two thousand yards in advance of their nearest support. The sacrifice the night before of the 1st/7th Queen's had apparently not been enough to placate whatever gods had decreed the elimination of the 44th (Home Counties) Division.

At the morning conference with Horrocks it was agreed that no daylight attempt either to clear more gaps in the minefield or to pass armour through the existing ones to the closer support of the Queen's was feasible, and that the coming night held only two alternatives. Either 22nd Armoured Brigade should try yet again to get through February, or a totally different action should commence to the north – an attack on the western end of the Munassib Depression by the 50th Division, in which it could be supported by the 4th Light Armoured Brigade which had so far seen practically nothing of the fighting.

These alternatives were put by Horrocks to de Guingand for communication to Montgomery (who at the time of the call was at a meeting with Alexander), and half an hour later de Guingand phoned back to say that the second alternative was preferred. The plight of the Queen's was appreciated but further support for them must be provided by the other 44th Division brigade – 132nd. The tanks of 7th Armoured Division must be preserved, certainly for the pursuit when the break-out took place, perhaps even for transfer to XXX Corps and employment there.

There had been something of a crisis during the night and plans might well have to be changed.

That crises in human affairs are often caused by lack of communication is doubtless a commonplace but is nevertheless true, and during the morning of October 24th in XXX Corps's area, communications in one important aspect had been unnecessarily complicated.

Freyberg's requests that 8th Armoured Brigade should support his own armour in an attempt to 'get the battle moving again' had had first to be passed by his own Tactical Headquarters to XXX Corps headquarters, who then passed them to X Corps and thus down to 10th Armoured Division – who replied by the same channels; and as both Lumsden commanding X Corps and Gatehouse commanding 10th Armoured Division had been out of touch – Lumsden in the northern corridor and Gatehouse on Miteiriya Ridge – delays were inevitable and protracted.

The same lack of communication had also caused a degree of confusion inside X Corps itself.

Gatehouse on Miteiriya Ridge had seen both the losses incurred by 9th Armoured Brigade when they had tried to move down the western face, and also what he considered to be evidence of impending German counter-attacks. In the circumstances it was imperative that his armour should give what defensive support it could to the New Zealanders, and when Freyberg told him that, despite Lumsden's opinion, there *was* a clear gap through which armour could move towards the New Zealand right flank, he ordered 24th Armoured Brigade to make their way as soon as they could across behind 8th Armoured Brigade and up on to the ridge on their right; and in due course 47th Royal Tank Regiment began the move.

But in the meantime, orders had arrived from Lumsden, sent while he was still up in the northern sector and direct to 24th Armoured Brigade as he could make no contact with Gatehouse on the ridge. The brigade were indeed to move across behind 8th Armoured Brigade – but not then to swing west to take position in support of the New Zealanders, but to continue into and across the Highland Division sector in order to help 1st Armoured Division forward along the northern gap, all in accordance with the Army Commander's earlier instructions. In the resultant confusion from these conflicting orders, hesitation grew, time was wasted, what little momentum had been gained was lost, and the tank crews drew back into themselves and took comfort in immobility. There is some attraction in the old soldier's cynical maxim 'Never obey the latest order; it's already been cancelled!' to men who know only too well that one false or unlucky move can result in themselves and their three or four closest companions being burnt to death in a steel box.

It is also arguable that had 24th Armoured Brigade carried out Lumsden's orders, they would have compounded confusion in the Highland Division sector to a disastrous extent.

General Wimberley, anxious to locate his forward units and ensure that they were both supported and supplied to the best possible extent, had set out shortly after first light to visit them himself:

> We had not been out long, when somewhere about the Red Line, on the 1st Black Watch front, I was trying to find Roper Caldbeck. There were some shells and mortar-bombs flying around, and I had just started off in my Jeep to go where I had been told Roper now was, when I felt myself sailing into the air, and then, for a time, knew no more . . . at the time I thought it was a mortar-bomb scoring a direct hit on my Jeep; perhaps more probably it was a mine. Anyhow I lay on the sand, and when I became conscious again, I suppose in a matter of seconds, I could not for a minute or two move hand or foot, in fact for a second or two I thought I was dead and coming to in another world. However, in a few minutes I was up to find myself practically unhurt, I had had some skin removed in various places, and was a bit bruised as I had been blown quite a long way from the remnants of the Jeep.[5]

Two of the other occupants of the jeep had been killed and the other seriously wounded, and although Wimberley had been extremely lucky, he was nevertheless out of action for the rest of the morning, and the separate formations of his division thus without control above brigade level. One of the results was that when he returned to the active area shortly after noon, he found that arguments between his own brigade and battalion commanders and those of the 2nd Armoured Brigade about the positions reached by their respective formations were growing heated, and although attempts had been made during the morning to clear away some of the enemy posts blocking the way to the Oxalic Line, it was obvious that a major attack must be organised if the armour in the northern corridor were to have any chance of breaking out.

The mechanics of this attack were comparatively simple to set out. From reserve the 2nd Seaforths were brought up, all remaining Valentines from 50th R.T.R. marshalled in support and as much artillery as was available in the area briefed to supply cover; and it was here that the problems began. The commander of 2nd Armoured Brigade, Brigadier Fisher, was still adamant that his forward units were much further forward than Wimberley's men said they were, but also that Wimberley's 1st Gordons were not on the Blue Line at Aberdeen as Wimberley claimed.

This part of the argument was complicated by the fact that the armour had named that vital area 'Kidney' from its contour shape on the map, believing it, moreover, to be a raised plateau instead of a depression which it in fact proved to be.

Time was short, tempers were brittle, argument reached the pitch when prestige began to assume more importance than fact, to such an extent that when the commander of XXX Corps's artillery offered to carry out a swift survey and settle the matter of exact locations, his offer was brusquely rejected by both sides. Even more importantly, Brigadier Fisher would not allow his own artillery to take part in the cover for the infantry attack as it would, he claimed, be shelling his own formations. Wimberley then suggested that as Fisher would not order his tanks forward to reach the Gordons at Aberdeen (Kidney) on their own, perhaps he would allow them to follow one of Wimberley's battalions which would be sent up to clear the way – but this was also rejected on the grounds that Fisher was not a part of Wimberley's division, not even a part of the same corps. He could only accept orders from his own commanders.

What would have been the position if 24th Armoured Brigade, operating solely under Lumsden's orders and without reference to Leese, Freyberg or Wimberley (or Gatehouse, for that matter) had in fact moved into and across the Highland Division sector during the morning is, of course, now impossible to state; but in view of the reigning confusion and the lack of understanding which still existed between infantry and armour – at least when they were separated into corps – it seems unlikely that the results would have been satisfactory.

Orders for 2nd Armoured Brigade in fact arrived in time for them to act in support of the attempts by the Seaforths to clear two enemy strongpoints just ahead, and although the regimental commanders complained that they had not been given adequate time to prepare, the 9th Lancers and the 10th Hussars did set out behind the Jocks who in a gallant daylight attack took both their objectives at a cost of eighty-five casualties – including all the officers and the sergeant-major of one company, which was led forward on its last charge by the company clerk.

Meanwhile, away to the north the Australians had begun to drive forward on their own left flank in order to reach the Oxalic Line across their whole front. Their supporting Valentines of 40th R.T.R. had closed up during the night and once daylight came drew a great deal of enemy fire, and the position was not helped when a squadron of Mitchells, briefed to attack the suspected location of an enemy headquarters, unloaded their bombs instead on the unfortunate 2nd/13th Battalion. But the 2nd/17th Battalion now came up from the rear in support and drove towards the junction between 20th and 26th Brigades, and when to the south the Seaforths had gone into their attack it would seem that the right hand regiment of the 2nd Armoured Brigade, the Bays, followed along the 2nd/17th's tracks.

But dust and confusion still had a part to play. The 9th Lancers lost contact with the Seaforths quite early and veered north-east towards the Australian sector, the Bays ran into minefields and were shelled by enemy anti-tank guns, some reputedly 88mms, lost six Shermans and promptly pulled back, veered south and ran into the 9th Lancers; together they edged their way carefully forward through the mine-fields, their sappers walking in front, guiding them roughly along the axis between the Highland Division and the Australians. Only the 10th Hussars kept contact with the Seaforths and were thus well away to the south, but nevertheless Brigadier Fisher, still under the impression that his brigade had started out from a position some 3,000 or more yards further west than it actually had, felt that the movements of his squadrons justified an evening report to the effect that two of his regiments were at last on their final objective – the northern hinge of the Pierson Line – with one slightly behind. They were in fact still well short of it and, having lost in all some twenty Shermans between them, they withdrew another 500 yards after dark.

But with his main armoured brigade reputedly out past the Oxalic Line, General Briggs, commanding the 1st Armoured Division, brought forward the riflemen of the 7th Motor Brigade, and by midnight they were closing up behind the forward positions.

The Australians and the Highlanders might have known different, but from the reports reaching General Montgomery during the evening of October 24th, he had every reason to believe that matters were progressing very satisfactorily in the northern corridor.

He did not, however, feel the same confidence in matters further south.

Crises caused by lack of communication will also be magnified by basic misunderstandings on the part of one or other of those concerned, especially if no attempt can be made to clear up that misunderstanding.

General Lumsden was the senior armoured commander in Montgomery's army at that time and, as has been mentioned, relations between them were cold almost to the point of being glacial. Not only were there differences in personality and upbringing to cause misunderstanding between the two men, but the distaste and scorn which Lumsden would seem to have felt for Montgomery at the time of Alam Halfa had undergone a change during the interval – and not a change for the better. According to an officer who saw a lot of both of them,

> Herbert Lumsden had very great abilities, there's no question about it – but the effect on Herbert Lumsden of Monty was like a stoat on a rabbit. He'd freeze up, become . . . not himself; and Monty saw him in this frozen-up state. Herbert was scared stiff of Monty.[6]

This was no condition in which the commander of the Eighth Army's main striking force could explain certain inalienable facts to the Army Commander, especially as the latter's misunderstanding of those facts would seem to have been of long duration.

During the First World War – the last time that Montgomery had been connected in any way with massed armour launched against strong defensive positions – the main and indeed original purpose for armour had been to protect infantry against machine-gun and rifle fire. Against such fire, tanks were invulnerable and apart from mechanical breakdown only the hastily adapted tactics of the German artillery ever stopped them. Throughout the British Army, therefore – with the exception of the armoured units themselves – the belief had been fostered that the role of armour in such a battle as Alamein was to lead and protect the infantry, who would follow up and consolidate ground won. And although the existence of minefields had necessitated an initial reversal of the leading roles, once the XXX Corps infantry reached the Oxalic Line and the sappers had cleared the minefields behind it, it was thought that the armour should have little difficulty in breaking out.

This was the philosophy behind the scheme to launch X Corps out on to the Pierson Line and then further forward towards Skinflint; but it took little account of the development of specialised anti-tank guns and formations, and of the training of both German and Italian field artillery in the same role. Lumsden was well aware of the dangers which would face his armour once they attempted to move out past the front infantry line, and he said so – somewhat elliptically – to Freyberg:

Playing with armour is like playing with fire. You have got to take your time about it. It is like a duel. If you don't take your time you will get run through the guts. It is not for tanks to take on guns.[7]

As it happened this was a conclusion to which Freyberg himself was also coming, as were those other Commonwealth commanders who had seen much of the desert fighting, and during the daylight hours of October 24th considerable doubts grew in the minds of the XXX Corps divisional commanders as to the ability of the X Corps armour to break out, even at this second attempt, unless their own infantry cleared the ground before them of all enemy artillery. And even had there been time to set up such an operation, there were hardly enough infantry left to carry it out, especially in view of the 'crumbling' battles they would then be expected to fight.

There was also far too little co-ordination between the staffs of the New Zealand infantry and its attached armour (of XXX Corps) and of the 8th and 24th Armoured Brigades (of X Corps), both of whom were expected to attack the enemy from adjacent sectors though in different directions.

The plan called for a programme of timed artillery concentrations starting at 2200, dropping at first just in front of the right hand, 5th New Zealand Brigade positions, and then extending in front of the advancing armour until both brigades of X Corps were on the positions along the Pierson Line, running north–south some 3,000 yards to the west. Meanwhile, the New Zealand artillery would fire a creeping barrage from the left hand, 6th New Zealand Brigade area, to the south – and behind this the New Zealand Cavalry and the remains of John Currie's 9th Armoured Brigade would advance and from a protective screen running west–east from the southern end of the Pierson Line back to the infantry positions at the bottom of Miteiriya Ridge. The supporting infantry of 10th Armoured Division – 133rd Lorried Infantry Brigade – would come up and take over the positions held by 5th New Zealand Brigade on the right, who would then be free to follow their own armour southwards in the exploitation role ordered by Montgomery, while the 133rd infantry then followed their own armour out towards the Pierson Line.

It is difficult to believe that even with the state of training to which Montgomery had brought the Eighth Army by that time, so complicated a series of manoeuvres could have been successfully carried out, even with the closest possible co-operation between all brigade and divisional staffs concerned. As it was, both Gatehouse and his tactical headquarters were so mobile that Freyberg was unable to make much more than fleeting contact during the afternoon with his fellow divisional commander in the operation, while Gatehouse's divisional headquarters were so far back that the staff there were often unaware of latest developments and thus unable to make valid decisions even when news of those developments arrived via first XXX Corps and then X Corps H.Q.s.

As the afternoon wore on and doubts as to the viability of the plans for the night's operations grew in Freyberg's mind, he warned his 5th Brigade commander that he expected considerable delays in the programme, and shortly after dusk rang General Leese and, to quote from the *Official History of New Zealand in the Second World War*, 'started an argument that has echoed down the years'.

The operation could not be a success, said Freyberg, because the 10th Armoured Division was not 'properly set up' and was in any case being commanded from too far back – which was perhaps an unfair reflection upon Gatehouse's character but not upon the administration for which he was responsible. Leese, worried by such a report from so highly regarded a source, managed to make contact with Lumsden and tactfully pass on the warning – and was further worried by Lumsden's reaction, which was rather to the effect that as neither he nor anyone else high in the armoured command had much confidence in the plans for the night's operations, he was not surprised at Freyberg's comments. By the time Leese had thought matters over and decided he should report all this to Army Head-quarters, Montgomery had retired for the night and de Guingand absorbed the information himself, hoping that news would improve as the night wore on.

If anything, it got worse.

As soon as dusk fell the whole of Miteiriya Ridge became a scene of intense activity and, as command was so divided, soon one of equally intense confusion. On the forward slope, XXX Corps in-fantrymen and heavy weapons crews emerged both to stretch cramped limbs and, more urgently, to try to improve their defences; from immediately behind them supply parties hurried to and fro across the crest ferrying food, water and ammunition to their comrades in the front line, and soon they found themselves part of a growing, busy throng as X Corps sappers with their own infantry covering parties began clearing more lanes for the armoured advance, due to start shortly after 2200. And the situation of everyone there was soon much complicated as the Axis gunners, having spent the late afternoon and early evening restocking the ammunition dumps and resting their crews, opened fire on the ridge in the confidence that their exertions would not be wasted. Having spent the day in apparent inactivity, what could the British armour do except attempt to come over the top that night?

Time did nothing to improve the situation. The New Zealand sappers had gone forward as early as possible to clear the gaps for their Divisional Cavalry on their drive south, but were delayed by the enemy artillery and were thus still out working when their own guns opened up with the covering barrage, mortally wounding their commander and causing some other casualties. It also fell on some of the most forward infantry positions and thoroughly disorganised one company of the 26th Battalion which, not surprisingly, retired precipitately and was unavailable as a fighting force for some hours.

But two squadrons of the Cavalry did get out and their Bren-gun carriers and light tanks moved slowly through the gaps, out past the minefields and despite small-arms fire, occasional anti-tank fire and the loss of a couple of tanks on scattered mines, one of the squadrons pushed south nearly two miles before halting to await support.

Unfortunately for them, their supporting armour from 9th Armoured Brigade were blocked by the movements of one of the 8th Armoured Brigade regiments – the Staffordshire Yeomanry – who instead of first moving behind the ridge and down through a gap on the right, found the gap through the left-hand 26th Battalion area and used that. Their Crusaders drove across the intended route of the 9th Brigade and reached a spot about 500 yards clear of the minefield, but in a south-westerly, not westerly, direction; and then they too halted to await their fellow squadrons from their own brigade.

But by now, Brigadier Currie, anxious to get his heavier tanks out to support the divisional cavalry, and furious at the blocking of their intended route, had personally reconnoitred a path over the crest and around the edge of a minefield, and sent the Grants and Shermans of the 3rd Hussars off, followed after a short delay by the Warwickshire Yeomanry. The first formation these came across was the Staffordshire Yeomanry, whom they helped to clear up some machine-gun posts and sent off to the west, while they themselves drew away south-westwards and eventually made contact with the cavalry.

Meanwhile, the second regiment of 8th Armoured Brigade, the Nottinghamshire Yeomanry, had been trying to get out and join the Staffordshires, but their soft-skinned supply columns had come up first on the left behind the ridge where they turned to await their heavy squadrons coming up further to the right. Unfortunately, they had hardly pulled to a halt when a random enemy shell or mortar-bomb hit one of the leading vehicles which happened to be carrying petrol. The flames spread rapidly through the columns as the vehicles were packed nose to tail and also double banked, and the resultant inferno attracted the attentions of practically every enemy gun and aircraft in the vicinity. Soon some twenty-five lorries were ablaze, petrol drums and tanks exploding, small-arms ammunition crackling furiously, mortar-bombs and shells erupting in a pyro-technic display as spectacular as it was disastrous. Valiant attempts were made to drive some of the rear vehicles clear, but as several of these promptly blew up on mines bordering the cleared gaps, most of the vehicles were reduced to smoking wrecks by morning.

Needless to say, the holocaust effectively halted the advance of the tanks of the Notts Yeomanry, who in their turn blocked the advance of the third regiment of 8th Armoured Brigade – the 3rd R.T.R. – and in the circumstances and especially in view of the attention the flames were attracting, Brigadier Custance ordered both formations to disperse as much as they could and await further instructions.

As for the movements of 24th Armoured Brigade, the squadrons of both of their leading regiments – 41st and 47th R.T.R. – had already been dispersed as confusion had overtaken their mine-clearance force. It would seem that these had at first begun clearing a gap through the wrong minefield, then lost contact with their reconnaissance party which, although they had advanced through the correct minefield, had come under heavy fire and promptly retired. As a result the sappers did not commence their appointed task until nearly an hour after they were supposed to have completed it, and even then they soon abandoned it when mistaken warning of an enemy counter-attack through their area reached their commanding officer. As he led his men back up towards the crest, he then lost contact with both his own infantry covering party and also his wireless truck.

It was a most unfortunate chapter of accidents, in view of which it is hardly surprising that at about midnight Freyberg rang Leese to say that as far as he could see 10th Armoured Division were sitting about doing nothing, or that shortly afterwards Custance rang Gatehouse to suggest that in view of the evident disorganisation of his brigade, the advance should be abandoned. Gatehouse passed this message on to Lumsden with the recommendation that it should be accepted, and it seems that Freyberg overheard it and again rang Leese . . . who then reported the whole matter to de Guingand.

In fact de Guingand had already received a call from Lumsden to the effect that as both his divisional and brigade commanders felt that the armoured attack for that night should be called off, he, Lumsden, was inclined to agree; and in the circumstances de Guingand felt that the occasion had arisen when one of the Army Commander's strictest edicts must be disregarded. Telling both Leese and Lumsden that they should report to Army Tactical Headquarters at 0330, he went along to General Montgomery's caravan and woke him up.

Presumably General Leese went along to the conference worried about the situation in general, but confident that little fault would be found with the performance of his own command. General Lumsden, however, must have viewed the immediate prospects with reluctance and his own long-term prospects with foreboding – although possibly by this time he would have welcomed any opportunity to leave Montgomery's command.

They found the Army Commander sitting in front of newly marked-up maps, showing the reported positions of the crucial formations in XXX Corps's sector. On the right, the known Australian positions showed the firm holding of the northern corner of the Oxalic Line – but also the main strength of 1st Armoured Division out through Kidney and thus on to the top end of the Pierson Line. Montgomery's inference that their infantry support from the 7th Motor Brigade was at that moment either out with the armour or was closing up to it – and that both armoured and infantry brigades must be under heavy attack – was thus so reasonable that no one challenged it.

In the extreme south of the sector, according to reports, matters were also going well, with the New Zealand Cavalry and the 9th Armoured Brigade out on their intended objectives, and the New Zealand infantry poised to commence their southward exploitation. Only along the length of the Miteiriya Ridge did the map indicate any difficulties, where 10th Armoured Division were stuck and their commander, General Gatehouse, apparently unable to drive his squadrons out into the battle.

But overall, the situation looked by no means hopeless and both Leese and Lumsden gave their own opinions on the battle's progress without, apparently, contradicting any of the assumptions shown on the map. Inevitably, Lumsden found himself defending Gatehouse and, indeed, repeating his divisional commander's arguments of the morning to Freyberg. Later, Montgomery was to record in his diary:

> Gatehouse had said that he did not care about the operation and that if he did get out he would be in a very unpleasant position on the forward slopes of the Miteriya [sic] Ridge; his Division was untrained and not fit for such difficult operations; he wanted to stay where he was. Lumsden was inclined to agree with Gatehouse.[8]

From Lumsden's previous utterances it seems likely that that last sentence was something of an understatement, but whatever arguments were put up by the X Corps commander they were of no avail. Quietly but firmly Montgomery insisted that the plan would be adhered to, the armour must break out over the ridge, reach the Pierson Line and shield the infantry during their 'crumbling' operations. He then dismissed Leese, and

> spoke very plainly to Lumsden and said I would have no departure of any sort from my original plan and orders; I was determined that the armour would get out from the minefield area and out into the open where it could manoeuvre; any wavering or lack of firmness now might be fatal; if Gatehouse, or any other commander, was not 'for it' and began to weaken, then I would replace him in command at once.[9]

There are different versions of exactly what happened next, but it would seem that while the conference had been going on, Gatehouse, still awaiting a decision from Lumsden regarding his request made some three hours before that the attack across Miteiriya be abandoned, made his way back from the ridge where he had spent most of his time since his armour had reached it, to his Divisional Headquarters still back near the Springbok Track.

Here he at last made contact with Lumsden who told him of the recent meeting and the Army Commander's inflexible demand that Gatehouse's brigades cross the ridge, make their way down through the minefields and out on to their designated positions on the Pierson Line; and this order Gatehouse refused to accept or obey. As he wrote later, Gatehouse then had no course but to report his attitude direct to Montgomery by telephone, which he did, apparently opening the conversation with the unlikely query, 'What the hell's going on here?'

In the tense atmosphere brought about first by the circumstances, secondly by the anger which Gatehouse undoubtedly felt at what he considered to be the misuse of his armour, and thirdly by the annoyance his opening remarks and general lack of deference almost certainly caused Montgomery, there was ample opportunity for misunderstanding – compounded almost immediately by Montgomery's accusation that Gatehouse was fighting his battle from far too far back, and must immediately move himself and his headquarters up closer to the front. To the end of his days, Montgomery insisted that he had ordered Gatehouse to adhere to the original plan and get his armour out on to the Pierson Line; but Gatehouse was equally insistent that the Army Commander had at last seen the danger of sending six armoured regiments clanking downwards through an unlifted minefield at night, to find themselves in open country at dawn – and had agreed that only one regiment should attempt it. This should be the Staffordshires who were already out and could stay there, protecting the right flank of the New Zealand Cavalry and the 9th Armoured Brigade.

Presumably as a result of these misunderstandings, four hours later Montgomery wrote that all was now well, with both 2nd Armoured Brigade and 24th in position on the Pierson Line, one regiment of 8th Armoured Brigade out and on its way to its position on the left of the 24th and the returned flank on the left firmly held by Freyberg's armour.

It was to be some hours before he was disabused of this optimistic impression.

In the absence of General Gatehouse from the area of Miteiriya Ridge it is hardly surprising that the strongest personality in the area became invested with the aura of command over all present . . . and in the circumstances Bernard Freyberg was hardly likely to deny himself any opportunity to push X Corps armour out to assist his own, XXX Corps, infantry.

What influence he brought to bear on Brigadier Custance is impossible now to assess, but the latter, having received no firm reply to his request to be allowed to abandon the advance, was by 0230 reassembling the two regiments of his brigade still behind the ridge, and urging them out in support of the Staffordshires. By 0330 the leading formations of 3rd R.T.R. were feeling their way out through the mine-gaps in the area of the 6th New Zealand Brigade on the left and from then until 0500 both their tanks and those of the Nottingham-shire Yeomanry 'streamed out' to the southwest. By the time greyness was spreading into daylight from the ridge behind them, the 3rd R.T.R. were beginning to fill the gap between the Staffs and the 3rd Hussars of Currie's 9th Armoured Brigade, while the Notts Yeomanry were following through and swinging up to the right as they cleared the minefields.

There was also a lot of movement at the western edge of the ridge. Brigadier Kenchington, commanding the R.T.R. regiments of 24th Armoured Brigade, had remained largely in ignorance of the con-ference and arguments which had been taking place at high level and, in the absence of any contrary instructions, was still intent upon getting his 83 Shermans and 48 Crusaders out and on to the Pierson Line, however much behind time they might be.

By about 0400 reports came to him that at least one gap was clear through the main minefield on the right, and soon after 0500 his leading squadrons, hastily assembled from their dispersed positions, came over the crest of the ridge and down the forward slope. Their objective was some 3,000 yards in front of them, and they were intended to link with 2nd Armoured Brigade on the right and the Notts Yeomanry of the 8th Armoured Brigade on their left – so when, as the light grew, they saw large numbers of Shermans and Crusaders grouped some two miles away to the north, they assumed, correctly, that these were the tanks of the 2nd Armoured Brigade and, incorrectly, that they were all now on Pierson.

Moreover, less than 1,000 yards to their left they could see the Staffordshires moving out of a hollow in which they had evidently spent the night and, in company with the first Grants of the 3rd R.T.R. to arrive, advancing slowly to the west. Although the tank crews of the 24th Armoured Brigade could not see them, on the extreme left flank of those advancing Grants were some Shermans of the 3rd Hussars, the right hand formation of Currie's 9th Armoured Brigade, the other units of which were facing roughly south. Behind Currie's tanks, the lightly armoured Stuarts and carriers of the New

Zealand Cavalry were prudently retiring to the shelter of the ridge.

But the move of 8th Armoured Brigade to reach their positions at the southern end of Pierson was not to go unchallenged. Random mines claimed three of the Hussars' tanks and accurate anti-tank fire quickly reduced six of the Staffordshires' Crusaders to blazing wrecks . . . and it was while this was happening that Gatehouse's order to Custance that only one regiment of the brigade should be sent forward and the other two retained behind the ridge, at last got through.

By 0615 those orders had reached the regiments themselves and, to quote from the New Zealand *Official History*:

> . . . through some misunderstanding all three obeyed the latter part of the order with such alacrity that by seven o'clock the whole of 8th Armoured Brigade was in cover of the ridge, while several tanks of 3rd Hussars in error conformed with the withdrawal.[10]

They had withdrawn laterally across the rear of the remaining squadrons of the 3rd Hussars and of the other regiment of Currie's command, the Warwickshire Yeomanry (the Royal Wiltshire Yeomanry, after their ordeal during the opening twenty-four hours of battle, had handed over their few remaining tanks to the Warwickshires and retired from the fray), and these were thus to find themselves as the sun came up with their right flank unsupported, and spread out in a long arc facing south-west and south in low ground overlooked by enemy artillery. However, as there did not for the moment seem to be any well-organised opposition immediately ahead, John Currie decided that his safest course would be to assume the offensive and move further forward – an admirable decision foiled only by the fact that he was now short of both fuel and ammunition.

His suggestion to Freyberg that he should send his squadron back behind the ridge for re-supply was accompanied by the revelation (to Freyberg) that 9th Armoured Brigade were once again out front on their own, and as Freyberg's attempts to obtain information about the intentions of 10th Armoured Division were proving unsatisfactory, Currie was ordered to remain where he was for the moment, in order 'to discourage enemy counter-attacks' – a duty at which 9th Armoured Brigade proved successful, as none developed while they were there.

By now it was nearly 0800 on the morning of October 25th, and Montgomery, back in the Army Headquarters and still confident that his orders were being satisfactorily carried out, issued more detailed instructions for the employment of the X Corps armour. Having now reportedly broken out through the minefields and reached the

Pierson Line, it was 'to locate and destroy the enemy's armoured battle groups, and to ensure that the operations of the New Zealand Division south-west of the Miteiriya Ridge were not interfered with by enemy armour from the west'.

Three hours later, still with the assurance from the commander of the 1st Armoured Division, General Briggs, that 2nd Armoured Brigade were actually on the northern end of Pierson and that 24th Armoured Brigade were in contact on their left – and unaware that 8th Armoured Brigade had retired behind the ridge – Montgomery issued the next round of orders.

In the north, Briggs was to take over command of 24th Armoured Brigade which then with his own 2nd Armoured Brigade would 'act offensively against any enemy armoured battle groups' they encountered; in the south, all three regiments of 8th Armoured Brigade were to form a line down to the junction with 9th Armoured Brigade which would continue to face southwards, holding the flank. Gatehouse would command all this southern armour, the 5th New Zealand Brigade would follow down and support 9th Armoured Brigade in their exploitation to the south, and Brigadier Lee was to confirm his 133rd Brigade as present to hold the vacated positions along the ridge.

These orders were issued at 1030, after which Montgomery turned his attention from such purely tactical matters to confer with his superior officer, General Alexander, who had arrived to pay him a visit and collect the next list of Montgomery's requirements – and it was while these talks were in progress that the news arrived from XIII Corps's area that the 7th Armoured Division had been unable to penetrate the February minefield, and the subsequent decision made not to pursue that particular objective.

Other news arrived, too. With daylight Brigadier Fisher had at last been forced to accept that his 2nd Armoured Brigade was not, in fact, on the end of the Pierson Line, and that Kidney was still at least 1,000 yards further on to the west; and in an endeavour to correct the situation he sent both the Bays and the 9th Lancers further forward and at last out beyond the front infantry defences. They had hardly reached the edge of Kidney when they found themselves under 88mm. fire, the Bays lost eight Shermans in as many minutes, the Lancers lost two Crusaders and attempts by the third regiment of the brigade, the 10th Hussars, to outflank the enemy gun positions faded in the face of evidence of enemy counter-attack.

Soon 2nd Armoured Brigade were once again back behind the Oxalic Line . . . and on this occasion accurate reports were quickly in Montgomery's hands. By the time the Army Commander bade farewell to Alexander, he was aware of the fact that some of his plans were not going quite as well as he had believed; and having arrived at

Freyberg's headquarters at 1130 and listened to the latest reports from Lumsden and Leese, who had both been summoned there, he had by noon learned that other parts were also in disarray.

Despite the successes which had attended the infantry, it seemed that the armour were still unable to break out and perform their shielding role. Whether it was a case of 'could not' or 'would not' was for the moment immaterial – what mattered now was that the battle was 'fizzling out', all momentum was dying and unless something was done to enliven it again the enemy would be given time to stiffen what defences were still in their hands and build new ones; in which case the tasks carried out since the evening of October 23rd would all have to be done again.

Those present were agreed that this must not be allowed to happen, and three of the four – Freyberg, despite his junior rank compared with that of Leese, Lumsden and Montgomery, was also in attendance – felt that the correct solution would be a continuation of the battle by the same methods as used so far. The proposed exploitation to the south by the New Zealanders should for the moment be postponed, and instead another massive artillery and infantry attack should be mounted to clear the ground in front of XXX Corps for another 4,000 yards, in the hope that the armour might then be able to break out from there.

But Montgomery disagreed. Such a course would be too obvious, and it almost smacked of dancing to the enemy's tune; it certainly smacked of reinforcing failure instead of success.

An entirely different approach to the battle must be adopted, directed along an entirely different axis. New factors must be introduced.

One new factor was, in fact, already being introduced, but on the other side of the line. Generalfeldmarschall Rommel was returning to take command of the Panzerarmee Afrika.

5 · *Pause for Reflection*

During the first fifteen minutes of the Battle of Alamein, the known German and Italian gun positions opposite the XXX Corps front had each received nearly one hundred 4.5- or 5.5-inch shells or their equivalent weight in 25-pounders, and although this concentration caused relatively few casualties in men, it smashed a large number of the guns and wrecked the main Panzerarmee communications. Moreover, the Wellingtons which soon arrived overhead were equipped to jam the Axis wireless in addition to dropping their bombs and so, once the main barrage preceding the infantry attack began and the thick pall of smoke and sand cloaked the area, the only information to come back was brought by German runners – usually wounded – and this was, obviously, fragmented and extremely limited.

There was no word at all from any of the forward Italian positions, for although many of them had fought bravely, they tended to disintegrate immediately they attempted withdrawal. Those right at the front were all either killed or captured and at least one Italian regiment – the 62nd of the Trento Division – seemed virtually to have disappeared. The German front-line infantry also suffered severely as a large part of the 382nd Regiment of Lungershausen's 164th Division had been overrun, but as the night wore on it became evident that most of the posts back in the main defensive area were not only still in existence, but were defending themselves stoutly.

At Panzerarmee Headquarters on the coast near El Daba, therefore, there was for some hours ignorance as to the extent of the enemy penetration of the minefields, and doubt even as to whether the thrust in the north by the Eighth Army was the main one or, as many thought, only a feint. General Stumme had thus to spend some hours drawing deeply upon his reserves of experience and self-confidence, exhibiting his normal calm to all with whom he came into contact despite the mighty sounds of battle which came thundering in from just a few miles away to the east. He did, however, refuse permission for either German or Italian artillery to reply to the

British bombardment by shelling probable enemy concentration areas, only too well aware of the fact that his slender reserves of ammunition did not allow for wastage should he have been deceived and the areas empty.

It would be time enough to reply in force to the enemy assault when he had gathered evidence of Montgomery's real intentions, and it was with this in mind that he left his main headquarters shortly after dawn to visit 90th Light Division's Tactical H.Q. along the road to Sidi Abd el Rahman. To Westphal's suggestion that he should follow Rommel's example and take with him both an escort and a signals truck, he replied jovially that he would not be long and that he certainly would not venture into danger; his driver and Oberst Buechting from the staff would be all the company he required, and his car adequate to carry them.

But at 90th Light H.Q. Stumme found that the situation was just as obscure as it had been further west, although there was news from 15th Panzer H.Q. away to the south-east. Here, apparently, 115th Panzergrenadiers were heavily engaged – with Scotsmen it was thought – and there was also news of more panzergrenadiers even further south in action against New Zealand troops. However, reports were still somewhat vague and uncertain, so Stumme decided that an investigation further forward was both justified and safe.

In this he was mistaken. Shortly after setting out, the car came suddenly under machine-gun fire so accurate that Oberst Buechting in the back was immediately killed by a burst through the head. The driver, with admirable despatch, swung the car around and headed back at high speed, and it was not until he arrived at 90th Light H.Q. that Obergefreiter Wolf realised that his only passenger was the dead Buechting, and that General Stumme, whom he had last seen standing on the running-board and hanging on to the rear door, was no longer present.

Parties were immediately sent out to find the missing general but they all ran into enemy fire, and soon the message was passed back to Westphal that the Commander-in-Chief had been either killed or taken prisoner. Until such time as his successor was appointed, Westphal was once more *de facto* commander of the Axis armies facing the main enemy in North Africa, and his experience in similar circumstances during the previous year can have done little to console him. As it was, a shadowy picture of the battle was at last emerging from the darkness and confusion, and he could only hope that by the time it became clearer, someone else would have arrived to take the relevant decisions.

According to reports at last coming in from 15th Panzer Division, an Italian and a German battalion had disappeared completely in the northern sector, 'wiped out', according to one report, 'by drunken negroes with tanks', while to the south violent battles were being fought by both Italians and Germans against the Scotsmen. From the Miteiriya Ridge area came confused reports that the ridge itself had been lost, that tanks were already attacking positions in front of it but that positions were still held on the eastern face by some of the 164th Division stalwarts; and that when 15th Panzer units had come up against their first Sherman, they had been impressed by its size and apparent invulnerability, and shaken by its fire-power.

During the late morning came news from the southern front that enemy tanks in large numbers had penetrated the forward minefield and overwhelmed many of the Folgore units, but that other Folgore units nearby with men from the Ramcke Brigade were available for counter-attack. They were awaiting orders but in view of the mass of armour which the British had thrown in in the south, it could still be that here was where Montgomery intended the main breakthrough to take place, so care must be exercised not to waste force in small packets. Certainly 21st Panzer and the Ariete must remain where they were.

This was the picture which had emerged by the time when, to Westphal's relief, General der Panzertruppe Wilhelm Ritter von Thoma arrived during the afternoon from Deutsches Afrika Korps Headquarters to take command in Stumme's absence – and Westphal had some sympathy for the new Commander-in-Chief's explosion of anger when the picture was exhibited. To von Thoma's startled eyes, he appeared to be taking over a static line which had already been breached in several places, with no mobile reserve in hand which could be moved up to seal those breaches – and to a man trained lately in Rommel's tactics and anyway of Rommel's temperament, this was inexplicable.

But for the moment, explanations must wait. Whatever the situation, counter-attack was essential in at least one area, and to ensure that it was carried out speedily and with utmost force, von Thoma immediately left Panzerarmee Headquarters for 15th Panzer, to organise and oversee a thrust by the 8th Panzer Regiment towards the area in the northern sector which all his tactical instincts told him would be crucial.

He was not at that time to know that other eyes had marked that area down, too; one set naming it Kidney and the other Aberdeen.

Rommel had by this time been at a convalescent home at Semmering in the mountains near Vienna for nearly three weeks, and although every comfort had been heaped upon him together with the devotion of the extremely competent medical staff – and the presence of his wife and son – it had been by no means a time of unalloyed relaxation. His mind too often returned to the desert which had

1 The Cairo Conference, August 5th, 1942: (front row) Field Marshal Smuts,
Winston Churchill, General Sir Claude Auchinleck, General Sir Archibald Wavell;
(back row) Air Chief Marshal Sir Arthur Tedder, General Sir Alan Brooke,
Admiral Sir Henry Harwood, the Rt Hon. Richard Casey

2 Revitalised command: Winston Churchill with Generals Alexander and Montgomery in the desert, August 23rd, 1942

3 After Alam Halfa: Brigadier 'Pip' Roberts introduces an Italian prisoner (far left) to an unimpressed General Montgomery. Wearing the topee is Mr Wendell Wilkie, President Roosevelt's personal representative.

4 Lieutenant-General Montgomery with his corps commanders, Lieutenant-Generals Leese (XXX Corps), Lumsden (X Corps) and Horrocks (XIII Corps)

5 Lieutenant-General Leese (second from right) with his divisional commanders, Major-Generals Morshead (9th Australian), Wimberley (51st Highland) and Pienaar (1st South African)

6 General Montgomery in the Grant tank from which he watched the progress of the battle

7 Montgomery with the two corps commanders whose formations were to advance over the same ground, at night and shrouded in dust; even had they been close friends there would have been difficulties

8 One of the Shermans that tipped the balance

9-10 Some of the men who commanded the tanks (Major-General Alec Gatehouse
   on the right) . . . not always to the satisfaction of the Army Commander

11–12 Throughout the battle it was always the infantry who had to take – and hold – the ground

13-14 After Alamein Montgomery wrote, 'We could not have won the battle in
twelve days without that magnificent Australian Division'

15 Hollow triumph: Rommel about to receive his baton from the Führer,
September 30th, 1942

16 Manifest defeat: General von Thoma reports to General Montgomery after his
capture, November 4th, 1942

occupied it so completely for the last eighteen months, and to the men who had served under his command and who now stood in such danger.

He could read the reality behind the euphoria of the news broadcasts and the daily newspaper headlines, and even more clearly see through the cheerful optimism which bubbled across the surface of the letters he received from Westphal and Stumme, especially when they obviously avoided answering certain specific questions he had asked in his own letters to them. He was, as he later wrote, 'incapable of attaining real peace of mind', and as conscious as everyone else connected with the Panzerarmee of the approach at the end of October of the full moon period.

But perhaps, as most intelligence reports had indicated, another month would go by before Montgomery was ready?

During the afternoon of October 24th he was disabused of this hope. Generalfeldmarschall Keitel, Hitler's chief sycophant on the O.K.W. staff, rang up to inform Rommel that the long-awaited assault had opened the previous evening, that the British were attacking with unprecedented force both on the ground and in the air, and that General Stumme had disappeared. Was Rommel well enough to return to the desert and take up again the reins of command?

No one who knew Rommel could have doubted the answer, but the next few hours were spent in deep anxiety as Keitel would certainly not take the responsibility for such an important order himself. But in the evening the telephone rang again and this time it was the Führer himself on the line: could Rommel start for Africa immediately? He was to ring Führerhauptquartier before taking off in case the situation should have eased, but in the meantime urgency was the note for all action.

Rommel drove immediately to Wiener Neustadt where his airplane had been ordered for 0700 the following day, and before midnight the Führer had called him again to confirm that his presence was obviously vital at El Alamein. He was at Rome by 1100 on October 25th (by which time Montgomery was at Freyberg's headquarters recasting his plans), listening grimly to the latest news from von Rintelin. 'I knew there were no more laurels to be earned in Africa,' he was to write later of his return to the desert, 'for I had been told in the reports from my officers that supplies had fallen far short of my minimum demands.'[1]

He crossed the Mediterranean via Crete to Qasaba, continued the journey in his faithful Storch and arrived at Panzerarmee H.Q. just after dusk – to take up the battle again 'with small hope of success'.

General Stumme's body in the meantime had been found, alongside the track leading forward from 90th Light Division H.Q.

Apparently he had hung on to the side of the car for as long as possible after Wolf had turned it around, but then suffered a heart attack (his blood pressure had really been too high for tropical service) either before or immediately after falling off. It is doubtful whether his sudden death gave the British any great advantage, for it took place so early in the battle that the time had not been reached for vital new decisions; and anyway, German staff efficiency had quickly filled the breach.

But there were, of course, far too many other breaches which even German staff efficiency could not fill. They could do nothing about the fact that there was apparently only three days' petrol issue available instead of the thirty days' supply which in the circumstances would be necessary if defeat were to be averted. They could do nothing about the fact that after a day spent on limited counter-attacks 15th Panzer Division had only 31 panzers still fit for action, and that recovery teams were finding it almost impossible to carry out their duties in the face of the storm of fire which swept the operational area at the slightest signs of movement upon it; or the fact that the overwhelming superiority of the enemy artillery, augmented as it was so frequently by air bombardment, was having its effect upon the morale of even the German element.

> I slept only a few hours and was back in my command vehicle at 0500 October 26th, where I learnt that the British had spent the whole night assaulting our front under cover of their artillery, which in some places had fired as many as five hundred rounds for every one of ours. Strong forces of the panzer divisions were already committed in the front line. British night-bombers had been over our units continuously. Shortly before midnight the enemy had succeeded in taking Hill 28, an important position in the northern sector.[2]

Rommel drove first of all out towards the scene of this latest attack – a relatively small and gentle rise which, however, in that flat and desolate landscape gave observation over what was evidently going to be a crucial area in the days to come. Elements of both Littorio and 15th Panzer had attempted piecemeal counter-attacks against the position, but already the enemy were well dug in with their heavy weapons to hand so it would be necessary to launch a concerted attack to regain the position.

Orders were issued, the 90th Light Division and Rommel's own *Kampfstaffel* brought up to help; and under Rommel's personal direction the attack went in at 1500 – immediately to be blanketed under a concentration of fire which reminded Rommel of his days on the Western Front twenty-five years before. Soon all his assault force was halted and taking refuge in whatever cover they could find – at which the guns ceased their thundering and bombers arrived overhead to make the position even more precarious; and from then on at least eighteen bombers arrived once an hour to keep up the pressure. An attempt by Italian and German dive-bombers to attack enemy supply columns and give reassurance to the unhappy Axis troops failed tragically; attacked by some sixty Allied fighters the Italians jettisoned their bombs over their own lines and the Germans were caught over their target by an intensity of anti-aircraft fire never seen before in Africa.

Sick at heart, Rommel returned to his command truck and then to his headquarters where Westphal had been preparing the latest intelligence reports.

From them, Rommel came to one specific conclusion and upon it decided to take a major risk. Despite the previous opinion registered by his intelligence staff, he came to the conclusion that Montgomery's main assault was concentrated in the north; he would now order 21st Panzer Division, part of the Ariete and most of the southern artillery to come northwards to help seal off the enemy drives. If he was wrong, the move would have eaten up much precious petrol – but in this regard Westphal could provide a modicum of good news. The tanker *Proserpina* with 2,500 tons of petrol aboard was due in Tobruk the following day, followed closely by the *Tergesta* with another 1,000 tons of fuel and 1,000 tons of ammunition; this would give him an extra six days' supply under battle conditions, more if he could divine exactly where his panzers should go at any particular time.

The petrol could also give him a little more room to manoeuvre. Surely he could still rely upon slowness of thought at British command level, and upon the inability of British armour to fight a mobile battle? With all his panzer forces in the north, perhaps he should allow the British tanks to come through the minefields and then smash them in a battle of manoeuvre in the area south of El Daba? It would certainly be a better idea than throwing his main force into the battle area *en masse* in an attempt to regain lost ground, for there they would be subject to both British artillery and British bombing.

His evening report to the Führer's H.Q. again stressed the danger to the entire Axis army unless there was an improvement in the supply situation, but his letter to Dearest Lu, though regretting the shortness of their time together, was by no means despairing.

But the night of October 26th/27th was even noisier than the previous one. Relays of British bombers flew along the coast road, circled the battle area, found the 21st Panzer Division on its northward move and seriously delayed it, though casualties were light; and at 0200, yet another furious barrage opened along the northern sector of the front and the sky grew 'bright with the glare of muzzle-flashes and shell-bursts'.

By dawn it became evident that the enemy had improved their

position around Hill 28, and were also attacking again at their original break-in point to the south-west (around Kidney). During the morning Rommel drove down the Telegraph Track to behind Tel el Aqqaqir and watched the unending barrage, the continually repeated air bombings, anxiously awaiting news of the arrival of his panzers from the south and considering their best employment.

This proved to be a waste of mental energy. During the morning had come the dreadful news that both *Proserpina* and *Tergesta* had been bombed and sunk, the former just outside Tobruk.

> At 1430 I drove to Telegraph Track again, accompanied by Major Ziegler. Three times within a quarter of an hour units of the 90th Light Division, which had deployed and were standing in the open in preparation for the attack, were bombed by formations of eighteen aircraft. At 1500 our dive-bombers swooped down on the British lines. Every artillery and anti-aircraft gun which we had in the northern sector concentrated a violent fire on the point of the intended attack. Then the armour moved forward. A murderous British fire struck into our ranks and our attack was soon brought to a halt by an immensely powerful anti-tank defence, mainly from dug-in anti-tank guns and a large number of tanks. We suffered considerable losses and were obliged to withdraw. There is, in general, little chance of success in a tank attack over country where the enemy has been able to take up defensive positions; but there was nothing else we could do.[3]

Only seventy tons of petrol arrived that day – flown in by the Luftwaffe – and this was hardly enough to move the newly arriving formations into positions from which they might block further enemy attempts to break out. So far from enticing the British armour forward into a mobile battle, there was nothing his panzers could do but act as mobile artillery and help to hold a static line.

> In the evening we again sent S.O.S.s to Rome and to the Führer's H.Q. But there was now no longer any hope of an improvement in the situation. It was obvious that from now on the British would destroy us bit by bit, since we were virtually unable to move on the battlefield. As yet, Montgomery had only thrown half his striking force into the battle.[4]

It might perhaps have been truer to say that as yet Montgomery had been unable to devise a method whereby he could *get* more than half his striking force into the battle; but since the midday conference at Freyberg's headquarters on October 25th, he had been giving deep thought to the problem. Another side of the problem, of course, was that at the same time as he was reorganising his armour (for by now he had decided that this would be essential) he must also retain the initiative and 'make the enemy dance to his own tune'.

For this second purpose, he decided that he must use the best instrument still left in his armoury, and this was undoubtedly the 9th

Australian Division. Already it had been clearly illustrated that the infantry were more likely to achieve their objectives than the armour, and of these the Australians had suffered the fewest casualties and had more reinforcements available. Moreover, they were in exactly the right position to open a new offensive in an entirely new direction, and one to which the enemy must immediately react.

Instead of continuing the attack westwards, the Australians would now drive north towards the coast from their exposed right flank, cutting both the road and the railway and, in so doing, isolating the Bersaglieri Battalion and the Germans of the 125th Regiment in the 'nose' of the salient. The armour and infantry of 1st Armoured Division (2nd and now 24th Armoured Brigades and the 7th Motor Brigade) would guard the new left flank of the Australians to the west and at the same time help and protect the Highlanders clearing away the last obstacles up to Oxalic, while at the same time the New Zealanders and Gatehouse's 10th Armoured Division (which now consisted only of the 8th Armoured Brigade and the 133rd Lorried Infantry) would consolidate behind Miteiriya Ridge, the infantry patrolling vigorously, the armour preparing to withdraw for re-organisation.

The sooner it could all start, the better, and as it happened General Morshead had already foreseen the necessity for his men to drive at least some way in the new direction. About 2,000 yards due north of the northern corner of XXX Corps's break-in, held by his own 26th Brigade, lay the high point marked on the British maps as Point 29 (and on the German maps, Hill 28) from which observation both of his own positions to the south and the ground to the north past the railway and road as far as the sea could be obtained. For the safety of his own men the position should be quickly taken and as early as the morning of the 24th he had told Brigadier Whitehead to prepare a plan for its capture.

As always, the Australians had begun patrolling in front of their positions as soon as they were established, and early on their first morning they had captured a few prisoners, one of whom still possessed a map of the minefields in the area. Then at dusk on the evening of the 25th, they watched a German reconnaissance party approach their own positions and indeed penetrate well into them before being attacked and captured – to provide amongst the prisoners the commanding officers of both the 125th Regiment and its 2nd Battalion. Both carried important documents and one of them typified a response often met with in German prisoners; whereas the Italians very often knew nothing of value to their captors and were anyway not interested in much besides their immediate evacuation from the battle area, German prisoners, reacting apparently to military discipline, seemed automatically to try to do their best to answer all questions fully and accurately, especially when these were put to them by an obviously senior officer.

As a result of these two episodes, two companies of the 2nd/48th Australian Battalion set out at midnight October 25th/26th, overcame all opposition and reached their first objective 1,000 yards ahead dead on time, their third company racing through in carriers to arrive nine minutes later on Point 29 itself and find that the preceding artillery barrage had so stunned the Germans there that the fight lasted barely two minutes. In view of the fact that the Australian gunners had nearly 16,000 rounds of ammunition, mostly 25-pounder, at their disposal, this was not altogether surprising.

Matters did not go quite so well on the Australians' right flank in the attempt to broaden the drive northwards, for 2nd/24th Battalion met strong opposition from the Germans of the 125th Regiment, and although the leading Australian company did reach the objective, they had then to fall back as their support could not get through. Nevertheless, ground had been won, over 200 Germans captured and the northern edge of XXX Corps's break-in now curved back in a shallow crescent from Point 29 to Tel el Eisa. It also confirmed Montgomery's opinion that the drive to the north would compel the enemy's attention, for as has already been related, during the whole of the next day (26th) Rommel threw his forces against the penetration, always to see them founder against the Australian defences and suffer under the artillery and air bombardments. The 'crumbling' process was undoubtedly working.

To the south of the Australian positions, however, matters were not proceeding smoothly, principally because of argument and confusion. There was still disagreement between the Highlanders and the 2nd Armoured Brigade as to where their respective forward units were, and General Wimberley was anxious to clear the whole way up to the Oxalic Line, still in part tantalisingly just beyond his reach. Moreover, his northern flank was still appallingly congested, with the tanks, trucks, guns and men of the armoured brigade continually milling around amongst his own infantrymen, and it was here that he wished to make his most important advance – to Aberdeen and the still-isolated company of the 1st Gordons of whom nothing had been seen since they advanced through the Red Line barrage on the first night.

But because of the presence of the armour and their insistence that they were in positions which the Scots disputed, no artillery cover for the advance to Aberdeen could be agreed and in some desperation Wimberley sent in a silent attack about an hour before midnight. It ran almost immediately into serious opposition, but at least found the missing company – away to the right of the advance, thirsty, tired, almost out of ammunition but still in being. But at dawn Aberdeen was still not wholly in the Highlanders' hands.

All other Oxalic objectives in the Highlanders' sector had been captured, however, by the morning of October 26th. Stirling had been attacked by the 5th Black Watch with some of the 46th R.T.R. Valentines in support, but they found the defences vacated and, surprisingly, two demolished 88mm. guns and a few small guns still in working order; and further south the 7th Argyll and Sutherland Highlanders at last secured Nairn after a stiff fight. Except for part of Aberdeen, the Scots were therefore closing up along the whole length of their line.

What had been noticeably missing, however, was still co-operation from the armour and as a result some opportunities had been lost.

General Briggs had decided that an attempt should be made to occupy at least in part the vital Kidney feature (still believed by many to be a ridge) and he proposed to send in the reserve battalion from the 7th Motor Brigade, the 2nd Rifle Brigade, but when news of this proposal reached General Wimberley he pointed out that the riflemen would be attacking over the same ground and at the same time as his Gordons. There seemed to be an obvious and advantageous solution to the problems posed – that the Rifle Brigade should follow the Gordons, clearing routes for their own vehicles at the same time so that once the Gordons reached Aberdeen, the riflemen could leap-frog through them and occupy Kidney.

But as the two parties could still not agree as to where either of them were or where their respective objectives lay, the men from 7th Motor Brigade were held back until after dawn when they attempted a daylight advance which, not surprisingly, ran immediately into stiff opposition. Their reports insisted that this was coming from Nairn, but this locality was so far off their intended route that there was from this particular débâcle an advantageous outcome; Army Command at last lost patience with the bickering over map reading and insisted that at a specific time that day, flares should be fired from advanced positions upon which cross-bearings would be taken.

The result was a severe jolt to the self-esteem of the armour, who were nowhere as far west as they claimed and whose navigation was thus demonstrated as inferior to that of the infantry – and even the infantry had not been as accurate as could have been wished.

But before that problem was cleared up, the armour had been attempting to reorganise itself for the next phase of the battle. Gatehouse's division moved out of the New Zealand area during the night of the 25th/26th, both 8th Armoured Brigade and the 133rd Lorried Infantry making their way to the rear, while 24th Armoured Brigade moved specifically over into 1st Armoured Division area. In view of the night's operations on 51st Highland Division front it was not, of course, possible for the R.T.R. regiments of the brigade to move directly north from the positions they had reached in front of the end of Miteiriya – so instead they went back across the ridge, then right back to the Springbok Track and up forward again via Star track. It took them the whole of the night of October 25th/26th – their third without sleep – and they were all exhausted upon arrival.

By the morning of October 26th, then, the Australians had extended the bridgehead northwards as far as Point 29 which they held firmly, the 2nd and 24th Armoured Brigades and the 7th Motor Brigade of 1st Armoured Division were at least on or just behind the Oxalic Line in the Kidney area, and except for Aberdeen, Oxalic itself was held down to the western end of Miteiriya Ridge – which was itself held along its crest. South of the South Africans the 4th Indian Division still held their anchor position at the bottom of XXX Corps's sector, their activities and by now somewhat restive spirits confined to raiding, their chief contribution to the battle so far being the repeated information that whatever else the enemy opposite might be doing, they were certainly showing no signs of withdrawal.

The attack by XIII Corps infantry on Munassib during the night of the 25th/26th (which it will be remembered had been preferred to the continuation of the attempt to punch a hole through the February minefield) had been almost as great a disaster as the previous attempt in the same area at the end of September. Two battalions from 69th Infantry Brigade set off after dark, and although the 6th Green Howards took part of their objective and 45 Folgore prisoners, the 5th East Yorkshires soon found themselves being shelled either by the enemy or by their own supporting artillery, lost over a hundred men and promptly retired to their starting line.

The action did, however, distract attention from further south where the two unfortunate Queen's battalions of 131st Brigade had endured a grim day of heat and exposure, west of February. The survivors quietly withdrew during the night into the bridgehead between February and January where 22nd Armoured Brigade had at least dug some defences, though the infantry were not to have the consolation of armoured protection for very long. The following night one of them awoke

> . . . just in time to see the last squadron of Sherman [*sic*] tanks belonging to the 7th Armoured Division rumbling away down the minefield gap, their wireless aerials whipping in a thin arc against the grey dawn sky as they bucked and lurched down the uneven track. There was not enough room inside the bridgehead which, as I learned later that day, was only about 500 yards deep at its furthest point, for the tanks to deploy. Besides, they were needed to regroup and stand by to reinforce the main attack in the north.

But it was a cheerless moment to face the dawn on an empty stomach and know that the total defence in the extreme south of the sector was two infantry brigades, strung out along some 2,000 yards of front, with the badly knocked-about remnant of the Free French Brigade in reserve somewhere to our left rear.[5]

But by now Rommel had withdrawn 21st Panzer, a major part of the Ariete and most of the artillery from the south, and Montgomery, too, was concentrating all the Eighth Army strength in the north. To all intents and purposes the battle in the original XIII Corps area died away after Munassib, and what troops were left down there spent the days in desultory mortar and small-arms exchanges with the equally unenthusiastic troops opposite, the nights in patrolling and reconnaissance through the minefields, awaiting news from the north.

No one has ever caught the air of irrelevance, of unreality, which can in daylight pervade large sections of a battlefield better than did Tolstoy in his description of Borodino. Fierce conflict might occupy one corner of the field with companies of men locked in combat, anguish and death . . . but within only hundreds of yards wagon trains are being unloaded in haste but no evident peril, squadrons gravely manoeuvre, batteries fire into apparently empty air, men march and countermarch. Even more men stand about waiting for orders, crowd around water-points or ration-trucks or – far more likely and more often – lie down and go to sleep.

This is an aspect of battle not often described and even less often appreciated. Even less appreciated is the difference made to the picture of conflict when later remembered, by a posture of offence instead of defence, of a condition of low instead of high morale, and especially of a final result of failure against that of success.

To Rommel and indeed to many of his men, the events of October 26th left a pattern in their memories of unceasing turmoil – of counter-attacks flung back time and time again, of shattering bombardment and of a long succession of implacable air attacks:

> The British resisted desperately. Rivers of blood were poured out over miserable strips of land which, in normal times, not even the poorest Arab would have bothered his head about. Tremendous British artillery fire pounded the area of the attack.[6]

Reports on the British side, however, especially of the early part of the day, seem to have been about an entirely different set of circumstances, enacted under entirely different conditions. To them, October 26th was a day of comparative peace and quiet. The Australians, certainly, were subjected to some shelling during the day, but compared to the counter-bombardment which they could themselves call up immediately they located the enemy batteries, it was insignificant. The first Axis counter-attacks of the day had come in against the base of the new salient where the Australian 2nd/13th Battalion were still in positions they had occupied and been strengthening ever since they took them in the first night's assault – and even there the M13s and Semoventis of the Littorio Division turned away under the heavy shelling which caught them long before they could wreak much damage.

During the morning, the axes of the counter-attacks edged northwards towards the newly won ground around Point 29, and at first the Australians there found their movements between the still shallow defences somewhat circumscribed by mortar and small-arms fire; but once their own observers had passed the requisite information back to the gunners and these had come into action . . . again, danger passed.

Early in the afternoon, an undoubtedly serious concentration of panzers, infantry carriers and guns appeared to the west and northwest, shell-fire increased, and groups of infantry could be seen deploying; but a few curtly worded sentences into the microphones by the Australian observers brought first the scream and crash of heavy and accurately directed shells, and shortly afterwards the roar of aircraft and the equally shattering explosions of 500-pound bombs. Gradually the enemy groups disintegrated, the shell-fire slackened, trucks and guns were seen withdrawing away to the west, and by late afternoon it was quite evident that the counter-attack had been called off – without, from the Australians' point of view, ever seriously developing.

On the other sectors of XXX Corps's front, the picture was the same. The area held by the newly found Gordons was rather unfairly subjected to random shelling, as was the newly taken Argyll and Sutherland position at Nairn, but Valentines of 40th R.T.R. encountered no problems in moving north to support the Australians, although 2nd Armoured Brigade, also ordered to move north to cover the western flank of the new Australian positions, found themselves still in argument as to their exact positions. When they did move they came under fire either from Aberdeen or from some of the counter-attacking forces further north, at which point they withdrew through the 7th Motor Brigade positions back to their starting point. The tank crews of 24th Armoured Brigade, not surprisingly, were either fast asleep or attempting to replenish their fuel tanks and ammunition racks in such an exhausted state that their presence amid the marching Highlanders, hard-working sappers, disgruntled truck-drivers and infuriated staff and liaison officers threatened to reduce confusion to chaos.

Further south on Miteiriya Ridge, the New Zealanders and their close friends of the 9th Armoured Brigade spent the day under intermittent shell-fire, observing and reporting enemy movements away to the west, occasionally calling down artillery concentrations whenever the panzers approached too close or congregated into worthwhile targets. After their efforts during the opening phase of the battle, the Kiwis were enjoying something of a well-earned rest.

To Montgomery also, October 26th was a day for little movement, but much deep thought and concentration. The basic changes to be made in the original plan were clear in his mind, and it was now necessary to decide upon the details – and in this regard, he had to bear in mind the cost of the battle so far.

According to de Guingand, casualties to date amounted to 4,643 in XXX Corps, 455 in X Corps and 1,037 in XIII Corps. Overall, this was by no means an exorbitant price to have paid for the gains made, but in detail it posed some problems. Infantry were making by far the greatest contribution to victory, and as the most trustworthy arm infantry must provide much of the power in the newly planned operations; unfortunately, infantry had borne the brunt of the battle so far and were critically short of reinforcements. The Australians had lost nearly one thousand men, as had the New Zealanders, while the Scots had lost nearly double that number – and the most realistic attitude to take was that the casualties had been from amongst the best, whose replacement in quantity was evidently difficult and in quality might prove impossible.

Another obviously realistic attitude to take was one of deep scepticism towards intelligence figures regarding Axis losses. According to the latest reports, Rommel's forces had been depleted by the staggering figure of 61,000 men, 530 tanks and 340 field guns, which if true would have left the Panzerarmee in shreds; and those responsible for producing the estimates must have been slightly puzzled as to why Eighth Army were not already well into Cyrenaica.

As they were still barely past the Oxalic Line, however, their Army Commander issued during the morning a general directive to help them along the way.

The Australians would renew their drive to the north during the night of October 28th, and until then the other infantry of XXX Corps would do little but solidify the existing front, facing west, and fight off counter-attacks. The armour left in the area would move to act as shield to the Australians but would not attempt to move out beyond artillery protection, and this would be augmented at all times by the close co-operation of both bomber and fighter squadrons.

The original Australian positions would now be taken by General Wimberley's reserve formation, the 152nd Brigade, while further south the New Zealanders would be withdrawn entirely from the battle, their places along the ridge being taken by the South Africans who would side-step to the right and thin out the line in general, *their* places being taken by the 4th Indian Division following the same procedure.

So far as XIII Corps were concerned, General Horrocks was to ensure that 7th Armoured Division suffered no more losses, and was regrouped to enable it to move north immediately word was received that 21st Panzer was doing the same. All moves should be completed by dawn of October 28th, and all formations should then be standing by to put new plans into operation; but in the meantime only shielding measures were to be taken, and energies conserved for a major offensive in the near future.

It is ironic that during the proposed 'quiet period' when recuperation and reorganisation were the intended order of the day, the fiercest and certainly the most famous action of the Battle of Alamein was to be fought.

It took time, of course, for General Montgomery's detailed orders to be disseminated down to the levels at which many of them would come into operation, and meanwhile there were phases of existing operations to be completed.

The Australians, for instance, on the night of October 26th/27th, were intent upon straightening the line eastwards from Point 29 back towards Tel el Eisa and fighting off the stalwarts of Lungershausen's 125th Regiment, equally intent upon recapturing the ground lost the previous night. This led to some fierce close fighting during the hours before midnight, but after midnight the Australians managed to disengage for long enough and at sufficient distance for their one great superiority to come into action. Shortly after 0200, as Rommel noted, Australian artillery opened fire along the northern sweep of their front to such effect that afterwards their patrols went forward almost without opposition, and by dawn all their objectives were taken together with 41 stunned and shocked German prisoners and one intact 88mm. gun.

To the Australians' south, General Briggs was making strong efforts to get his armour out into that shielding role that the Army Commander was still requiring, but he had decided that even before his armour could disentangle itself from the confusion amongst the Highlanders, he must secure a firm base for them further forward. To achieve this, he would send two rifle battalions of the Motor Brigade forward, one on each side of the Kidney feature, to attack and occupy areas from which they could dominate the enemy anti-tank posts, thus creating a passage through which the armour could pass. Both 2nd and 24th Armoured Brigades would then at last be out in the open and the Motor Brigade units could connect up and follow them, while units of 133rd Lorried Infantry Brigade moved into the vacated positions – 'Woodcock' about a mile north-west of Kidney, 'Snipe' a similar distance to the south-west.

The commanding officers of both rifle battalions – 2nd King's Royal Rifle Corps in the north, and 2nd Rifle Brigade in the south – had had brief opportunities for reconnaissance during the morning, but as the flare-firing exercise had not by then been conducted the doubts as to locations of both start lines and objectives persisted. Even after the experiment there was still some uncertainty because the armoured formations were reluctant to accept the evidence, so when at 2130 the Bren carriers of the K.R.R.C. set off, they were forced after a while merely to follow the artillery barrage, despite the fact that it was not falling in what they considered to be the right direction.

On the way they came across an entirely unexpected post held by the Gordons and some equally unexpected enemy anti-tank posts from which they collected nearly a hundred prisoners, and when daylight came they found themselves in open ground, quite obviously not Woodcock, fully exposed to enemy fire. It seemed to the commanding officer that they could serve no useful purpose there, so he ordered a withdrawal which eventually took them back through the Gordons' outpost to a position east of Kidney, not far from where they had started out.

Lieutenant-Colonel Victor Turner, commanding the 2nd Rifle Brigade, had been so uncertain of the locations of his start line and his objective – and conscious of the differing opinion regarding these of the commander of the 1st Black Watch for whom Turner had considerable respect – that in the evening of the 26th he had reported his anxiety to 7th Motor Brigade H.Q. where, however, he was told that it was too late to change arrangements.

He therefore issued orders that his force was to follow the line of the artillery barrage which in the event proved to be some 45° north of the line as calculated by his own navigating officer. Zero hour was 2300, the barrage opened five minutes before and the change in direction delayed the advance of the infantry and engineers by ten minutes. Little opposition was experienced over the first 1,000 yards at which point they came up against wire, but this, on examination by the engineers, proved only to surround a dummy minefield.

During the next 1,000 yards, the infantry captured some twenty prisoners and saw several other enemy troops scattering in front of them, leading them over the crest of a ridge to an area about 500 yards further forward. Here Colonel Turner halted his force, disposed them for immediate defence and fired the success rocket to bring forward the heavy weapons.

These had been left with the second-in-command of the battalion,

Major Pearson, and had been waiting on the start line for nearly an hour during which time they had been subjected to random shelling and been bombed at 2330 by a lone aircraft. This set fire to two of the vehicles and caused casualties to which the doctor was at that moment attending, and as Pearson immediately gave the order to advance, the convoy started off without their medical officer or the ambulances.

The trucks and guns found the going very bad, with long ridges of soft sand which sucked the wheels down to the hubs and turned the comparatively short journey into a nightmare of sweat and frustration. But by dint of much hard work and considerable determination, 19 of the 27 6-pounder anti-tank guns arrived at the chosen position together with their ammunition trucks, and all were off-loaded by 0345. The empty trucks left, again under Major Pearson, two hours later, by which time Colonel Turner's force were endeavouring to take up their positions, despite a small but confused battle taking place in their midst.

In the dark, Colonel Turner had halted his force in the middle of what later proved to have been a German engineers' dump, about 800 yards to the north-east of a leaguer of enemy tanks and trucks. When C Company's Bren carriers fanned out to take their positions, they had climbed a shallow ridge where they found wire and also some dispirited Italian soldiers who gave themselves up. But there was a gap through the wire, and as there appeared to be a group of about 150 equally dispirited-looking soldiers some 500 yards beyond it, the carriers made their way through – to find themselves in the middle of the leaguer, which promptly sprang into active and hostile life.

The prisoners bolted – to be shot down indiscriminately by both sides – the carriers hastily retreated with the loss of one of their number, but leaving one enemy truck ablaze and sufficient dismay and confusion in the leaguer for its commander to decide to seek further security. It lay, he thought, away to the north, and in order to attain it the entire force formed up and began an advance to the north-east – to run very quickly into the south-west corner of Snipe, where both C and B Companies of Turner's force were just siting their first anti-tank guns. In the ensuing fracas an Italian self-propelled gun was destroyed and a German medium tank set alight, from which one valiant crew member jumped into a convenient trench and sniped at British positions until shortly after dawn when a grenade put an end to his activities.

Dawn also revealed their position to 300 embattled riflemen.

They were dispersed inside an oval of scrub-covered desert whose longer axis ran north-east and south-west for just over 1,000 yards, its shorter axis being half that length. The usual undulations and small dips provided cover for most of the guns, and soft sand at the bottom of most of them scope for improvement. An abandoned German dug-out just west of the centre point provided Turner with head-quarters, around which B Company's five anti-tank guns were deployed in the south-easterly sector covering the angles 90° to 225°, C Company's four guns to the south-west covering 225° to 315° and A Company's four guns in the northern sector facing north-west and north. Alongside A Company's guns were six more from 239th Battery of the 76th Anti-tank Regiment, covering the north and north-east sector, under command of Lieutenant Alan Baer.

This battery had been detached to join Colonel Turner's force late in the evening, with the cryptic valediction from the regiment's second-in-command, 'From all the signs, I should think it highly probable that you are in for a death or glory affair!' – a point of view which gained force as daylight grew.

Although the night's action had died down except for those of the lone sniper, the enemy force from the southern leaguer had drawn only a little way back to the south-west – and now the riflemen could see the security which its commander had been seeking – a solid and menacing-looking German leaguer about 1,000 yards away to the north. As this was coming rapidly to life, all gun crews along the north-west quadrant braced themselves for action and watched closely for the first signs of movement. These when they came, however, provided the riflemen with both surprise and relief, for instead of turning towards them both the German and Italian forces began to move off westwards, thus exposing the vulnerable sides of their armoured vehicles.

This provided a temptation which could not be withstood despite the danger that yielding to it would bring, and fire on the panzers was immediately opened. In return the position itself was heavily shelled and for nearly half an hour the whole northern sector of Snipe was a chaos of smoke, blown sand and explosion – but when the last of the enemy withdrew out of range the reports which came into Turner's headquarters claimed that six German panzers, eight Italian tanks and two Semoventi guns had been destroyed, and two German panzers hit – and moreover, smoking remains of several could still be seen to confirm the tally, while enemy recovery teams were at work towing others away. On the debit side, three of the anti-tank guns had been put out of action, and one had proved to have been sited in such soft sand that it had almost buried itself by its own recoil. But the action had clearly demonstrated that hard-hitting anti-tank guns, well sited and well dug in, could extract an extortionate price from any panzer force which might try to eliminate them.

On the other hand, of course, the action had also revealed, first to the local enemy and soon to Rommel, that there was a powerful

British force apparently isolated some 1,000 yards into their own positions; heavy counter-attacks must be expected shortly.

As it happened, however, the first danger came from behind.

The original plan called for the armoured brigades to come out to the support of Woodcock and Snipe at about dawn – but as the Woodcock force was obviously nowhere near their objective, the 2nd Armoured Brigade remained more or less where they were. But 24th Armoured Brigade received word that 2nd Rifle Brigade were on Snipe and at 0730 they breasted a protective ridge and saw, some 2,000 yards in front of them and surrounded by a zareba of burnt-out Italian and German panzers, a well-sited concentration of guns upon which they promptly opened fire. This was, as the writer of the most detailed account of this action says, with massive understatement, ' . . . galling':

> In an attempt to stop it, Turner sent out his Intelligence Officer, Jack Wintour, on the dangerous mission of making his way to our tanks in a bren-carrier. This Wintour accomplished. He succeeded in abating the fire of the leading squadron, but the remainder of the brigade continued to bombard their friends. The irrepressible Wintour then calmly returned.[7]

Shortly afterwards the tanks of the 24th Armoured Brigade began advancing westwards towards Snipe – but the Rifle Brigade crews along the southern quadrant of the position could see some 25 panzers, all with long-barrelled guns with 'muzzle brakes' – presumably Mark III or IV Specials – moving into hull-down positions behind a ridge about 1,500 yards away, from which to attack the advancing Shermans. The gun crews opened fire at once again into the vulnerable sides of the panzers – to see the nearest three brew up almost immediately, their crews machine-gunned as they jumped clear by the approaching Shermans who at last appreciated the true position.

By 0830 the leading squadrons of the armoured brigade had actually moved into the Snipe position, much to the discomfort of the riflemen and especially the anti-tank gunners of the 239th Battery, for the Shermans attracted devastating shell-fire from the German gunners who seemed to be using a new technique. One of the hull-down panzers would drop a smoke shell as near as possible to one of the tanks, and immediately the 88mm. anti-tank guns and the heavy panzer guns would shell the smoke – larger and much more visible than the camouflaged Shermans. Within a quarter of an hour seven Shermans were blazing, the whole area had become a confusion of smoke, fire and shell-bursts, and that basic fact of armoured warfare was yet again patently obvious: against dug-in guns or hull-down tanks, stationary vehicles in open country – however well armoured – were too vulnerable to live. To everyone's relief the order was given for the Shermans to withdraw, which they did about 0900 – to cause yet another revelation.

As the Shermans drew away to the east, fire was opened upon them by panzers and guns some two thousand yards away to the north. The nearest anti-tank guns to these attackers were those of 239th Battery, but it was only under pressure from one of the Rifle Brigade officers that Sergeant Binks was persuaded to open fire at such an extreme range; but he hit and stopped one of the panzers with his third shot, and harried another which came out to tow away the casualty. The British undoubtedly now had an effective anti-tank weapon.

What the men in Snipe lacked, however, were two important services. Some men had been killed and more had been wounded – and the medical officer and his ambulances were still back at the start line, unable in daylight to move forward. Even more important, the attached gunner observation officer had disappeared during the night, and in the developing circumstances his presence and expertise would have been very useful. In the folds and dips of the desert

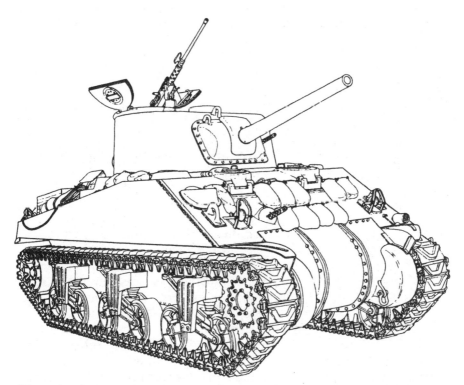

Figure 4   Medium tank M4 (Sherman): weight 32 tons; armour 25mm.–55mm.; engine 460 h.p.; maximum speed 23 m.p.h.; armament one 75mm., one ·30 in. machine-gun, one ·50 in. machine-gun; crew 5

surrounding the embattled riflemen, slight though they were, were now congregating enemy units with guns and panzers which neither anti-tank guns nor small-arms could hit – and the crying need was for the kind of dropping artillery blanket protection which was proving so effective elsewhere along XXX Corps's front. A gunner observation officer could moreover have cured another problem which was besetting Turner's force, and at 1036 he sent out a message clarifying it. 'What we most need is artillery support. We have a suspicion that our own artillery is landing on us.'

Moreover, it was quite obvious that if action on the scale so far experienced were to continue all day, another urgent need would be for more ammunition, so in an attempt to solve all their problems at once, three carriers under an officer and a sergeant made a dash for the eastern ridge behind which waited their support, carrying the more severely wounded. Unfortunately, neither they nor the convoy held in readiness by Major Pearson were ever able to get back through the storm of fire which greeted everything which showed itself over the crest, and by mid-morning it was quite evident to the men at Snipe that they were on their own, at least until darkness fell.

It was soon equally evident that this was a point not lost upon the enemy, and by 1000 Italian infantry were moving in groups nearer to the western perimeter and forming up for attack. Turner briskly instructed one of the Scout carrier platoons to 'see them off' (which they did by driving straight at them with Bren-guns and rifles blazing) while some readjustments were taking place within Snipe itself, for more danger was now threatening from the south-west. By enormous effort and at some cost two guns were therefore quickly moved down into the sector, but as Bren carriers were the only vehicles now left in the area and as they had no towing hitches, the guns had to be pulled out of the soft sand with ropes attached to the tracks – and the movement above ground churned up clouds of sand which were promptly shelled by the enemy, causing on this occasion the loss of one officer and three riflemen.

But the movement of the guns proved worthwhile almost immediately for as they settled into their new positions, thirteen Italian M13s came over the western ridge, while away to the south more than twenty panzers moved out of their hull-down positions apparently intent upon attacking the Shermans of the 24th Armoured Brigade, now themselves hull-down behind the eastern ridge opposite.

The Italian tanks were quickly dealt with as all the guns along the western flank opened up together. Four M13s were hit in the first salvo and the remainder scuttled back behind their ridge – a not unreasonable course of action, for the M13s had been vulnerable even to the old British 2-pounders, and for them to advance against the new 6-pounders was suicidal.

But in the meantime, an interesting case of what Colonel Turner was later to refer to as 'cross-trumping' was taking place along the southern perimeter. As the panzers crossed their ridge and came out into the open towards the 24th Armoured Brigade positions, they once again exposed their sides to the watching riflemen, one of whom, Sergeant Calistan, was to prove as accurate a shot with his 6-pounder as had Sergeant York with his rifle in the Argonne twenty-four years before. Within a few minutes of setting out, the panzer commander had been forced to detach half his force to attack the Snipe position from which such dangerous fire was coming, only to find that now the vulnerable sides of this force were exposed to the guns of the hull-down Shermans of 24th Armoured Brigade.

The range was long, but the nerves of the gunners remained steady, neither set switching their fire to the panzers actually attacking them but concentrating instead upon those crossing their sight-lines towards the other target. Soon at least eight of the panzers were alight, others were going to their aid and attempting to tow them out of danger, while others had turned under the weight of fire and were back under cover again. The longed-for co-operation between armour and infantry – admittedly of the same division in this case – seemed at last a reality.

Conditions inside Snipe, however, were by now serious. More men had been killed and many more injured, and as the heat grew the lack of skilled medical attendance, of much more than shell-dressings in the way of medical equipment or of water to spare for washing wounds, added considerably to their sufferings. Flies covered the bodies of the living, and as the heat rose towards noon so did the intensity of enemy fire.

Six of the carriers were hit during a burst of shelling just before midday, their flames adding to the heat and fury, their smoke drifting across the gun positions and confusing the gunners. There were not so many of these now, and many gun crews were made up to strength by officers whenever danger threatened, or by other gunners running over from unthreatened positions. Six guns had now been knocked out, leaving but thirteen to cover a 2,500-yard perimeter – but from all reports written about this action, morale everywhere remained astonishingly high. Many of these men had taken part in previous desert battles and had known the frustration of trying to fight off panzer attacks with inadequate weapons. Now, in their own hands, they had a battlewinner – and few of them would have exchanged their fate with another's; they were professional soldiers of a famous regiment, in the type of action for which they had long trained.

The shortage of ammunition, already a general problem, now tended to become acute in the south-western sector. Two jeeps, driven by one of the company commanders and a corporal whose gun had been put out of action, were used to redistribute what ammunition there was, driving everywhere through thick dust, heavy shelling and a torrent of machine-gun fire.

Then shortly before 1300, the shelling concentrated, the machine-gun fire increased and from over the ridge to the south-west appeared eight Italian M13s and a Semoventi self-propelled gun – doubtless encouraged by the fact that all but one of the defending guns in the southern sector had fallen silent.

Unfortunately for the Italians, the exception was Sergeant Calistan's, although at that moment one of his crew was lying badly wounded and the others were all away from the gun, scrounging ammunition from the nearest wrecks. Realising the danger and the predicament, Colonel Turner and Lieutenant Toms raced to Calistan's assistance, the colonel taking post as loader and observer, Toms as No. 1 to Calistan as layer; together they waited until the M13s were within 600 yards.

Calistan's expertise combined with their own thin armour proved fatal to the Italian tanks. He had picked off five of them and the self-propelled gun before they had closed to 400 yards, and was prevented from making a clean sweep right away by the fact that only two rounds of ammunition were left – a difficult situation as the remaining three M13s, gallantly manned, were still advancing, their machine-guns pouring in fire on the defiant gun-post. Lieutenant Toms turned and raced for a jeep some hundred yards behind him, drove to the nearest wrecked gun and with the strength of desperation threw aboard every round he could find. He arrived back behind Calistan's gun in a storm of machine-gun fire which set the jeep's petrol-tank alight as he pulled up, but with total disregard of the flames, Turner and a corporal who had run across to help lifted the ammunition clear and flung it towards the gun. As he turned for the last time, a shell fragment pierced Turner's helmet and cut deep into his skull causing the blood to pump out over his face and blind him.

But the three remaining tanks were now within 200 yards and their machine-gun bullets were whining close by the sweating men, deeply denting the thin gun-shield. It was now all up to Sergeant Calistan, but he apparently refused to be hurried; with the clarity of movement of a top-class soloist, he took his time and scored a hat-trick – all three tanks bursting into flames as he hit them, the crews perishing to a man inside.

'Hardly miss 'em at that range,' he is reputed to have said much later. 'Poor bastards!'

'After this,' says the Rifle Brigade history, 'there was a comparative lull' – but 'comparative' would seem to have been the significant word.

Random shelling and mortar fire continued all the afternoon, more men and officers were wounded. Colonel Turner recovered full consciousness for a time and insisted on visiting the gun positions, but a combination of pain, loss of blood and the increasing heat began to give him hallucinations, and towards the end he had to be kept in the headquarters dug-out by force. As six of the other ten occupants were also wounded conditions inside were difficult in the extreme, especially as nearby shelling blew in clouds of sand and the flies were everywhere. By 1600, the majority of the officers had been killed or wounded, all gun positions were commanded by N.C.O.s and most of them had been hit at least once – and now trouble came from yet another source.

General Briggs, commanding 1st Armoured Division, was faced with a dreadful dilemma. He was well aware of the situation and the condition of his men on Snipe and the need to get help to them, but he also knew that his armour would be needed during the next offensive stage of Montgomery's plan (and it should be remembered that the battle being fought by the Rifle Brigade battalion was taking place during a designated 'quiet' period). He was also aware of what had happened to the Shermans of 24th Armoured Brigade when they had reached Snipe during the early morning, and what had happened since to everything else which showed itself over the protective ridge behind the position.

He could not send armour out to help – at least not in daylight. But he would try to grant Turner's repeated request for artillery support, so 2nd Armoured Brigade were ordered to help supply it and their attached artillery of the 11th R.H.A. edged up to the crest with their Priests – 105mm. howitzers mounted in M3 tank chassis – and opened fire. It was unfortunate that the armour had still not identified correctly either their own position or that of their forward infantry, for the heavy shells smashed viciously down into the Snipe area, adding considerably to the difficulties there.

'During an unpleasant day,' Colonel Turner's narrative records sadly, 'this was the most unpleasant thing that happened.'

By this time Rommel, who it will be remembered was watching this action from his place along the Telegraph Track, had put together his main counter-attack against the whole of the northern front. Units from the 90th Light Division moved cautiously in from the west towards the Australian positions just south of Point 29, while parallel and further south (across the original Woodcock area) a force estimated at thirty German and ten Italian tanks advanced to attack the positions held by some of the 2nd Armoured Brigade. Those in the north immediately disappeared into a storm of artillery fire and shortly afterwards were thoroughly dispersed by bombing, while those crossing Woodcock would seem to have been destroyed by their own lack of intelligence.

Presumably they had only just arrived in the area and certainly they had been most inadequately briefed, for they advanced in open phalanx, at least seven of them crossing in front of the remaining four guns of the 239th Battery on Snipe at less than 200 yards' range. The action was as spectacular as had been Sergeant Calistan's in the south, the battery's tally being nine panzers destroyed and several hit, while one of A Company's nearby guns claimed another four destroyed though it is probable that one or two of these were duplicated by the 239th.

But now the second wave of Rommel's counter-attack was launched, and from it fifteen panzers were detached specifically to assault the north-western face of the Snipe position, in which by that time only two guns were left to defy them – those of Sergeant Hine and Sergeant Miles – though frantic attempts were made by Lieutenant Holt-Wilson to turn one of the nearby guns around to help. Between them the three guns had thirty rounds of ammunition left.

Making good use of ground, the panzers crept nearer and nearer, their machine-gunners sweeping the gun positions whenever their turrets gave them a sighting, driving the gun crews first in behind the screens, then as the range closed and the bullets penetrated, into the shelter of nearby trenches. Sergeant Miles was himself hit and his crew pinned down, but when the three leading panzers were about a hundred yards from Miles's gun, Sergeant Swann crawled the fifty yards from Battalion Headquarters under intense machine-gun fire, loaded the gun, aimed and fired it.

In rapid succession he scored two hits on the leading panzer whose crew promptly baled out, while Sergeant Hine waited until another Mark III was within one hundred yards and then hit it with a shot which went clean through and hit the third Mark III about ten yards behind it. This third panzer backed away into a hull-down position and continued to pump machine-gun fire over the Snipe position until it apparently ran out of ammunition, a pursuit in which it was joined by all the other panzers of this particular assault, none of which thereafter exposed itself sufficiently for the gunners to get a shot at it.

A kind of stalemate thus resulted and at 1844 the adjutant, Captain F. W. Marten, sent out a signal to 7th Motor Brigade H.Q. reading 'Twenty tanks lying doggo in valley to the north of us at about one thousand yards. We are being swept by machine-gun fire. Expect attack at any moment.'[8]

Fortunately none developed in strength but in the meantime other signals were being sent to and fro. The Rifle Brigade codes had been burnt earlier in view of the close danger in which the headquarters lay, so clear though somewhat veiled language had to be used, and the first orders to be received were to the effect that 'friends' would come out to take the place of the riflemen 'at dinner time'. The riflemen should wait and see the said 'friends' comfortably in place, after which their own transport would arrive to take them home.

To the reasonable query as to whether it would be an early or late dinner, the reply was 'the fashionable time' – with which the riflemen had to be content despite the possibility of misunderstanding; but in the meantime there was work for the survivors to do. About 1900 the light began at last to drain from the sky, and by 1940 the panzers had all withdrawn to the north-west where a few were incautious enough to remain silhouetted against the pale evening sky. At them were fired the last few rounds of anti-tank ammunition, 'more of a gesture of relief than with any hope of hitting them' – but to everyone's gratification one hit was scored, the last of a remarkable day.

Back towards the headquarters dug-out now began to close the survivors of the outlying posts, all still crawling under a horizontal screen of machine-gun bullets from the static enemy posts around, many dragging wounded comrades between them. Lieutenant Holt-Wilson went around the gun positions to make sure that every gun had been either destroyed by the enemy or had had its breech-block removed, while the wounded were loaded on to the remaining jeeps and Bren-carriers, and sent off into the darkness. The one carrying Colonel Turner and Major Bird eventually made its way to the dressing station of the Highland Division, the others reached their own lines but not before running through a minefield laid that morning across their line of withdrawal, fortunately without further injury to the wounded. And the remaining fit riflemen on Snipe settled down to await 'the fashionable time'.

Eight o'clock came and went, half past eight, nine o'clock. All around them they could hear the sounds of German recovery teams and ambulances at their rescue work, and not surprisingly they did nothing to interfere. By 2130 there was no sign of either the 'friends' or their own transport and someone was heard to remark that it looked as though headquarters were on a bloody diet, at which the decision was taken to commence withdrawal at 2230 if there was still no sign of relief.

The survivors of A and B Companies therefore set out on foot at this time, but shortly afterwards the British artillery opened up on the enemy positions with exactly the kind of barrage for which the riflemen had been praying all day. One of its effects was that the panzers moved out of the leaguers, straight towards Snipe – so rather hastily and still without seeing any of the 'friends', Battalion Headquarters and the remaining men moved out, leaving behind them a scene which daylight would reveal as one of quite astonishing desolation, and also of considerable mystery. A month later a committee of inquiry into the action examined the scene and counted the wrecks of 34 tanks or self-propelled guns – and no one has ever been able to establish how many of both had been towed away.

Immediate losses among Colonel Turner's force amounted to about a hundred killed and wounded but many of the wounded, including both Turner and Major Bird, recovered to fight again. When General Montgomery heard of the action and had time to assess its results he was, of course, delighted. Turner received the Victoria Cross, Sergeant Calistan was recommended for one but received the Distinguished Conduct Medal instead; several D.S.O.s and lesser awards were made, but perhaps the highest accolade came from Rommel himself, for the men on Snipe must have contributed greatly to that 'murderous British fire' which 'struck into our ranks' and brought his heaviest counter-attack against the XXX Corps salient to a halt. It was certainly the Snipe action which caused him to conclude: 'There is, in general, little chance of success in a tank attack over country where the enemy has been able to take up defensive positions.'[9]

The non-arrival of the 'friends' had been due to inexperience and poor navigation, not to neglect.

Despite the events of the previous few hours around Snipe, the opinion was still held at command level that the front in general was 'quiet' for the moment and that nothing much remained to prevent the occupation of the Kidney area which had been so troublesome in the past. Now at last Brigadier Lee's 133rd Lorried Infantry Brigade could prove its value, taking over the positions and duties of 7th Motor Brigade including, of course, Woodcock and Snipe.

But exhaustion among the front-line formations was by now taking its toll, and tempers were very short. When Lee arrived at 7th Motor Brigade H.Q. he could elicit very little useful information, and when some time later he met both Lumsden and Gatehouse (who was coming up to take over this part of the front on Montgomery's latest instructions) Lee was told that he must make his own arrangements, but that all he had to do as far as Woodcock and Snipe were concerned was to 'walk through'.

He was, however, to be given ample artillery support – and it was this which crashed down on the panzers and drove them out towards Snipe. By this time, of course, the arranged relief hour had long passed, Turner and the wounded were already home and the fit Rifle Brigade survivors were walking out. Somewhere they must have passed their relief – the 5th Royal Sussex – but these in any case did not reach as far west as had the riflemen, digging in before dawn some 1,000 yards to the south-east of the recent battlefield.

As for the other battalions of Lee's brigade, the 2nd Royal Sussex in the centre of the advance reached the Kidney feature satisfactorily, but their colonel was killed and as the night wore on and daylight began they found themselves pinned down by small-arms and mortar fire from ridges away to the west.

The fate of the 4th Royal Sussex, however, was more complicated. Theirs had been the task of 'walking through' to Woodcock, but the unending confusion in the minefield gaps held them up twenty minutes behind their barrage, after which they went forward and attacked 'in good order and aggressive spirit' the first opposition they encountered. It was unfortunate that this was a post in Aberdeen held by the Gordons, but the episode had been inevitable ever since the planned axis of the Sussex advance had been laid straight across it.

The advance continued when at last proper identification had been achieved, but the battalion then came under heavy fire from the left flank and the company sent to deal with it was practically annihilated as it had run unexpectedly into an alert panzer leaguer.

Eventually, Lieutenant-Colonel Ronald Murphy considered that he had led what was left of his battalion as far as Woodcock (he had, in fact, reached the eastern edge) so he halted them and deployed them for defence, to find that the ground was rock hard so at dawn the slit-trenches were still far too shallow. Moreover, both German and Italian armoured units were close at hand, the wireless had broken down, and there was little sign of 2nd Armoured Brigade units which, they had been assured by Lumsden, would be up at first light to support them.

Those units were, however, on the move – though too far to the north. The Yorkshire Dragoons were already in action against an unexpectedly strong panzer attack which overran them and then turned south towards Woodcock, while still further north the 9th Lancers were moving towards Point 33, followed closely by the Bays; and from this vantage point both cavalry units in due course watched the panzers sweep across the ground held by the 4th Royal Sussex, knocking out the anti-tank guns easily as they had not yet been dug in, killing about sixty of the Royal Sussex, including Colonel Murphy.

Half an hour later they also watched the melancholy spectacle of 300 disconsolate infantrymen being marched off into captivity. But by then the cavalry were under orders to move back again as part of a general reshuffle of units, for General Montgomery had now completed his detailed plans for the next phase of the battle.

It was the morning of October 28th.

6 · *The Crumbling Process*

> It is clear that we now have the whole of Panzer Army opposite the Northern funnel and that we shall never get the armoured divisions out that way. I have therefore decided to make this a defensive front, to be taken over by XXX Corps. 1 Armd Div. and 24 Armd Brigade to be withdrawn into reserve.[1]

These were the basic conclusions and decisions which General Montgomery communicated to his two northern corps commanders and their chiefs of staff at a meeting held at 0800, October 28th. The Australians would continue their drive northwards to the coast that night, using the occasion also as a means of annihilating any enemy units they could draw into the battle, and for this purpose they would be given as much artillery as could be spared from all other sectors, plus the instant co-operation of British and South African bomber squadrons when required.

Then at a moment to be decided by the Army Commander – probably the night of October 30th/31st – XXX Corps infantry would drive north-westwards from the original Australian west-facing front towards Sidi Abd el Rahman while armoured car regiments would break south-westwards from the flank of the advance to circle around and cut enemy communication and supply routes. The armoured divisions would be held in check until opportunity arose for them to be used either against any unexpected pockets of enemy resistance or, in the event of a clear breakthrough, to race ahead and block an enemy retreat until such time as infantry and artillery could come up and complete his destruction. The only armour to be embroiled in the immediate battles to the north would be the infantry support squadrons of 23rd Armoured Brigade, whose Valentines had already contributed much to the infantry advances.

The Army Commander's main problem at this point, of course, was where the infantry for this crucial drive along the coast would come from and, equally important, who would command it. There were, in fact, two divisional generals who had, in Montgomery's opinion, the experience, the co-ordinating staffs and the aggressive drive for such a task, but one of them was the Australian commander, General Morshead, who was already deeply committed. Fortunately the other one, General Freyberg, was calling for lunch.

Over it, Montgomery told his visitor what would be required of him.

First, Freyberg's own 6th Brigade, who had left Miteiriya Ridge during the previous night and were now to have a few days' rest and recuperation lying in the sun and swimming close to Army H.Q., would be called up to take over the western face of the Australian salient through which the drive to the coast would take place. Then for the advance itself, in view of the casualties already suffered by the New Zealand battalions, Freyberg would be fed with brigades brought up from the south – first the 151st Durham Light Infantry (under the newly promoted Brigadier Percy) from the 50th Division, then the 152nd Brigade from the Highland Division, then the 131st Queen's Brigade from the 44th Division, and then if necessary the Greek Brigade. John Currie's 9th Armoured Brigade would cover the southern flank of the advance and would be given top priority of all tank replacements, and one or other of the armoured divisions would be deployed further to the south either to shield or to exploit as occasion demanded. In which respect, as it was now obvious that 21st Panzer Division were no longer in the south, John Harding had been ordered to bring Roberts's 22nd Armoured Brigade up into the Alamein sector.

General Montgomery, of course, would have the final decision upon the exact timing of the break-out, but in the meantime General Freyberg would have a great deal of work to do as the detailed movements of several brigades of infantry and almost two armoured divisions through an area already severely congested would have to be worked out, and time was short. They parted immediately after lunch and Freyberg in due course made his way to XXX Corps headquarters to discuss his problems further with General Leese.

He found when he got there that events during October 28th on XXX Corps's front had been very similar to those of the previous day. The combined South African and Royal Air Forces had continued to dominate the air above the battlefield, and their contributions to the ground battles had been generous and often conclusive in that they both identified danger of counter-attack as it appeared, and then neutralised it by bombing before it could properly develop. The two surviving Royal Sussex battalions, although neither of them so aggressive or so far forward as had been the 2nd Rifle Brigade the day before, attracted a certain amount of attention from the enemy though not enough to cause them to vacate their positions, which was fortunate as behind them the 8th Armoured Brigade were taking over from the 2nd Armoured Brigade, and neither of them had much time to spare for any troubles in which the infantry might find themselves.

Further north, New Zealand artillery formations were moving into the Australian sector, while the gunners already there, again aided by the combined air forces, broke up Rommel's repeated efforts during the day to mount an effective counter-attack against Point 29.

Altogether October 28th was another day during which the generals planned and their staffs endeavoured to administer, when the infantry dug in and kept their heads down, when the armour argued and exchanged places, and the shell and the bomb arbitrated. And at sea another Axis tanker, the *Louisiano* with 2,000 tons of petrol aboard, was sunk by torpedo, thus adding to Rommel's anger and anxiety when eventually the news reached him – and it was no consolation to him that with 271 fewer armoured vehicles in running order than when the battle had started, Panzerarmee Afrika's daily consumption of petrol was less than had been predicted. It was also on the 28th that the writer of the Panzerarmee narrative recorded that their counter-attacks were continually failing under heavy defensive fire, then developing into tank duels in which the British tanks 'firing from hull-down positions at over 2,000 yards range simply outshot our tanks'.

By midday Rommel had become aware of the concentration of force taking place along the northern flank of the Eighth Army positions, so he had moved 90th Light further along the coast with their head-quarters east of Sidi Abd el Rahman and brought all German for-mations except the Ramcke Parachute Brigade up from the south. The whole of the Afrika Korps was now in the quadrant curving from north of the Kidney feature to the coast, with the Bersaglieri and the 125th Regiment of Lungershausen's 164th Division still holding the salient pointing forward towards Tel el Eisa; and during the afternoon they all at some time or other shelled the Australian positions which bulged ominously to the north.

The majority of the officers had also had opportunity to read an Order of the Day issued by Rommel early that morning, to the effect that they were now all engaged upon a battle of life and death, that all orders were to be obeyed without question and that any soldier who disobeyed would be court-martialled regardless of his rank – a re-minder of their duties which many considered both unnecessary and offensive.

Then at nine o'clock in the evening came the stroke for which they had been waiting all day – a tremendous enemy bombardment of the area around 'Hill 28', eventually concentrating on the positions of the 2nd Battalion, 125th regiment:

> The British launched their assault at about 2200. The weight of this attack was something quite exceptional. However, by concentrating every gun in the area, we managed to break up the British attacks, which were

mainly made from Minefield I. Further to the north, in the gap between Minefields I and H, British tanks and infantry succeeded in making a penetration. The battle raged at this point with tremendous fury for six hours, until finally 11/125th Regiment and the XI Bersaglieri Battalion were overrun by the enemy. Their troops, surrounded and exposed to enemy fire from all sides, fought on desperately.

Army H.Q. had meanwhile been moved farther to the west. I spent the whole of that night with a number of my officers and men on the coast road roughly in line with the old H.Q. site, from where we could see the flash of of bursting shells in the darkness and hear the rolling thunder of the battle. Again and again British bomber formations flew up and tipped their death-dealing loads on my troops, or bathed the country in the brilliant light of parachute flares.

No one can conceive the extent of our anxiety during this period. That night I hardly slept and by 0300 hours [October 29th] was pacing up and down turning over in my mind the likely course of the battle, and the decisions I might have to take. It seemed doubtful if we would be able to stand up much longer to attacks of the weight which the British were now making, and which they were in any case still able to increase. It was obvious to me that I dared not await the decisive breakthrough but would have to pull out to the west before it came. Such a decision, however, could not fail to lead to the loss of a large proportion of my non-motorised infantry, partly because of the low fighting power of my motorised formations and partly because the infantry units themselves were too closely involved in the fighting.[2]

Rommel was beginning to look over his shoulder.

The Australian attack on the night of October 28th/29th had not in fact been as tactically successful as Rommel's account indicated. The 2nd/15th Battalion drove north for some 3,000 yards from the top of the Point 29 salient, overcame several enemy posts and took 130 Italian and German prisoners at comparatively low cost, though among those killed had been their own colonel. Away to the right a somewhat depleted and exhausted battalion, the 2nd/13th which had been in the thick of the recent battles, reached their first objective, the Fig Orchard, on a north-easterly drive from the base of the salient but there they found themselves being heavily mortared in positions anyway strewn with anti-personnel mines.

Two nearby enemy posts were attacked, the first at high cost as a mortar-bomb had exploded right in the middle of the platoon, the second by a patrol of ten men under command of a corporal. First they attacked two machine-gun posts with grenades and bayonets, then rushed across to the mortar post which the machine-guns had been protecting and captured the crew, whom they then took with them to the final objective carrying the three captured weapons.

But an attack by 2nd/23rd Battalion in the ground between those two advances supported by Valentines of 46th R.T.R. developed – to quote from the official Australian history – 'into the type of muddle for which there were several derisive epithets in common army parlance'. One company of infantry advanced riding on the Valentines, but some of these missed the marked gaps and had tracks blown off as a result, others behind tried to dodge around and ran on to other mines, and in the meantime the enemy gunners, alerted by the barrage which had by now gone far ahead of the tanks, pumped fire into the area. Casualties were heavy – and crippling, for the commander of the armour and all his squadron leaders were killed or wounded so communications broke down between infantry and armour at battalion level, and were then further confused when the brigade commanders of both the Australian infantry and the British armour went forward themselves to find out what had happened, and lost touch with their headquarters.

Yet despite these mishaps, 2nd/23rd captured a German position with six guns and 160 men, and the survivors of one company actually reached the railway line but were then forced back. At dawn the battalion were dug in about 1,000 yards in front of their original positions, but it was some hours before they had linked up with the 2nd/15th on their left and the 2nd/13th on the right, and even then contact was tenuous. But if the overall attack had not gained its full objectives, the three battalions had between them taken over 200 prisoners and killed an unknown number of enemy soldiers, and yet another demonstration of Allied air and artillery superiority had been given to a worried Axis command.

The advance had also given the Australians at the tip of the salient a commanding view over the ground leading to the coast, which would allow them accurately to plan the next operation; and it also gave them during that morning a certain amount of amusement. Evidently the exact extent of their success had not been appreciated by the enemy and several Axis vehicles drove unconcernedly into the new Australian lines, some carrying ammunition, some carrying food; none, unfortunately, carrying beer.

The following daylight hours (of October 29th) along the length of the main front passed with the same comparative lack of major action as had the previous two days, though another succession of counter-attacks was launched against the western face of the new salient. This was now held by men of the 2nd/17th and 2nd/15th Australian Battalions, and the assaults on their new positions were so hammered by artillery as they formed up, and then beaten back by anti-tank, mortar, machine-gun and rifle fire as they approached, that when evening fell, to quote from the Australian historian, 'It could be seen that dreadful casualties had been inflicted on the attackers.' Grey and khaki-uniformed bodies dotted the sand, wrecked vehicles burned, their ammunition racks spitting violently in the flames or tearing the vehicles apart with shattering explosions; smoke wreathed up into the short twilight, small stretcher-parties moved between the dark clumps, bearing away their sad burdens.

'Crumbling' was still paying off.

That night the 2nd/23rd Battalion mounted another attack to take some of the ground that had eluded them the night before, to find that the first 1,000 yards had been evacuated – so with no more losses they were level and in contact with their brother battalions on each side. On the morning of October 30th, therefore, the maps showed just that one small advance, the reports told of little but patrol activity, and the men at the front watched carefully not only the occasional enemy movements, but also the comings and goings of their own commanding officers and their adjutants whose activities, they had learned long ago, foreshadowed their own dangerous employment by but a few hours.

In this they were prescient, for on the night of October 30th/31st began an action in the Australian sector to contend in ferocity with that of the 2nd Rifle Brigade on Snipe. It was also, from the point of

Map 10   Australian attack, night of October 30th–31st

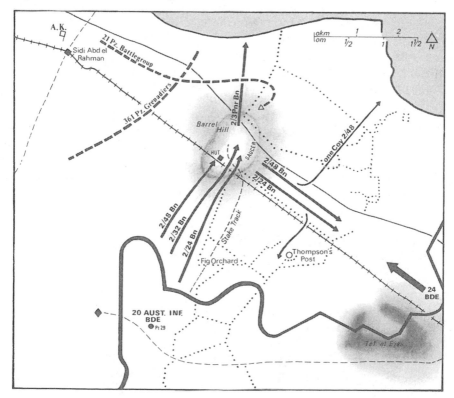

view of sheer planning, one of the most complicated small operations in the history of warfare.

The tactical idea behind it was to eliminate the Axis positions in the salient pointing back towards Tel el Eisa, in particular the strongpoint known as Thompson's Post, but undoubtedly the main purpose was to continue the 'crumbling' process against the Axis troops, and to draw as many of them as possible into a battle of attrition.

From the narrow salient now stretching up past Point 29, the 2nd/32nd Australian Battalion would drive north-eastwards and ensconce themselves across both the railway and the road at a locality known as Barrel Hill, while close behind them would follow the 2nd/48th Battalion on the left and the 2nd/24th on the right. These two battalions, using the 2nd/32nd Barrel Hill position as a base, would then turn sharp right and during the second phase of the operation drive south-east down along and between the railway and the road until they were north of Thompson's Post, at which point 2nd/24th would turn right and attack the post itself, while 2nd/48th sent a detachment out to the left to try to reach the sea.

Meanwhile, the men of the 24th Australian Brigade, who had not moved from their positions north of Tel el Eisa since they had opened the Battle of Alamein with their diversionary raids seven nights before, would drive forward to hold enemy attention to the east, while back at the 2nd/32nd positions astride the railway and road, the 2nd/3rd Pioneer Battalion would drive northwards to try to reach the sea some 5,000 yards west of the 2nd/48th detachment, thus forming a pocket in which, theoretically, the Bersaglieri and the remaining men of the German 125th Regiment would be trapped.

The task for the Pioneers – whose first infantry action this would be – was complicated by the direction that they should first of all regard themselves as reserves for the other three battalions engaged in the operation. To quote again from the official Australian history:

> The 2nd/3rd Pioneer Battalion therefore received instructions (aptly described by its historian as the IF plan) that it was to be ready to help the 2nd/32nd Battalion to take its objective if required; if not, then to be ready to help the 2nd/24th take Thompson's Post, if required; if not then to be ready to help the 2nd/48th take the defences from the road to the sea; if not required for any of these things, then to carry out its original role of advancing north from the firm base to the coast.[3]

As one fairly senior officer concerned with this operation remarked reflectively to another with whom he had been a fellow student at Staff College, 'If we had put in this solution to the problem at Camberley, we should certainly have been failed!'[4]

A detailed engineering plan was drawn up regarding the clearance of mines and the gapping of the railway embankment which ran in places some four feet above the desert level, to allow not only the infantry heavy weapons through, but also supporting Valentines from 23rd Armoured Brigade; and the plan for supporting artillery for the various phases of the operation – one of which at least would require a *receding* barrage with the infantry walking towards it from the far side – was of a complication that only a gunnery genius would fully appreciate. Australian, New Zealand and Highland Division artillery regiments were to take part, augmented by field batteries from the armoured divisions and medium guns from XXX Corps, giving a total of 312 field guns and 48 medium guns scheduled to fire some 64,000 rounds; it would undoubtedly be a noisy night, and was being preceded by an afternoon of swelling uproar as fighter-bombers roamed the coastal area searching for targets, while shortly before dusk three squadrons of Bostons and Baltimores arrived overhead and dropped 85 tons of bombs into what by any reckoning was a restricted area.

They successfully cloaked the sounds of the men of the 2nd/32nd moving up to their start line, but these arrived just a few minutes late and had to race forward to catch up with their supporting fire as it crashed down in front of them. They had nearly 2,000 yards to cover to the railway line, but the air-bombardment and the artillery had left few pockets of resistance on their direct route, so the 2nd/32nd were at the railway line on time, having taken prisoner nearly 175 men of the German 1/361st Battalion. Against rather heavier opposition they then crossed the 400 yards to the road and thus reached the further lip of their base, which now formed a saucer of about 500 yards' diameter in which was contained a concrete hut. This had probably originally been a maintenance store but it now housed some German wounded together with three German medical officers and their orderlies who, with a scrupulous adherence to the rules of war which would undoubtedly have been approved by their commander, worked steadily on through the days which followed alongside Australian counterparts who now moved in with them, ministering to the wounded of both sides without discrimination.

Behind the 2nd/32nd came the men of the 2nd/48th and the 2nd/24th followed eventually by those of the Pioneer Battalion, all of whom lost some men mopping up a few posts on the flanks of the original advance, two platoons of the Pioneers surviving a potentially disastrous attack on one post by but a narrow margin. They had attacked independently and from different directions and were only saved from annihilating each other by what their historian delicately calls 'the inimitable profanity of their language'.

Both 2nd/24th on the right and 2nd/48th on the left had swung to the south-east on time, but as 2nd/48th moved up to their second-phase start line they came under machine-gun fire and had to send out a company to quell the post to the north from which it came – and in the darkness and confusion 2nd/24th found themselves apparently alone; but promptly at 0100 the covering barrage crashed down along the line of the advance, and 2nd/24th set out on their 2,250-yard drive to the first objective north of Thompson's Post. As the guns firing their cover were pointing almost straight at them, the advancing infantry had to keep at least 600 yards back from the curtain of fire, and in doing so they thus lost much of its protection. Before very long, both battalions – for the 2nd/48th soon came up on the left – were fighting vicious actions with diminishing strength against stern and intelligent opposition.

On the right the leading company of the 2nd/24th ran into three posts early in the advance which all had to be stormed with grenade and bayonet, after which the company had to swing left to help the reduction of another post which held an 88mm. These actions left gaps through which the follow-up companies ran into devastating machine-gun fire which killed one company commander and wounded the other, then killed or wounded every subaltern or warrant officer who took over, at the same time reducing the already shrunken platoon strengths even further. On two occasions enemy machine-gun posts were silenced by lone men attacking with grenade and Bren-gun after the rest of the platoon had been put out of action – and when at last Colonel Weir brought his headquarters through to consolidate on that focal point north of Thompson's Post, his battalion had been reduced to 84 men!

The ordeal of the 2nd/48th was no easier. They reached their objective after two hours during which time one of the companies had been reduced to five men, including the sole surviving officer who had himself been wounded. Their right hand company had on occasion crossed to help the left hand companies of 2nd/24th and taken part in their ferocious battles, though these had not been lacking on their own sector, where one of their sergeants had also led an attack which put an 88mm. out of action.

The 2nd/48th reserve companies, too, had come forward through the remnants of the attacking companies, and faced the same devastating fire. One young subaltern led a bayonet charge against successive machine-gun and mortar posts which were holding up the whole company, and in doing so took fifteen prisoners – but when he came to lead them back he found that he had only two men beside himself left from his platoon, and when he arrived he found that he now commanded the whole company – of five men. As for the other assaulting company, there is no point in trying to improve upon the official version:

Hammer had heard no word from Robbins, whose company had pressed on close to the objective, because Robbins had been killed and all his platoon commanders and his headquarters men had either been killed or wounded. The company had been caught in open ground as it approached the end of its advance and 16 men were killed assaulting the objective. When Robbins had been killed and the officers commanding the other two platoons severely wounded, Sergeant Kibby took command and organised an attack on the objective with the survivors, perhaps a dozen men, in converging groups. The attackers were forced to ground within 20 yards of it. Kibby jumped up and charged, hurling grenades which silenced the post, but not before he had been caught by the enemy's fire, which cut off the life of a soldier whose gallantry in this and earlier actions at El Alamein could not have been surpassed.[5]

Shortly after Sergeant Kibby's gallant action (for which he was later awarded a posthumous Victoria Cross) Colonel Hammer came up and discovered that his battalion had been reduced to 41 (including himself), and that all his communications had been wrecked. He therefore decided to cross the railway line to try to find Colonel Weir and decide what to do, and while doing this fought a small action on his own during which he took two prisoners and was shot through the face. And on arrival at the 2nd/24th headquarters, he found that Colonel Weir had departed upon the most desperate venture of the entire operation.

Incredible as it may seem now – though probably not so incredible as it did then – the first message Weir had received once his communications had been re-established with headquarters back behind the original lines, was that it had been reported that Thompson's Post was unoccupied – so the proposed barrage to cover his attack had been cancelled, and would Weir please investigate and verify the report, occupying the Post should it prove to be true! And in response to what has been called 'a fearful mandate' Weir himself had set out with fifteen men to find out.

They reached the outer wire and indeed penetrated it without incident, but with great care as all concerned were deeply sceptical about the grounds upon which the operation was being mounted. Inevitably some heavy foot kicked a stone or a rifle clinked on a buckle, challenges rang out and the next moment the night erupted with all the noise and confusion of a close-quarter battle. But it was one in which at least one side had no wish to linger and Weir and his men were back through the wire at very short notice (leaving one man dead and another wounded but with a medical orderly already bringing him out) and right back on the railway line listening to Hammer's message within an hour.

However proud they all might have been of Australia's fighting reputation – and Heaven knows they had themselves contributed enough to it – there was no point in some 120 men, most of whom had been wounded at least once, attempting to hold a position which warranted the presence of at least one whole battalion, and preferably the best part of two; and within a very short time both groups were making their way back towards the 2nd/32nd positions. The survivors of 2nd/48th went straight away – taking with them some 200 German prisoners – but the trials of 2nd/24th were not yet over. On their way back south of the railway line, they went through a minefield planted with aerial bombs and two of them detonated, killing twelve men and wounding sixteen among whom was Colonel Weir. Most of the wounded were stretcher cases, like the greater proportion of the 264 wounded suffered by the two battalions during those few hours of action.

By now the 2nd/32nd men had been able to carry out a certain measure of consolidation. Engineers had cleared wide gaps through the approaches from the south, but their bulldozer and the truck containing much of their explosive had been blown up on mines and they had to tackle the job of gapping the railway embankment with pick and shovel. In this they had been assisted by some of the Pioneer Battalion so the gap was through in four hours and by 0400 the infantry heavy weapons were up and in position, despite the fact that the locality of the gap had been under enemy fire almost from the moment work was commenced.

Even more valuable than the heavy weapons, however, was the arrival of the 289th Battery of 6-pounder anti-tank guns, manned by Rhodesians, who now joined the three troops of the 9th Battery of the 2nd/3rd Anti-tank Regiment. In the dark, the various troops were disposed to cover every segment of the northern semi-circle, but except for those few guns sited south of the embankment, there was little broken ground to provide any cover, and the crews set to to dig themselves in.

The arrival from the east of the exhausted survivors of the 2nd/48th and 2nd/24th (they took position respectively north and south of the railway on the eastern lip of the saucer) at least clarified one point. None of the IFs now obtained and the Pioneers could therefore set out on their prime task – that of attempting to reach the coast to the north – although in this they could apparently no longer have the support of either the battery of anti-tank guns or the platoon of medium machine-guns which they had originally been promised.

This diminution of strength does not seem to have depressed the Pioneers in any way, for they were typical of their breed and independent to the point of bloody-mindedness. They were also extremely tough physically despite the fact that they were, in general, older men than those usually serving in combat formations. One of their company commanders, Major Rosevear, typified in several ways both the maturity and the outlook of the men he commanded: his biographical note states that he was born in Tasmania on June

6th, 1900, and served as a lance-corporal during the First World War with the Australian infantry; but it then adds with studied neutrality, 'When he enlisted under the name of H. G. Brown in 1916 Rosevear gave his year of birth as 1895.'

Now Rosevear and his companions awaited their orders to move out and the bombardment to give them cover, and both arrived at 0430. There was now so little time left for the leading company to advance the required 3,000 yards and then to dig in before dawn that no attention was paid to strict formation or last-minute briefing, and the platoons were off immediately, very close behind their artillery cover.

Captain Owens's company led through quite heavy fire and reached the first objective 1,500 yards in front on time, having collected 30 prisoners and three machine-guns on the way, and then at 0500 Captain Stevens's company went through them and drove on towards the coast. They were prevented from reaching it by their own barrage, which unaccountably ceased advancing some 1,200 yards short of their objective (some of their shells had been dropping short anyway) but maintained the curtain of fire until dawn was obviously near. Abandoning the idea of reaching the sand-dunes, Stevens thereupon ordered his men to dig in and took stock of his situation. It was not promising; his signals officer had been badly wounded so he had no communications either with his commanding officer or with Captain Owens behind him, and his Artillery Forward Observation Officer's truck had been blown up and the officer himself was missing – and as the light grew it revealed that there was little likelihood of reinforcement or supplies getting through to him while daylight lasted.

Like the infantry they had left behind them, the Pioneers were disposed in various positions at the bottom of a saucer with the enemy around three-quarters of the rim – and it was quickly evident that that enemy objected strongly to their presence. Machine-gun and rifle fire harassed the Pioneers' every movement, occasional mortar-bombs exploded in their midst and there was no doubt that soon heavier weapons would be brought to bear, so Captain Stevens – whose command, it is interesting to note, now constituted the right flank of the Eighth Army – sent out a patrol to enfilade the opposition from the flank.

It was not a success. The lieutenant in charge was badly wounded, all the N.C.O.s were hit and half were killed, and at the end only four men got back unscathed; and after another hour's increasingly heavy attack, the entrenched survivors were interested to see a German officer rise to his feet some 200 yards away and walk towards them carrying a white flag. Their continued resistance was, he suggested, a waste of time and of life. The Pioneers had no hope of relief or reinforcement, and as an alternative to annihilation surrender was surely no dishonour, no reflection upon their courage; and as he had tried hard to make both his tone and his suggestion reasonable and persuasive, the Oberleutnant may well have been upset by his reception. According to the *Official History*, remarks 'not in the best of taste' were addressed to him, the basic tenet of which was, 'If you want us, come and get us.'

By noon, Stevens's company was completely invested and shortly afterwards the Germans sent in an infantry attack accompanied by some light tanks in front of which they put down a smoke-screen – and as ammunition stocks in the post were all but exhausted, the remaining pioneers used the smoke as cover for escape. About half got away, the others being taken prisoner; Stevens himself lay in the sun all day apparently dead and covered with someone else's blood, but after dark he crawled some distance, then rose shakily to his feet and walked back to the main lines. Owens's company in the meantime had also been overrun, and by mid-afternoon Rosevear's company was under attack, as was the whole of the Saucer.

But the 2nd/32nd had now received yet another reinforcement which would add considerably to their powers of resistance. Since 0300 on October 31st, 32 Valentines of 40th R.T.R. under Lieutenant-Colonel J. L. Finigan had been groping their way carefully up the 'Stake Track' past the Fig Orchard on the western side of Thompson's Post, and by first light had reached the railway line. The engineers preceding them had suffered several casualties, they had themselves lost some tanks on the way up and as they turned westward along the line they promptly lost another two; Colonel Finigan thereupon decided to lead his squadrons forward on foot, and it was while doing so that he met Colonel Hammer, nursing his very painful face wound, and learned the details of the situation.

Finigan's original orders had been to support Hammer's battalion, and although he had hoped to find them more to the east than they were, he saw no reason to adjust those orders in any way. Bringing his tanks on across the railway line, he deployed them to the west of the 2nd/48th positions, his northern flank across the road – and as the light was growing fast, his men now had time and opportunity to assess their situation.

This, one of their number had no hesitation in describing as 'distinctly dodgy'. The Valentines were in a salient overlooked on three sides by enemy forces on higher ground, and if in the immediate neighbourhood there were many doubtless indomitable friends, these had the advantage that they were able to dig both themselves and their guns into some sort of shelter. The tank crews, on the other hand, had no choice if they wished to defend themselves but to sit in their thinly armoured vehicles standing some seven and a half feet above ground, of which the highest nearby rise was the four-foot railway embankment behind them.

By the time it was full daylight it was quite obvious that anyone within 3,000 yards who cared to glance in their direction could not fail to see them, and one person who did so promptly reported the fact to Rommel, adding that in standing where they did the Valentines effectively cut off the German troops in Thompson's Post and their Bersaglieri comrades.

Rommel by this time had long abandoned any faint hope he might once have held of winning the battle outright, and was now even suspecting that his idea of holding the enemy in position until they ran out of energy and determination was also doomed to disappointment. In order to preserve some part of his army and the lives of the devoted men he had led for so long, he had therefore ordered a reconnaissance of the Fuka positions some seventy miles back, and been quite encouraged when reports told of the possibility of strong defences in the north, and ground so broken in the south on the edge of the Qattara Depression that no attacking armoured force could penetrate there.

But this still left him with the almost insuperable problems of the movement back itself, for there was hardly enough fuel to move his armoured divisions that far, let alone for transport to lift the non-motorised formations who might therefore have to be sacrificed. Even before those problems were faced, however, there would be the equally intransigent task of disengaging his most valuable troops from the battle in which they were already deeply committed, without letting enemy forces flood through and overwhelm the entire Panzer-armee, mobile and non-mobile units alike.

Air support in far greater strength than was available at the moment would be required in any circumstances, and especially in the face of the present almost complete domination of the skies by the enemy – but when applied to, Kesselring could hold out little or no hope for even the smallest increase. Already he was being pressed to release some of the Luftwaffe formations for service on the Russian Front in an apparently important battle raging around Stalingrad, and there was even doubt that the morale of the Luftwaffe crews here in the desert could stand much more of the strain of this continual conflict. That Italian pilots sometimes failed to press home attacks had long been accepted, but during the last few days reports had come to him of Stuka pilots jettisoning their bombs indiscriminately over friend and foe alike – and nowhere near their targets – immediately Hurricanes or Tomahawks appeared.

Morale among even his trusty soldiers was sagging, too. Under the devastating artillery barrages which fell upon every assembly of Axis troops, counter-attack after counter-attack had broken up – sometimes before they had even begun to advance – and an ominous account of over a hundred infantrymen of 15th Panzer Division giving themselves up to British patrols in the central area told its own story. Even the 21st Panzer Division under their new commander, Generalleutnant von Randow, were showing signs of depression – not all that surprisingly in view of the fact that every day since their arrival in the north they had been bombed at almost hourly intervals by squadrons of eighteen British or South African bombers, flying in those imperturbable formations already dubbed 'Party Rally raids' by the cynical recipients.

But 21st Panzer Division still constituted the most reliable armoured formation at his disposal, and during the night of October 28th/29th he had ordered their withdrawal from the line to give him some sort of mobile reserve, to be replaced at the front by the now battered and attenuated remains of the Trieste Motorised Division with their 34 outdated M13s. As for the only other Italian division in which he had much faith – the Ariete – they were all back in the south and he only hoped that with the support of the Ramcke Brigade and the Folgores they would be able to hold out if Montgomery decided, after all, to mount a major assault down there.

Not that this was likely. Captured British documents and the obvious concentration of Eighth Army strength in the north supported his growing conviction that their commander intended to drive along the narrow coastal strip of Egypt, in the belief that the use of a properly laid road would compensate for the restricted width of the advance and the lack of space for wide manoeuvre – at which, after all, the British were not particularly adept. His own concentration of 90th Light Division in the north with their headquarters near Sidi Abd el Rahman, together with those units of Lungershausen's 164th Division which were still in their pre-battle positions, was the best counter to that design, and only time would show if the formations were strong enough to withstand the assault when it came, or nimble enough to extricate themselves if and when it became obvious that they were not.

At least there had been no casualties among the topmost commanders – other than Stumme. General Ritter von Thoma still commanded the Afrika Korps with cold efficiency and Bayerlein had returned from leave on the morning of October 29th and been immediately despatched to join him; von Randow with the 21st, von Vaerst with the 15th and Graf von Sponek with the 90th Light were all still alive and active, and instantly responsive to his demands. If only the same could be said of the Italians!

Generale Barbasetti had arrived at Rommel's headquarters on October 29th – in place of Maresciallo Cavallero who had been, fortunately for him, detained in Rome – and received the full blast of Rommel's anger, exacerbated at that particular moment by the arrival of the news of the loss of the *Louisiano*. Where were all the supplies that Rommel had been repeatedly promised? Where was the ammunition, the guns, the trucks and the reinforcements which weeks ago Il Duce had agreed were necessary and which Rommel had been almost pleading for ever since his return?

Above all, where was the fuel? And it was not the slightest good assuring him that it was on its way in heavily armoured Italian cruisers to Benghasi, as it would take too long to reach him from there and too much of it would be burned up by the transport bringing it.

Tobruk was the port to which all supplies must now be directed if they were to be of the slightest use, and if this entailed the Italian Navy's venturing into danger from Royal Air Force or Royal Navy torpedoes, it was no more than that in which the Panzerarmee had stood for months; in any case facing danger was what naval craft were built and bought for!

The tirade went on for some time and it was a discomfited, indeed outraged, Generale Barbasctti who eventually departed with whatever dignity was left to him, unaware that he was, in fact, lucky to get away when he did. Later that day as Rommel was conferring with Westphal and others of his staff, they were all suddenly electrified by a message to the effect that two British divisions had made their way through the Qattara Depression, scaled the sides and were now sixty miles south of Mersa Matruh and moving rapidly north-west! Air patrols were sent out, one of the Fascist reserve divisions alerted and the relief of 21st Panzer Division by Trieste delayed – until the following morning (October 30th) when, to quote Rommel's words, ' . . . we discovered that the whole story, which had come to us from Comando Supremo, was a pure invention.'

Italian popularity suffered even further diminution later that morning, first with the news that Trieste were now apparently too weak in numbers to take over all the 21st Panzer Division positions so that one German infantry battalion must stay where they were, and then that the Littorio Division grouped with the 15th Panzer Division had only 23 tanks to contribute to the mobile reserve which Rommel was endeavouring to put together.

This last exercise in itself was revealing a number of disturbing factors, such as that the entire Afrika Korps could muster fewer than a hundred panzers – including several Mark IIs – and now, as Rommel pointed out to Kesselring who arrived for a visit during the afternoon, those happy, carefree days when recovery teams could scavenge the battlefield for replacements or when numbers could be maintained with captured British tanks were but a dim memory.

The only good news during that day (October 30th) was that 600 tons of fuel had, after all, arrived at Tobruk (enough for twenty-four hours) but even this was dampened by reports that the R.A.F. were shooting up everything that moved along the coast road, so the petrol still might not arrive at the front.

So plans for that withdrawal must at least be drawn up and warning orders issued. Perhaps an opportunity would arise to whip the infantry out of the line under cover of darkness, load them into whatever transport could be found and race them back to the Fuka line with the panzer formations covering them, fighting a delaying action to give the infantry as much time as possible to dig themselves in. It was a slim hope, but perhaps the Gods of War would relent, perhaps the British were more tired than they appeared.

In the meantime, that mobile reserve must be formed – and it was while more attempts were being made to withdraw panzers from the line and replace them with infantry during the night of October 30th/31st that once again the massed British artillery in the north erupted, its opening salvo crashing down on positions held by remnants of the 1st/361st Battalion and almost annihilating them. Shortly afterwards all contact with them was lost as was that with one of the Italian artillery positions nearby, and from then on the night was filled with noise and fire from which very little useful – or even intelligible – information emerged until dawn, when a detached section of the 361st Grenadier Regiment reported not only the presence of enemy infantry patrols right up near the coast, but also a force of thirty heavy tanks between the railway and the road.

Rommel had, of course, been conscious all the time of the exposed position of the troops out in the Tel el Eisa salient, but had considered their presence there a positive check to enemy plans so long as they could be supplied and, if necessary, reinforced. Now it looked as though he might have left them there too long, so driving immediately to Sidi Abd el Rahman he set up a command post from which a relieving operation could be mounted, and sent for von Thoma to come up and form a battlegroup from elements of both 21st Panzer and 90th Light Divisions, augmented by some of Panzer-armee's mobile artillery.

Apparently the Afrika Korps staff found this direction almost incomprehensible, as it meant that von Thoma would be abandoning a central position commanding large forces in order to command small forces on the flank – though not so incomprehensible as did von Thoma himself when he arrived. Rommel had already set up the first attempt to get through to Thompson's Post, and he ignored von Thoma's presence and continued to direct the assault himself; by 1100 the panzers, artillery and infantry were assembling, the battalion commanders issuing their orders – and when at 1105 bombers arrived overhead and the British artillery opened fire yet again, it took the presence of Rommel to hold the group together and get it moving down towards its objective.

As they did so, they could see the British tanks also begin moving – towards them to form a shield between the railway embankment and the road. Perhaps they were even heavier tanks than they looked.

They were, of course, still the Valentines – now committing themselves to a battle in which their foes could destroy them at anything up to 1,200 yards whilst their own puny 2-pounders could do little until the panzers were within four hundred, and then only if they hit the vulnerable sides.

But the Australian infantry and the Rhodesian anti-tank gunners were with them and they themselves were, after all, infantry support tanks; no matter what the odds, they would not desert their friends, and in any case everyone in the Saucer had faith in both the main artillery behind them and in the R.A.F. – a faith in which they were not to be disappointed. The first assault at about 1130 consisted of fifteen panzers which rolled down upon them between the road and the railway with an infantry escort north of the road, but before it approached within hitting distance a flight of Bostons dropped a load of bombs on the panzers, and artillery had thoroughly dispersed the infantry.

But some of the panzers swung up to the north and through the remains of the 2nd/3rd Pioneer positions, then down again against the main defence, and soon the Valentines were being driven back towards the embankment. Two of the Rhodesian anti-tank guns were wrecked, and with the panzers driving implacably down between the smoking remains, the hard-pressed Valentine crews tried to beat them by movement – tempting the panzers forward towards one troop of Valentines while another manoeuvred to catch them from the flank. They scored some successes that way but at a dreadful price, and as the afternoon wore on the smoke from burning Valentines drifted over the confusion to mix with the blown sand and the heat-haze, to cut visibility drastically.

This could have been a saving factor for the Valentines had they wished to take advantage of it, but while they had ammunition and their guns could fire it they had to stay and wreak what damage they could – and there were other targets besides the seemingly invulnerable panzers. An 88mm. gun and its trailer were wrecked and at least one half-tracked vehicle set alight – and then somewhat to the defenders' astonishment, they saw that the attack was faltering, the panzers drawing back.

Perhaps they had run out of ammunition, perhaps they had been unprepared for such violent opposition, but as they went the German battlegroup left behind them in the Saucer four wrecked panzers and one burning furiously, the 88mm. gun and the remains of several lighter vehicles; but 21 of the Valentines had been knocked out including several which had brewed, and 44 crew members were dead. This was a heavy casualty rate for such a small armoured force, and the survivors were glad to receive orders to withdraw to the south of the railway line as daylight faded, though some of them were unable immediately to move even that far. Radiators and fuel tanks had been ruptured by hits, batteries cracked and the electrolite drained away, so fewer than ten Valentines were in the end to make the journey – but those that did found that they had that day earned the deepest respect and admiration of the Australians who had been watching them. 'The courage of these men', wrote the historian of the 2nd/48th Battalion in a judgment made by men who knew their subject, 'made their action one of the most magnificent of the war.'

The battle in the Saucer, however, was by no means over. Reports reaching General Morshead that day (October 31st) had revealed to him the losses sustained by the battalions of 26th Brigade during the last eighteen hours, and he decided that they must be relieved by the two battalions of the 24th Brigade which had seen so little action since the first night of the battle (the third battalion was the 2nd/32nd which could have been judged lately to have seen enough for the whole brigade). So during the night of October 31st/November 1st, Brigadier Godfrey brought his fresh battalions around and fed them up into the forward positions from which the exhausted survivors of 2nd/24th and 2nd/48th were withdrawn, thus considerably increasing the strength to support their brothers in the 2nd/32nd and their new-found Rhodesian friends.

They were in position by dawn to watch first of all an air battle in which British and American fighters shot down seven Stukas and chased away the remainder of a large group sent over to bomb them, then the regular shelling of yet another battlegroup forming up now under command of von Thoma and Bayerlein to mount the first of the day's attempts to relieve Thompson's Post. It came in just after midday – a battalion attack supported by panzers and sustained artillery cover which included at least eight 88mm. guns firing air-bursts above Australian positions – but was beaten off at the cost of twelve of the anti-tank guns which had been an especial target of the German attack.

Another assault came in at 1525, and this one developed into an almost continuous mêlée which showed no sign of flagging as the afternoon wore on, despite the solid and unyielding defence against which the attackers were hurling themselves. However, some of the panzers swung well north and through the dunes to make contact with Thompson's Post, and many were seen closing down on its northern side just about the time when a major disaster struck the men in the

Saucer. All day long the German artillery had been shelling their positions at intervals, and in the early evening a lucky shell hit the command headquarters, killing Brigadier Godfrey and three of his staff and severely wounding two others.

The brigade major took charge, but pressure from the north had been such that now there were no Australians across the road, and with the loss of the anti-tank guns the safest place for the bulk of the infantry was now obviously south of the embankment – and with their withdrawal there, the German corridor to Tel el Eisa was strengthened and the way opened for the withdrawal of the Axis troops in the salient.

This was still an idea to which Rommel was unresponsive. During October 31st both von Thoma and Bayerlein had suggested that the troops in the salient should be warned to ready themselves for immediate evacuation if and when the enemy blocking force were swept aside, but Rommel had then vetoed the idea, as so hasty a withdrawal would probably mean a loss of invaluable heavy weapons; anyway, a German presence at Thompson's Post could still prove a vexatious thorn in the enemy's side if it could be maintained.

But he had been away from the Sidi Abd el Rahman front checking on the situation further south (where he later recorded that waves of enemy aircraft, each of eighteen or twenty planes, had bombed Axis positions thirty-four times in less than eight hours) and on his return to the north on the afternoon of November 1st he went to see for himself the extent of the carnage wrought on that small battlefield across the road and railway line.

'Seven wrecked tanks lay around "The Hut" alone, and farther on we could see another 30 or 40 destroyed British armoured vehicles,'[6] he wrote, but he nevertheless listened without comment to one piece of von Thoma's report. The colonel of the battalion at Thompson's Post had made his way back to Sidi Abd el Rahman during the preceding night, and the impression he had left with Bayerlein was that although he and his men would stay there if so directed, there were not half so many of them now as there had been when the battle opened and most of the survivors had been wounded at least once; moreover the bulk of the defences had already been smashed by artillery fire.

Rommel at that particular time did not give specific orders regarding withdrawal, but at least he did not repeat his flat rejection of the previous day. In any case, he had other matters to consider. The supply situation was as bad as ever, and if there had been a temporary alleviation regarding fuel, ammunition was now running crucially short especially for the anti-tank guns. Only forty tons had arrived since the opening of the battle and, in contrast to the extravagance shown by the British, both Italian and German gunners had to exercise the shrewdest economy. Concentrated fire was a thing of the past, harassing fire the best which could be afforded.

But if supplies were not getting through, messages were still arriving from Rome:

For Field Marshal Rommel

The Duce authorises me to convey to you his deep appreciation of the successful counter-attack led personally by you. The Duce also conveys to you his complete confidence that the battle now in progress will be brought to a successful conclusion under your command.

Ugo Cavallero[7]

As there were indications that such easy optimism was just as prevalent at the Führer's headquarters, Il Duce's platitudes did nothing to soothe Rommel's temper or relieve his anxieties. These were mounting in the light of reports and assessments submitted by his intelligence staffs, who were becoming increasingly alarmed by indications that the enemy were grouping for yet another gigantic onslaught upon what had now become an attenuated and threadbare line of defences. British troops were massing again just to the south of the known Australian positions, and it seemed that thorough preparations for a devastating blow there had been taking place for some time.

In this the staffs were correct, though they were not to know of the diplomatic manoeuvrings which had been necessary before Eighth Army plans could take the shape they did, nor the political storm the course of the battle had been causing in the British camp during the last few days.

If Brigadier de Guingand's fortitude had been tested in the early morning of October 25th by the crisis which entailed the awakening of his chief, October 29th had called upon all his reserves of loyalty, imagination, tact and charm. It had been fortunate that he was so well-endowed with all of them.

Quite early in the morning the intelligence staff at Army H.Q. had collected from both field sources and Ultra a significant body of evidence to the effect that Rommel was concentrating 90th Light Division and a considerable proportion of his remaining armour opposite the Australian section of the front. It looked indeed to some of them as though he were abandoning his policy of 'corseting' the Italians with his German troops, and instead was withdrawing the latter and packing them solidly up into the coastal sector – directly in front of the proposed drive by the newly assembled forces under General Freyberg; and it struck several of them that an adjustment of direction would not only increase the chances of success, but also promise greater results.

If Freyberg's drive was directed more to the south than was currently planned, and hit the line of junction between the regrouping Italian and German forces, and especially if its main assault fell most heavily upon the Italians just south of that junction, it might break through completely and thus, if the X Corps armour followed up quickly and strongly enough, open up an opportunity for first pressing the Germans against the coast and then cutting them off with a short northward drive to the sea.

This was the suggestion put by de Guingand to Montgomery at the first morning conference on October 29th, and it was with some disappointment that afterwards he had to report to his colleagues, 'No, he won't have it' – a decision which added to growing worries among some of them that the battle was not going according to plan.

They were not the only ones either, for in both Cairo and Whitehall anxious eyes had been watching every development, and not always with the rocklike confidence of the man in charge. For Mr Churchill especially, the strain of leading his country for two and a half years of perhaps the greatest danger she had ever faced now reached its climax, for he realised quite clearly that if the attack at Alamein should fail his own career would be over and he would be toppled from power – which would then pass to others who would surely prove in the end to be lesser mortals than himself. Not only would his own life be reduced to waste and ashes, but the hardship and perils which his beloved country had faced since 1940 would be extended far into the future. The weight of the world sat on the Prime Minister's shoulders during that first week of Alamein, and on the morning of October 29th seemed likely to crush him, for news had arrived that despite Montgomery's assurance that Eighth Army would break through the enemy defences in less than a fortnight, here he was already *withdrawing whole divisions from the battle*!

The storm burst over Sir Alan Brooke's head early that morning. What was his protégé Montgomery doing, allowing the battle to peter out? Why was he taking troops out of the battle? Why did he say he would break out seven days after the break-in if he only intended to fight in a half-hearted manner?

'Haven't we got a single general who can win even one battle?' Churchill cried, and for a moment Sir Alan thought he was going to hit him.

The storm slackened under Sir Alan's stout defence of Montgomery's actions to date, but it flared up again at a Chiefs of Staff meeting in the afternoon and needed the cool common sense of the South African Field Marshal Smuts to calm the atmosphere; but later Brooke recorded that although during the conference he had maintained an exterior of complete confidence, he was by no means unworried himself. 'I had told them what I thought Monty must be doing . . . but there was just that possibility that I was wrong and Monty was beat.'[8]

If doubts existed at such a level, it was hardly surprising that questions were being raised much nearer the scene of action, where physical danger would be present if the Eighth Army collapsed – and it was in connection with these that de Guingand's resources were again tested.

When General Alexander arrived for the scheduled morning conference and report, he was accompanied this time not only by his own Chief of Staff, Lieutenant-General Richard McCreery, but also by the Minister of State in Egypt, Richard Casey; and the last-named bore with him a cable from Mr Churchill pointing out the imminence of the landings in North Africa, and the desirability of an obvious, overwhelming *and early* victory at Alamein in order to encourage the French in Morocco and Algeria to throw in their lot with the Anglo-Americans.

In response, Montgomery described the situation and his plans, and, according to de Guingand, 'radiated confidence'; but afterwards Casey drew de Guingand aside and asked him if he really was happy about the way things were going. According to the only witness present at that time, the Chief of Intelligence, Colonel Williams, Casey seemed unconvinced by de Guingand's protestations of confidence, and at one point mumbled something about cabling Churchill to warn him that bad news might be on its way – at which de Guingand exploded in a spectacular (and possibly feigned) burst of rage.

'For God's sake don't!' he exclaimed, adding, 'If you do, I'll see you're drummed out of political life!' – although what effect a soldier of de Guingand's standing at that time could have had on the position of a career diplomat – who in any case was not in political life as such – only de Guingand himself could have imagined. But it would seem that his momentary display of conviction had been enough to muzzle Casey for no such cable was ever sent, and after the Minister of State had left de Guingand could once again devote himself to the sphere of his military influence, especially to the matter of the forthcoming operation about which he and his colleagues still retained their early morning opinions.

They had learned shortly before the conference that in these opinions they had the agreement of General McCreery, who announced that he would certainly advocate in the strongest terms that General Freyberg's assault should not be delivered along the coast, but down in the area just north of Kidney Ridge; and de Guingand's diplomacy was once more called into action. Montgomery disliked McCreery (not least, one suspects, as the latter was such a strong supporter and friend of General Lumsden) and de Guingand knew that pressure from that particular quarter would thus be immediately counter-productive.

'I will go and talk to Monty about it again – don't you, for goodness' sake!' he pleaded. 'If one can persuade him it's his own idea . . . '

And although the subject was brought up during the conference to be brushed aside once again by Montgomery, de Guingand went back to see his chief after Alexander's party had left. How he put the case, whether or not he did manage to make Montgomery believe that it was all his own idea, it is now impossible to say – but when de Guingand emerged he did so with Montgomery's full agreement that the axis of Freyberg's attack would now lie along an extension of the original Australian sector's northern boundary, and not along the coast road. The sigh of relief which went up at Army H.Q. was echoed later by Bernard Freyberg himself.

'That's what I wanted to do originally,' he grunted; and promptly asked for a lot more tanks to be put under his command. It was a request he was frequently to make and almost as frequently to have refused, but the new scope of this operation undoubtedly entailed much more armoured participation, so much of the rest of the day was occupied by drawing up plans in more detail and to a greater scale than before. It seems that this was done to the Army Commander's satisfaction, for his diary entry for that night ends with the passage:

> The Armd Car Regts will be launched right into open country to operate for four days against the enemy supply routes.
> The two Armoured Divisions will engage and destroy the DAK.
> This, in effect, is a hard blow with my right, followed the next night with a knock-out blow with my left. The blow on night 31 Oct/1 Nov will be supported by some 350 guns firing about 400 rounds a gun.
> I have given the name 'SUPERCHARGE' to the operation.[9]

The assault opened in fact at 0105 on November 2nd, having been postponed for twenty-four hours at General Freyberg's request after he had observed how exhausted the attacking infantry were by the time they had arrived in their assembly areas. The Geordies of 151st Brigade, for instance, had been brought up from south of Ruweisat Ridge but failed to reach their bivouac area at Makh Khad on time, owing first to the difficulties of moving across almost unmapped desert which was nevertheless congested with both traffic and static military units, and secondly by what the New Zealand *Official History* calls 'the inertia of several bodies of 10 Corps who resisted being shifted to other areas'.

In the end, strong measures had to be taken at a high level to get these formations to move at all, for X Corps hubris was undimmed despite the events of the last few days and they still reckoned they were something of a law unto themselves. Even the squadrons of Pip Roberts's 22nd Armoured Brigade had not been made particularly welcome when they came up from XIII Corps's area, and now they waited in isolation around Imayid Station some miles east of El Alamein itself.

But during the extra period, granted somewhat reluctantly by General Montgomery, the units did get themselves sorted out and the infantry were waiting in their concentration areas on time. The 151st Brigade with the 28th New Zealand Battalion of Maoris attached

Map 11 *Supercharge*, November 1st–2nd

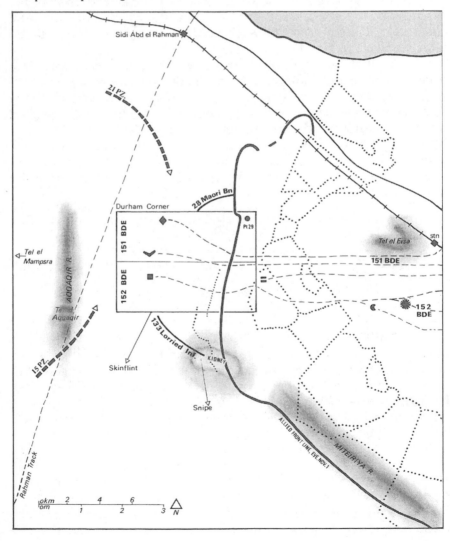

(they were to hold the first section of the northern flank of the advance), the minefield task force behind and following them the 44 Valentines of 8th R.T.R. were all grouped just south of Tel el Eisa, while to their south at the roots of the Two-bar and Square tracks were the Scots of 152nd Brigade, with 5th Seaforths on the brigade right, 5th Camerons on the left and 2nd Seaforths following to cover the south-western corner of the salient. The Royal Sussex Battalions of 133rd Lorried Infantry Brigade would follow to fulfil the same duties in the south as the Maoris in the north, and 38 Valentines of 50th R.T.R. would provide immediate armoured support.

In the plan of attack there was some similarity between *Supercharge* and the Australian section of *Lightfoot*, in that the shape of the advance was a rectangle some 4,000 yards wide and nearly 6,000 yards long which would take the assault from a line running south from just east of Point 29 along the line of the present defences towards Kidney, westwards to a line of similar length with its northern end almost on the Rahman Track. As with *Lightfoot* the advance would be covered by a powerful artillery barrage, this time from 296 field guns and 48 medium guns firing altogether some 54,000 rounds including, in specific places and at specific times, smoke rounds as direction indicators and tracer shells to demarcate brigade boundaries.

The minefield task forces were not so large as those for *Lightfoot*, as it was believed that this advance would not face such wide and concentrated mine-marshes, but what was expected was a scattering of those random, isolated patches of mines which had proved so troublesome before, so Scorpions were taking part in the advance.

Behind the infantry would follow first the 72 Shermans and Grants and 49 Crusaders of John Currie's 9th Armoured Brigade – still regarded by Freyberg as the only trustworthy armour in Eighth Army – then the 150 Shermans and Grants and 110 Crusaders of the two brigades – 2nd and 8th – of the 1st Armoured Division, still under General Briggs. When the armour had broken out through the advanced infantry positions, crossed the Rahman Track and reached the ridge north of Tel el Aqqaqir, it would all come under command of X Corps now concentrated on 'ground of its own choosing', and there General Lumsden would direct the armoured battle in which all that remained of 15th and 21st Panzer Divisions and of Ariete and Littorio would be destroyed.

In the meantime, armoured cars of the Royal Dragoons, the 12th Lancers and the 4th/6th South African Armoured Car Regiment would endeavour to break out through the northern or southern flanks of the advance, circle around well to the west of Tel el Aqqaqir and cause as much chaos and confusion in the Axis rear areas as possible.

As throughout the entire battle so far, the Royal Air Force and the South African Air Force opened the action and gave their unstinted support to their earthbound colleagues. During the evening of November 1st, Wellingtons with Albacores from the Fleet Air Arm bombed all known targets from Tel el Aqqaqir up to Sidi Abd el Rahman and westwards as far as El Daba, setting fire to several ammunition and supply dumps and thoroughly wrecking the Afrika Korps communications system.

On the ground, the infantry moved up to the line of cairns which marked the start line (General Wimberley was making sure that his Jocks at least would not suffer the confusion regarding position that had marred *Lightfoot*, and the 151st Brigade followed suit), Durhams shivering in their khaki drill but liberally coated with the fine pale dust through which they had marched, the Scots warmer in battle-dress and again wearing the St Andrew's Cross in white flannelette across their small-packs. Behind them the gunners waited, while as a safety precaution the two battalions of the 6th New Zealand Brigade who had been holding the line through which the attack would be launched, came quietly back; the opening barrage would fall very close to their recent positions.

At 0055 the infantry stepped over their tapes and walked forward, at 0105 the guns opened with yet another shattering bombardment with one shell bursting every twelve yards along the 4,000-yard line; dust and smoke plumed up in the now-familiar choking clouds, and as the men moved into them the guns lifted forward another hundred yards and from along the southern half of the assault came the high, piercing-sweet notes of the bag-pipes.

The Maoris on the extreme right flank met opposition almost from the start, the strongpoint just in front of Point 29 which was their prime objective proving strong indeed. One Maori company was practically wiped out in the initial assault, but the company on its left flank reached their objectives on time and dug in to form a base from which the survivors of the first company could be supported. This was as well, for the line of the Maori objectives had been slightly north of the path of the barrage and there were several enemy posts to be subdued by bayonet and bomb before the root of the northern flank of *Supercharge* would be securely linked to the Australians to the north.

South of the Maoris, the two assault companies of the 8th Durham Light Infantry broke quickly through a line of enemy posts to overrun a German tank recovery park and a medical dressing station, both occupied by men shocked almost to the edge of hysteria by the shelling. The first objective was reached on time but with the loss of about a hundred men and several of their officers, so the reserve company went through to reach the final objective (the corner near the Rahman Track) at about 0400, having collected nearly fifty prisoners en route. For the moment, however, they were out of contact with everyone as their wireless link had been destroyed, but the survivors of the other companies gradually came up, then the battalion heavy weapons, then New Zealand anti-tank and machine-gun platoons, and by dawn the 8th Durhams, though low in strength, were well established on their objectives.

On their right the 6th Durham Light Infantry, who had followed some 500 yards behind the 8th, met little opposition until they had passed the area in which the Maoris were fighting so hard, then came under heavy machine-gun fire from the north which it took a whole company to quell. But the other companies swung right to form a battalion front facing north between the corner of the salient and the intended positions of the Maoris though with a gap still between them, and again, anti-tank guns and heavy machine-guns quickly arrived. By dawn the Durham corner of the salient was secure.

On the left of the Durham Brigade sector, the 9th Durhams had met only a line of dug-in tanks and gun positions during the second half of their advance, and even these were not defended with great resolution as the barrage had been as effective here as on the right. They were on their final objective by 0400 and in touch with their brothers of the 8th, their heavy weapons and support anti-tank guns with them well before dawn. The Durham Brigade had therefore reached all their objectives on time at a cost to themselves of some 350 killed, wounded and missing, having taken the same number of prisoners who upon examination proved to be mostly from the Littorio and Trento Divisions, with a sprinkling from the 115th Panzergrenadier Regiment.

On the Durhams' left, the advance of the Scotsmen of 152nd Brigade had gone so like a drill that a fair picture of the night's proceedings can be gained from the signals sent by the brigade commander, George Murray, to General Freyberg:

0148   We are in touch with both battalions and everything appears to be going smoothly.

0218   There is light shelling and moderate machine-gun fire on our front. We have taken some prisoners, a mixture of Italians and Germans. Everything appears to be going according to plan.

0235   Newly laid minefield discovered.

0359   On our left flank our tanks are engaging enemy tanks.

0417   Both battalions have reached objective and are again in action with enemy tanks. Artillery concentration 'Roxbrough' called for and fired.

0525   Enemy tanks are melting away and battalions are getting supporting arms up. One Italian tank captured intact.

0535   Reorganisation of final objective is proceeding and battalions are
linking up. Right gap is through and left will be open as soon as small
minefield is cleared. Our casualties will not exceed 40 per battalion. [10]

Most of the Scots casualties had been suffered during assaults on
dug-in tanks, but even from these little real resistance had been
experienced while the few infantry posts they had encountered –
Italian or German – had been surrendered by men totally shattered
by the storm of fire which had passed over them. Whatever the
co-ordination between other arms, that between infantry and gunners
had now reached a state of near-perfection.

Between infantry and its immediate supporting armour co-
ordination was good, too. The Valentines had in places been held up
by uncleared minefields, and one troop of the 8th R.T.R. had missed
a marked route and was badly delayed as a result, but the tank crews
were determined to get through to their friends' support and by dawn
most of them had done so. On the Jocks' left flank, enemy tanks had
been reported holding up the formation of the south-facing front by
the 2nd Seaforths, but they seemed to 'melt away' when both guns
and Valentines came quickly into action, and well on time the
Seaforths had made contact with the 2nd Royal Sussex on their left,
whose line in turn was continued by the 5th Royal Sussex back to the
original Oxalic Line where it was now held by the 5th/7th Gordons.

XXX Corps infantry had undoubtedly completed all its primary
tasks in *Supercharge* well on time, and now it was up to the armour.
As the first assault armour (as opposed to the support Valentines)
due to come through was that of John Currie's 9th Armoured
Brigade, no one doubted that it would be with them as quickly as
determination, devotion and inspiring leadership could arrange.

It was going to need all of those qualities. Although orders had
made it plain that 9th Armoured Brigade were to have priority in all
tank replacements, it seems that as a result of the haste and strain of
battle conditions more effort had gone into providing quantity than
quality. Of the 123 tanks of various marks mustered that night, few
were new, and the Crusaders issued to the Royal Wiltshire Yeomanry
to replace their losses of that first night on Miteiriya Ridge were 'in a
deplorable state. Nothing fitted. Nothing worked. Guns, compasses
and radios were all faulty.' [11]

John Currie's brigade was therefore not in such a state as would fill
their commander's breast with pride and hope – except perhaps with
regard to the morale of his men, and here he faced an even more
'fearful mandate' than that accepted by Colonel Weir north of
Thompson's Post. At the briefing conference held by General
Freyberg on November 1st, the task for 9th Armoured Brigade – to
advance past the infantry objective, break through the enemy
defences before and immediately beyond the Rahman Track and

then hold open the gap against enemy counter-attacks until the heavy brigades of the 1st Armoured Division had gone through – was so obviously one of difficulty and danger that when Currie's time came to make comment, he rather diffidently suggested that by the end of the day his brigade might well have suffered 50 per cent casualties.

To this Freyberg had replied with studied nonchalance, 'Perhaps more than that. The Army Commander says that he is prepared to accept a hundred per cent.'[12]

And in the dead silence which followed this pronouncement, those who were not thanking God they were not standing in Currie's shoes wondered how far down his command he would allow the fiat to percolate.

In the event he told his regimental commanders and these passed it on to most of their squadron commanders, but it would seem that the rest of the brigade as they waited in their assembly area were accepting the action to come as just another in which they would undoubtedly be the 'sharp end' of the assault, and suffer accordingly; but they had been there before, and not very long ago.

The problem for the moment was to get there, for in addition to the general dilapidation of their tanks and armament, the darkness of the night was immeasurably increased by the clouds of dust churned up by every movement, far worse in their estimation than ever before. Traffic and exploding shells, to say nothing of the thousands of marching feet, had by now pulverised the surface of the desert all the way from Alamein Station where by 1900 on November 1st they were forming up, to the proposed new infantry line nearly fifteen miles to the west; dust at least a foot thick carpeted the route the whole way, and that night there was a head wind.

Except for the leading vehicles in each column, therefore, the three regimental groups were condemned to a long journey in choking fog with very limited visibility. The leading group consisting of the 3rd Hussars with 33 tanks (but whose column including support infantry, anti-tank gunners and supply trucks totalled nearly 300 vehicles) made their way along the Sun track between the road and the railway as far as the Diamond track, which they joined to pass south of Tel el Eisa and into the main approaches to the battle zone. They were followed along Sun by the 44 tanks of the Royal Wiltshire Yeomanry together with the Brigade Tactical Headquarters and the head-quarters of the support group and the New Zealand Divisional Cavalry, and these in due course turned off along the Boomerang track, while to the south the Warwickshire Yeomanry column of about 120 vehicles including 46 tanks travelled on their own along the Moon track.

Extensions to all these main (and now battered) tracks were being hurriedly cleared by the engineers in the new *Supercharge* salient, but long before they reached them the 9th Armoured Brigade were in trouble. Collisions in the dark between tanks and lorries usually led to the soft-skinned vehicle being damaged even if both had been crawling along at snail-pace, and however clean the filters were when the vehicles started out, the dust was so thick that it soon choked them and throttled the engines. By the time the regimental groups were moving into the battle area quite a number of their support vehicles were already trailing far behind.

Across the infantry start line and into the salient, matters, of course, worsened. By now the Axis gunners had recovered from the first shock of attack and when necessary resited their guns, and their harassing fire was dropping into the rear areas through which 9th Armoured were making their way – adding to the deafening effect of the British barrage, still roaring over their heads to drop in front of the advancing infantry. The leading tanks of all three regimental groups were passing their first objective by 0330 (at which time both infantry brigades had still about 1,000 yards to go to their final objective) but behind them they were already leaving the wrecks of some of their tanks and many of their support guns or trucks. The Hussars had lost six of their tanks, and their anti-tank support had become so disorganised by the shelling that they had had to pull off the route and thus drop well behind.

The Wiltshires ran into scattered mines which blew the tracks off two of their Crusaders and delayed them until a Scorpion was brought up by the engineers to ease their progress, and A Squadron of the Warwickshires missed their way as a result of the destruction of guiding lamps, found themselves in a blind end entirely closed by mines and obviously moving in the wrong direction, so they had carefully to turn around and make their way back to the main stream, followed in turn by the other squadrons, whose members became increasingly sarcastic as time went by.

But nothing was allowed to halt the main advance, and by 0515 the 3rd Hussars had reached the forward infantry positions on the right, having lost twelve of their tanks, all of their anti-tank guns – at least for the time being – and with their infantry support so crippled by casualties that there was obviously no point in taking them forward on the next, crucial stage of the battle. Within a quarter of an hour the Royal Wiltshires were up on the left less eleven of their tanks, but there was for the moment no sign of the Warwickshires who should by now have reached the Scottish positions – and the covering barrage for the 9th Armoured Brigade was due to start at 0545.

The commanding officers of both the 3rd Hussars and the Royal Wiltshire Yeomanry urged Currie to allow the programme to continue as scheduled and not to wait for the Warwickshires, but Currie was worried about the narrowness of the gap which would be opened if he attempted to break through with only two-thirds of his brigade, so he persuaded Freyberg to postpone their main assault for half an hour by which time, in fact, the Warwickshires had arrived. So as the moment for the second barrage of the night crept nearer, the bulk of the 9th Armoured Brigade were on their start line, ready to follow their covering curtain of fire as it jumped forward 100 yards every three minutes until it had taken them across the Rahman Track and on towards the low ridge with its identifying Tel el Aqqaqir hump towards the southern end.

It was a tense, indeed crucial moment, both for the tank crews and for the whole of Eighth Army. Shells still hurtled overhead but in nothing like a concentrated barrage for the moment, the tanks lined up as directed, the commanding officers walked between the tanks and talked to the crews, to the surprise of many John Currie's command tank edged up into the front rank, and as zero hour approached the crews waited, the engines idled. So must have waited the Light Brigade at Balaclava.

Then at 0615 the barrage roared out again and crashed in front, drivers revved their engines and the whole line moved forward. Crusaders led the advance of all three groups with the heavy Grant and Sherman squadrons just behind, and at first everything seemed to go well although the 3rd Hussars' commanding officer's tank went up on a mine shortly after starting, and the wireless in the one he promptly commandeered was useless. But apart from that mishap, the line of tanks moved forward behind their artillery cover, flushing shell-shocked German and Italian infantrymen from their posts, machine-gunning them if they showed signs of further aggression, directing them to the rear with a jerk of the thumb if they wished to surrender; occasionally, in the speed and confusion of the night, running them down and crushing them beneath the steel tracks.

Both Hussars and Wiltshires made out and passed the line of telegraph poles which marked the Rahman Track running diagonally across their path, and one of the tank commanders noticed with a pang of concern that the top third of the one nearest to him was silvered with the light of dawn. But then they were past and suddenly amid enemy anti-tank guns, some of which had already been wrecked by the barrage, others now close and spitting fire. On the right, the Hussars' Crusaders had no option but to charge, and in the resulting mêlée lost almost immediately the squadron commander's tank and with it all contact with the heavy squadrons behind.

On their left, the Crusaders of the Wiltshires met at first with astonishing success, crashing into the German 50mm. and the Italian 47mm. guns and knocking them over, at one moment the triumphant drivers crushing a whole line of enemy gun trails under their tracks in one triumphant charge. It seemed briefly as though they could do nothing wrong – like a winning football team – and when four German officers tried make a bolt for it in a scurrying staff car, the Crusader squadron commander took a pot-shot at them with his revolver and was astonished to see the petrol-tank explode and the car go up in flames.

But all the time, the silver was creeping down the telegraph poles and eventually the light touched the top of Aqqaqir Ridge. At this, as later described by one of the survivors, 'The whole world seemed to blow up,' for on and just behind the ridge had lain in wait the main enemy defences – 88mm. and 75mm. anti-tank guns against which the British tanks, silhouetted against the paling eastern sky, were as defenceless as had been the British infantry against the German machine-guns on July 1st, 1916, the first day of the Somme.

The comparison with that occasion and also with the charge of the Light Brigade at Balaclava now took a more tragic reality. The western horizon cracked with fire along its base, and first the Crusaders and then the Grants and Shermans glowed red hot where the heavy shells hit them, then slewed aside and brewed, their crews leaping for safety when they could, often turning back to try to rescue their trapped and agonised companions.

Then the Wiltshires, renewing their tradition of getting further forward than anyone else and with John Currie still among them and in the forefront of the battle, suddenly came under fire from the south – from tanks which they had thought to be the Warwickshires but which were in fact the 15th Panzer. The last of the Wiltshires' Crusaders brewed up, the heavy squadrons of both the Hussars and the Wiltshires fired smoke in order to cover escaping crews – as much in danger from the Durham infantry behind them as from the enemy machine-gunners in front – and John Currie strove to keep control of the battle by shouted word of command for by now all wireless sets were out of action through damage or injury to the operators.

On the left flank, the Warwickshires were out on their own owing to a navigational error which had taken them too far south, but their story was similar to those of the Wiltshires and the Hussars. At first in the dark they had won unexpected success against the lighter anti-tank guns, machine-gun posts and dug-in tanks, smashing the heavy weapons, herding the infantry away to the sides and rear, dropping grenades into gun-pits or open tank-turrets; but once the light grew they suffered the same fate as the others. First from the heavy anti-tank guns on the ridge, then from the panzers in the gap they had themselves left on their right flank came crippling fire which tore the Crusaders apart and brought both Grants and Shermans to a shuddering halt.

Thus, though they had bitten deeply into the enemy defences, were the tanks of the 9th Armoured Brigade brought to a halt – without having torn the hole through which 1st Armoured Division were to pass. They had, however, as one of them was to remark later, 'made a bloody big dent' and if 2nd Armoured Brigade came up now they should be able to deepen it and get through themselves.

This, at least, was John Currie's belief, and as Brigadier Lucas Phillips says in the most detailed account of this action written:

> All that he could see was a world of devastation – devastation of the enemy, indeed, their shattered guns sprawling at crazed angles, their detachments lying dead, but devastation of his own brigade also. As far as the eye could see lay the terrible record – tank after tank burning or wrecked, the smoke of their burning mingled with the cold mist, the crimson shafts from the eastern sky tincturing all objects with the hue of blood. Only here and there could he see a tank still defiantly shooting it out with the more distant guns and the tanks of the Afrika Korps. He was very angry, very bitter. In fulfilment of his orders, he was ready to sacrifice all if Fisher's brigade had been there to crash through whatever ragged breaches he had torn in the enemy's wall of guns.[13]

Of the 94 tanks which had followed him forward from the infantry defences, 75 had been wrecked, and of the 400-odd officers and men who had manned them, 230 were dead, wounded or missing – and the battle still raged, the enemy gun-line still existed and was doubtless being strengthened, and there was no sign of the two brigades who were surely supposed at this juncture of the battle to be sweeping through his ranks to complete the annihilation of the enemy defences, and so to justify the price his own brigade had paid so far.

In the circumstances, it is not surprising that the thought that should they attempt it they too might suffer the same fate as his own brigade hardly crossed his mind; or that possibly he had himself made a fatal misjudgment when he obtained that half-hour postponement of the advance.

Freyberg, of course, was almost as perturbed as Currie at the non-arrival of the leading formations of 1st Armoured Division in what they both considered the crucial area, and three times in fifteen minutes he had rung up Leese, to ask him to urge Lumsden, to order Briggs, to press Fisher, to get his tanks forward both farther and faster; the battle was still bedevilled by the problems of two corps, each with different structures, fighting on the same ground – two corps, moreover, between which existed some antagonism.

The other problems stemming from this anachronism still existed, too, and 2nd Armoured Brigade had spent the time since they had left their assembly area at 0230 grinding their way forward in choking clouds of dust through a confined area even more congested than the corridor through which they had tried to find a way on the opening night of the battle. Durham and Highlander supply parties were hurrying forward towards their comrades in action, engineers were still clearing minefields, gun-pits pocked the area at every turn, ambulances swayed and twisted towards and through their ranks, demanding precedence by the compassion of their task. And as before, the area was packed first with the tails of the two infantry brigades, then with the tail of the 9th Armoured Brigade – and through all this the tanks of three more regiments had now to make their way, followed closely by their own tails which added up to a total of over a thousand vehicles.

The wonder was not so much that 2nd Armoured Brigade were late, but that they got through at all – and in fact Fisher's tanks were in action very shortly after Freyberg's third call to Leese. On the right the Queen's Bays had passed the Durhams and were closing up to the Rahman Track, in the centre the 9th Lancers were also past the infantry front line; only the 10th Hussars on the left were still well behind, having been misdirected at one point and subsequently having been forced like the Warwickshires to back-track.

All three regiments as they came up through the half-light passed through heavy enemy shelling, streams of German and Italian prisoners sent back by Currie's tank crews and, as the light grew, the bursts of armour-piercing and H.E. shells which had missed the 9th Armoured. In front the ground was dotted with the flaming remains of Currie's tanks, and soon one of the regimental commanders saw Currie himself coming back so he went forward to meet him. He was bloody late, Currie told him, but 9th Armoured Brigade had made the gap and now it was up to him and his colleagues from 2nd Armoured Brigade to get forward through it as quickly as possible; and when, after looking at the scene of flame and chaos stretching out towards the ridge, the newcomer said, 'I have never seen anything, sir, that looks less like a gap!' Currie was very angry indeed.[14]

The fact remained that still along the line of the Aqqaqir Ridge lay a formidable enemy defence against which even the Shermans and Grants would dash themselves to pieces if they attacked it in daylight. Moreover, it seemed that there would very shortly be a perhaps even more important function for the newly arrived armour to perform than exploiting whatever success the 9th Armoured Brigade had won, for warnings were coming through from XXX Corps that intercepted signals indicated counter-attacks soon to be expected from 21st Panzer Division coming down from the north. With the presence of the 15th Panzer formations between the remnants of the Wiltshires and the Warwickshires, another could obviously be expected from the west – and at the very least, the Durhams and Highlanders would need protection.

There was another point to be considered, too. The ultimate task for 1st Armoured Division was to destroy the Axis armour 'on ground of their own choosing' – and if they chose now to do the job along the Rahman Track instead of across the Aqqaqir Ridge, they would have additional fire-power from the anti-tank guns of the infantry brigades close by, together, as it happened, with those which had been attached to the 3rd Hussars and which had just arrived.

It is still almost impossible to discover who made the decisions and how they were arrived at, and certainly one can have sympathy for all the commanders. Freyberg and Currie were both pleading for exploitation of the 9th Armoured Brigade's sacrifices, Montgomery's orders had been that 1st Armoured Division should follow through and fight on or beyond the ridge, Lumsden was certainly well aware of the unpopularity of both himself and his command in view of the failures of the past few days, even of the past few months. Yet at divisional and brigade level they faced the realities of the situation developing across the Rahman Track, and this would seem to have led to some dichotomy of thought.

As early as 0745 Freyberg had somewhat tartly suggested that 'a very senior officer' should be up front invigorating the armour, and perhaps as a result Lumsden himself arrived at 1st Armoured Division H.Q. just before 0800. He warned Briggs of possible counter-attack, but told him to push Fisher's 2nd Armoured Brigade forward to Currie's assistance – but by this time Fisher's observers had told him that both the Bays on the right and the 9th Lancers in the centre were already across the Rahman Track, despite the fact that the infantrymen could see quite clearly that they were not. Briggs, too, seems somehow to have been aware that Fisher was wrong and that the two regiments had, in fact, taken up hull-down positions in broken ground just forward of the Durham corner in which they were already engaged with panzers coming down from the north.

Not only could they not for the moment easily disengage to go further forward, but one suspects that General Briggs did not want them to despite the orders he was getting from above – and the resulting confusion probably explains a certain ambiguity which colours the logged record of a series of signals which passed between divisional and brigade commanders. At 0904, Fisher, increasingly worried by the differing pressures being exerted upon him, asked, 'Is it intended that I push on or stay?' to which Briggs replied, 'Your instructions are to destroy tanks and get into positions where you can' – which in the circumstances was hardly the clearest possible order.

Very shortly afterwards, Fisher replied, 'In accordance with orders, Brigade has taken up positions ready to take on attack from west or north. Being engaged by tanks and anti-tank guns.' And somewhat tetchily, Briggs then ordered, 'Destroy opposition and get on,' following it shortly afterwards with, 'We must have room. You must push on.'[15]

But by this time, not only were the Bays and the remnants of the 3rd Hussars together with some of the Valentines of 8th R.T.R. working themselves into sound defensive positions facing north, but 9th Lancers and the Wiltshires were together amid the Durham and Seaforths' forward positions facing west, and the Warwickshires, 10th Hussars and the 50th R.T.R. were exchanging shots with panzers away to the south-west on the Rahman Track. Moreover, all armour was now under command of X Corps as it had been decided to specify a time for this to happen – 0910 – instead of the perhaps long-drawn-out event of arrival on the 'chosen ground'.

It must be said that in their decision to fight what was to develop into one of the fiercest tank battles of the desert war where they did, the armoured commanders had the support of their subordinates. They all by now knew what would happen if they tried in daylight to assault a line of guns on or behind a ridge, and in case any of them had forgotten they could see what had happened to the 9th Armoured Brigade. Now they took hull-down positions wherever they could find ground broken enough to allow it, and waited for the enemy to come out and attack them; and as the sun rose higher in the sky, they could see to the north a new line of enemy anti-tank guns and a group of panzers already massing behind it.

The Bays and the remnants of the 3rd Hussars were very quickly to reap the benefits of their positions, for they had hardly taken them when a line of panzers and Italian tanks moved north on the far side of the Rahman Track, apparently to join the assembling force – and two panzers and three M13s were promptly put out of action.

But not all the counter-attacks were to be so easily dealt with, and soon afterwards some of the panzers taking part in what was probably an attempt to 'pinch out' the salient at its root, carefully probed forward until they found a gap between the Maoris and the 6th Durhams through which they might have penetrated into the salient itself. It is impossible now to be certain what first caused them to hesitate, but it may have been the sheer mass of vehicles, movement and apparent chaos with which they were faced, for by mid-morning the salient presented an astonishing sight.

Flat as a billiard table, it was packed with men, guns, ammunition and vehicles amid which German and Italian shells exploded constantly but with no perceptible pattern, raising more dust to add to the clouds already caused by the movement, and occasionally smoke when they hit and set vehicles alight. And some of the vehicles moving across the salient were now those of the 8th Armoured Brigade, still following their original *Supercharge* orders to make their way through to the support of 2nd Armoured Brigade in the break-out across the Aqqaqir Ridge – though by now their commander, Brigadier Custance, was aware that there had been modifications.

On the right flank of their advance were the Crusaders of the Staffordshire Yeomanry accompanied by their battery of R.H.A. 25-pounders – and it was someone amongst them who first became aware of the panzer threat along the northern flank of the salient. They immediately swung right and within a few minutes a small and entirely separate battle was being fought across a sector of the salient itself – while traffic still streamed forward under the two-way exchange of fire between the two protagonists, and eddied continually around the Staffordshires.

But soon this was just a small part of a much bigger conflict – the one, in fact, for which much of the planning of the battle had been directed, between the massed armour of X Corps and that of the Panzerarmee.

It raged from 1100 to 1300 on November 2nd, with the remaining panzers of 15th and 21st Panzer Divisions and the lighter tanks of Littorio (Ariete were all still down in the south) trying valiantly to eliminate the new salient by destroying the Crusaders, Grants and Shermans of the now concentrated 1st Armoured Division. At times it would seem that over 120 mixed panzers and Italian tanks were engaged in co-ordinated attacks on the northern, north-western and western faces of the salient, their first onslaught being supported by Stukas and all of them backed by as much artillery support as Rommel could organise, including the twenty-four 88mm. guns he still had in the vicinity.

But the British now were in the tactical position which they had so often envied their opponents. They held a strong defensive line with effective anti-tank fire to back up the already powerful Grant and Sherman armament, not to speak of the massive field artillery which 'on call' could interfere and blanket Axis concentrations as soon as they were identified. Above all, they had the constant support of the Allied air forces – British, South African and American – whose fighters made short work of the Stuka attacks and whose impeccable eighteen-bomber formations seemed almost permanently stationed over the battlefield. (They made seven appearances in those two hours.)

The desert, quivering in the heat haze, became a scene that defies sober description. It can be discerned only as a confused arena clouded by the bursts of high explosive, darkened by the smoke of scores of burning tanks and trucks, lit by the flashes of innumerable guns, shot through by red, green and white tracers, shaken by heavy bombing from the air and deafened by the artillery of both sides. Upon the British forces in the funnel – tanks, infantry and supporting arms – a 'torrent of shell and shot' was poured in from three sides. In the words recorded by the sober historian of the 9th Lancers, 'for hours the whack of armour-piercing shot on armour plate was unceasing'. Overhead, fierce conflicts were fought in the air as the Germans twice attempted to attack the British armour with Stukas, only to be fought off by the R.A.F.[16]

It was an unequal battle from every point of view, for not only did the British have complete domination of the air, but they could afford to lose tanks at a far higher rate than could their opponents; but above all, events had at last conspired to force the Afrika Korps to attack in daylight and across open ground, and as a result to suffer the kind of losses which they had so often in the past inflicted upon their opponents. By the end of the day, Afrika Korps was down to 35 panzers still in battle order and 20 Italian tanks, while the battered remains of over 100 still smoked on the battlefield from which it was quite evident that the exhausted recovery teams could rescue only a very small proportion.

Losses for that day among the British armour had by no means been small, of course, but 8th Armoured Brigade had not been heavily involved and were thus still strong, while Pip Roberts's 22nd Armoured Brigade had not been involved at all and now was ordered to assemble south of Tel el Eisa where, on orders issued by Montgomery early that morning, they would be joined by the 4th Light Armoured Brigade coming up rapidly from the south, thus to reconstitute under John Harding the whole 7th Armoured Division as it had begun the battle.

By evening all the British armour would be in the north, and its most experienced component poised for a crucial role. In addition, the early morning reports had revealed to General Montgomery one small but highly significant success away on the southern flank of the *Supercharge* salient, and this he was determined to exploit.

The approach march from the assembly areas to the start lines had not been comfortable for anyone, but it was probably less uncomfortable for the armoured car regiments than for anyone else. They were not marching through the thick dust, and on the other hand they were not choking in clouds flung up by huge wheeled or tracked formations clanking along in front. They were, however, conscious of the fact that they could not, like the infantry, individually fling themselves to the ground when shells burst nearby, nor find cover from shrapnel or splinter behind the flimsy sides of their vehicles. Ahead, the night was already full of the fire and sound of battle and for the men of A and C Squadrons of the Royal Dragoons it was something of a comfort that their path lay to the south where matters seemed quieter.

The leading car reached the end of the marked tracks and edged quietly ahead between anti-tank guns waiting to go forward, its commander making sure that the cars immediately behind were closing up and then directing the driver to lead off into the dark. The car promptly fell into a slit-trench and had to be abandoned.

Another car took the lead and quite soon the column of Daimlers and Humbers had passed through a line of infantry digging themselves in. The Dragoons were now in no-man's-land. The night was dark and in the immediate vicinity quiet, so they pressed ahead and were soon into enemy territory itself – a fact quickly made apparent to them when yet another leading car fell into a hole in the ground, this time the gun-pit of an 88mm. with its crew dead around it.

The column wound slowly on, a late moon now giving them a better chance to avoid trouble. At last they hit a track which seemed to lead in their desired direction, and after a short wait to allow the tail-enders to close up, they drove quickly forward:

> One or two more cars, including three petrol replenishing lorries, got stuck in slit trenches, but most of them pulled out when dawn broke and fought their way up to us. The enemy were too astounded to do anything as we came through, or else the Italian section thought we were Germans, and the German section thought we were Italians. They waved swastika flags at us with vigour and we replied with 'Achtung!' and anything else we could think of which, with an answering wave, would get us through their lines. As it grew lighter they stared and blinked at us. Although a warning artillery barrage had been going on all night they couldn't believe their eyes. They would goggle at us from short range, see our berets, bolt away a few yards, pause as if they didn't think it was true, and come back to take another look.[17]

The Dragoons sped through ammunition and stores dumps as dawn broke, and shortly afterwards found themselves amid the tents and dug-in trucks and lorries of a brigade or perhaps divisional headquarters. They shot up all standing vehicles, shot down any sign of opposition (there was very little, such was the element of surprise), collected a colonel and two majors as prisoners, and pushed on into the open spaces of the desert to set about their main task of raiding the Axis supply columns. They also sent off the essential coded signals to inform Eighth Army that at last one of their units had found a way through the enemy defences.

It was as yet just the first small trickle through the dam, but what could it portend?

Montgomery was determined that it should portend the final breakthrough and the destruction of the Panzerarmee – and following the military principle of reinforcing success, as soon as he had assimilated the morning situation reports for the entire front, he ordered Lumsden to shift as much as possible of the armoured weight to the south-west corner of the salient, as quickly as possible. Lumsden could not, of course, disengage 2nd Armoured Brigade or the remnants of the 9th from the ferocious battle now being fought in front of the Durhams, and the Staffordshires of the 8th Armoured Brigade must stay where they were until the northern face of the salient was secure – but the rest of 8th Armoured Brigade should skirt the southern edge of the main battle, leave 2nd Armoured Brigade to deal with 15th and 21st Panzer formations, and themselves endeavour to break through around or south of Tel el Aqqaqir.

But if a really large-scale breakthrough was to take place down there – say with the whole of 7th Armoured Division in addition to 8th Armoured Brigade – then more space would be required for deployment and manoeuvre, probably south of the salient itself, and infantry must secure it. Skinflint and Snipe both lay within striking distance of the battalions along the southern flank, and they should be taken as quickly as possible, certainly before the day – November 2nd – was out.

Neither of these moves, however, would solve the problem posed by the existence of that line of anti-tank guns on the Aqqaqir Ridge north of the Tel, and one way or another it must be destroyed. According to Fisher, his 2nd Armoured Brigade were on the Rahman Track and although they were fighting hard they did not seem to be suffering severe losses; when darkness fell their survivors should be able to advance under artillery cover and break that gun-line – and they could have infantry support for the operation from the rifle battalions of the 7th Motor Brigade who were now well forward in the salient. Lumsden should organise this for tonight.

As for the main Eighth Army long-term objectives, a breakthrough westward or southward was now imminent, so what was required immediately was the organisation of a balanced force both to make the final lunge and then to exploit it. The problem, of course, would again be posed by the shortage of infantry, though there were still a few reserves upon which Montgomery could draw.

Howard Kippenberger's 5th New Zealand Brigade had been waiting ever since it had been withdrawn from Miteiriya Ridge specifically to carry out an exploitation role, and they could be joined by 5th Indian Brigade from the 4th Indian Division which had hardly as yet been seriously engaged in the battle. In addition, the Durham Brigade was evidently in need of withdrawal from the salient for reorganisation, for Freyberg had reported that although their losses had not been unduly severe, their hold on the salient corner was not as firm as it might have been – not surprisingly in view of the armoured battle being fought all around them and of their own comparative inexperience. He had suggested that the two battalions of the 6th New Zealand Brigade at the base of the salient take over from them – and once this had happened, the Durhams could withdraw, reorganise, and quickly be ready for further employment.

A fourth brigade was also available and close at hand. The 154th Brigade of Argyll and Sutherland Highlanders, Black Watch and Gordons were already in position behind their brothers of 152nd Brigade holding the southern half of the salient, and could be launched through quite easily when the moment came.

But speed in everything was essential, and by noon – when the battle along the western edge of the salient was at its height – the staff officers were racing around the XXX Corps area with the orders, the commanders were barking at their adjutants and company commanders, the quartermasters were cursing their fate and shouting for more petrol, more trucks and where the hell had the ammunition column got to? And in view of the fact that the rush was causing such anomalies as XXX Corps issuing orders direct to Highland Division troops still supposedly under Freyberg's command, at Freyberg's suggestion a new and clear dividing line was agreed. He would still command all troops in the northern half of the salient, while the Scots in the southern half returned to their own divisional commander, Douglas Wimberley, who would assume responsibility for the immediate operations down there.

All this lightning change and replanning might easily have resulted in chaos, for the attack by the 2nd Seaforths and the Valentines of 50th R.T.R. on Skinflint was as a result first postponed from 1600 to 1800, then to 1830 and then back to 1815, which not unnaturally thoroughly confused the gunners. There were thus a couple of false starts which in normal circumstances could have spelt disaster – but in the event the men of the Trieste Division holding Skinflint showed no inclination to resist, over 100 giving themselves up immediately the Seaforths arrived. These thus took the post with no casualties at all, though four of the Valentines had been lost on mines or to shell-fire on the way up.

As for Snipe, the 5th Royal Sussex had planned for an advance supported by artillery at 1900, but long before then came signs that the Trieste formations there considered themselves already outflanked, so the Royal Sussex marched across (unfortunately losing seven men in a minefield on the way) and took at no cost the position for which the 2nd Rifle Brigade had fought so long and so valiantly.

Needless to say, not everything had gone as well elsewhere during that afternoon and evening (of November 2nd). Brigadier Custance had by midday managed to disengage the Staffordshire Yeomanry from the panzers on the northern flank and tried to drive southwestward through the positions held by the Camerons, but the German anti-tank guns were still lying in wait and although the 8th Armoured Brigade later claimed to have knocked out eleven enemy tanks, they lost six Crusaders themselves and made no progress.

There was thus, despite Brigadier Fisher's continued belief to the contrary, no live British armour west of the Rahman Track when darkness fell.

General Lumsden's plans for the attack that night on the enemy defences in front of and on the ridge were, to start off with, extremely ambitious. His original orders, given verbally at about 2000 on November 2nd, were to the effect that both brigades of the 1st Armoured Division were to advance due westwards under cover of the heaviest artillery barrage that could be arranged, while 7th Motor Brigade followed and then wheeled left to cover the armour's southern flank. But an hour later, under pressure either from his brigade commanders or perhaps Montgomery himself, he modified them to an advance at first by the motor brigade to a known area of resistance across the Rahman Track, followed by the 2nd Armoured Brigade who would pass through and on to high ground about a mile and a half further on, while 8th Armoured Brigade drove across on the left towards a similar area of high ground just south of Tel el Aqqaqir. If all went well, he suggested that 22nd Armoured Brigade which would have been brought down from Tel el Eisa would then swing even wider south and, perhaps with the other 7th Armoured Division brigade, drive up to the coast with Ghazal Station (see rear endpaper) as their objective.

Far too little time, however, had been allowed for reconnaissance or even proper briefing, and the Motor Brigade battalions – 2nd and 7th Rifle Brigade and 2nd King's Royal Rifle Corps – had already spent a very uncomfortable day being sporadically shelled in the salient, and generally hanging about awaiting orders and employment. The two Rifle Brigade battalions eventually assembled behind the Durham positions (now being taken over by the 6th New Zealanders) short of both men and vehicles and even somewhat uncertain of their exact objectives. Nevertheless, at 0115 on November 3rd the riflemen duly set out behind their hastily organised artillery cover, and the 2nd Rifle Brigade on the right (now commanded by Major Pearson) crossed the Rahman Track successfully after storming a couple of enemy posts, but then ran into fire from anti-tank guns which wrecked the carriers, and machine-gun fire from Italian tanks which drove the men to ground. There was obviously little chance of their own anti-tank guns coming up, and after the punishment the battalion had taken six days earlier on Snipe, plus the realisation that 7th Rifle Brigade had not caught them up on the left, it is not surprising that Pearson soon asked for, and received, permission to withdraw.

The 7th Rifle Brigade had met with even less success. They had been late at the start line and thus lost whatever advantage the singularly ragged artillery cover might have given them, ran into totally unexpected opposition before they reached the track which resulted in companies losing touch and finally, as control went, the men scattering. By daybreak on November 3rd, small groups of survivors of both battalions, some on foot and some in the remaining carriers, filtered back through the New Zealand line with all the stain of dismal failure visible in their faces and in their bearing.

The third battalion, the 2nd K.R.R.C., had attacked through the 5th Camerons on the south-western corner of the salient, their objective the area where the Rahman Track crossed over the Aqqaqir Ridge, just to the south of the Tel itself. Congestion behind the Camerons had delayed their arrival on the start line, which they crossed about an hour after their opening artillery cover had been fired, and as a result they found themselves up against solid opposition almost 1,000 yards short of the ridge. Here, too, there was some misunderstanding about the true objective so the riflemen, perhaps with the admirable intention of matching the deeds of their fellow Green Jackets a week before, dug themselves in and positioned their anti-tank guns as they came up for all round defence.

Dawn revealed their position more similar to that of the Pioneers in the Saucer than that of the 2nd Rifle Brigade at Snipe, for they were overlooked from the ridge (where they were supposed to be) and there were several enemy posts much nearer, one within a stone's throw. However, their wireless was still in operation and they managed to report their progress, though owing to some misinterpretation along the line, General Lumsden gained the impression that they had, in fact, reached their objective and were firmly in control of it.

As it was now obviously too late for the armoured brigades to advance to the ridge, and as he was at least aware that the objectives in the north had not been taken, Lumsden therefore instructed the 8th Armoured Brigade to try to 'feel their way' forward and around the south of the supposed K.R.R.C. positions, and he sent out the 4th/6th South African Armoured Car Regiment in a pre-dawn dash to attempt to swing around on the same course and join the Royal Dragoons. They were back some two hours later with accounts of minefields and strong opposition from all along the ridge – which was confirmed by infantry observers, but not believed by 7th Motor Brigade, 1st Armoured Division or X Corps.

The attempts by 8th Armoured Brigade, aided later by the 2nd, to obey Lumsden's orders to get forward came to little during November 3rd except the destruction of some enemy anti-tank guns between the track and the ridge at the expense of a great deal of ammunition, and the loss of three tanks in a well-intentioned attempt to rush the ridge and take the pressure off the unfortunate K.R.R.C. These remained where they were all day, unknowingly basking in high level approbation, for no doubts at all existed throughout the armoured command that they were actually on the ridge, and also by the afternoon that 8th Armoured Brigade formations were at least halfway towards them and well across the Rahman Track.

Though the report which went to the Army Commander outlining this situation was thus over-optimistic, there were other promising reports during the day which were quite true. From the XIII Corps sector came reports of fires and explosions behind the lines opposite which seemed to have no relation to any specific action, and the hopes they aroused were confirmed by air reconnaissance which told of long columns of marching men and convoys of vehicles moving north-westwards. Moreover, early in the morning the signal intercept service had reported that 90th Light Division headquarters had ordered one of its forward infantry battalions to send vehicles to help bring out the heavy weapons still held by 125th Regiment around Thompson's Post, and when Morshead ordered patrols out to hinder the movement, they reached Barrel Hill without opposition and found no enemy positions between there and the coast. Further south, the Australians along the western face of the Point 29 salient found that they could move about quite freely, and some of them even walked across to the nearest known German positions which they promptly ransacked for souvenirs.

There was no doubt, therefore, that the Panzerarmee was drawing back – but Montgomery wanted them held for a little longer where they were, so that he could slip the armour out and around from the south to cut off their withdrawal. Lumsden must therefore urge his armoured brigades to keep up the pressure all day – which they were certainly doing – and also to be ready to move quickly when darkness fell. Infantry from Wimberley's Highland Division would move forward in the late afternoon and take position just south of the valiant K.R.R.C. on Aqqaqir Ridge, thus gaining control of the Rahman Track to the south, and through that area the whole 1st Armoured Division would drive south-west and west, then swing north to pen the enemy against the coast.

The 7th Armoured Division would follow and swing out wider towards Ghazal Station, while the New Zealand Division with the 4th Light Armoured Brigade under command (it was still coming up from the south) would follow behind with Sidi Ibeid as their first objective, then Fuka or even Matruh should opportunity favour them.

November 3rd was obviously another day when speed of decision and action would be the keynote, a condition heightened as the morning passed and reports came in from Coningham's H.Q. that every aircraft which came in brought tales not only of enemy withdrawal in the south, but of dense traffic on the coast road and all tracks leading off it to known enemy centres. Needless to say, every fighter and fighter-bomber that could climb into the air was out attacking these routes, especially the main road from Daba back as far as Matruh – but, significantly, they were up against far more opposition than they had met of late, for Me 109s and 110s were out guarding the traffic in unexpected strength.

So the orders went out, the plans were laid for the night's operations which, it was confidently expected, would result in the long-awaited break-out, the freeing of the entire Eighth Army from the morass of minefields and close enemy defences in which they had been confined for so long, the release into the open desert and the thrills of a triumphant chase.

Such was the atmosphere of excitement and euphoria that no notice was taken in the higher echelons of command of the increasingly worried pronouncements of the men at the front, especially the forward artillery observers, that the whole of the length of the Aqqaqir Ridge and especially the ground around the Tel was still occupied by German anti-tank formations, and that neither the K.R.R.C. nor any of the 8th Armoured Brigade tanks were even across the Rahman Track.

General Wimberley, like all the other divisional commanders that day, had a very busy time indeed. He now had three attacks to launch in the course of twelve hours, two of them each by one of his own beloved Scots battalions and one by the 5th Indian Brigade, and whatever he and his staff could do to ensure that they all succeeded at the smallest possible cost would be done. He checked that start lines were agreed and marked out as clearly as possible, that battalion commanders were adequately briefed and were given time to pass necessary information on to their men – and above all that adequate artillery cover was laid on for each advance, properly organised and accurately planned.

He was thus astonished, then bewildered and finally infuriated when he was rung up by XXX Corps's commander, General Leese himself with whom Wimberley was on close and friendly terms, to be told that General Briggs had heard of his detailed plans and was protesting vigorously. The proposed barrage to protect the first of Wimberley's attacks – that by the 5th/7th Gordons from the Skinflint area to just south of Tel el Aqqaqir – would, claimed General Briggs, fall far too close if not actually upon the positions held by the K.R.R.C.s, having on its way caused untold losses among the advanced formations of 8th Armoured Brigade!

Nothing that Wimberley said, no other authority which he quoted could change the instruction that the artillery cover must be cancelled, for General Briggs persisted in his claim and in it he was supported by General Lumsden. Wimberley was moreover ordered that the Gordons and the Valentine crews of 8th R.T.R. who would be accompanying them should be told of the reasons for their lack of cover, and that their task was simply that of advancing through areas already taken by the armour to a location already held by British infantry.

The only alleviation of the order which Wimberley could extract was that the guns could put down smoke to guide the Gordons towards their objective – and late in the afternoon, the force set out with the Jocks riding on the leading Valentines. For the first twenty minutes progress was excellent, then the Valentines passed through the last smoke-screen to drive forward into a setting sun which effectively blinded the drivers and tank commanders, and a storm of vicious anti-tank and machine-gun fire which swept down from the ridge upon them, putting 20 tanks immediately out of action with 27 of their crew members including seven officers; and by the time they had pulled back, 98 of the Gordons were killed, wounded or missing.

What rubbed salt into an already grievous wound was that even while the men and the tanks were undergoing their ordeal, 1st Armoured Division rang up the Highland Division H.Q. to say that the artillery cover should be allowed to proceed after all, as information had just come in from which they concluded that their infantry and tanks were perhaps not quite so far forward as had been believed.

Later that night Wimberley spoke again to General Leese on the subject of another of the attacks, and sounded so despondent over the loss of his Gordons that Leese himself was worried. 'Surely now you, Douglas, of all people are not going to lose heart!' he said, at which Wimberley rallied – and at least had no trouble in ensuring that the other two attacks were properly covered by artillery.

That by the 11th Indian Brigade took a great deal of organisation, for the 1st/4th Essex on the right were only given their orders at 1915, and then had to find and cross the start line which was a long way away at the far end of the crowded and congested salient. The 3rd/10th Baluchs were supposed to take the left flank but could not be found so the reserve battalion, the 6th Rajputana Rifles, took their place and – despite all this – the attack went in on time at 0230 on November 4th and was completely successful. The Essex took 100 exhausted Panzergrenadiers prisoner, found another eighty on their objective on the Rahman Track some three miles south of Tel el Aqqaqir, and was joined there quite quickly by both the Rajputanas and the Baluchs who followed through without opposition.

As for the third attack by the 7th Argyll and Sutherland Highlanders on Tel el Aqqaqir itself, by dawn they were on their objective with no casualties at all, to find it and indeed the length of the ridge abandoned. The Afrika Korps, indeed the whole Panzerarmee, had withdrawn during the night, leaving behind in the Alamein defences just a few stragglers, some wrecked artillery, random areas of unexploded mines and a considerable number of ingenious booby-traps.

The Battle of El Alamein was over, and all that remained was for Eighth Army to organise its effective exploitation.

7 · *Break-out and Pursuit*

However grimly and realistically Rommel and his staff may have regarded the progress of the battle before November 2nd, the impact of *Supercharge* and the immediate consequences shook them severely.

They had foreseen the size and timing of the attack but been deceived as to its location, for they had, of course, no means of knowing of Montgomery's last-minute change of mind. They had therefore expected it in the north, driving out of the Australian salient south of Hill 28 towards Sidi Abd el Rahman, and no reports which might have corrected the misconception arrived for some time, as R.A.F. aircraft fitted with radio-jamming equipment had been operating in the area and the pre-assault bombing had wrecked several vital communication centres.

Rommel's staff had even contributed to their own mystification, for in an attempt to distract British attention from the main task they had arranged for an artillery programme to be fired to the south of the expected danger area. This fell into the *Supercharge* area but was so meagre by British standards that it was hardly noticed by Freyberg and his troops who assumed it was nothing but Axis reaction to their own barrage – but it helped to mask what was really happening down there.

Rommel, therefore, had made no immediate alterations to his plans to deal with the expected British assault when the *Supercharge* barrage opened, merely ensuring that 21st Panzer and 90th Light were properly deployed to seal off the attack if and when it broke through towards Sidi Abd el Rahman, and it was not until nearly dawn, when some of the communications had been restored, that the true location of the new battle was realised. Even with German efficiency some confusion thus resulted and the first attacks on the salient by 21st Panzer from the north and 15th Panzer with tanks from Littorio and Trieste from the west were both uncoordinated and hastily mounted.

Several of the panzer commanders, moreover, especially from 21st Panzer Division, now came up against the Sherman for the first time and were dismayed to find themselves outgunned – and by a tank apparently impervious even to the fire from their previously infallible 88mm. anti-tank shield. They also found themselves for the first time in an action in which their orders gave them no latitude to draw back behind that anti-tank shield but insisted that they stay in front and hammer out a victory against the enemy by themselves, without infantry of their own to consolidate their advances, without – so far as they could see – an enemy infantry position for them to assault; just that line of huge, invulnerable tanks supported by massive artillery fed from inexhaustible ammunition dumps, while enemy bombers cruised implacably overhead, unloading steel and high explosive upon them with devastating impartiality.

It was a shattering experience for the morale of the men, and for the structure of the formations themselves. Nearly 120 German panzers and Italian tanks were drawn into the battle fought out on the afternoon of November 2nd along the western and northern faces of the *Supercharge* salient – and at the end of it only 35 panzers and 20 Italian tanks were still runners; and all present were well aware that the British still had vast reserves of both tanks and guns to draw upon.

That evening Rommel decided he must withdraw the Panzerarmee from the battle to new lines from which he could fight delaying actions until either his own forces were strengthened or Mont-gomery's forces tired – or ran out of supplies. From his staff he therefore obtained details of the artillery and anti-tank defences still in position behind which he could manoeuvre, from von Thoma he gathered the sobering truth about the remaining strength of Afrika Korps – and from his own experience he drew the conclusion that if he acted quickly and with resolution, a major part of his army could still be saved to fight again.

The first problem was that of immediate disengagement. Ariete must come north to add their armour to what was left of the Afrika Korps and thus form a screen behind which the infantry could get away – accepting the fact that the Italian tanks could not return to the south, whatever the developments down there; and he ordered the infantry of X Corps – Pavia and Brescia – to pull back to their pre-Alam Halfa positions. Bologna and Trento infantry in the centre would draw back to the line of the Telegraph Track, leaving rearguards of course, and he would organise transport to begin lifting them further back during the night of November 3rd. Priority was to be given to Italian troops 'as their fighting value is smaller' – but 'not a single German soldier is to be left behind', especially not from the Ramcke Brigade who with the Folgores would have been holding the line in the south.

Thompson's Post and the whole Tel el Eisa salient would also now be completely evacuated, the troops there drawing back first to the line of the Telegraph Track and thus helping 90th Light to hold the northern extremity of the Panzerarmee defences.

Much of this could be put in hand immediately, so that by the evening of the next day (November 3rd) the mass of the Italian infantry of Panzerarmee would be poised ready for deployment or further retreat as circumstances dictated, while the mobile formations of the Afrika Korps, plus the Ariete and 90th Light Divisions, formed in the north a protective screen which could – indeed must – hold the enemy east of a line running south through Ghazal Station while the rest of the army got away. In the meantime, no British armour must be allowed to cross the track, and those armoured cars which had reputedly broken through must be found and destroyed – or at least driven away from the supply routes.

Having drawn up the orders and seen that they were despatched and understood, Rommel then reported his intentions to Rome and Berlin, and spent the next few hours listening anxiously for sounds of a repeat of the previous night's violent bombardment.

But there was little except local action, and by morning the mass of Italian infantry were moving back out of close contact with the enemy, some reports even indicating that troops from Littorio and Trieste once they had left their front-line positions were streaming away out of control. In the centre, too, positions previously held by the Bologna Division had been totally evacuated, so Ariete were ordered to wait just north of the Deir el Qatani area in case they should be needed to plug vital gaps.

Otherwise, all moves seemed to be proceeding smoothly, and shortly after 0900 on November 3rd Rommel drove along the coast through dense traffic, mostly belonging to Italian supply and administration formations which he had ordered back to Fuka. For the moment there was an unaccountable absence of enemy aircraft, but he did not doubt that they would soon be overhead – although perhaps they were even now attacking the Italian infantry movements down in the south. At about 1000 he received reports from General von Thoma and Oberst Bayerlein; the British armour were still deployed around the north-western and western faces of their new salient, facing the line of anti-tank guns behind which waited the thirty-odd panzers which still remained to the Afrika Korps. It seemed for the moment that the enemy intended no aggressive moves; presumably Montgomery was reorganising his artillery for yet another massive bombardment, preceding yet another step forward by his infantry and armour.

Perhaps, then, *now* was the moment to begin the main withdrawal from the battle, first to whatever defensive positions the Fuka Line could provide, then to whatever defensive positions the rest of the

North African desert might provide for a weakened and poorly supplied army battling against a Juggernaut. Unless he was prepared to throw away the lives of his men in a pointless sacrifice, this was a course which he would have to take sooner or later – and the moment seemed propitious.

Shortly after 1030 Rommel made the decision. The disengaged Italian infantry should continue their march to the rear towards Fuka, after their supply services, and as much transport as possible must be sent down to them. Ariete must come further north, instructions must be given to 15th and 21st Panzer Divisions to be ready to move back to the area south of Ghazal as soon as darkness fell, for the 90th Light to move back along the coast towards El Daba, and for the anti-tank formations of 164th Division around the salient to be ready to slip away immediately they received the order to do so, some time after midnight. Down in the south, Ramcke Brigade must be warned to be ready to move out during the night, and Folgore told to do so during the first quiet period after sunset.

To protect these moves, every aircraft the Luftwaffe could get into the sky must be made available, in fact they should be there now as it surely would not be long before the R.A.F. arrived over these dense streams of traffic, of which Rommel was himself at that moment a vulnerable member.

At which reflection yet another of the 'Party Rally' formations arrived overhead and it was only by some frantic driving that he and his escorts arrived back at his headquarters just after midday. His staff immediately began issuing the detailed orders for the night's withdrawal, and it was after the bulk of them had been sent off that he was handed the Führer's reply to his report of the night before:

To FIELD MARSHAL ROMMEL

It is with trusting confidence in your leadership and the courage of the German–Italian troops under your command that the German people and I are following your heroic struggle in Egypt. In the situation in which you find yourself there can be no other thought but to stand fast, yield not a yard of ground and throw every gun and every man into the battle. Considerable air force reinforcements are being sent to C.-in-C. South. The Duce and the Comando Supremo are also making the utmost efforts to send you the means to continue the fight. Your enemy, despite his superiority, must also be at the end of his strength. It would not be the first time in history that a strong will has triumphed over the big battalions. As to your troops, you can show them no other road than that to victory or death.

ADOLF HITLER[1]

The Führer had spoken. And issued a death warrant.

It was a bitter blow to Rommel, not only in that the order if obeyed would mean the end of the Panzerarmee and especially of his beloved Afrika Korps, but also that his military judgment was being overruled at the level from which he had always in the past received support. For the first time in the African Campaign he did not know what to do, for unlike his fellow generals on the Russian Front, he had not yet learned the occasional necessity of disobeying the Führer, or the techniques of doing so without placing his own life and those of his family in jeopardy.

The Führer's directive could hardly have arrived at a more inopportune moment, too, for although the orders for the retreat had gone out, there was undoubtedly time for Rommel to cancel them – and in doing so to condemn his army to destruction. He rang von Thoma who reported tersely that Afrika Korps had now only 24 panzers left and that they must withdraw to regroup, and when he had heard the message from Hitler, suggested temporising along the lines that 'minor withdrawals for tactical adjustments' would surely not constitute disobedience of a direction at strategic level.

But Rommel knew that this would be neither practicable nor acceptable and having always in the past insisted upon unconditional and meticulous obedience from his own subordinates, saw the dangers in not applying the same principles to himself. Whatever his own feelings upon the matter, he must issue orders implementing the Führer's directive, commanding every formation to stand firm and be prepared 'on instructions from the highest level' to fight to the last man and the last round of ammunition; and if it proved difficult as a result of orders which had already gone out to persuade men who had already glimpsed their release from intolerable conditions to return to face them again, then the sternest measures would have to be used.

Some time was spent drafting a reply to Hitler's edict, accepting that all formations would be ordered to stand firm where they were, but pointing out that losses in German infantry to date approximated to 50 per cent, in artillery 40 per cent, that only 24 panzers were now left to Afrika Korps and that the Littorio and Trieste Divisions had been to all intents and purposes wiped out; and Rommel's A.D.C., Leutnant Berndt – a long-term Nazi Party member – was despatched to the Führer's H.Q. to attempt to point out to him that unless he changed his directive Panzerarmee Afrika would quickly be destroyed, and that great harm had befallen it already.

But in the meantime, the orders went out: 'I demand all possible efforts to be made to retain possession of the present battlefield, so that operations now in progress may be brought to a victorious conclusion.' Although there were undoubtedly several formations, especially among the Italians, who might choose to take little notice of the order, there would still be many staunch and patriotic Germans who would feel it their duty to obey, whatever the consequences.

The problem, however, would be getting the orders to them while it was still practicable for them to be obeyed, for 'order-counterorder' was quickly producing its inevitable chaos. Some of the administrative and supply services had long foreseen the ultimate necessity of a retreat, and lorries had been loaded and dumps prepared for destruction even before Rommel's first set of orders had gone out – and by the time he set about trying to reverse them, the road convoys were already on the move and the dumps were burning. Communications were still poor, enemy aircraft still ranged the battlefield shooting up every unit, static or mobile, they could find, messages failed to get through, wireless was still being jammed.

By the time darkness fell on the evening of November 3rd, Panzerarmee was unbalanced, the German element uncertain of their roles, the majority of the Italian infantry, one suspects, determined to get away from the scene of their recent ordeals before the next phase brought them even more suffering. Along the southern portion of the Aqqaqir Ridge and the Rahman Track stretching down from it, the 164th Division formations found that the Italians whom they had been 'corseting' had gone, that the gaps left were far too wide for them to cover without reinforcement and that all transport had disappeared; and as apparently their commander did not receive the later 'standstill' order, they marched out that night having repulsed the attack by the Gordons, and before either the 5th Indian Brigade or the Argyll and Sutherlands had arrived.

To the north, too, 90th Light were by dawn back as far as Ghazal, while 15th Panzer were back about six miles west of the Aqqaqir Ridge, their left flank on a twelve-foot-high rise called Tel el Mampsra adjoining the right flank of 21st Panzer Division, which in turn curved north-east as far as the railway line. Somewhere to the south of 15th Panzer lay the Ariete with what was left of the Trieste Motorised Division, mustering between them almost a hundred tanks – but at the best only M13s, all of them in need of service and maintenance.

As has been suggested before, military affairs occasionally acquire an impetus of their own, and little or nothing can be done to check it, even the direct interference of one of the most powerful men in history.

Dawn on November 4th brought Eighth Army the news of victory in the long hard-fought battle, heavy early morning mist, and a traffic jam in the salient which surpassed all previous experience.

With the concentration in the north of all Eighth Army armour (in fact of the major part of Eighth Army's fighting strength) the armoured formations themselves had reverted with one exception to their original divisions – the 1st Armoured Division consisting of Fisher's 2nd Armoured Brigade and the 7th Motor Brigade, the 10th Armoured Division (under Gatehouse) consisting of Custance's 8th Armoured Brigade and the 133rd Lorried Infantry Brigade, and John Harding's 7th Armoured Division consisting of Roberts's 22nd Armoured Brigade and the 131st Lorried Infantry Brigade newly formed from the Queen's battalions; and all of them, plus the 4th Light Armoured Brigade now attached to Freyberg's New Zealanders in place of the annihilated 9th Armoured, were trying to get through and out into the desert by the exit most likely to be mine-free, the *Supercharge* salient:

> Little if any attempt seems to have been made at a higher level to co-ordinate the confusion that was bound to arise from so many divisions struggling to push out through the bottle-neck of the salient area. It would have been hard enough if all had been under the command of the same corps; with two different corps, who were not on the best of terms anyway, both trying to carry out the same task in the same area, it was chaotic. There is no other word to describe the incredible confusion of that dark night in a sea of dust. Vehicles of every formation were travelling in every direction on every conceivable track, looming up in front of each other from unexpected directions out of the thick, stifling pall of dust.[2]

Obviously, the first tanks likely to get away from such confusion would be the ones who had fought along the western face, and Fisher's 2nd Armoured Brigade with the divisional commander General Briggs and the surviving riflemen of the 7th Motor Brigade were ready to move at dawn – if only they could see where they were going and what stood against them. It was nearly 0800 before the mist disappeared, and shortly afterwards the armoured cars of the 12th Lancers moved carefully forward, followed by the Shermans and Grants of the Bays, the 9th Lancers and the 10th Hussars, across the Rahman Track at last, up and over the northern end of the Aqqaqir Ridge – to see in front of them and barring their route to El Daba the remaining Afrika Korps panzers and anti-tank guns, grouped on each side of the rise of Tel el Mampsra.

There was never any great doubt as to what the end of the ensuing battle would be, but neither was there any doubt that the Afrika Korps rearguards would resist to the last. One of their first shells wrecked the tank in which General Briggs was travelling and quite soon after several more tanks were ablaze – and with an appreciation that every vehicle which could move would be required during the next few days, Briggs ordered the armour back while artillery came up over the ridge behind them to deal with the Afrika Korps anti-tank fire. Slowly but inexorably, the line of panzers and guns was smashed, and towards noon it was seen that some of the panzers were drawing back and a few of the guns were being towed away – and as the British tanks and trucks drove cautiously towards the Tel, they saw amid the wreckage of the battle and the groups of German infantrymen and gunners rising reluctantly with their hands in the air from hastily dug trenches, the tall, weatherbeaten figure of a German general, dressed in a correct field uniform with epaulettes and decorations, standing beside a burning tank, impervious to the heat, the sand, the bullets which still whistled close.

General der Panzertruppe Wilhelm Ritter von Thoma had decided that he would soldier no more under a regime of 'unparalleled madness' and that if his men were to be expected to stand firm and fight against obviously overwhelming odds, then he should be there with them. He had taken his *Kampfstaffel* into the forefront of the battle and seen it destroyed around him.

By this time, a much bigger battle was also being fought some seven miles to the south.

The 'Desert Rats' – John Harding's 7th Armoured Division – had spent the night in the salient itself and at 0630, their planned advance having been twice delayed, the Crusaders and Grants of the 22nd Armoured Brigade felt their way out of the south-west corner into and through the positions taken by the 5th Indian Brigade a few hours before. They drove further down the Rahman Track and just after 0800, as their leading troops were turning west into the desert, they came under fire from 88mm. guns, well sited to cover the track, which obviously had to be destroyed or chased away.

As Pip Roberts deployed his tanks and brought up his artillery, however, orders arrived from General Harding that he should 'push aside' the enemy force and get past it, but when Roberts sent forward his armoured cars – two troops of the 11th Hussars – to find a way around and start cutting enemy communications up towards El Daba, they found no open space but instead a lot more enemy tanks and guns.

Roberts had, in fact, bumped into the Ariete Division with its hundred-odd Italian tanks together with most of the remaining Italian XX Corps artillery, and some random tank and infantry units from Littorio and Trieste, who on their northern flank were in touch with the 15th Panzer Division. Quantitatively it was undoubtedly a formidable force, and qualitatively in many ways as well, for if its tanks were mostly of the type which justified their pejorative title of 'mobile coffins', the Italian troops themselves were the best of Rommel's allies and their artillery was as good as any in the Panzerarmee.

It therefore very soon became evident to Harding that Roberts would be unable to leap-frog his brigade away to the left to get around this enemy block, and that the whole of 7th Armoured

Division would be engaged. The Queen's battalions of the Lorried Infantry Brigade (44th Division had at last been liquidated) had by now cleared the salient to come down in support of the armour, gun batteries wheeled into position and all preparations for a set-piece battle began.

It raged throughout the whole of the morning, on through the noonday haze and well into the afternoon – and neither side made any appreciable troop or armoured movements during the entire time, both apparently prepared to leave the battle to the gunners; but as at last the light began to fade, the Italian and German forces fell back and Roberts's tanks drove forward to take the field upon which they counted the shells of but 29 Italian tanks, a few guns and some 450 prisoners. What had happened to the rest of Ariete remained for a short time something of a mystery.

Meanwhile, however, the 8th Armoured Brigade and 133rd Lorried Infantry of Gatehouse's 10th Armoured Division, originally ordered to drive westwards between the 1st Armoured to the north and the 7th to the south, had by midday extricated themselves from the confusion of the salient, and were about to drive across to Tel el Aqqaqir when new orders arrived from Lumsden: instead they were to drive south, circle around the battle being fought there, and attempt to cut off the remnants of the Panzerarmee with a drive up to the coast at Galal, thirty miles to the west. As they were adjusting their line of march to this new direction, they were caught by one of the few successful Stuka attacks of the whole battle and thoroughly dispersed – and by the time they had reassembled to move off it was late afternoon. The leading squadrons drove down the Rahman Track towards the area of the dying battle fought by Harding's troops, whereat Brigadier Custance decided to pull off to the east and leaguer for the night, his men being, in his opinion, untrained for movement during the dark hours.

Thus by the end of the first day of the break-out after Alamein, the 1st Armoured Division under General Briggs had only advanced some five miles to Tel el Mampsra (for after the surrender of von Thoma they hardly moved at all), 10th Armoured Division under General Gatehouse was still east of the Rahman Track, and 7th Armoured Division under General Harding, although it had destroyed or at least dispersed Rommel's last major armoured force, was still in the area of the battle only two or three miles west of the track. Lumsden's X Corps had not, therefore, achieved much success if their object had been to cut off the remnants of the Panzerarmee.

On the other hand, they had held in place a significant part of the remaining enemy strength, and if circumstances allowed them to continue to hold it there was every reason to believe that it would be destroyed.

But if a 'cutting off' operation was intended, there was now another Allied force well positioned to carry it out.

Bernard Freyberg had been convinced that the enemy were cracking as early as the afternoon of November 3rd, and as soon as news of the Argyll and Sutherlands' occupation of Tel el Aqqaqir had reached him, he was off on a personal reconnaissance of the country to the south of the Tel to find a way through for his two brigades and the remnants of the 9th Armoured Brigade, plus the 4th Light Armoured Brigade which he had prised out of Montgomery as replacement for John Currie's force after their sacrifice in front of Aqqaqir Ridge.

Satisfied as to its practicability, Freyberg had then to contain his soul in patience while his own 6th Infantry under Brigadier Gentry with Currie's remaining tanks disengaged themselves from the northwest corner of the salient, Howard Kippenberger's 5th Brigade came across from the base of the salient, and 4th Light Armoured Division, whom he wanted to lead his force at last out into the open (he intended to drive straight to Fuka, fifty-five miles to the west), arrived from their latest reported position close to Alamein Station!

It is astonishing what men can do when motivated with enthusiasm. The Royal Scots Greys and the armoured cars of the 2nd Derbyshire Yeomanry managed to thread their way through the confusion of the salient by shortly after 0800, and although the rest of the 4th Light Armoured still tailed back past Tel el Eisa they were determined to get into the battle, for down in XIII Corps's area they had seen very little action.

The brigade were with Freyberg by 1000, and at 1030 he sent their armoured cars away down the Rahman Track to discover and report on the action being fought there by his old friend John Harding and his Desert Rats. Soon afterwards he sent the Stuarts and Grants of the Greys to support the cars, and by midday both his infantry brigades were up and he was holding a conference with the brigade commanders – during which reports came in that the Greys were themselves in action, away to the south and west of the main battle which they had by-passed.

It was time to move – and to move fast, for Freyberg wanted to be clear by nightfall not only of the entire Alamein battlefield, but also of the interfering and often confining restrictions which proximity to other divisions – especially armoured ones – so frequently brought about. He set out with his Tactical Headquarters early in the afternoon, assured that the rest of his force would follow as soon as they had collected and stowed away water and rations for eight days, 360 rounds for each field gun and petrol for 200 miles – and embedded in his thoughts was the declaration by Brigadier Gentry of the 6th Brigade that every man in the force had been waiting for three years for such a victory and such an advance as now stretched before them, and would willingly travel all night without sleep – and the next day if necessary – in order to consolidate it.

In his diary, Freyberg wrote late that night:

> We began to pass through enemy positions and tanks of the Panzer Divisions that would fight no more, burning transport, and large calibre guns. It was a change much appreciated to speed across open desert away from the dust heap of the Alamein front. As the Div. swept south-westwards the guns of the tanks and arty were in action to the north where the British armour were fighting the Panzer rearguard. 4 Lt Armd Bde were ahead. Behind them marching apparently quite cheerfully were columns of PWs with a solitary armoured car or truck as an escort, carrying a few wounded and a single guard armed with a Tommy gun. We passed an infantry (or artillery) position almost intact with guns in position and ammunition boxes empty . . . [3]

They passed through Sidi Ibeid and hit the old Barrel Track, but when he judged they were south of El Daba Freyberg halted the head of the column to allow the rest of his force to catch up – especially in view of the fact that a signal had just come in reporting indications that Rommel's remaining armour were also making for Fuka, and he felt that he would need more strength than he had at present should he come across them there.

It was midnight before Kippenberger's brigade came up, and they had hardly reported when a small battle broke out at the tail of the column where an enemy force of about seventy men, most probably from the Ramcke Parachute Brigade, attacked presumably in the hope of capturing transport with which to make their escape to the north. Mortars and heavy automatic machine-guns played their parts in this brief but violent encounter, and at the end of it the raiders got away with some vehicles and eight prisoners, leaving behind them seventeen of their own men killed. They had killed eight of the New Zealanders and wounded twenty-six, and set light to an ammunition truck which then acted as a beacon for the 6th Brigade and the rest of Freyberg's force as it came up – but the incident confirmed Freyberg's opinion that he must keep his force concentrated in this open, unmapped, unknown and featureless waste, dotted with wrecked vehicles, sewn with old and now-forgotten minefields – and populated again, as it had been during those far-off days of the June retreat, by random bodies of troops who might or might not prove to be hostile when contact was made.

He would wait to see what daylight brought before continuing his drive to Fuka.

Daylight brought confusion to the whole desert area, chiefly because late in the previous afternoon (November 4th) either common sense or loyalty to his men had overridden Rommel's sense of duty to the Führer. Until then the orders to stand firm had been holding fast the 90th Light Division, what little remained of the two panzer divisions and the Ariete conglomerate, in a position where at least two-thirds of them were being systematically annihilated by the British artillery – but after a conversation with Bayerlein who had yet again been put in command of the Afrika Korps, Rommel decided that further sacrifice was pointless.

The staff were told to pack and move the headquarters back to Fuka as quickly as possible, and it seems that Rommel and Bayerlein themselves raced around the battlefield releasing the formations from their ordeals – and in no uncertain terms, for Rommel accepted that this was to be an affair of *sauve qui peut* in which those who could climb aboard vehicles might get away, those left without transport almost certainly would not.

The result had been the sudden disappearance of organised resistance in front of the British armoured divisions who were, not unnaturally, relieved, and as darkness was near only too glad to retire into leaguer until dawn. But plans for the next day were being drawn up at Eighth Army and X Corps headquarters on the assumption that Panzerarmee would still be present to give battle on November 5th, and the first orders which went out were based on that assumption. Briggs and Harding were to continue their battles, Custance to drive for Galal, and Freyberg for Fuka.

But then reports came in from both the R.A.F. and the armoured car and raiding units (for both the L.R.D.G. and the S.A.S. were out now watching and occasionally attacking the coast road) of Axis traffic streaming westward in even greater density, and realisation that Rommel had ordered a general retreat dawned upon the headquarter staffs. Now everything must be directed towards cutting off as large a portion of the Panzerarmee as possible, and speed would be the keynote.

Briggs and Harding were now to drive their respective divisions west-north-west to the coast, Briggs aiming for El Daba and Harding on his left to hit the road a few miles to the west; Gatehouse was to take his headquarters and his lorried infantry along the top of the Escarpment to where the road climbed it just west of Fuka, and Custance was to follow as quickly as his tanks would roll to support him there; and Freyberg, who would now be transferred from XXX Corps to X Corps and thus come under Lumsden's command (so much for his hopes for independence) would drive parallel to Gatehouse and then curve around to the north towards Maaten Baggush and capture for the R.A.F. the string of landing-grounds near Sidi Haneish.

All armoured car units – and now in addition to the Royals both the 3rd and 4th South African Armoured Car Regiments were out – would concentrate near Fuka and attempt to block the road up the Escarpment.

The headquarters of the armoured divisions received their emended orders in good time and by 0700 Briggs's armoured brigade (2nd, under Fisher) were on their way to El Daba with the riflemen of 7th Motor Brigade on their heels. They met no opposition until they were on the outskirts of the village when an 88mm. opened fire and killed the officer who had taken von Thoma prisoner the day before, and the armoured brigade then swung around to cut the road west of the village while the riflemen mounted an attack along the road from the east; by 1230 El Daba had been taken with about 150 stragglers and the 88mm.

On the 1st Armoured Division's left flank, Pip Roberts's 22nd Armoured Brigade had kept pace, quickly realised that El Daba had been evacuated and then learned from their 11th Hussar reconnaissance troop in front that the road where they were aiming for it was almost deserted, and that to catch a sizeable bag they would have to sweep much further west. Without waiting for orders, Harding therefore pulled back into the desert and drove slightly south of west on a course which would take the 7th across the Barrel Track and – though he did not know it then – the path of the New Zealanders.

It was left to the 8th Armoured Brigade under Brigadier Custance to reap whatever profits were to be earned that day, oddly enough because it would seem that Gatehouse had failed to pass on the 'emended' order. B Squadron of the 11th Hussars had led them off at 0600, and after a brush with an enemy column more intent on getting away than staying and fighting – and twice crossing the route of the 7th Armoured Division without, apparently, noticing any sign of them – they arrived at Galal, their original objective, and ensconced themselves across both road and railway by about 1100. A small enemy column arrived soon afterwards and was collected and shepherded away by the 3rd R.T.R., and then just after midday the head of quite a large force was seen driving unconcernedly towards them from El Daba, which they had obviously vacated just before Fisher's troops had arrived.

Not unlike the Support Group of the 7th Armoured Division at Beda Fomm twenty-one months before, the 8th Armoured waited in their hull-down positions and, at exactly the right moment, opened fire with every gun they had. The result was spectacular and rewarding, for after less than an hour's hectic confusion the whole enemy column had been captured or destroyed, 14 panzers and 29 Italian tanks having been accounted for, four guns, over 100 vehicles in running order and nearly 1,000 prisoners; and shortly afterwards 11 more tanks and several more vehicles were found abandoned to the south. All that Brigadier Custance now required was petrol for the captured vehicles and some organisation to deal with his prisoners; it was a problem which would grow.

Freyberg's column had in the meantime continued on their way towards Fuka, but very shortly after starting out they caught up with what later proved to be the remains of 15th Panzer Division, and the Grants of the Greys fought a brisk and successful battle with them. By the time the Germans managed to disentangle themselves and draw away, the Greys had put five panzers out of action and captured two intact – and at about the same time, the 1st K.R.R.C. riflemen with the column rounded up several hundred German and Italian infantry-men, including the commander of the Trento Division and most of his staff, who had been blundering about the desert for the last two days.

Successes such as these, however, bred their own problems and by noon Freyberg's force was strung out over many miles of the Barrel Track, and some at least of his manpower had to be diverted to guard duties. By this time, too, his new orders had reached him (though not, apparently news of his transfer to Lumsden's command) and shortly afterwards the head of his column arrived at the fencing around a marked minefield which ran south from the Fuka Escarpment – and when they felt their way up it they found that the only obvious gap was covered by the guns of at least two highly efficient German rearguards. By 1500 some of the leading tanks were through, but it was quite obvious that it would be a long time before the rest of Freyberg's force were west of the minefield, and until then Fuka was open for the survivors of Panzerarmee to use as refuge or channel.

They were arriving often four vehicles abreast on and alongside the narrow ribbon of the road, every truck, tank, gun-limber and lorry full or covered with troops of whom very few were still in cohesive formations. As a general rule discipline held firm, perhaps because stern measures had been taken during the first hours of the retreat – and were known to have been taken. Rommel himself had arrived at Fuka during the early hours of November 5th and watched with anger and sorrow in his heart as the troops flooded in, knowing as he did by now that there were no prepared defences here, no 'Fuka Line', no rest for his exhausted men. The enemy aircraft were bombing and machine-gunning the packed roads, and during that afternoon they found Rommel's H.Q. by wireless intercept and bombed it twice, driving Rommel and Westphal into slit-trenches nearby; and still the traffic came in, though for the moment the rearguards held the nearest enemy force back from the top of the pass.

Then came news of yet another outflanking force further out in the desert and Rommel knew that he must go further back, to Mersa Matruh for the moment – but then where? And how far?

He and his headquarters moved out after dark:

It was a wild helterskelter drive through another pitch-black night. Occasional Arab villages loomed up and dropped behind us in the darkness, and several vehicles lost contact with the head of the column. Finally, we halted in a small valley to wait for daylight. At that time it was still a matter of doubt as to whether we would be able to get even the remnants of the army away to the west. Our fighting power was very low. The bulk of the Italian infantry had been lost. Of the XXI Corps, part had been destroyed after a stiff resistance against the overwhelmingly superior British, and part of it had been overtaken in its retreat and taken prisoner; the vehicles which we had repeatedly demanded for them from the Italian Supply H.Q. had not arrived. The X Italian Corps was on the march south-east of Fuka, short of water and ammunition and, to be quite frank, with no hope of escaping to the west . . .

As for the XX Italian Motorised Corps, it had been practically wiped out on the 4th November – no more than a few companies and detachments remained in the hands of the Corps' staff . . .

The only forces which retained any fighting strength were the remnants of the 90th Light Division, the Afrika Korps' two divisions – now reduced to the strength of small combat groups, the Panzer Grenadier Regiment Afrika and a few quickly scratched-together German units, the remains of the 164th Light Division. Tanks, heavy A.A. guns, heavy and light artillery, all had sustained such frightful losses at El Alamein that there was nothing but a few remnants left.[4]

They still had one or two factors on their side, however, such as that adrenalin tends to flow faster into the veins of men escaping from a trap than into those closing it, and that they now constituted a tightly knit mass imbued with one single aim. They were also travelling along the only road in the locality; and their luck was about to change.

The outflanking force which had precipitated Rommel's retirement from Fuka was Pip Roberts's 22nd Armoured Brigade which Harding had sent off on his own responsibility on a 'long hook' aimed past Fuka. They had been delayed for a short time by the passage in front of them of the tail of Freyberg's force, and then again when they, too, ran into the minefield which was holding up the New Zealanders away to the north. For well over an hour the 11th Hussars hunted for a way through or around – and then some of the attached engineers discovered that the minefield was a dummy – one, moreover, which had been laid by the British during the June retreat.

By this time Roberts had received clear orders – he was to help Freyberg take the Sidi Haneish airstrips – but it was nearly 1800 before his brigade were across the dummy minefield, the lorried infantry brigade (131st) which should have been with him were still some fifteen miles behind, and he was very short of petrol. Sending out the Hussars to reconnoitre the immediate surroundings, he ordered his brigade into leaguer and hoped that both his infantry and his petrol lorries would be up soon.

To the north of Roberts's brigade, Freyberg was still unaware that the minefield which had been holding his force up was a dummy and so was still trying to get the last units of 4th Light Armoured Brigade and his two infantry brigades through a gap under enemy fire. The presence of the hostile guns and all the reports he had received during the afternoon convinced him that strong enemy forces were occupying Fuka and he had no wish to expose his men to another such action as they had experienced at Minqar Qaim, now only a short way away. The bulk of his armour had got through the gap in full daylight, so just before dusk under cover of an attack towards the guns by the armour and smoke fired by the main artillery, 5th Brigade rushed through (the fences had been widened but no suspicions aroused by the fact that nothing else had been found in the vicinity) – but he held 6th Brigade back in reserve. They would all, he decided, now dig in and wait to see what tomorrow would produce.

During that morning (of November 5th) General Lumsden had realised that Rommel's forces were slipping away, and that the comparatively short hooks being made by three of the divisions under his command were unlikely to prove profitable – but there was still another at his disposal, for after their capture of El Daba the 1st Armoured Division had gone into leaguer to the west of the village, where they were counting their prisoners and trying to organise their despatch to the rear. At 1430 they received from X Corps orders that 2nd Armoured Brigade should move off 'at once' on a long, seventy-mile dash to Bir Khalda where they should be by dawn, poised and ready to drive up and capture Mersa Matruh, thirty-five miles away to the north – and with the base, perhaps a major part of whatever was left of Panzerarmee Afrika.

Brigadier Fisher was by this time feeling the effects of the strain of battle and perhaps this explains the delay, for nearly six hours were to pass before the 12th Lancers led the armoured formations off, and when darkness fell two hours later they found themselves still amongst the coastal maze of slit-trenches, old gun-pits, minefields and criss-crossing tracks, all still carrying traffic from every conceivable formation travelling in every direction. Nevertheless, the brigade struggled on and by dawn the leaders had travelled fifty-five miles in twelve hours – which in the circumstances was a thoroughly commendable performance – but they were fifteen miles short of Bir Khalda and the tail of the division was still twenty-three miles behind; and shortly after 0900 (November 6th) the whole division came to a halt through lack of fuel, its leading tanks still short of their dawn objective.

It was 1100 before their B echelon support arrived with petrol for two of the armoured regiments (that for the Bays had gone astray and was stuck in soft sand) and 1330 before those which had been refuelled could start out again, which they did under the brigade second-in-command, as Brigadier Fisher had finally succumbed and gone back to base with the empty petrol trucks.

By this time, Freyberg's force were all through the dummy mine-field and driving for the top of the Escarpment overlooking Sidi Haneish and Maaten Baggush. They had run into an enemy column on the way, and after a brisk running fight cut off its tail and collected about five hundred prisoners including one hundred Germans from the 90th Light Division – and to their left, 22nd Armoured Brigade had refuelled about midday and were aiming for the landing grounds along the top of the Escarpment to the west of Sidi Haneish, below which, according to their reconnaissance troops of the 11th Hussars, was a considerable body of enemy troops, probably the last of the 21st Panzer Division.

Back to the east, Gatehouse's 10th Armoured Division with the 8th Armoured Brigade contentedly counting its profits, had been visited by Montgomery during the morning (he had come up to 'apply some ginger') and curtly told to close up along the coast road, clear all the rear area of enemy stragglers – and send every drop of petrol they could spare across the desert to Briggs's 1st Armoured Division; but at about this time, another factor began to complicate the problems facing the Eighth Army in its pursuit of the beaten enemy.

Quite early in the morning pilots returning from flights along the coast had given warning of low cloud moving in from the sea, and by 1000 heavy rain was falling along the coastal strip and moving inexorably inland. By noon the recently captured landing-grounds at El Daba were unusable and fighters could only operate from the all-weather strips back behind Alamein, wheeled vehicles except on the road were sinking to their hub-caps and tracked vehicles were emptying their petrol tanks even more rapidly than usual, at one time Shermans needing three gallons to travel one mile. By afternoon the rain had developed into a steady downpour and every formation not on the road was bogging down. The experience of the New Zealanders was typical of all:

> On the escarpment plateau widening pools filled the hollows where the sand lay deep, turning them into morasses impassable to most vehicles and then overfilling, gouged channels down to lower levels. Only on the rocky ridges was travel possible, but many of these soon stood isolated like islands in the sea of rain. From the escarpment, miniature water-falls cascaded down to the coastal plain to form streams which swept across the

road and railway towards outlets through the sand dunes on the beach.

As the New Zealand brigades drove north towards the road, first the trucks with only rear-wheel drive, then those with four-wheel drive, fell behind. As each truck sank to its axles in the wet sand, the men aboard dismounted from the shelter of cabs and canopied trays and, in the cold persistent rain, dug channels for each wheel. With camel thorn, sand trays, discarded enemy tents, or anything that would help the wheels to grip placed in the channels, the men hauled and heaved their trucks to firmer ground. At first the tracked tanks and carriers were able to tow some of the wheeled vehicles, but soon too many trucks were immobilised and even the tracked vehicles were finding the going treacherous. The rearmost vehicles, driving over ground whose crust had been churned up by those in front, were the first to succumb, so that before long the brigade columns were stretched out over many miles of desert. By late afternoon the men in charge of most of the heavy trucks carrying troops and stores had given up the struggle and the advance slowly ground to a standstill.[5]

Yet another complication was that the weather also seriously affected wireless communication. A large number of the vehicles in Eighth Army were now equipped with sound, reliable transmitter/ receivers, but present conditions caused gross over-use of the facility as everyone tried to inform their commanders of their individual plight and request assistance, and then as even heavier storms swept in from the north, severe atmospheric interference brought about a complete signals black-out. Command from Army down to company level became powerless to effect the onward movement of troops, as it had only the roughest idea of where they were, lacked all means of communication with them – and could have given nothing but empty exhortations to 'get on', if they had. So the command fumed, and the troops cursed the weather and the conduct of the war with sardonic impartiality.

Ironically, though November 6th was the day when the last possibility of cutting off Rommel's forces slipped from Eighth Army's grasp, it was also for Panzerarmee a day of dejection and, at some levels, of near-panic. The weather, of course, contributed to the former, for a condition of sodden misery does not make for the clarity of vision which could see extra possibilities of escape through the pouring rain – but the latter was caused by the realisation that their next backstop was Mersa Matruh, that it was filled with workshops and stores which had been built up over the weeks and, as the port was quite evidently indefensible, as much of this as possible must be destroyed in the extremely short time before evacuation further west.

And how much further west, how soon, and what was awaiting them there? One narrow road as far as Sollum which they knew to be so heavily and systematically mined on each side that it would be dangerous if not impossible to move even a metre off it, routes to the south threading their ways through uncharted minefields on sand already pulverised by months of traffic and now turned by the rain into quagmires, and most ominous of all for those who stayed on the road, two winding passes up the steep escarpment at Halfaya and Sollum where they would almost certainly be bombed – and could be blocked and destroyed by any sizeable enemy force which reached the tops before them.

Yet Rommel himself was by no means despondent, and from his writing one gathers the impression that he was assuaging the pain of defeat and retreat by concentrating on the technical problems of getting his army back into some form of safety – and arguing with his superiors. Hitler's reluctant agreement that Panzerarmee should be allowed to pull back as far as Fuka had arrived the morning after Rommel had issued the relevant orders, as had a similarly grudging missive from Mussolini which ended with the order, 'You must, however, make certain that the non-motorised units are withdrawn too . . . ' without, of course, indicating where either the transport or the petrol for the operation was to be found.

November 6th gave Rommel a short respite from direct command problems and even a little good news, for he was told that 5,000 tons of petrol had arrived at Benghasi – though as he had so often pointed out Benghasi was a long way away; and less than a hour later came news that half the petrol had been destroyed in an air attack. But 2,500 tons gave him some ground for confidence and the loss of the other 2,500 an extra edge to his tongue when in the afternoon an emissary from Maresciallo Cavallero, Generale Gandin, arrived to inquire about plans for the future.

'This,' wrote Rommel later, with some relish, 'suited me very well.'[6]

With fewer than twenty tanks, fewer than twenty anti-tank guns, fewer than fifty field guns, fewer than five thousand men, far less than adequate transport for them all and practically no petrol – Rommel informed the Generale – there was no point in making plans for anything except a retreat as far and as fast as possible, endeavouring occasionally to hinder the enemy but not attempting anywhere to give battle. There was nothing, he insisted, except their own logistic difficulties to stop the British driving straight through into Tripolitania if they wished to, and only British hesitation had allowed Panzer-armee remnants to escape this far or might now allow them to slip away deep into Libya where they might, if they were lucky, be given opportunity to reorganise. In respect of which, he hoped to have them there within the week, and Il Duce's message brought by Gandin that he expected the Italo-German forces to stand on the frontier and deny so much as a metre of the Italian Empire in North Africa to the foe, was a waste of breath. Empty, bombastic breath, true, but nevertheless a waste.

Generale Gandin departed as shaken as Barbasetti had been a few days previously, and Rommel, having released a great deal of his nervous tension, resumed the task of organising the retreat. To the south-west with their backs to the Charing Cross minefields, 15th Panzer were watching with some apprehension the movements through the murk of a body of 'about a hundred tanks' which in the event remained away to the south in soaking isolation all night, while to the south-east the remnants of 21st Panzer, brought to a halt through lack of petrol near Qasaba but with the Voss rearguard group out just beyond it, reported that British tanks from the famous 7th Armoured Division were groping their way towards them.

In the circumstances there was nothing the 21st could do but rely upon their own expertise and luck – and neither deserted them. They drained the petrol from all bogged and damaged vehicles, fought off the approaches (by Roberts's 22nd Armoured Brigade) by prodigal use of their remaining ammunition, pulled back after dark having demolished every vehicle and gun they could not take with them, and made their way westwards through that pitch-black and torrential night, arriving at Charing Cross shortly after dawn – having met and been replenished by a supply column en route! How it happened only the Gods of War might explain.

November 7th brought more surprises, not all as welcome. The stores at Matruh proved disappointing, the bulk having been plundered by earlier arrivals most of whom had pressed on west-wards, or destroyed during the previous day's panic; what was left – for instance a warehouse full of Italian boots – though useful was rarely able to meet the most pressing requirements. On the other hand, it was late in the day before conditions improved sufficiently for the mass of the enemy armour to make any really threatening moves, though 90th Light rearguards at Gerawla were forced back a short distance after probing attacks had been made on them during the late afternoon; otherwise the British seemed for the moment to be indulging in one of their 'pauses for regrouping'.

What had been most welcome to Rommel was the arrival of Generalleutnant Karl Buelowius as Chief Engineer to the Panzer-armee, for the little man was a positive genius at demolitions and booby-traps, at any device, in fact, which would prove a nuisance to and so delay a pursuer. He seemed totally undeterred by the tactical situation into which he was being plunged, positively relishing the intricacies of the tasks which would face him.

Welcome too – though for reasons of personality not so welcome as Buelowius – was the unexpected arrival of Generalmajor Hermann

Ramcke with six hundred of his men, after an epic crossing of the desert from their battle positions south of Ruweisat Ridge. They had ambushed and captured a British supply column and its lorries, and the Generalmajor greeted Rommel with a peculiarly metallic and sardonic smile, metallic as his false teeth were of stainless steel, sardonic because his Fallschirmjäger Brigade was really a Luftwaffe unit and had made themselves highly unpopular with their airs and demands among the soldiers; and Ramcke made few bones about his suspicion that the army had deliberately deserted them as a result.

But their valour was unquestioned and an addition of six hundred such fighting men would come in especially useful at that moment, for Rommel had made another decision. The weather was holding the enemy back now, but they would presumably start moving again as soon as the desert surface dried out; so he would whip his forces out of Matruh that very night on a seventy-mile dash along the road which would take them to Sidi Barrani and within striking distance of those vital passes at Sollum and Halfaya.

They began moving even before dusk with the fighting formation vehicles, partly by accident and partly by design, mixed in with the flood of more expendable traffic and so suffering less concentrated attack from enemy air forces – which in any case seemed now to be more interested in the congestion building up through and below the passes; and when daylight came on the morning of November 8th there was a 25-mile queue along the coast road, solidly jammed up against Halfaya and Sollum by the sheer rapidity and efficiency of the retreat. Fortunately, although there was still some disorder among the administrative and non-combatant formations on the run, cold discipline was now ruling at the tail of the column, strengthened by rising hopes of escape.

Then at midday two further aspects of the war in North Africa assumed significance, one strategic and the other tactical. There had been rumours of great events at the other end of the Mediterranean since early morning, and shortly after 1100 came confirmation; huge invasion fleets had entered the western end of the Mediterranean and landed Anglo-American forces in vast numbers at Oran and Algiers (and others further west at Casablanca) – which raised the possibility, however remote, that any rebuilt Panzerarmee might be caught and crushed between two Colossi. More immediately and much closer to home, Rommel's trusted quartermaster, Major Otto, informed him that the press of traffic below the Escarpment would require two days to clear through the passes if the enemy air attacks were to continue on such a scale, even if none of their ground forces intervened.

Obviously, this latter problem concerned Rommel most for the moment, and that evening he drove across to assess the situation for himself – and was forced to agree with Otto. The traffic was in fact moving with admirable efficiency with control points manned by picked officers who kept the vehicles moving, ruthlessly jettisoned damaged or broken-down trucks, guns or even tanks, and dealt effectively with drivers whose nerve broke under the bombing.

But it was obvious that more risks would have to be taken if the combat units at the end of the queue were to be saved for the trials to come. Whatever remained of the Italian XX Corps, therefore, escorted by the 3rd Reconnaissance Battalion, must immediately break away to the south, skirt the eastern end of the Escarpment and drive for Habata – and from there watch the British and do everything possible to keep them from the tops of the passes; even the staunch remains of the Afrika Korps might have to go the same way to reduce the pressure along the road – though they were now reduced to four panzers, all badly in need of service and maintenance. Down on the plain the 90th Light would continue to provide the rearguard.

And now Rommel had another minor but irritating problem to deal with. Il Duce was still clamouring for defence of the Italian Empire, and Cavallero had ordered the Pistoia Division and a few other random battalions to the Egyptian–Libyan frontier, including even the Giovani Fascisti (Young Fascist) Division of virtually untrained youngsters from Siwa – and asked that Rommel should take them under command. His reply was curt and dismissive; he had neither transport nor administration to spare for such an addition to his forces as the Pistoia, and as for the Giovani Fascisti, if they managed to escape from Siwa he suggested that they go straight to Mersa Brega where they could be employed refurbishing the defences from which the Afrika Korps had emerged eleven months before, on their victorious advance first to Gazala and then to Alamein. For there was no doubt in Rommel's mind that that was the nearest position in which Axis forces might offer some resistance to the Eighth Army – and perhaps not even there.

By the morning of November 9th there were still a thousand vehicles waiting on the plain below the Halfaya and Sollum Passes, despite the night's operations which had been surprisingly successful – and now the plan must be to get them and everyone else in the area up and over the top, then back into Cyrenaica. Motor-cyclists raced away from his headquarters whipping in every unit and straggler they could find as far back as Sidi Barrani, 15th and 21st Panzer Division units after all drew back and started up the narrow hair-pin bends, 90th Light pulled their rearguards further in as enemy armour probed along towards them – and all day long the Kittyhawks machinegunned between the cliff-tops and Spitfires attacked along the plain. That night Wellingtons and Halifaxes bombed the top of the Escarpment and on towards the frontier around Capuzzo.

In the meantime, Rommel had had an opportunity to assess the strength of the army left to him:

> For manning the Sollum front we had 2,000 Italian and 2,000 German fighting troops with 15 German anti-tank and 40 German field guns, and a few Italian anti-tank guns and several Italian field guns.
>
> For the mobile reserve we had 3,000 German and 500 Italian fighting troops with 11 German and 10 Italian tanks, 20 German anti-tank guns, 24 anti-aircraft guns and 25 field guns.[7]

The most important thing was to get them all out – and that morning British armour and New Zealand infantry were reported assembling in force south of Buq Buq, obviously about to launch a concerted drive along the coast. The orders were issued, 90th Light efficiently and almost invisibly drew in their outer rearguards and by midday they were driving up the Sollum Pass, their passage marked by explosions as Generalleutnant Buelowius's engineers blew the road to pieces, or tumbled the bordering cliffs where they existed across it. By late afternoon the division, once again the rearguard of Panzerarmee, were watching with some curiosity from the top of the Escarpment as the leading Stuarts (of the 4th Light Armoured Brigade) felt their way through the mined approaches to the bottom of Halfaya. Three of them blew up.

To the west, the remainder of Panzerarmee were flooding back into Cyrenaica, few units bothering with interim halts at such places as Sidi Azeiz or Bardia but driving straight for Tobruk; and by this time, Rommel had no plans for remaining there for anything but the briefest pause.

He had now had time to draw some conclusions with regard to the Anglo-American invasion of North Africa and the obviously imminent arrival of their forces in Tunisia, and he wished to make them known to higher authority or at least to discuss the ramifications of the development with them. To his mind, there was now no chance whatsoever of holding General Montgomery's forces back anywhere in Libya or Tripolitania longer than it would take them to bring up artillery and supplies, and organise a holding frontal attack combined with a hook by armour around to the south. Admittedly, the British general seemed to be showing exceptional caution in the advance so far, and there seemed still to be a characteristically British slowness of thought and deliberation about every move the Eighth Army made; but with American industrial power and American armies behind them, they could afford to take their time.

Nowhere east of Tunisia itself was there a single position in which a defence line could not be outflanked from the south by armoured or even motorised formations (with which it was quite evident that Rommel himself was not going to be supplied) and moreover, even the Tunisian frontier would have to be abandoned. Not until the Gabes–Wadi Akarit position was reached ninety miles inside Tunisia, in Rommel's opinion, could a defence line be formed which could not be turned. But there Montgomery could be held at bay and, providing troops and supplies arrived from Germany in sufficient quantities to keep the Anglo-American forces back in Algeria, *and providing his own forces too were properly supplied and reinforced*, then a real blow could be prepared and launched against the British which would throw them back to the east.

Nowhere short of Gabes could such a plan come to fruition, nowhere short of Gabes could the implacable progress of the Eighth Army be halted – and if the High Command were not prepared to allow what was left of the Panzerarmee to retreat there, and then to provide him with the human and industrial material with which to rebuild it, then the best and quickest solution to the problems which faced them all – in Berlin and Rome as much as in Tunis or Tobruk – would be to organise an evacuation along Dunkirk lines for his own force and also for any in Tunisia, and abandon the North African theatre once and for all.

This, in fact, was what the Axis Powers would have to do in the long run anyway, for with Anglo-American naval power controlling the Atlantic, Anglo-American industrial potential growing at a rate which Germany and an Occupied Europe could never match, and American manpower now available to swell the hostile armies and air forces, North Africa was already a dwindling asset and would soon become a bleeding and costly burden.

But to his requests that Maresciallo Cavallero and Generalfeldmarschall Kesselring come out to Africa to discuss these matters with him he received reply that they were both too busy, and to his requests for directions as to the immediate future he was told that as he apparently lacked the means to obey Il Duce's instructions to hold the enemy back in the Halfaya region, then he must so delay them that preparations now being made for a defensive line at Mersa Brega would be completed. There he would find awaiting him not only the Giovani Fascisti Division, but also the La Spezia infantry division and the Centauro armoured division, both of which were at that moment being organised for despatch to the front.

The fact that the rate of retreat might depend upon the military prowess of the enemy far more than on any other factor did not seem to have entered the minds of Comando Supremo, though the events of the next few hours might cause them to wonder. On the night of November 10th/11th New Zealand infantry stormed Halfaya Pass and by the morning leading units of the 4th Light Armoured Brigade were up at the top, taking prisoner three batteries of German artillery and a large detachment of the Pistoia Division who had shown little desire to live up to their regimental motto 'Valiant unto Death'.

British forces were then suddenly reported south of the Gambut airfields, and when they were identified as leading units of the 7th Armoured Division Rommel ordered all rearguards in the frontier area back as quickly as possible. By noon on the 11th they were at El Adem and turning into Tobruk where they hoped to stop for a while – both to rest and reorganise and also to get away the thousands of tons of supplies still there – and to Rommel's fury he found that the transport planes which had flown in had brought him not petrol, but an extra 1,100 men for whom he had neither transport nor am-munition, even for the rifles and light machine-guns which was all they brought with them.

That night reports came back of serious traffic jams ahead through the uncleared minefields and defensive positions around Gazala (although the first of the refugees from Alamein had already passed through Benghasi) but during the following morning (November 12th) British armoured cars and light tanks were seen at Acroma, and the possibility of heavier tanks sweeping around and cutting the Via Balbia to the west was too great. With no further hesitation Rommel ordered everybody out and into the Jebel country as quickly as they could get there.

Tmimi, Martuba, Derna – the names recalled the two advances and the one retreat of the last twenty-one months – and by the evening of the 14th both the panzer divisions and the 90th Light were past them and on their way to Barce. There had been bombings and breakdowns, accidents and narrow escapes (though Buelowius's demolitions and booby-traps held off the closest pursuit) and as ever the nagging worry of petrol shortage. Cavallero had sent forward the German Air Attaché Ritter von Pohl with instructions that Cyrenaica must be held for at least a week longer (he knew better than to come up with such a message himself) and Rommel took the opportunity to point out that sixty tons per day would not save an army whose most miserly quartermaster agreed that they needed two hundred and fifty. This at least brought them a further sixty tons that day which allowed them to move off the following morning – but November 15th very nearly proved to be the day of final disaster for the original formations of the Afrika Korps.

Early in the morning as they were just clearing Giovanni Berta, 90th Light suddenly found themselves under attack from Stuarts and armoured cars, so with the fear that heavier tanks would soon be along they raced off down the coast road – but another Mediter-ranean storm swept in from the sea, the battered roads cracked and churned under the weight of traffic, and attempts to move off them floundered into mud. By the evening they had only the smallest margin of petrol left – and 15th and 21st Panzer Divisions on the

Maraua road were stranded, still short of Barce, with none at all.

What made the position even more infuriating was that panic somewhere had gripped the staff, and they had turned several petrol ships back from Benghasi in case their precious cargo fell into enemy hands, in addition to ordering one tanker already in port to leave with still a hundred tons aboard; and they then compounded their sins by ordering the demolition of the ammunition dump at Barce just as the troops who could put it to good use were about to enter.

Fortunately the rains (and Buelowius) delayed the pursuers even more than the pursued, and by November 18th, 90th Light were in Benghasi at last with a reaguard back at Benina, 21st Panzer were down at Ghemines, 15th further south at El Magrun with the 33rd Reconnaissance Battalion forward at Sceleidima, while Rommel and his headquarters had reached Zuetina by the coast and the first formation of Centauro to arrive were forward at Antelat. The Ramcke Brigade were already working on the defences on the coast at Mersa Brega, while La Spezia and Pistoia formations extended the line inland.

Rommel, however, was still both worried and angry. The British were at Msus, their armoured cars attacking his scanty rearguards – and ever present in his mind was the possibility of outflanking forces cutting off his own still to the north by a thrust down the Trig el Abd, similar to the one which had destroyed Bergonzoli's army in the very first desert offensive. A British convoy with a strong naval escort had also been reported off Derna, and in the supposition that it was en route for Benghasi yet more Italian shipping laden with petrol – this time naval destroyers – had been turned back, some of the stores there had been burnt, more loaded on to barges which were sunk as soon as they put to sea – and the harbour and dock installations destroyed or severely damaged even while 90th Light were still holding the port. As no further purpose would be served by them remaining there, he ordered them south the following day and watched with sorrow and anguish as they and the other units to the north filtered back, hundreds of their vehicles on tow and all in a condition of battered disrepair. By the night of November 23rd/24th, all the Axis troops were back in the Mersa Brega positions, close to where they had started out so adventurously ten months before.

But ten months before he had had at his disposal two excellent and well-equipped panzer divisions and an adequate stock of both fuel and ammunition; now there was nothing but the tattered remains of those divisions plus the totally inexperienced Centauro armour, to provide a flank guard to a static position into which equally inexperienced Italian infantry were being fed, easy prey to enemy armoured and motorised columns who could cut them off by a simple swing around the south.

It was essential for them to be stationed further back, so in an attempt to get the demand for a stand between Brega and El Agheila cancelled he sent off one of the more intelligent Italian officers, Generale de Stefanis, commander of the XX Corps, to Rome to try to explain the realities of the situation there. In the meantime, Kesselring and Cavallero were at last available to see him, and they and Maresciallo Bastico arrived at Arco dei Fileni (Marble Arch, some fifty miles west of El Agheila) for what Rommel hoped would be a reasoned discussion.

Both the meeting and de Stefanis's trip to Rome were a waste of time. Even while de Stefanis was away a directive arrived from Hitler confirming Il Duce's order that the Mersa Brega line was to be held at all costs, and promising massive reinforcements of men, guns and tanks to ensure that it was; and it was quite obvious at the Marble Arch meeting that the generals all knew of the instruction and would not countermand it, even though they also knew that the promises which accompanied it would not be kept – if only because everything which came across the Mediterranean now would go via Tunis and there be requisitioned for the battle against the new invaders. And as an added twist of the knife in Rommel's soul, he was informed that he and his force would once again revert to Maresciallo Bastico's command!

Having made the position clear, the visitors then attempted to assuage the bitterness with flattery, assuring Rommel of their admiration for his feat in bringing his army back eight hundred miles along a single roadway without major loss. It was surely a feat unique in the annals of warfare – but when Rommel asked pointedly what Bastico advised him to do if the 7th Armoured Division chose to ignore the Brega and Agheila positions and just drive past to the south on their way to Tripoli, his question was met with sullen silence.

Then followed a minor but intensely irritating episode which deeply affected Rommel, revealing in stark relief the scale of the reverses he had suffered. The night after the meeting at Marble Arch, in order to obtain some relief from worry and tension he attended a cinema show put on for the headquarter staff and troops; the films were light and trashy but there was also a newsreel, weeks old, which, as a vengeful fate would have it, showed Rommel at the Berlin press reception making that ill-fated assertion, 'We have the door to all Egypt in our hands. What we have, we hold!' Even Rommel's presence and the deep loyalty the majority of the audience felt for him could not restrain the sardonic laughter which greeted the declaration.

Much worse was to follow. The next day came the decisions made over his head after the Marble Arch meeting. Il Duce demanded not only that the Mersa Brega line be held but that Rommel should launch an attack against the British as soon as possible – supported, he announced, by a strongly reinforced Luftwaffe which even Kesselring admitted would not be available. Moreover, in the event of a British attack coming before Rommel's, then Bastico alone was empowered to give an order to retreat – an order, Comando Supremo directed, that he was only to give in the direst emergency.

Enough was enough; not only had Rommel's pride been deeply hurt, but he was tired and the illness from which he had not fully recovered when he returned to Egypt was plaguing him again. He would return to Europe, hoping that a brief respite there would do him good, and also that he could secure an interview with the Führer and explain to him the realities of the situation in Africa.

He was quite confident that General Montgomery would not attempt any serious challenge to the Mersa Brega positions in the short time he would be away.

In this Rommel was quite justified; General Montgomery had not the slightest intention of attacking the Mersa Brega–El Agheila positions until he had amassed enough strength in the area to be assured of victory, and indeed, enough to take his forces well on their way to Tripoli. There was to be no repeat in 1943 of the riposte of January 1942 or of Rommel's first lightning success of April 1941 – and in taking every possible measure to ensure against such reverses the Army Commander had the support of every man under his command, especially those who had taken part in either or both of the previous débâcles. The magic of Rommel's name, his reputation for rebounding with unexpected strength and brilliant exploitation from every reverse, had contributed greatly to the caution with which the X Corps divisions had pursued him, and the wariness with which even now the armoured cars and light tanks of 7th Armoured Division watched and approached the Mersa Brega positions.

That caution had not, of course, been the sole reason for Eighth Army's failure to 'put the whole Panzerarmee in the bag' – the expressed intention of General Montgomery at and before the time of the break-out. Lack of training, lack of trust, and logistical problems had all contributed, especially the first two at the beginning.

Montgomery had trained the infantry of Eighth Army specifically for the 'break-in' battle and they had succeeded admirably. His instructions for the training of the armour had resulted in their concentration on what Gatehouse had called 'a static role', more as mobile artillery than as a rapidly moving striking force, and the experiences of both 1st and 10th Armoured Division during the battle had not led them to believe that the Army Commander would allow them a great deal of individual responsibility afterwards. In this they were quite right, for it was Montgomery's nature to try to keep a tight personal control on every battle – and even with the break-out achieved the relationship between himself and General Lumsden was neither happy nor relaxed. As a result the original X Corps divisions made short hooks to the coast – one of which it should be remembered was the most successful of all – and only the column under the trusted Freyberg and the 7th Armoured Division from XIII Corps under the equally trusted John Harding made thrusts likely to prove really effective.

These two were defeated first by the accident of the dummy minefield and then by logistics, the rain dealing a final blow to their hopes.

As far as logistics were concerned, one of the problems facing the supply columns was that for those first crucial days everything had to be channelled out through that narrow *Supercharge* salient, feet deep in dust and getting deeper every hour, pocked with trenches and gun-pits, dotted with wrecked vehicles and guns, still treacherous by reason of the random undiscovered mine, and choked with traffic coming back the other way. The conditions were not helped by bad traffic control as the best men were up forward, and bad driving discipline because the battle had been won now, and euphoria ruled.

And very soon one of the iron rules of war made itself felt – the further a victorious army advances, the longer its lines of communication and supply; all Eighth Army's problems would indeed have been eased had they caught Rommel's forces before they had reached Fuka.

Once they – and the leading British formations – were over the frontier, Montgomery had then to cope with yet another perennial problem, shortage of infantry, exacerbated now by the demand from the Australian Government that as the battle had been won, General Morshead and his division should return home in order to play their part in the defence against the new danger in the Pacific. The men who had 'crumbled' the enemy and held the northern salient, who had isolated Thompson's Post and won time for the launching of *Supercharge*, would not be available for the pursuit. It was a heavy loss, but it had been expected; at least the New Zealanders would remain, as would the 4th Indian and, of course, General Wimberley's Highlanders.

Nevertheless, Montgomery had felt it necessary to call a pause at the frontier because of the difficulties of supply and also for reorganisation – only armoured cars, some light tanks and some artillery units would immediately go on into Cyrenaica, in formations not dissimilar to those of the Jock Columns of the first desert campaign. Freyberg's force must rest and reorganise, 7th Armoured Division replace its more battered and worn tanks and vehicles with fresh ones with a view to carrying on the pursuit, 1st and 10th Armoured Divisions concentrate on clearing up the whole of the area east of the Wire. After all, between them they had contributed largely to victory in a hard-fought battle lasting twelve days, and in a further six days had chased the remnants of the famous Panzerarmee two hundred and fifty miles; it was not surprising that organisationally they were somewhat out of breath, and anyway there were prisoners to be marshalled back, and thousands of weapons, vehicles and dumps littering the Western Desert of Egypt which must be quickly checked and when possible put to good use.

But contact with Rommel's forces had to be kept, of course, and on November 14th four columns were sent out under command of 7th Armoured Division. Each had detachments of field, anti-tank and anti-aircraft guns and engineers, and the first was grouped around the armoured cars of the 12th Lancers. Their task was to drive for Martuba and capture the landing-ground there, and when the R.A.F. had taken over to drive on to Derna for the same purpose.

The second column was detached from the 4th Light Armoured Brigade and contained a troop of Grant tanks, and their task was to follow the first column to Martuba but then to proceed along the main road through the Jebel Akhdar to Benghasi. The other two columns were to drive hard for El Adem, then on November 15th to take the southern route through Tengeder, capture the landing-ground at Msus and then probe down towards Antelat. Every column contained men who had been over the ground before, and every column commander was instructed that his main task was to report every action fought and every contact made with the enemy, as quickly as possible.

These had been the forces, backed by remarkably little else on the ground, which had chivvied Rommel's Panzerarmee remnants out of Tobruk, the Afrika Korps through the Jebel, and finally the combined Italo-German forces back into the Mersa Brega positions. They had, however, been fully supported by the R.A.F. who had sent in parties to clear landing-strips as soon as they were captured, driven the German fighters out of the sky and guarded the army formations from Stuka attacks. And every night the bombers were out (including the American heavy bombers) over Tobruk at first, then Benghasi and Tripoli, sinking Rommel's supply ships, and robbing him in one week of nearly 10,000 tons of fuel.

As soon as it had become obvious to General Montgomery that Rommel and what remained of his forces were going to get away, he reasoned that they would not stop to give battle before the El Agheila positions. With this in mind, as soon as he had attended to organisational plans to ensure that some pressure at least was kept up on the retreating enemy, he turned his mind to the problems of defeating them there.

The first was to get the forces and the men he wished to command them assembled in the forward area. With the success of XXX Corps in the recent battle to recommend him, General Leese was the obvious choice of commander for the next one, which would, equally obviously, be a corps, not an Army, battle. Leese must therefore move up as soon as possible into the forward area, and his new XXX Corps divisions would be the 7th Armoured, the 51st Highland and the New Zealanders. X Corps was nominally already in the Jebel, although only formations of the 7th Armoured Division – to be transferred anyway – were there with the command; which was to change. After the difficulties between Army and X Corps commands during Alamein, not even McCreery would press for General Lumsden's retention within Eighth Army.

General Horrocks therefore would take over X Corps, now composed of 1st Armoured and the 4th Indian Divisions, and as soon as XXX Corps were in place, Horrocks would establish his command in and around Benghasi as an insurance against another of Rommel's explosive counter-attacks should the enemy forces somehow gather sufficient strength to mount one. If they did not, then X Corps would be available for exploitation of XXX Corps's breakthrough.

By November 29th, Montgomery's plans for the battle were complete. Two brigades of the Highland Division would drive frontally against the Mersa Brega position down the coast road, 7th Armoured Division plus the third Highland brigade would attack the enemy line some ten miles to the south at Bir es Suera and drive for the Via Balbia between El Agheila and El Mugtaa, and the New Zealand Division, still with the 4th Light Armoured Brigade under command, would make a huge left hook to the south, cut through between Sidi Tabet and Marada and drive for Marble Arch or even Nofilia. The main operation would begin on the night of December 16th/17th, but the New Zealanders with so much farther to go – probably over very difficult country – would leave their assembly point at El Haseiat two or three days before.

There were thus at most eighteen days for 7th Armoured and the Highlanders – and only fourteen for the New Zealanders – to organise themselves again for battle, and for the Army Q Branch to solve all the problems of supplying them with whatever they would need to defeat Rommel again and drive him back perhaps another hundred miles. No time must be wasted.

The Gods of War now favoured the Eighth Army. The harbour facilities at Benghasi were not so badly damaged as had been feared, traffic control was improved and strictly enforced to keep the convoys moving, and although petrol supplies presented a problem, ammunition dumps abandoned during the retreat through the Jebel eleven months before were found virtually undisturbed. Supplies poured in through the harbours of Tobruk and Benghasi, were brought up further every day by rail from the Delta as the line was repaired (it was in use as far as Matruh – 130 miles from Alamein – by November 14th) and trucked on from there. General Montgomery had no doubt that all would be well on time.

So far as General Leese was concerned, matters were proceeding quite well for him too. The line his forces had to breach swept from Mersa Brega on the coast around to Maaten Giofer some forty miles away on the Agheila–Marada track, then down along it for ten miles to Sidi Tabet. Salt marshes, broken ground and soft sand would undoubtedly make it difficult for tanks or wheeled vehicles to manoeuvre, and minefields would certainly cover the gaps between them – though by no means as thick or as wide as those his infantry and engineers had recently conquered.

In any case, the crucial movement would be that by General Freyberg's force around the flank, and there luck was favouring them. The armoured cars of the King's Dragoon Guards and the specialists of the Long Range Desert Group had provided the answers to the most pressing problems, and the latter would also furnish guides for the New Zealanders, leading them over the first hundred miles of comparatively good going to Chrystal's Rift (named after the K.D.G. captain who discovered and reconnoitred it). The K.D.G. would then take them through the rift, with the L.R.D.G. taking over again afterwards and leading them on as far as Fortune would allow. The men were rested and keen (the Highlanders had even held a review with the officers in kilts), more Shermans were arriving, and there would again be no shortage of ammunition.

Then on the evening of December 9th, reports from Highlander patrols told of movements behind the enemy lines which looked remarkably like withdrawals; by the evening of the 12th it was quite evident that Rommel and his forces were getting out.

Rommel's visit to Europe had not been a success. He had left Libya on the morning of November 28th and was at the Führer's head-quarters at Rastenburg by 1600, having called in briefly at Wiener-Neustadt to speak to his wife on the way. His reception first by Keitel and Jodl was wary and cool, and then at 1700 by Hitler chilly in the extreme, even when Hitler had recovered from his astonishment that Rommel should have left Africa without receiving his permission to do so.

But at first he had at least received attention while he recounted the course of the battle at Alamein and events since and, at the end, praise. His conduct of all operations, Hitler announced and the surrounding court nodded in agreement, had been faultless and indeed unique.

But when Rommel went on to suggest that although delaying actions might be fought in the desert or in Tunisia for a while, it should be accepted that in the end Africa would have to be abandoned, the storm broke. Retreat and evacuation was all that his generals ever suggested, the Führer screamed; he had had exactly the same trouble last year with the generals on the Russian Front and had had to insist the armies stayed where they were – and now they were suggesting the same thing about Stalingrad. But they would stay where they were and consolidate the victories he had already given them in the east – and so would Rommel in Africa.

There would be no retreat from Mersa Brega, there would be no more throwing away or abandoning of valuable weapons – which in view of the fact that Rommel claimed that 10,000 of his 15,000 men were unarmed was the only possible explanation – and most important of all, there would be no more thought of leaving Africa. Such an abandonment would weaken Mussolini's position to such an extent that he could be overthrown and Italy might then break the Pact of Steel; or even switch to the other side.

Germany's attention and indeed her destiny were now directed to the east. Here battles were being fought which reduced the affairs in North Africa to the level of skirmishes, and the Führer had no time and little patience for them; it was the duty of the men he sent there to execute their responsibilities properly, to vanquish the Reich's enemies and to do so without distracting his mind with unnecessary trifles.

Yes – all right! Rommel needed more weapons, more supplies and more men. But the person most responsible for the North African theatre and everything that happened in the Mediterranean was Il Duce, and Rommel should return to Rome immediately accompanied by Reichsmarschall Goering who would argue Rommel's case, bring the whole of his persuasive personality to bear on the problem and see that Rommel was properly supported.

With which Rommel was dismissed – to spend the next two days in Goering's specially furnished train, listening to the fat fool's pluming self-approbation, to his boasting, to his bland dismissal of all Rommel's troubles as caused by his own exhaustion and weakness which had, according to the Reichsmarschall, induced in him a spirit of debilitating pessimism. Even the fact that Frau Rommel joined the train on November 29th served only as temporary relief, and by the time they had arrived in Rome, Rommel was even more depressed than when he had left Africa.

In Rome, his suggestion that his forces should retire to Tunis and join the newly strengthened forces there to form a powerful striking force with which to administer a spectacular defeat upon the Anglo-Americans – which had for a time in the train received Goering's approval – was curtly rejected by Kesselring on the grounds that enemy air forces based at Tripoli, Algiers and Malta would make Tunisia uninhabitable. But somewhat to his surprise, Mussolini and the Italian generals were at last sufficiently realistic to see that if Rommel's forces remained too long in the Mersa Brega positions, they would be lost; and by now the majority were Italians.

He should, they agreed, make all necessary plans for a retreat to Buerat where, they assured him, some fortifications already existed, others would now be built as soon as materials and labour could be sent there, and the non-motorised infantry at Mersa Brega should go as quickly as possible. The Afrika Korps, with their panzer strength now up to fifty-four, the reconstituted Ariete and the Centauro should stay in the Mersa Brega–El Agheila positions until the enemy attacked, then retreat to the Buerat Line as slowly as possible using every conceivable device and tactic to inflict damage and loss upon their pursuers. Ample petrol stocks would be built up and there would be no further shortages.

This slightly more realistic attitude in Rome was at least a partial relief though Rommel arrived back in Africa a profoundly depressed man. The Buerat Line might be a step in the right direction but it was a very short step, and would in any case be dependent not only upon the authorities in Rome keeping their promises about sending petrol, but the Royal Navy and the Royal Air Force allowing it to arrive.

There was, as it happened, enough fuel immediately available for the operation of withdrawal to commence, and on the night of November 6th the first of the Italian infantry pulled out. Orders had been issued that this was to be done as quietly and unostentatiously as possible, so Rommel was infuriated and then very worried when he learned that the lorries transporting them had driven off with headlights blazing, their cargoes cheering and singing, presumably with relief. But no immediate reactions were forthcoming from the enemy side of the line, and on the next night the Giovani Fascisti went back, followed on the 8th by the Pistoia; and the Ariete and the armoured divisions would have followed immediately had there been any petrol left.

Enough did arrive during the following days to lift the armour at least back to El Mugtaa, and as on November 11th it became apparent that the Highland Division opposite the Mersa Brega front were about to attack, the orders went out, the rearguards were posted, the main formations drew away and by midnight the Via Balbia was again filled with panzers and guns driving westwards.

In fact, on the evening of November 11th the Highland Division were merely mounting a heavy raid, that being all which could be managed in the time.

When the reports had reached General Montgomery that Rommel seemed to be about to withdraw, he had advanced the date of the main attack by forty-eight hours to the night of the 14th/15th, thereby screwing even tighter an already tight schedule. Nevertheless, the artillery cover was fired on time – falling for the main part on vacated positions – and both the Highland Division and the 7th Armoured drove in along their allotted paths.

They met little direct resistance from enemy strongpoints or even artillery, but they quickly ran into minefields sewn now with anti-personnel mines, and along roads or tracks infested with the most ingenious booby-traps that Generalmajor Buelowius could devise. At one point in the pursuit which followed, C Squadron of the 11th Hussars were feeling their way through the wadis and ditches to the south of the Via Balbia:

> Here, in extremely difficult country, a minefield had been laid with such skill and care that its mines were practically impossible to see, and 'C' ran into it without the slightest warning. The car in which Lieutenant J. French was leading No 3 Troop fell a victim first, when the explosion which wrecked the car killed outright Trooper C. F. Blakey, and wounded both French and Trooper Whittard. Only then was it discovered that both the two remaining cars were already right in the middle of the mines, with the result that the whole Troop was immobilised for the remainder of the day.[8]

It took engineers with special equipment four hours to clear a way out for the first car, for every mine was found to have been booby-trapped and there were some detonating mechanisms which had been buried so deep that the detectors were unavailing. Eventually, the first car was driven out with both the commander and gunner tip-toeing in front of each wheel searching for signs of further ground disturbance – and when a second car tried to creep out along the first's tyre-tracks it promptly blew up on a mine which had been hidden deep under those which had been removed:

> Daybreak on December 16th showed that the enemy had fallen back, and 'A' Squadron reached Marble Arch at noon, despite the fact that both the road and its verges were so heavily mined that the armoured cars were forced to pick their way cross-country over broken ground and bogs.[9]

But infantry-carriers, gun-limbers or tanks needed roads or hard desert surfaces and now the war was moving into very different country. There were flower-decked meadows to rejoice the artistic heart, but the flowers grew in soft soil and what hard ground there was usually lined the sides of ravines. As a result the Highland Division's progress had been reduced – along and abreast of the road but almost without active enemy resistance – at times to one mile an hour, by the combination of booby-traps and broken ground.

The New Zealanders had completed their hook successfully – though without all their armour as the soft going used so much petrol that they outran their supplies – but they ran into the 15th Panzer Division cannily positioned to hold the road open for the 21st Panzer, still defending the defile at El Mugtaa against the Highlanders. There was a brisk engagement, broken off when Rommel issued orders for a full retreat to Nofilia, just enough petrol having arrived for this to take place.

Again the Italo-German forces escaped, and the New Zealand historian admirably summed up:

> The high hopes of cutting off even some of the retreating enemy had come to nothing, partly because greater speed was possible along the road than across the desert, partly because the enemy was well-seasoned and adopted the orthodox safeguards of flank and rearguards, and partly because of the difficulties of deploying by night in unknown country at the end of a long and tiring move . . . [10]

This was to be the story all the way, and there is no doubt that Buelowius thoroughly deserved the promotion and tributes which Rommel later awarded him. He turned the advance of Eighth Army in the closing days of 1942 into a snail-paced nightmare, and saved Rommel's forces from the dire straits into which petrol shortages – for none of Comando Supremo's promises were kept – threatened to plunge them. They were back in Nofilia by December 16th, out two days later and into Sirte where they were left in peace until Christmas Day when 15th Panzer, who were serving there as rearguards, had suddenly to abandon their festivities and move out fast in the face of a movement towards them by tanks of 7th Armoured Division. They, and indeed all of Rommel's forces, were back in the Buerat defences by the last day of the year.

They were to be left there, occasionally bombed by the R.A.F. or the American heavy bombers but undisturbed by ground forces other than raiders against their lines of communication, until the middle of January – for Montgomery had been caught in a logistic trap.

Tobruk was now 800 miles to the rear and, in addition to the thousand or more tons of supplies a day the Army needed, the air forces wanted forward all-weather fighter strips as quickly as possible and even more solidly constructed strips for bombers; and Montgomery was as keen as they were that they should have them. Very quickly Benghasi was open and supplies were pouring through – but even Benghasi was 300 miles from Nofilia and nearly 450 from

Buerat – and who knew what Buelowius would have done to the roads as he had passed over them?

But 230 miles beyond Buerat lay Tripoli, an even bigger port than Benghasi, and if it could be taken quickly then the demolitions might be as quickly dealt with, and the logistic problems which had so beset Eighth Army since they had crossed the Egyptian frontier would be solved.

But how to get there?

At least four divisions would be needed to be certain of breaking the Buerat Line – or even successfully outflanking it in this new kind of country – and in order to ensure full support in case of accident, at least two more divisions would be needed close at hand. XXX Corps would therefore consist of 50th and 51st (Highland) Divisions, 7th Armoured and, of course, the New Zealanders; Horrocks could bring his 1st Armoured Division and the 4th Indian up into the El Agheila area while Leese assembled his divisions between there and Nofilia and only armoured cars and Stuarts with light artillery would operate further forward.

But the tonnage of stores needed to sustain six divisions would strain transport to the limit, and when the advance began the problems would increase – and could not long be borne. Montgomery's calculations made it quite clear that once his forces began to move forward against Buerat, they would have only ten days in which to reach and secure a new source of large-scale supply.

Tripoli in ten days . . . or he would be forced to bring his army back in a withdrawal which would reawaken memories of past misfortunes, would damage the victorious image of the Eighth Army and might even affect morale within it. He and they must therefore take their time now and thus be invincible when the moment for battle arrived.

So through the last days of 1942, the divisions moved into their assembly areas, the ships unloaded at Tobruk and Benghasi, and the long columns of trucks and lorries roared continuously along the narrow roads which the engineers were labouring all the time to keep passable; while up front even more engineers still risked their lives every minute dismantling Buelowius's masterpieces, and losing 170 of their number while so doing.

And further up in front, the armoured cars of 11th Hussars, the King's Dragoon Guards and the Royal Dragoons, and the Stuarts and R.H.A. Batteries attached to them, moved carefully along the roads and winding tracks leading up to and across the Buerat positions, exchanging shots with their opposite numbers of Rommel's reconnaissance battalions, sometimes losing cars, sometimes lives. And waiting for the next onslaught to begin.

There was no *feu de joie* among the Germans as 1942 died, and if the few British present who had witnessed the fireworks twelve months· before could at least reflect that they were now some three hundred miles forward of where they had been then, they had arrived by a peculiarly circuitous route.

And in human terms, a costly one. At Alamein alone Eighth Army had lost 13,500 in killed and wounded and the enemy must have lost at least half that number in their defensive battle. Heaven alone knew how many on both sides had been lost on the way there – or since.

There were so many gone – some to graves, some to hospitals, some to prison-camps, some to other theatres of war; a tiny fraction even back to civilian life. Of those who were gone for ever, some had been fools, some incompetent, some just unlucky; but amongst them, on both sides, had been the bravest and the best.

Appendix
Forces Engaged at the Battle of Alamein, October 23rd–November 6th, 1942

Allied Forces

Commander-in-Chief, Middle East General the Hon. Harold Alexander

EIGHTH ARMY
Lieutenant-General Sir Bernard L. Montgomery

X Corps – Lieutenant-General Herbert Lumsden

1st Armoured Division – Major-General R. Briggs
2nd Armoured Brigade
7th Motor Brigade

10th Armoured Division – Major-General A. H. Gatehouse
8th Armoured Brigade
24th Armoured Brigade
133rd Lorried Infantry Brigade

XIII Corps – Lieutenant-General Brian G. Horrocks

7th Armoured Division – Major-General A. F. Harding
4th Light Armoured Brigade
22nd Armoured Brigade
131st Infantry Brigade (after November 1st)

50th Infantry Division – *Major-General J. S. Nichols*
69th Infantry Brigade
151st Infantry Brigade
1st Greek Infantry Brigade

44th Infantry Division – Major-General I. T. P. Hughes
131st Infantry Brigade (until October 30th)
132nd Infantry Brigade

Fighting French Brigade – Brigadier-General P. Koenig

XXX Corps – Lieutenant-General Oliver Leese

4th Indian Division – Major-General F. I. S. Tuker
  5th Indian Infantry Brigade
  7th Indian Infantry Brigade
  161st Indian Infantry Brigade

51st (Highland) Division – Major-General D. N. Wimberley
  152nd Infantry Brigade
  153rd Infantry Brigade
  154th Infantry Brigade

9th Australian Division – Major-General L. J. Morshead
  20th Australian Infantry Brigade
  24th Australian Infantry Brigade
  26th Australian Infantry Brigade

2nd New Zealand Division – Major-General B. C. Freyberg, V.C.
  5th New Zealand Brigade
  6th New Zealand Brigade
  9th Armoured Brigade

1st South African Division – Major-General D. H. Pienaar
  1st South African Infantry Brigade
  2nd South African Infantry Brigade
  3rd South African Infantry Brigade

23rd Armoured Brigade Group – Brigadier G. W. Richards

German and Italian Forces

PANZERARMEE AFRIKA
General der Kavallerie Georg Stumme (until October 24th)
Generalleutnant Wilhelm Ritter von Thoma (until October 25th)
Generalfeldmarschall Erwin Rommel

Deutsches Afrika Korps – Generalleutnant Wilhelm Ritter von Thoma

15th Panzer Division – Generalleutnant Gustav von Vaerst
  Panzer Regiment 8
  Panzergrenadier Regiment 115
  Panzerjäger Abteilung 33
  Machine-gun Battalion 8
  Reconnaissance Battalion 33
  Artillery Regiment 33

21st Panzer Division – Generalmajor Heinz von Randow
  Panzer Regiment 5
  Panzergrenadier Regiment 104
  Panzerjäger Abteilung 39
  Reconnaissance Battalion 3
  Artillery Regiment 155

90th Light Division – Generalleutnant Theodor Graf von Sponek
    Infantry Regiment 155
    Infantry Regiment 200
    Infantry Regiment Afrika 361
    Panzergrenadier Regiment Afrika
    Panzerjäger Abteilung 190
    Reconnaissance Battalion 580
    Artillery Regiment 190

164th Infantry Division – Generalmajor Carl-Hans Lungershausen
    Panzergrenadier Regiment 125
    Panzergrenadier Regiment 382
    Panzergrenadier Regiment 433
    Reconnaissance Battalion 220
    Artillery Regiment 220

22nd Parachute Brigade – Generalmajor Hermann Ramcke

Corpo d'Armata X – Generale di Corpo d'Armata Edoardo Nebba

Brescia Division – Generale di Divisione Brunetto Brunetti
Pavia Division – Generale di Brigata N. Scattaglia

Corpo d'Armata XX – Generale di Corpo d'Armata Giuseppe de Stefanis

Ariete Armoured Division – Generale di Brigata Francesco Arena
Littorio Armoured Division – Generale di Divisione Gervasio Bitossi
Trieste Motorised Division – Generale di Brigata Francesco La Ferla
Folgore Parachute Division – Generale di Divisione Enrico Frattini

Corpo d'Armata XXI – Generale di Corpo d'Armata Enea Navarini

Trento Division – Generale di Brigata Giorgio Masina
Bologna Division – Generale di Divisione Alessandro Gloria

Notes

Crown copyright material throughout this book is reproduced by permission of the Controller of Her Majesty's Stationery Office.

Prologue

1 Quoted in Alun Chalfont, *Montgomery of Alamein*, Weidenfeld and Nicolson 1976, p. 5.
2 Field Marshal the Viscount Montgomery of Alamein, *Memoirs*, Collins 1958, p. 32. This and all subsequent extracts from this title are reproduced by permission of Viscount Montgomery of Alamein.
3 Chalfont, op. cit., p. 113.
4 Montgomery, op. cit., p. 35.
5 Ibid., p. 36.
6 By permission of Sir Denis Hamilton on behalf of the Montgomery Archive.
7 Montgomery, op. cit., p. 83.
8 By permission of Sir Denis Hamilton on behalf of the Montgomery Archive.
9 By permission of Sir Denis Hamilton on behalf of the Montgomery Archive.
10 Quoted in Alan Moorehead, *Montgomery*, Four Square 1958, p. 79.
11 Quoted, ibid.
12 Quoted, ibid.
13 Quoted, ibid., p. 80.
14 By permission of Sir Denis Hamilton on behalf of the Montgomery Archive.
15 Crown copyright, quoted in Chalfont, op. cit., p. 95.
16 Crown copyright, quoted, ibid.
17 Crown copyright, quoted, ibid., p. 99.
18 Quoted in Ronald Lewin, *Montgomery as Military Commander*, Batsford 1971, p. 11.

1 *'A cool and refreshing breeze'*

1 Quoted in Major-General I. S. O. Playfair *et al.*, *Official History, The Mediterranean and Middle East, Vol. III*, H.M.S.O. 1960, p. 319.

2 Winston S. Churchill, *The Second World War, Vol. IV*, Cassell 1951, pp. 421–2.
3 Quoted in Nigel Nicolson, *Alex, The Life of Field Marshal Earl Alexander of Tunis*, Weidenfeld and Nicolson 1973, p. 157.
4 Major-General Sir Francis de Guingand, *Operation Victory*, Hodder and Stoughton 1947, pp. 136–7.
5 Field Marshal the Viscount Montgomery of Alamein, *Memoirs*, Collins 1958, p. 103.
6 De Guingand, op. cit., p. 139.
7 Vladimir Peniakoff, *Popski's Private Army*, Pan 1957, p. 211.
8 Quoted in Alun Chalfont, *Montgomery of Alamein*, Weidenfeld and Nicolson 1976, p. 156.
9 *The Rommel Papers*, ed. B. H. Liddell Hart, Collins 1953, p. 268.
10 Ibid., p. 247.
11 Quoted in Fritz Bayerlein, 'The Battle of Alam Halfa', in *History of the Second World War, Vol. III*, ed. Barrie Pitt, Purnell 1967, p. 1152.
12 *Rommel Papers*, ed. Liddell Hart, p. 285.
13 Quoted in Correlli Barnett, *The Desert Generals*, Pan 1962, p. 321.
14 By permission of Sir Denis Hamilton on behalf of the Montgomery Archive.

2 *Daffodil, Hyacinth, Snowdrop and Tulip*

1 Vladimir Peniakoff, *Popski's Private Army*, Pan 1957, p. 174.
2 General Sir John Hackett, letter to author, July 18th, 1978.
3 Gordon Landsborough, *Tobruk Commando*, Cassell 1956, p. 95.
4 Fitzroy Maclean, *Eastern Approaches*, Pan 1956, p. 201.
5 Peniakoff, op. cit., p. 198.

3 *Prelude to Battle*

1 By permission of Sir Denis Hamilton on behalf of the Montgomery Archive.
2 By permission of Sir Denis Hamilton on behalf of the Montgomery Archive.
3 Fritz Bayerlein, 'El Alamein', in *The Fatal Decisions*, ed. Seymour Freidin and William Richardson, Michael Joseph 1956, p. 90.
4 Ibid., p. 91.
5 Ibid.
6 David Irving, *The Trail of the Fox*, Weidenfeld and Nicolson 1977, p. 198.

4 *El Alamein: The Onslaught*

1 Major-General D. N. Wimberley, 'Scottish Soldier', Vol. II, p. 41, unpublished.
2 Quoted in Field Marshal Lord Carver, *El Alamein*, Batsford 1962, p. 109.

3 Ibid., p. 123.
4 George Greenfield, 'The Fighting at Alamein', in *History of the Second World War, Vol. III*, ed. Barrie Pitt, Purnell 1967, p. 1173.
5 Wimberley, op. cit., p. 43.
6 Quoted in Nigel Hamilton, *Monty, The Making of a General, 1887–1942*, Hamish Hamilton 1981, p. 790.
7 Quoted in Ronald Walker, *Alam Halfa and Alamein, Official History of New Zealand in the Second World War 1939–45*, Historical Publications Branch, Department of Internal Affairs (Wellington) 1967, p. 304.
8 By permission of Sir Denis Hamilton on behalf of the Montgomery Archive.
9 By permission of Sir Denis Hamilton on behalf of the Montgomery Archive.
10   Quoted in Walker, op. cit., p. 312.

5 *Pause for Reflection*

1 *The Rommel Papers*, ed. B. H. Liddell Hart, Collins 1953, p. 304.
2 Ibid., p. 306.
3 Ibid., pp. 309–10.
4 Ibid., p. 310.
5 George Greenfield, 'The Fighting at Alamein', in *History of the Second World War, Vol. III*, ed. Barrie Pitt, Purnell 1967, p. 1173.
6 *Rommel Papers*, ed. Liddell Hart, p. 306.
7 Brigadier C. E. Lucas Phillips, *Alamein*, Pan 1965, p. 224.
8 Major R. H. W. S. Hastings, *The Rifle Brigade in the Second World War*, Gale and Polden (Aldershot) 1950, pp. 175–6.
9 *Rommel Papers*, ed. Liddell Hart, p. 310.

6 *The Crumbling Process*

1 By permission of Sir Denis Hamilton on behalf of the Montgomery Archive.
2 *The Rommel Papers*, ed. B. H. Liddell Hart, Collins 1953, pp. 311 12.
3 Barton Maughan, *Tobruk and El Alamein*, Australian War Memorial (Canberra), p. 709.
4 Brigadier C. E. Lucas Phillips, *Alamein*, Pan 1965, p. 249.
5 Barton Maughan, op. cit., p. 715.
6 *Rommel Papers*, ed. Liddell Hart, p. 315.
7 Ibid., p. 316.
8 Quoted by Arthur Bryant, *The Alanbrooke War Diaries 1939–43: The Turn of the Tide*, Fontana 1957, p. 423.
9 By permission of Sir Denis Hamilton on behalf of the Montgomery Archive.
10 Quoted in Lucas Phillips, op. cit., p. 273.
11 Ibid., p. 278.
12 Ibid., p. 270.
13 Ibid., p. 287.

14 Ibid., p. 292.
15 Quoted, ibid., p. 294.
16 Ibid., p. 298.
17 Quoted in Field Marshal Lord Carver, *El Alamein*, Batsford 1962, p. 168.

7 *Break-out and Pursuit*

1 Quoted in *The Rommel Papers*, ed. B. H. Liddell Hart, Collins 1953, p. 321, footnote.
2 Field Marshal Lord Carver, *El Alamein*, Batsford 1962, p. 184.
3 Quoted in Ronald Walker, *Alam Halfa and Alamein, Official History of New Zealand in the Second World War 1939–45*, Historical Publications Branch, Department of Internal Affairs (Wellington) 1967, pp. 445–6.
4 *Rommel Papers*, ed. Liddell Hart, pp. 339–40.
5 Walker, op. cit., pp. 445–6.
6 *Rommel Papers*, ed. Liddell Hart, p. 341.
7 Ibid., p. 347.
8 Brigadier Dudley Clarke, *The Eleventh at War*, Michael Joseph 1952, p. 270.
9 Ibid., p. 271.
10 Major-General W. G. Stevens, *Bardia to Erfidaville, Official History of New Zealand in the Second World War 1939–45*, Historical Publications Branch, Department of Internal Affairs (Wellington) 1962, p. 57.

Index